S0-BON-545

KANSAS CITY, MO. PUBLIC LIBRARY

0 0001 4555029 9

RAMOS

MV/SC

AN

INQUIRY

INTO

THE SCRIPTURAL VIEWS

OF

SLAVERY.

BY

ALBERT BARNES.

Τὴν Ἰλευθερίαν ἑλοίμην ἂν ἀντὶ ὧν ἔχω πάντων καὶ ἄλλων πολλαπλασίων.
XENOPH. *Anab.* lib. i. c. vii. 3.

NEGRO UNIVERSITIES PRESS
NEW YORK

Originally Published in 1857
by Parry & McMillan

Reprinted 1969 by
Negro Universities Press
A DIVISION OF GREENWOOD PUBLISHING CORP.
NEW YORK

Library of Congress Catalogue Card Number 68-58048

PRINTED IN UNITED STATES OF AMERICA

MV-N
261.8
B261i

CONTENTS.

	Page
INTRODUCTION	5

CHAP. I. *Reasons why the appeal on the subject of Slavery should be made to the Bible* 19

   1. The Bible is the acknowledged standard of morals in this nation 21

   2. The subject of slavery is one on which the Bible has legislated, and there is, therefore, a propriety that we should ascertain its decisions 22

   3. The question whether slavery is right or wrong can only be settled by an appeal to the Scriptures 23

   4. Great reforms, on moral subjects, do not occur except under the influence of religious principle 25

   5. Because it is by such an appeal that the advocates of slavery endeavour to defend the system 28

CHAP. II. *What constitutes Slavery?* 38

   (1.) Not a mere condition of apprenticeship 40

   (2.) Not to be confounded with the condition of a *minor* . 41

   (3.) Not merely a governmental affair 42

   (4.) Not a mere relation in which legislative bodies alone are concerned 43

   (5.) Does not pertain wholly to a legislature to regulate . 43

   (6.) Not a condition like that of the serfs of Russia, &c. . 44

   (7.) Not the kind of property which a man has in his wife or child 46

   1. Is wholly involuntary on the part of the slave . . . 50

   2. Is property claimed in that which belongs to him, but which he is not at liberty to resume to himself . . . 50

   3. Is a right of property in all that pertains to the slave . 51

   4. Is a right of property in his services without equivalent or compensation 52

   5. Involves the right to *sell* him as the master pleases . . 54

   The true question stated 56

3

4.25
MV-N
752640
KANSAS CITY (MO.) PUBLIC LIBRARY

4 CONTENTS.

Page

CHAP. III. *Slavery in the time of the Patriarchs* . . . 58
   Meaning of the words denoting servitude in the Scriptures . 64

CHAP. IV. *Slavery in Egypt* 81
   I. The resemblance between the servitude of the Hebrews in
      Egypt and slavery now 83
   II. Whether the interposition of God, in that case, was such as
      to make it proper for us to derive any conclusions as to his
      will in regard to slavery 96

CHAP. V. *The Mosaic Institutions in relation to Servitude* . . 105
   § 1. What the argument which is relied on is 107
   § 2. What the Mosaic institutions in regard to servitude were . 112
   § 3. Comparison of the Mosaic institutions in relation to slavery
      with those existing in the United States 160

CHAP. VI. *Hebrew Servitude in the time of the Prophets* . . 203
   1. The inquiry in regard to the condition of the native in-
      habitants of the land of Palestine 206
   2. There was no foreign traffic in slaves 210
   3. The prophets felt themselves at liberty to animadvert upon
      the injustice of slavery, &c. &c. 213

CHAP. VII. *The relation of Christianity to Slavery* . . . 229
   I. There is no evidence that Christ himself ever came in con-
      tact with slavery 242
   II. The manner in which the apostles treated the subject of
      slavery 249
      § 1. They found it in existence when they organized churches
         out of the limits of Judea 249
      § 2. The apostles did not openly denounce slavery as an
         evil, or require that those who were held in bondage
         should be at once emancipated 260
      § 3. The question whether the general conduct of the apos-
         tles is consistent with the belief that they approved of
         slavery and desired its perpetuity 304
         The case of Onesimus, the servant of Philemon . . 318
      § 4. The principles laid down by the Saviour and his apos-
         tles, are such as are opposed to slavery, and if carried
         out would secure its universal abolition . . . 340
CONCLUSION 376

INTRODUCTION.

THE subject of slavery is one in which all men have an interest, and which all have a right to discuss. It pertains to a great wrong done to our common nature, and affects great questions relating to the final triumph of the principles of justice and humanity. Wherever wrong is done to any human being, there is no improper interference if the conviction is expressed by any other one. Wherever principles are held which have a tendency to produce or perpetuate wrong, it is a right which all men have, to examine those principles freely. The race is one great brotherhood, and every man is under obligation, as far as he has the ability, to defend those principles which will permanently promote the welfare of the human family.

These obvious principles have a peculiar applicability to our own land. Our country is one. What promotes the honour of one portion of the nation, promotes the honour of the whole ; what is dishonourable, in like manner pertains to all.

Pre-eminently, the subject of slavery pertains to the republic, as such. There are no interests of our common liberty or religion which are not affected by it ; there is nothing which our fathers valued, and which we have been taught to prize,— no principles of justice, or humanity, or equal rights, or industry, or morals, which are not more or less affected by this institution. If it be a good institution ; if it be in accordance with the divine arrangements for the welfare of society, it is the duty of every man to defend it, and to seek its extension in the world. If it be contrary to the principles of the Bible, and if its tendency be evil, he is under no less obligation to

5

lift up his voice on this subject, and to do whatever he can, that truth and justice may prevail. Every citizen at the North whose situation is such, or who has secured such a reputation that his arguments will receive respectful attention, owes a duty to his Southern brethren which he should not fail to discharge, and should not die without giving utterance, in the best way he can, to his convictions on the subject of American slavery. It may be little that the testimony of any one individual can accomplish, but by the accumulation of numerous testimonies, and the multiplication of appeals and arguments, the conviction may gain ground all over the nation that slavery is wrong, and the means may be devised for its entire removal. As one having a common interest in whatever affects the welfare of my country, in the prevalence of true religion, and in opposing whatever seems to me to militate against the gospel, I desire to discharge this portion of my duty to my generation, however humble my individual influence may be, and to record my convictions on a subject of so much concern to our whole land.

The work which is now submitted to the public, is limited to an examination of the *Scripture* argument on the subject of slavery. This is done because this seems to me to be the most important department of the general argument respecting slavery, and because it better falls in with my whole studies and habits of investigation than any other question pertaining to it. There are questions in regard to the general subject—its relations to agriculture and commerce; its political bearings; its influence on the means of national defence and security, and kindred topics, which I do not feel competent to examine, and which can be much better pursued by those who are familiar with the science of political economy than by one whose studies have had a different direction. To a man, however, who has spent more than twenty years in an almost exclusive study of the Bible, it may be permitted to examine the teachings of that book on a subject so important as this is ; and whatever may be the inference as to the strength of his argument, there are none who will charge him with a departure from the proper sphere of his duty.

I have been led to the discussion of the Scripture question in this manner, by the following considerations :— (*a*) Because the institution of slavery is defended by many individuals of respectable names, and by entire bodies of men, by an appeal to the Bible. (See ch. 1.) (*b*) Because, although there have been some professed investigations of the Scriptures on this subject, evincing considerable research, submitted to the public, yet they did not any of them furnish so full and thorough an examination as seemed to me to be desirable. Believing that the spirit of the Bible is against slavery, and that all the arguments alleged in favour of it from the Bible are the result of a misunderstanding of its true spirit, and that the honour of religion demands that that argument should be placed fairly before the world, I was desirous of doing what I could to make the teachings of the Bible seen and appreciated by my fellow-men. (*c*) Because it did not appear to me to be proper to preach on it so fully as would be necessary if I had gone into a thorough examination of the subject in my pulpit instructions; and besides this, the critical nature of many of the investigations is little fitted to the pulpit. Nor if I had deemed it proper to make this a more prominent subject of my preaching, could I have reached one of the main objects which seemed to me to be desirable. The people to whom I minister will bear me witness that I have not concealed my views from them on the subject of slavery. I have endeavoured to give it the place which it appeared to me it ought to occupy in my ministrations in the circumstances in which I am placed. But my lot is not cast in a slaveholding community. I do not know that I have an advocate of slavery in my church, or that there is one who statedly attends on my ministry who would willingly be the owner of a slave. I confess also that it seems to me that any one topic, except the cross of Christ, however important in itself, may be introduced too frequently into the pulpit, and that undue prominence in preaching is given to this in many churches where slavery does not exist. I do not suppose that this occurs too frequently in those places where slavery *does* exist; but where the pen is free, and a man may make his voice heard beyond the bounds of his own congregation, however important it may be that he should make his views decidedly understood in reference to every form of national sin, and should exhibit the fair teachings of the Bible on every subject in the proper proportions, it is better to endeavour to influence the public mind in some other method than by making any one topic a very constant subject of discourse in the pulpit. Slavery, though a great evil, is not the *only* evil in the land. Its influence is indeed vast, and there is no part of the republic that is wholly free from it, but there are other bad influences in our country also. I will not undertake to say *how* prominent a minister should make this topic in communities where slavery exists, and where he is called constantly to address those who sustain the relation of master and slave; nor will I venture to say that *I* should be in any way likely to be more faithful in this respect if my lot were cast there, than I fear is the case with most of those who reside there, but I may be allowed to suggest that the prominent evils which we should assail in preaching are those which are near, and not those which are remote; those which directly pertain to our own people, rather than those which pertain primarily to a distant community; and those in reference to which we may expect immediate action on the part of those who hear us, in forsaking their own sins, rather than such topics as will lead them to judge of others who are living in wickedness. (*d*) I have been led to adopt this course because it was in this way only that I could hope in any manner to influence those whom I desired to reach. I have already said that I am not accustomed to preach to many such. But I would hope that there are not a few who may be willing to examine an argument on slavery, if proposed with candour, and if pursued with a manifest desire to know what is the teaching of the Bible. There are, I am persuaded, not a few such men in the slaveholding portions of our country. I have never indeed been at the South, but my situation has given me an opportunity of becoming acquainted with not a few Southern gentlemen, and that acquaintance has been such as to induce me to believe that there are large numbers there who would examine with candour an argument proposed on this subject. Indeed, I have been led to apprehend that there are many there who, in this respect, are much in advance of many at the North, and that among these are many who exhibit a degree of candour which we do not always find in those portions of our country in which slavery does not exist. There is a hesitancy at the North in speaking of it as an evil; a desire to apologize for it, and even to defend it as a scripture institution, which by no means meets the convictions of the great body of men at the South, *and for which they do not thank us.* They regard slavery as an unmixed evil— as the direst calamity of their portion of the republic. They consider it to be contrary to the spirit of the Bible. They look upon it as a curse in the midst of which they were born; as an evil entailed upon them without their consent, and which they desire above all things to get rid of. They remember with little gratitude the laws and cupidity of the mother country by which it was imposed on them, and the Northern ships by which the inhabitants of Africa were conveyed to their shores; and they little thank the professors in Theological Seminaries, and the pastors of the churches, and the editors of papers, and the ecclesiastical bodies at the North, who labour to convince the world that it is not an evil, and that it is one of the designs and tendencies of Christianity *to rivet the curse on them for ever.* Such men ask for no defence of slavery from the North. They look for a more manly voice—for more decided tones in behalf of freedom, from those whom God has favoured with the entire blessings of liberty, and they ask of us that we will aid them to free themselves from a burden imposed on them by the joint wickedness and cupidity of our fatherland and the North; not that we will engage in the miserable business of attempting to convince the world that the South must always groan under this malediction, and that even the influence of Christianity will be only to make the evil there eternal. There have been more published defences of slavery from the Bible at the North, than there have been at the South. A Christian man can look with some respect on a defence of slavery at the South—for they who are there live in the midst of it, and it is natural for us to love and defend the institutions in the midst of which we were born; but what respect can we have for such a defence emanating from the North?

It is a subject of not unfrequent complaint, that, in the examination of this subject, the adversaries of the system endeavour to show that slavery *as it exists* in our own country is contrary to the Bible, instead of confining themselves to the naked question whether slavery *in the abstract* is right or wrong. They are willing to admit that there are many '*abuses*' in the system as it now exists; that there is much that is oppressive and unjust in the laws; and while they regard slavery in itself as not inconsistent with the Bible, they admit that there is much in the system in our own country which they will not undertake to defend. They maintain that the controversy should be confined to the naked question whether slavery in any form is inconsistent with the Bible, and that it is unfair in this argument to make an appeal to slavery as it now exists, in determining the morality of the institution. Thus Dr. Fuller, in accordance with language often used by good men at the South, says:— " What I am writing about is slavery, but let no one suppose that I am defending all the slave laws." "In reference to the laws of South Carolina I am not called to express myself in this discussion. Suffice it to say, that most of them are virtually repealed by universal practice. The law, for example, forbidding slaves to assemble without the presence of so many white persons, is a dead letter, whenever the meeting is for religious purposes." "It is not of the slave laws, but of slavery, I am speaking; and the character of this, according to the eternal principles of morality, is not affected by any human enactments."* Thus also the conductors of the Princeton Biblical Repertory say:—"We have little apprehension that any one can so far mistake our object, or the purport of our remarks, as to suppose *either that we regard slavery as a desirable institution*, or that we approve of the slave laws of the Southern states. So far from this being the case, the extinction of slavery, and the amelioration of those laws, are as sincerely desired by us as by any of the abolitionists." "It follows necessarily, from what has been said, that all those laws which are designed to restrict the master in the discharge of the duties which flow from his relation to his slaves; which forbid his teaching them to read, or which prohibit marriage among them, or which allow of the separation of those who are married, or which render insecure the possession of their earnings, or are otherwise in conflict with the word of God, are wicked laws; laws which do not find their justification in the admission of the right of ownership in the master, but are in direct contravention of the obligations which necessarily flow from that right. If the laws of the land forbade parents to instruct their children, or permitted them to sell them to the Turks, there would be a general outcry against the atrocity of such laws; but no man would be so absurd as to infer that having children was a great sin. Parents who complied with such laws would be great sinners, but not parents who did their duty to

---

* Letters to Dr. Wayland, pp. 158, 159, 211.

their children.   In all other cases, men distinguish between
the relation, whether of kings and subjects, of lords and
tenants, of parents and children, and the laws just or unjust,
which may be made respecting those relations. *If they
would make the same distinction between slaveholding and
the slave laws, they would see that the condemnation of the
latter does not necessarily involve the condemnation of the
former as itself a crime.*"

In reply to this, I would make the following remarks:
(*a*) The very question—the only one that is of any practical
importance to us—is, whether slavery as it exists in the
United States is, or is not, in accordance with the principles
and the spirit of Christianity.   As an abstract matter, there
might indeed be some interest attached to the inquiry whether slavery, as it existed in the Roman empire in the time
of the Apostles, or in Europe in the middle ages, was in
accordance with the spirit of the Christian religion; and it
cannot be denied also that for us there may be *some* interest,
and for others *great* interest, in the question whether slavery
as it exists in India or in Brazil, is in accordance with the
principles of the Bible, but neither of these are the questions
which are fairly before the American people.   When the
inquiry respects any particular institution, it is proper to look
at that institution *as it exists*, not *as it might possibly exist:*
—for that is the only question which it is of much importance to examine.   When an inquiry pertains to the temperance reformation, or to the morality of gambling, it is proper
to look at these things *as they actually are,* for the object is
to ascertain whether it is desirable to make any change in
them.   This is especially important if an evil is of long
standing; if it is incorporated into the customs and habits of
a people; if it is sustained by the laws; if it affects the welfare of millions of human beings.   When Christianity first
made war on idolatry, the immediate and most important
question which came up to be examined, was not, whether
some modified form of idolatry might not be consistent with

the new system of religion, or whether there might not be found in some community a form of idolatry which Christianity could consistently tolerate, but whether the idolatry with which Christianity then came in actual collision was consistent with its principles. In examining the morality of the stage, shall we not examine it as it *is*, not as it possibly *might be;* shall we not look at its practical working to know whether it is a good or a bad thing? Is it not right to ask whether the principles of the Bible sanction the drama as it is? Is there any other question respecting it that is of immediate practical importance? (*b*) It is not improper to regard slavery as it exists in the United States as *a fair illustration* of the tendency of the system. It exists here in the best age of the world, and in the land most distinguished for intelligence, and for wisdom in making and administering laws. The laws pertaining to the system here may be regarded as those which long experience has shown to be necessary. It may be presumed that, amidst the prevalent intelligence of this land, the best measures have been adopted, or those which are *regarded* as the best, to make the system of slavery as perfect as possible. The laws in the several slave states are those which experience has shown to be necessary that the system may be perpetuated; that this kind of "property" may be as secure as possible, and that the institution may be made to contribute as much as possible to the wealth and comfort of the community in which it prevails. In the free states it is proper to look to the laws existing there in regard to common schools, to real and personal property, to the administration of justice, to apprenticeship, as *a fair expression* of the nature of the institutions there—as showing what experience has demonstrated to be adapted to secure the best working of the system—as an *exponent* of the real value and character of the system at this advanced age of the world. What shall forbid us, in like manner, to regard the laws and customs which are found necessary at the South, as *a fair illustration* of the

system—as an *exponent* of what slavery is in the best age
of the world, and under the guidance of legislative wisdom
and experience? That some of the laws may be so modified
as better to secure the ends in view; that some that are
harsh may be repealed consistently with the best working
of the system, need not be denied—just as in the farther
progress of society in free states some of the modes of punishment may be modified with advantage; but still, in the main,
in the one case and the other, the *existing* laws may be
regarded as what the best wisdom of the world has been able
to devise to make the system as perfect as possible. I have
therefore, in this Inquiry, freely appealed to the existing
laws in the Southern states, *not for the purpose of casting
reproach on those portions of our country where slavery
exists,* but for the sole design of ascertaining what the system
is, and of examining the question whether a system which *so*
develops itself is in accordance with the Bible. (*c*) If *any*
system of slavery is sustained by the Bible, it may be presumed that that which exists in the United States, is. This
is a Christian land—a land, to a degree elsewhere unknown,
under the influence of the Christian religion. In what
country could we hope that slavery would exist in a milder
or better form than in the United States? Our institutions
have grown up under the influence of Christianity. Not
a few of the legislators of the land have been pious men.
Not a few of the owners of slaves are pious men, and are
gathered into Christian congregations under the instruction
of men abundantly able to explain the doctrines of the
Christian system. It could hardly be hoped that a state
of society could be found, in which slavery could be
better developed, and where its developments would more
accord with the principles of the Bible, than in our own
land. Why then is it not fair to appeal to slavery as it
is, and to inquire whether the system as it now exists
is in accordance with the Bible? Is it not as impracticable to form an ideal system of slavery that shall be free

from all objections, and that shall be in all the laws and customs by which it is sustained in entire conformity with the New Testament, as it is to perfect the drama so that it shall be wholly free from objection on the score of morals? (*d*) The advocates of slavery themselves appeal to the Bible to show the propriety of slavery as it exists in the United States. When the question is agitated whether slavery is right or wrong, they almost uniformly make their appeal to the Scriptures to sustain themselves in the practice of it. The appeal which they make to the Bible is not to prove that slavery as it existed in Palestine in the time of Moses was right; or that slavery in Greece and Rome was right; or that slavery in India, Cuba, or Brazil, is right; but *to vindicate themselves in the practice*—to show that slavery in our own land cannot be regarded as wrong, and especially to show that the position taken by many that slavery *is a sin*, is not sustained by the Bible. When we make an attack on slavery as it exists in the United States, and endeavour to show that it is an evil—that it is morally wrong—that it ought to be abandoned—they make their appeal at once to the Bible. Why is this, but to defend slavery as it exists in this country? If this is *not* the drift of the argument, why do they not at once admit that slavery here, as it actually exists, is wrong, and enter on the foreign question whether some imaginary form of slavery could be vindicated? What can be the pertinency or propriety of such an appeal to the Bible as is almost uniformly made at the South, and frequently at the North, unless it is proper to bring American slavery *as it is* by the side of the Bible, and to inquire whether, with all its developments, it is or is not in accordance with the word of God? If the advocates of slavery would take this ground, and admit that the system of American slavery *is in fact* contrary to the Bible, the field of debate would be much narrowed. But as long as, in arguing this question, the appeal is made at the South to the Bible, it cannot be wrong to press the question with earnestness whether

American slavery *as it is* is sanctioned by the word of God. The main question is not about the 'abuse' of the system—for it might be a question whether there *is* any abuse of it possible, that is, any degree of oppression and wrong which the principles of the system do not sanction—but about the thing as it is fairly developed in our country. For what *is* the 'abuse' of slavery? When you have taken away a man's liberty; when you have made him a piece of property, and refused him the right of citizenship, and the right in his wife, his children, and himself; when he is to be wholly at the will of another, what precisely is to be understood by the 'abuse' of the system? What law of the South can be referred to which can be distinctly shown to be an 'abuse' of the system, in the sense that the *principles* of the system do not lead to it, or that it is not necessary in order to sustain it? It may be fairly doubted whether there is a single law or custom at the South which can be shown to be a violation of the fundamental principle of slavery; and if this be so, then it is proper to make the appeal to the Bible to inquire whether *this* system of laws and customs is in accordance with the revealed will of God. So the advocates of the system make their appeal when it is attacked; and so it is right for us.

I may be permitted to add another prefatory remark. I have *endeavoured* to conduct the argument with candour, and with a kind and Christian spirit. In noticing the arguments of the advocates of slavery, and of those who have in any manner used the language of apology for it, I have not designedly given any representation of their views which would diminish their force; nor have I been conscious of evading an argument because it seemed to present an unanswerable objection, or a material obstacle, to the views which I entertain. I have not sought to gain any thing in the argument by the use of hard names; or by imputing bad motives; or by assuming that every thing connected with slavery is wrong; or by the supposition that tne slaveholder is necessarily a bad man. I have aimed not needlessly to offend any one. To a candid examination of the views expressed by the advocates of slavery, no one can reasonably object ; and if I have been enabled to evince the spirit in this argument which I have desired to do, no one will have just occasion to be offended with the manner in which this discussion has been conducted. If I have betrayed any other than a kind spirit, and have used any other than kind words, it has been contrary to my design.

I anticipate that in some of the views expressed in this work, I shall be found to differ from not a few of my friends ;—but it is one of the conditions of our friendship that each one is at liberty to express his opinions with entire freedom. I expect to be found to differ from not a few of the wise and good of the land ;—but it would be impossible to discuss any subject on morals in respect to which this would not be the case—and the truly wise and good are accustomed to expect that this may occur. All such will admit that the points discussed in this work are of great importance to the best interests of humanity : to me it would be a matter of high gratification if the discussion in these pages should be found to be such as to contribute something towards promoting uniformity of views and feelings on one of the most momentous questions which this age is called to investigate, and which enters more deeply into the permanent welfare of our country than any other.

AN INQUIRY

INTO THE

SCRIPTURAL VIEWS OF SLAVERY.

CHAPTER I.

Reasons why the appeal on this subject should be made to the Bible.

THERE are perhaps no questions of more importance to our country than those which pertain to the subject of slavery. The fact that after the existence of more than half a century of freedom in this land, there should be in the midst of us now a number nearly equal in the aggregate to the white population at the time of the Declaration of Independence, is of itself most remarkable in history; and is so anomalous, and so at variance with all our principles, that posterity will inquire for the reasons of such an occurrence. This number, already so large, is increasing in certain parts of our country in a ratio fearfully alarming, and the effects of the system are felt, and must be felt, in every portion of the Republic. There is nothing connected with our national interests which is not affected more or less by slavery. It enters into the representation in our national legislature; it is connected with great questions of industry, literature, agriculture, commerce, and morals; it is intimately allied with religion. The entire South is identified with it; and by the ramifications of business, of education, of commerce, and of manufactures, there is not a town, a school-district, or a parish in the North, which is not

19

directly or remotely affected by it. As a part of a great nation—one great confederated people—we of the North have the deepest interest in all the questions that pertain to the weal or wo, the perils or the faults of any part of our country —for we share the common honour or the dishonour of the Republic. Belonging to the same race with those who are held in bondage, we have a right, nay, we are bound to express the sympathies of brotherhood, and to " remember those who are in bonds, as bound with them." But there is a deeper interest still which we have in this subject; a more perfect right which we have to express our views in regard to it. The questions of morals and religion—of right and wrong, know no geographical limits; are bounded by no conventional lines ; are circumscribed by the windings of no river or stream, and are not designated by climate or by the course of the sun. They are questions which no existing compacts or constitutions forbid us to examine ; and though there *are* rights which one part of a country has which are not to be invaded by others, yet there are no enclosures within which the questions of right and wrong may not be carried with the utmost freedom.

At the same time, this subject should be approached with calmness and candour. There is no one thing pertaining to the welfare of our common country, which is beset with so many difficulties, and which is so much fitted to make men of all classes feel their need of the " wisdom which is from above." Hitherto, all " the wisdom of the wise" has been confounded in regard to it, and if there is any question that is fitted to bring the whole intellect of this nation—including that of judges, senators, counsellors, and the ministers of religion, at the feet of Infinite wisdom, it is the question respecting African slavery. How is the evil to be arrested ? How is that unhappy people among us to be restored to freedom, and elevated to the dignity and the privileges of men ? How is a foreign race with so different a complexion, and in reference to which so deep-seated prejudices and aversions exist in every part of the land, to be disposed of if they become free ? These, and kindred inquiries, have hitherto baffled all our wisdom. It may do *something* towards answering them, if we can settle the grand preliminary question whether slavery is right or wrong ; an evil *per se*, or only an evil incidentally and by abuse ; a good institution which God designs to be perpetuated, or an institution which he regards as evil, and which he designs that the principles of his religion and his own Providential dealings shall ultimately destroy.

In the examination of this subject, on which I propose now to enter, the appeal will be made wholly to the Bible, for the following reasons :

1. The Bible is the acknowledged standard of morals in this nation. To an extent wholly unknown in other lands, it is allowed here to settle all questions of right and wrong, and its decisions, when clearly ascertained, are conceded to be final. It is not indeed directly made the basis of legislation, and it cannot be denied that there are departures from its principles in many practical views which prevail, yet still it maintains an ascendency on all questions of morals which no other book can acquire, and which, by the mass of this nation, will be conceded to no other authority whatever. There are few writers on morals, and probably none of reputation, who would undertake to defend a position that was plainly *against* the teachings of the Bible. It may be safely affirmed that there is not a legislative body that would take the ground of openly legislating against the Bible ; there is not a judge on any bench who would pronounce a decision that would be clearly contrary to a principle laid down in the Sacred Scriptures ; there is not a department of government that would not admit that if the Bible has settled a question, it is final. It is to be regarded as an elementary principle in the questions which come before the public mind in this nation, that on subjects in relation to which there are clear principles in that book, the intellect, and the heart, and the laws of this great people will bow reverently before that high authority. It is proper therefore to bring this question before this admit-

ted standard in morals, and I shall regard it as a safe position, that if the people of this nation were convinced that slavery is contrary to the Bible, they would at once institute a train of measures which would effectually remove the evil. We may carry a clear decision of the Bible to any class of our citizens, expecting that the authority will be respected, and that the obligation to obey it will be conceded. This sentiment is recognised at the South as well as at the North ; and by candid men there as well as elsewhere it is admitted that, if slavery is contrary to the Bible, it *must* be abandoned. Thus it is said in the Southern Quarterly Review, for October, 1845, p. 334, "Greatly the most important view of the subject [slavery] is the religious one. For assuredly if slavery be adjudged a sin, if it be condemned by the revealed will of God, then in Christendom it cannot continue to exist. It is the duty of every man, making the laws of God the rule of his conduct, to use all practicable efforts to abolish whatever violates them."

2. The subject of slavery is one on which the Bible has legislated, and there is, therefore, a propriety that we should ascertain its decisions. An institution of servitude of some kind early existed in the world. The most ancient and venerable men whose names the Sacred History has trans- mitted to us, were in some way connected with it. There are numerous statutes on the subject in the Mosaic code of laws. The Prophets often refer to it. Servitude had an existence in the time of the Apostles, and they often came in contact with it in their attempts to spread the Gospel. They have repeatedly alluded to it in their writings, and have laid down principles in regard to it which they evidently designed should be understood to be the settled laws of the Christian religion. In fact there is scarcely any one subject to which there is more frequent allusion in the Scriptures, in some way or other, than to slavery ; and it cannot be that a subject should so early attract the attention of the Great Legislator whose laws are there recorded, and be so often referred to,

without ever laying down any *principles* which may be regarded as decisive in regard to his views. It is to be presumed that it is *possible* to ascertain whether God regards it as a good institution or an evil one; an arrangement in society which he meant his religion should contribute to sustain and perpetuate for the good of the race, or an institution which he intended it should ultimately abolish.—There is, therefore, perfect propriety in carrying the appeal to the Bible; and there can be few things more important than to ascertain what are the teachings of the Bible on the subject. If slavery be in accordance with the principles of the Bible, and be the best thing for society, there is then an increasingly large part of the world that is neglecting to avail itself of the advantages which might be derived from the institution, and that is falling into dangerous error on a great question of morals—for there can be no doubt that there is a growing conviction in the world that the institution is not one which it is desirable to perpetuate for promoting the welfare of mankind.

3. There is little approximation to a settlement of the question whether slavery is right or wrong on other grounds than an appeal to the Scriptures. Apart from the influence of the Bible, it may be doubted whether any advance is made towards a settled and uniform judgment on this subject. Considerations of humanity or policy have done something indeed to change the views of men in regard to the slave *trade*, and by common consent this has come to be regarded as *piracy;* but it may be doubted whether these considerations have done any thing to affect the question about *slavery itself* in slaveholding communities. No progress was made towards its abolition in the Roman empire by the influence of these considerations. Slavery flourished in its extremest rigour under the highest advances made in Roman policy, and in the brightest days of Roman jurisprudence, and it was only by the application of religious principle that it was ever permanently affected in the empire. In England, it was by the power of religious principle in Clarkson, Wilberforce, and

their fellow-labourers, that slavery was abolished, and not by considerations of policy or mere humanity. In our own country, it may be doubted whether any considerable progress has been made in determining whether slavery is to continue or not, by mere political considerations. The convictions of the great mass of our fellow-citizens in the slaveholding part of our country in regard to the evils of slavery, are not more decided than were those of Jefferson, and though since his views were so firmly expressed there has been an opportunity of observing the effects of the system for half a century, yet slavery has a hold on the country at large not less tenacious than it had then. It is indeed not difficult to show the impolicy of the system. It is easy to show the superior prosperity of those portions of our country where it does not exist. It is easy to point to the exhausted soil; the wasted fields; the diminished population and wealth; the comparative destitution of schools, colleges, and churches; the ignorance, degradation and corruption of morals which slavery engenders; and it is easy to fortify all this by the splendid declamation of Southern statesmen themselves about the impoverished condition of their country,* but still almost no

---

* The following eloquent remarks by two Southern gentlemen in Congress, furnish at the same time a mournful description of the effects of slavery on the condition of a country; show the comparative influence of freedom and slavery; and illustrate the argument which might be derived from the tendency of slavery, to show that God does not approve of the system. The first extract is from a speech of the Hon. Mr. Clowney, of South Carolina. He says :—

"Look at South Carolina now, with her houses deserted and falling to decay, her once fruitful fields worn out and abandoned for want of timely improvement or skilful cultivation; and her thousands of acres of inexhaustible lands still promising an abundant harvest to the *industrious* husbandman, lying idle and neglected. In the interior of the state where I was born, and where I now live, although a country possessing all the advantages of soil, climate and health, abounding in arable land, unreclaimed from the first rude state of nature, there can now be found many

advance is made towards admitting that the system is evil. Almost no efforts are put forth to remove it. No conclusions against it are derived from the disapprobation which the God of Providence is placing upon it by these results of the system, and if the inquiry is ever settled it must be by bringing it to a standard which all will admit to have authority to determine great questions of morals.

4. Great reforms on moral subjects do not occur except under the influence of religious principle. Political revolutions, and changes of policy and of administration, do indeed occur from other causes, and secure the ends which are desired. But on subjects pertaining to right and wrong; on those questions where the rights of an inferior and downtrodden class are concerned, we can look for little advance except from the operation of religious principle. Unless the inferior classes have power to assert their rights by arms, those rights will be conceded only by the operations of conscience, and by the principles of religion. There is no great *wrong* in any community which we can hope to rectify by

---

neighbourhoods where the population is too sparse to support a common elementary school for children. Such is the deplorable condition of one of the oldest members of this Union, that dates back its settlement more than a century and a half, while other states, born as it were but yesterday, already surpass what Carolina was or ever has been in the happiest and proudest day of her prosperity."

The other extract is from a speech of the Hon. Mr. Preston, of South Carolina.

"No Southern man can journey (as he had lately done) through the Northern States, and witness the prosperity, the industry, the public spirit which they exhibit—the sedulous cultivation of all those arts by which life is rendered comfortable and respectable, without feelings of deep sadness and shame as he remembers *his own neglected and desolate home.* There, no dwelling is to be seen abandoned—not a farm uncultivated. Every person and every thing performs a part toward the grand result; and the whole land is covered with fertile fields, with manufactories, and canals, and railroads, and edifices, and towns, and cities. We of the South are mistaken in the character of these people when we think

new considerations of policy, or by a mere revolution. The relations of slavery are not reached by political revolutions, or by changes of policy or administration. Political revolutions occur in a higher region, and the condition of the slave is no more affected by a mere change in the government than that of the vapours in a low, marshy vale is affected by the tempest and storm in the higher regions of the air. The storm sweeps along the Apennines, the lightnings play and the thunders utter their voice, but still the malaria of the Campagna is unaffected, and the pestilence breathes desolation there still. So it is with slavery. Political revolutions occur in high places, but the malaria of slavery remains settled down on the low plains of life, and not even the surface of the pestilential vapour is agitated by all the storms and tempests of political changes. It remains the same deadly, pervading pestilence still. Under all the forms of despotism; in the government of an aristocracy or an oligarchy; under the administration of a pure democracy or the forms of a republican government, and in all the changes from one to the other, slavery remains still the same. Whe-

---

of them only as pedlars in horn flints and bark nutmegs. Their energy and enterprise are directed to all objects, great and small, within their reach. The number of railroads and other modes of expeditious intercommunication knit the whole country into a closely compacted mass, through which the productions of commerce and of the press, the comforts of life and the means of knowledge, are universally diffused; while the close intercourse of travel and of business makes all neighbours, and promotes a common interest and a common sympathy. How different the condition of these things in the South! *Here* the face of the country wears the aspect of premature old age and decay. No IMPROVEMENT IS SEEN GOING ON, nothing is done for posterity. No man thinks of any thing beyond the present moment."

It is true that these gentlemen attribute these effects to the tariff, but *the facts* in the case are the things of chief importance here. Other persons see different causes at work than the tariff, and the period will arrive when the true cause will be seen by all the inhabitants of the slaveholding states.

ther the master is hurled from the throne, or rides into power on the tempest of revolution, the down-trodden slave is the same still, and it makes no difference to him whether the master wears a crown or appears in a plain republican garb; whether Cæsar is on the throne or is slain in the Senate house. Slavery, among the Romans, remained substantially the same under the Tarquins, the Consuls, and the Cæsars; when the tribunes gained the ascendency, and when the patricians crushed them to the earth. It lived in Europe when the Northern hordes poured down on the Roman empire, and when the Caliphs set up the standard of Islam in the Peninsula. It lived in all the revolutions of the middle ages—alike when spiritual despotism swayed its sceptre over the nations, and when they began to emerge into freedom. In the British realms it has lived in the time of the Stuarts, under the Protectorate, and for a long time under the administration of the house of Hanover. With some temporary interruptions, it lived in the provinces of France, through the Revolution. It lived through our own glorious Revolution; and the struggles which gave liberty to millions of the Anglo-Saxon race did not loosen one rivet from the fetter of an African, nor was there a slave who was any nearer to the enjoyment of freedom after the surrender at Yorktown, than when Patrick Henry taught the notes of liberty to echo along the hills and vales of Virginia. So in all the changes of political administration in our own land, the condition of the slave remains unaffected. Alike whether Federalists or Republicans have the rule; whether the star of the Whig or the Democrat is in the ascendant, the condition of the slave is the same. The pæans of victory when the hero of New Orleans was raised to the presidential chair, or when the hero of Tippecanoe was inaugurated, conveyed no note of joy, no intimation of a change, to the slave; nor had he any more hope, nor was his condition any more affected when the one gave place to his successor, or the other was borne to the grave. And so it is now. In the fierce contests for rule in the land; in the questions about changes of administration, there are nearly three millions of our fellow-beings who have no interest in these contests and questions, and whose condition will be affected no more, whatever the result may be, than the vapour that lies in the valley is by the changes from sunshine to storm on the summits of the Alps or the Andes.

The reason of this is, that these questions of revolution do not go into these humble vales of life. It is only *religion* that finds its way down and effects changes there; and the only hope, therefore, of producing revolutions on this great subject is, by bringing the principles of the Bible to bear upon it. The suggestions, therefore, in the argument which I propose to conduct, will not refer to the political bearings of slavery, but to the naked question whether the institution is in accordance with the Bible. I should feel myself incompetent to go into a proper examination of the former question; I may accomplish some good if I can do any thing to determine what is truth in regard to the latter.

5. The appeal will be made solely to the Bible, because it is by such an appeal that the advocates of slavery endeavour to defend the system. In popular speeches; in sermons; in the solemn acts of Presbyteries, synods, conventions, conferences, and assemblies; in formal treatises in defence of slavery, in pamphlets and reviews, the appeal is constantly made to the Sacred Scriptures. In popular illustrations of Scripture, in newspaper articles, in learned commentaries, and in the formal opinions of erudite professors at the North and the South, such a melancholy general expression of opinion that the Bible lends its sanction to slavery prevails, that it has come almost to be regarded as a settled matter. A few selections from those opinions will illustrate the propriety of an appeal to the Bible, and will show that the prevailing method of interpreting the Bible on this subject is such as to call for an examination of the meaning of the Scriptures, involving whatever talent may

be found adapted to such an inquiry, and whatever patient labour such an investigation may demand. The extracts will be mere brief selections designed to exhibit the prevailing mode of speaking and writing on the subject among intelligent religious men.

The following is the declared opinion of Rev. E. D. Sims, Professor in Randolph Macon College, a Methodist institution :—

"These extracts from holy writ unequivocally assert the right of property in slaves, together with the usual incidents of that right, such as the power of acquisition and disposition in various ways, according to municipal regulations. The right to buy and sell, and to transmit to children by way of inheritance, is clearly stated. The only restriction on the subject, is in reference to the market, in which slaves or bondmen were to be purchased.

"Upon the whole, then, whether we consult the Jewish polity, instituted by God himself; or the uniform opinion and practice of mankind in all ages of the world ; or the injunctions of the New Testament and the moral law ; we are brought to the conclusion, that slavery *is not immoral*.

"Having established the point, that the first African slaves were legally brought into bondage, the right to detain their children in bondage follows as an indispensable consequence.

"Thus we see, that the slavery which exists in America was founded *in right*."

The following sentiment was expressed by the late Rev. Wilbur Fisk, D. D., President of the Wesleyan University in Connecticut, a name standing deservedly high in the church.

"The relation of master and slave may, and does, in many cases, exist under such circumstances, as free the master from the just charge and guilt of immorality.

"1 Cor. vii. 20—23.—This text seems mainly to enjoin and sanction the fitting continuance of their present social relations ; the freeman was to remain free, and the slave, unless emancipation should offer, was to remain a slave.

"The general rule of Christianity not only permits, but, in supposable circumstances, enjoins a continuance of the master's authority.

"The New Testament enjoins obedience upon the slave as an obligation due to a present rightful authority."

The following resolutions of different religious bodies of the South may be regarded, without impropriety, as expressing the prevailing sentiment at the South in regard to the sanction which the Bible gives to slavery.

HOPEWELL PRESBYTERY, SOUTH CAROLINA.

1. "Slavery has existed in the church of God from the time of Abraham to this day. Members of the church of God have held slaves, bought with their money, and had them born in their houses; and this relation is not only recognised, but its duties are defined clearly, both in the Old and New Testaments.

2. "Emancipation is not mentioned among the duties of the master to his slave, while obedience 'even to the froward' master is enjoined upon the slave.

3. "No instance can be produced of an otherwise orderly Christian being reproved, much less excommunicated from the church, for the single act of holding domestic slaves, from the days of Abraham down to the date of the modern abolitionist."

HARMONY PRESBYTERY, SOUTH CAROLINA.

"Whereas, sundry persons in Scotland and England, and others in the north, east, and west of our country, have denounced slavery as obnoxious to the laws of God, some of whom have presented before the General Assembly of our church, and the Congress of the nation, memorials and petitions, with the avowed object of bringing into disgrace slaveholders, and abolishing the relation of master and slave: And whereas, from the said proceedings, and the statements, reasonings, and circumstances connected therewith, it is most manifest that those persons 'know not what they say, nor whereof they affirm;' and with this ignorance discover a spirit of self-righteousness and exclusive sanctity, &c.; therefore, Resolved,

1. "That as the kingdom of our Lord is not of this world, his church, as such, has no right to abolish, alter, or affect any institution or ordinance of men, political or civil, &c.

2. "That slavery has existed from the days of those good old slaveholders and patriarchs, Abraham, Isaac, and Jacob, who are now in the kingdom of heaven,) to the time when the

apostle Paul sent a runaway slave home to his master, Phile-mon, and wrote a Christian and paternal letter to this slave-holder, which we find still stands in the canon of the Scriptures—and that slavery has existed ever since the days of the apostle, and does now exist.

3. "That as the relative duties of master and slave are taught in the Scriptures, in the same manner as those of parent and child, and husband and wife, the existence of slavery itself is not opposed to the will of God; and whosoever has a conscience too tender to recognise this relation as lawful, is 'righteous overmuch,' is 'wise above what is written,' and has submitted his neck to the yoke of men, sacrificed his Christian liberty of conscience, and leaves the infallible word of God for the fancies and doctrines of men."

CHARLESTON UNION PRESBYTERY.

"It is a principle which meets the views of this body, that slavery, as it exists among us, is a political institution, with which ecclesiastical judicatories have not the smallest right to interfere; and in relation to which, any such interference, especially at the present momentous crisis, would be morally wrong, and fraught with the most dangerous and pernicious consequences. The sentiments which we maintain, in common with Christians at the South of every denomination, are sentiments which so fully approve themselves to our consciences, are so identified with our solemn convictions of duty, that we should maintain them under any circumstances.

"Resolved, That in the opinion of this Presbytery, the holding of slaves, so far from being a sin in the sight of God, is nowhere condemned in his holy word—that it is in accordance with the example, or consistent with the precepts of patriarchs, apostles, and prophets, and that it is compatible with the most fraternal regard to the best good of those servants whom God may have committed to our charge; and that, therefore, they who assume the contrary position, and lay it down as a fundamental principle in morals and religion, that all slaveholding is wrong, proceed upon false principles."

SYNOD OF VIRGINIA.

"The committee to whom were referred the resolutions, &c., have, according to order, had the same under consideration—and respectfully report, that in their judgment, the following resolutions are necessary and proper to be adopted by the Synod at the present time:

" Whereas, the publications and proceedings of certain or ganized associations, commonly called anti-slavery, or abolition societies which have arisen in some parts of our land, have greatly disturbed and are still greatly disturbing the peace of the church, and of the country; and the Synod of Virginia deem it a solemn duty which they owe to themselves and to the community to declare their sentiments upon the subject; therefore, Resolved, unanimously,

" That we consider the dogma fiercely promulgated by said associations—that slavery, as it exists in our slaveholding states, is necessarily sinful, and ought to be immediately abolished—and the conclusions which naturally follow from that dogma, as directly and palpably contrary to the plainest principles of common sense and common humanity, *and to the clearest authority of the word of God.*"

The following is from the church in Petersburg, Virginia, 16th November, 1838 :—

" Whereas, the General Assembly did, in 1818, pass a law, which contains provisions for slaves, irreconcilable with our civil institutions, and solemnly declaring slavery to be a sin against God—a law at once offensive and insulting to the whole Southern community ; Resolved,

1. " That, as slaveholders, we cannot consent longer to remain in connection with any church where there exists a statute conferring a right upon slaves to arraign their masters before the judicatory of the church—and that, too, for the act of selling them without their consent first had and obtained.

2. " *That as the Great Head of the church has recognised the relation of master and slave, we conscientiously believe that slavery is not a sin against God, as declared by the General Assembly.*

3. " That there is no tyranny more oppressive than that which is sometimes sanctioned by the operation of ecclesiastical law.''

Thus also the Presbytery of Tombecbee, in a formal letter to the General Conference in Maine, expresses the following sentiments :—" In the Bible the state of slavery is clearly recognised, but the condition of the slave, like that of all society, is left to be regulated by the civil policy of the state, or country in which it exists.   Abram, the friend of God, had slaves born in his house, and bought with money." "Jacob held slaves, without the least remorse of conscience, or reproof from God." "It was no sin for a priest to purchase a slave with money." "The Bible warrants the purchase of slaves as an inheritance for children for ever." "That slavery is not a moral evil, is evident from the fact, that it is nowhere condemned by the Redeemer, or his apostles, in the New Testament." "The Bible makes slavery a part of the domestic circle; it is associated with husband and wife, parents and children."

Views similar to these are expressed in an article in the Princeton Biblical Repertory, for April, 1836—an article which was reprinted at Pittsburgh, on the eve of an important meeting of the General Assembly of the Presbyterian church, by Southern gentlemen, and which was understood to give great satisfaction to the friends of slavery in the South. The following extracts will show the views of the writer, and illustrate the inclination of those who look favourably on the system, to sustain their views by the authority of the Bible.

"It is on all hands acknowledged that, at the time of the advent of Jesus Christ, slavery in its worst forms prevailed over the whole world. The Saviour found it around him in Judea; the Apostles met with it in Asia, Greece, and Italy. How did they treat it? Not by the denunciation of slavery as necessarily and universally sinful. The subject is hardly alluded to by Christ in any of his personal instructions. The Apostles refer to it, not to pronounce upon it as a question of morals, but to prescribe the relative duties of masters and slaves."—pp. 275, 276. "An obvious deduction from the fact above referred to, is, that slaveholding is not necessarily sinful."—p. 277. "The argument from the conduct of Christ and his immediate followers seems to us decisive on the point, that slaveholding, in itself considered, is not a crime."—p. 279. "But what stronger argument can be presented to prove that the sacred writers did not regard slaveholding as in itself sinful, than that while they condemn all unjust or unkind treatment (even threatening) on the part of the masters toward their slaves, they did not condemn slavery itself."—p. 280. "That many of the attributes of

the system as established by law in this country are condemned, is, indeed, very plain ; but that slaveholding in itself
is condemned, has not been, and cannot be proved."—p. 281.
" It is admitted by these distinguished moralists [Dr. Channing and Dr. Wayland] that the Apostles did not preach a
religion proclaiming freedom to slaves; that Paul did not
assail slavery ; that the Gospel did not proclaim the unlaw-
fulness of slaveholding ; it did not forbid it. This is going
the whole length that we have gone in our statement of
the conduct of Christ and his apostles."—p. 282. " The
Apostles did not condemn slavery; they did not require
emancipation ; they recognised slaveholders as Christian
brethren."—p. 285. " Slavery was tolerated among the
ancient people of God. Abraham had servants in his family
who were ' bought with money.' The Mosaic institution
recognised the lawfulness of slavery. Our argument, from
this acknowledged fact, is, that if God allowed slavery to
exist, if he directed how slaves might be lawfully acquired,
and how they were to be treated, it is in vain to contend that
slavery is a sin, and yet profess reverence for the Scriptures."—p. 287. " Slavery is a question of circumstances,
not a *malum in se*."—p. 292. " As it appears to us too
clear to admit of either denial or doubt, that the Scriptures
do sanction slaveholding ; that under the old dispensation it
was expressly permitted by divine command, and under the
New Testament is nowhere forbidden or renounced, but, on
the contrary, acknowledged to be consistent with the Christian character and profession, (that is, consistent with justice,
mercy, holiness, love to God and love to man,) to declare it to
be a heinous crime, is a direct impeachment of the word of
God."—pp. 297, 298.

" Slavery," says the Hon. J. K. Paulding, (in his work
entitled " Slavery in the United States," pp. 14, 15,) " is
made the subject of express regulation in the social institutions of the Jews, and this without a single expression of
disapprobation on the part of the divine Lawgiver." After
quoting several passages from the books of Moses on the subject of slavery, he also adds, (pp. 19, 20,) " Here is a direct
sanction of rights corresponding in all respects with those of
the holders of slaves in the United States. They were
originally ' of the heathen' when purchased ; their posterity
was ' begot in the land ;' and they have descended ' as an
inheritance to our children.' It is difficult to conceive how,
with these authorities before them, the Abolitionists can

persist in maintaining that slavery is contrary to the law of God." "There is no authority derivable from the New Testament, which justifies the assertion that slavery is contrary to the law of God."—p. 24. "Slavery existed almost universally at, and ages before, the Christian dispensation, and it is *not even discountenanced there,* much less denounced as contrary to the law of God."—p. 26.

Dr. Fuller, in his letters to Dr. Wayland, says, "The Old Testament did sanction slavery. And in the Gospels and Epistles the institution is, to say the least, tolerated. You admit some sort of slavery to have been allowed in the Old Testament, and suffered by Jesus and his apostles. A man who denies this will deny any thing, and only proves how much stronger a passion is than the clearest truth. But if this point be yielded, how can it be maintained that slave-holding is itself a crime?"—pp. 3, 4. And again: "I undertake to show that the Bible does, most explicitly, both by precept and example, bear me out in my assertion, that slavery is not necessarily, and always, and amidst all circumstances, a sin. This is the position to be established, and the entire reasoning (reasoning which, if the premises be true, really seems to me to commend itself at once to every man's conscience) is this, WHAT GOD SANCTIONED IN THE OLD TESTAMENT, AND PERMITTED IN THE NEW, CANNOT BE SIN."*

To these extracts may be added, for an illustration of the prevailing manner in which the subject is regarded, the following views of Professor Stuart, than whom there is not one of higher or more deserved authority in this land, in all questions pertaining to the interpretation of the Scriptures. These views are copied, not because I would wish to convey the impression that Professor Stuart is or would be either the advocate of slavery, or the apologist for it, but to show the importance of a thorough inquiry into the actual teachings of the Scriptures on this subject. The following is Professor Stuart's letter to Dr. Fisk:

"ANDOVER, *April* 10, 1837.

"REV. AND DEAR SIR:—Yours is before me. A sickness of three months' standing, (typhus fever,) in which I have

---

* Fuller and Wayland on Slavery, p. 170.

just escaped death, and which still confines me to my house,
renders it impossible for me to answer your letter at large.

"1. The precepts of the New Testament, respecting the
demeanour of slaves and their masters, beyond all question,
recognise the existence of slavery. The masters are, in part,
'*believing masters;*' so that a precept to them, how they are
to behave, as *masters*, recognises that the relation may exist,
salva fide, et salva ecclesia, [*without violating the Christian
faith or the church ;*] otherwise Paul had nothing to do but
to cut the band asunder at once. He could not lawfully and
properly temporize with *malum in se*, [that which is in itself
sin.]

"If any one doubts, let him take the case of Paul's sending
Onesimus back to Philemon, with an apology for his running
away, and sending him back to be a servant for life. The
relation did exist—may exist. The *abuse* of it is the essential and fundamental wrong. Not that the theory of slavery
is right, in itself. No. 'Love thy neighbour as thyself'—
'Do unto others that which you would that others should do
unto you,' decides against this. But the relation, once constituted and continued, is not such a *malum in se* as calls for
immediate and violent disruption at all hazards. So Paul did
not counsel.

"2. 1 Tim. vi. 2, expresses the sentiment that slaves, who
are Christians and have Christian masters, are not, on that
account, and because *as Christians they are brethren*, to
forego the reverence due to them as masters. That is, the
relation of master and slave is not, as a matter of course, abro-
gated between all Christians. Nay, servants should, in such
a case, *à fortiori*, do their duty cheerfully. This sentiment
lies on the very face of the case. What the master's duty is in
such a case, in respect to *liberation*, is another question, and
one which the apostle does not here treat of.

"3. Every one knows, who is acquainted with Greek or
Latin antiquities, that slavery among heathen nations has
ever been more unqualified and at loose ends than among
Christian nations. Slaves were *property* in Greece and
Rome. That decides all questions about their *relation*.
Their treatment depended, as it does now, on the temper of
their masters. The power of the master over the slave was,
for a long time, that of *life and death*. Horrible cruelties at
length mitigated it. In the apostle's day, it was at least as
great as among us.

"After all the spouting and vehemence on this subject, the

good old Book remains the same.   Paul's conduct and advice are still safe guides.   Paul knew well that Christianity would ultimately destroy slavery, as it certainly will.   He knew too that it would destroy monarchy and aristocracy from the earth, for it is fundamentally a doctrine of *true liberty and equality*.   Yet Paul did not expect slavery or aristocracy to be ousted in a day, and gave precepts to Christians respecting their demeanour, *ad interim*.

     " With sincere and fraternal regard,
        " Your friend and brother,
                " M. STUART."

These extracts, with the considerations which have been suggested, will show, it is believed, the propriety of the course which I propose to pursue in this argument.   By the results of such an investigation, the people of this land ultimately *must* and *will* abide.   He that shall contribute any thing, however humble, to influence the public mind in coming to a right decision on so momentous a question, will not have lived in vain.

CHAPTER II.

What constitutes Slavery?

THE issue of the question about the lawfulness of slavery must depend materially on the answer which is given to the question, What constitutes slavery? Until this is determined, it is impossible to arrive at any settled views on the inquiry whether it is right or wrong.

The true inquiry here is, what are the essential features of the system? What distinguishes it from all other relations of life—from the relation of a child, a minor, an apprentice, a day-labourer, a serf, a 'villein' under the feudal system? Slavery has *some* features which resemble certain things in other relations, and the attention is sometimes fixed on these features of resemblance, forgetting what constitutes the peculiarity of the system, and then an argument is constructed to prove that slavery is recognised in the Scriptures just as those other relations are; that the duties in the one case are prescribed as they are in the other; and that this relation in society is designed to be as permanent, and is in itself as lawful, as the others. It is undeniable that in the relation of slavery there is *something* in common with the relation of apprenticeship, of a minor, of a subject under an arbitrary government, of those who are transferred from one government to another, as " by the treaty of Vienna, a large part of the inhabitants of central Europe changed masters,—as Saxony was transferred to Prussia, Belgium was annexed to Holland, and as Louisiana was transferred from France to the United States,"* but still the question is, whether the *peculiarity* of slavery is found in all these relations and transfers? In the condition of a slave, also, there

---

* Bib. Repertory, 1836, p. 294.

٠s *some* resemblance to that of the serf of Russia, and the 'villein' under the feudal system; but still the world is accustomed accurately to distinguish their condition from that of slave, and it does not define slavery to say that it is the condition of a serf or a ' villein.' There is still *something* essential to it which is not reached by these terms.

The importance of ascertaining accurately what slavery is, may be seen by referring to some of the definitions which have been given of it. From these it will be seen that, according to some of the different views which are held of its nature, it is easy to construct an argument in its defence. Paley's definition is this : " I define slavery," says he, "to be an obligation to labour for the benefit of the master, without the contract or consent of the servant."* Substantially the same is the idea of the author of the article before referred to in the Biblical Repertory, and as this may be regarded, without impropriety, as expressing the sentiments of those who apologize for slavery, or who regard it as consistent with Christianity, it is important to quote the words of the writer at length. He says, "Neither inadequate remuneration, physical discomfort, intellectual ignorance, moral degradation, is essential to the condition of a slave. Yet if all these ideas are removed from the commonly received notion of slavery, how little will remain. All the ideas which essentially enter into the definition of slavery are, deprivation of personal liberty, obligation of service at the discretion of another, and the transferable character of the authority and claim of the master. The manner in which men are brought into this condition; its continuance, and the means adopted for securing the authority and claim of masters, are all incidental and variable. They may be reasonable or unreasonable, just or unjust, at different times and places."— p. 279. " Slavery, in itself considered, is a state of bondage, and nothing more. It is the condition of an indi-

---

* Moral Philosophy, book iii. ch. 3.

vidual who is deprived of his personal liberty, and is obliged to work for another, who has the right to transfer this claim of service, at pleasure."—p. 289. In discussing the question whether the nature of *property* enters into the idea of slavery, the writer remarks that, "a man has property in his wife, in his children, in his domestic animals, in his fields and forests," and goes on to observe that, "where it is said that one man is the property of another, it can only mean that the one has a right to use the other *as a man*, but not as a brute or as a thing.—When this idea of property comes to be analyzed, it is found to be nothing more than *a claim of service either for life, or for a term of years*."—p. 293. According to this view, slavery is comparatively a harmless thing. No one should be alarmed at the idea of being himself a slave, or of having his children reduced to this condition ; and no one should regard slavery as essentially an undesirable condition of society, and still less as having in it any thing that is morally wrong. The idea of regarding a slave as a chattel or a thing is expressly discarded, and all the *property* which it is supposed there can be in the slave is that harmless possession which a man has in his wife and children. If this be the just idea of slavery, then it would hardly be worth while to argue the question whether it is right or wrong, or whether it is, or is not, in accordance with the Bible. It may be remarked here only that this is a view which will calm the feelings, allay the suspicions of guilt or responsibility, save from the compunctious visitings of remorse, and meet the wishes of all those south of 'Mason's and Dixon's line' who desire to preserve this domestic institution in its purity. Whether this is the true notion of slavery, however, it may be well to consider. I would observe, then,

(1.) That slavery is not a mere condition of apprenticeship, or that the service which a slave is bound to render to his master is not that which the apprentice is bound to render to his employer. There may be *something* in common, but all men make a distinction between them. Even in the system of 'apprenticeship' in the West Indies, there was an accurate, and a very obvious distinction, between that condition and the state of slavery which this was intended to supersede. An apprentice is bound to his master; he works for him; his time is his; and the master avails himself of whatever physical strength or skill the apprentice may have, or may acquire while he is with him —and so far there is that which the relation has *in common* with slavery. The relations resemble each other also in the fact, that the apprentice is usually placed in this condition without being consulted, or in accordance with the will of another. But this relation is designed to be temporary; it is for the good of the apprentice himself; it contemplates his own future usefulness and happiness, and there is *a full equivalent* supposed to be rendered for his labour. The care of the master over his morals and habits, and the instruction which he is expected to receive in the employment to which he designs to devote his life, are regarded as an ample compensation for any service which he can render. The master, in fact, avails himself of no unrequited labour of the apprentice; has no claim of property in *him;* has no power to continue the relation beyond a specified period; and has no right to transfer the apprentice to another. The condition is one also that is consistent with a regular advance in knowledge of all kinds, and in which the master has no control over any of the other relations which the apprentice may sustain, or into which he may choose prospectively to enter. In all this it differs from *slavery.*

(2.) Nor is slavery to be confounded with the condition of a *minor.* There are many things indeed that are common between slavery as it has always existed, and the condition of those who are under age. A minor, like a slave, has no right to vote; is not eligible to office; cannot be held in law by contracts which he makes, and in his time and labour is subject to the will of another. But we never confound the two conditions, and never suppose that the description of the one is a correct representation of the other. Nature, not force, has made the condition of a minor. In the arrangement, his own good is consulted. The whole arrangement is with reference to his own future welfare. It contemplates his being ultimately raised to all the dignities and rights of a citizen, and nature has secured, in the affections of those under whom minors are commonly placed, the best possible pledge that their interests will be sacredly regarded. Slavery does none of these things.

(3.) Nor is slavery merely a governmental affair—an assertion of power like that under a hereditary monarchy, or like a transfer of a portion of a people from one government to another, by treaty.* There may be much in common between such a condition and slavery, but we never confound them—except where we wish to throw dust in order to render the subject obscure. The authority asserted over the slave is often hereditary ; the power is claimed of making laws for him without his consent, and without representation ; the power over him is an usurped power ; it deprives him of the rights of a freeman, and he is transferred from one master to another without his consent—as the inhabitants of Poland, Belgium, Louisiana, Canada, Florida, and Normandy have been, or as the Cherokees, Choctaws, and Seminoles have been removed from Georgia and Florida, to the country west of the Mississippi. But we never think of confounding these things with slavery. Slavery is the right of an individual owner, not the operation of a government. It is control over the individual, and not over the mass. It contemplates properly no arrangement for masses *as governed*, but of individuals *as owned*. It transfers none by communities, but sells them as individuals. It is not the mere power of making laws for others,

---

* See Biblical Repertory, 1836, p. 294.

or of commanding their services for war; it is the power of controlling their time, a claim on their whole earnings, and of receiving all the avails of their skill and labour. It is not the right of transfer by treaty or conquest, but the power to *sell* them. The idea of slavery is not that of suffering the de privation of rights as a community, but as individuals; and if laws are ever made for them regarded as a community, it is not because they are considered as any part of the govern ment, but only to guard the rights of those who own them. In every essential feature slavery is removed from the aspect of being a governmental affair; for while it has some things in common with such an arrangement, still the world makes an accurate distinction between them. Besides, it would settle nothing as to the question of right and wrong to show that it was a mere governmental transaction. There are great questions of right and wrong in relation to the govern-ment of Nero, and the conquests of Attila, and the authority claimed by the Emperor of Morocco, or by the Sultan, as really as in relation to the rights claimed by the master over the slave.

(4.) Nor is it a mere relation in which legislative bodies alone are concerned.* It has indeed a relation to governments, and the makers and administrators of the laws have much to do with it. It is, indeed, a relation between man and man—for the slave *is* a man, and is, in some respects, regarded as such. But the usual relations in civil life are those of compact and agreement; of buying and selling; of commerce, appren-ticeship, marriage, mutual aid, in regard to which each party is voluntary, and each party has guarded rights. Nothing of this kind occurs in slavery. There all is involuntary on the part of the slave, and he is never considered and treated as a neighbour, or an equal. In no respect does the law regard him as on a level with the master.

(5.) Slavery is not a thing which pertains wholly to a legislature to regulate, and with which an individual, or an

---

* See Biblical Repertory, 1836, p. 293.

association expressly organized for that purpose, or an ecclesiastical body have no right to interfere, or in reference to
which they have no right to express an opinion. There *are*
respects, indeed, in which the subject pertains to legislative
bodies, and in *those* respects others cannot interfere with
their peculiar prerogatives. The bad laws which they have
made, they only can unmake. The actual *legislation* which
may be at any time demanded to remove the evil, or to correct
abuses growing out of the laws, pertains only to them. Others
can no more usurp the place of the legislator, in respect to
this, than they can in respect to any thing else. But the
points on which slavery touches on the legislative body are
few and unimportant, compared with its other relations to
society. Men are not made slaves by legislative acts, but by
individual rapacity and wrong. Legislatures do not own
slaves, unless it be in a corporate capacity, and rarely then.
The slave is the property of an individual, and his relations
are to him. That individual is *a man*, not a *legislator;* and
it is right to reason with him as a man, as a neighbour, as a
member of the church, as a father and a brother, or as a
minister of the gospel. In each and all of these respects, it
is right to bring the subject before his conscience, and to reason and remonstrate with him, as himself responsible to God.
And it is the right of any one to do it who *is* a man, whether
in his individual or associate capacity—for the slaveholder
holds *a man* in bondage, and claims him as his property.
Between these two *individuals*, therefore, no legislator has
a right to interpose a barrier, and to say that *this* subject
pertains to *us*, and that no individual or association has a right
to intermeddle with it. It does not define slavery, therefore,
to say that it is a relation which has been instituted by a
legislature for the good of the community, requiring one class
of people to engage in the service of another.

(6.) Slavery is not a condition like that of the serfs of
Russia, or like the 'villeins' of the feudal system. It has
something in common with those relations, and in some

aspects may not be more oppressive or degrading, but still it is to be accurately distinguished from them.   In the relation of the 'villein' of the feudal system there was an obligation of service to the lord ; the time, and talent, and skill of the vassal were his ; the villein had none of the rights of a freeman, implied in the power of making laws, eligibility to office, or the administration of justice ; and there was the possibility of being transferred with the soil from one master to another. The same is substantially true of the condition of the serf. But the ' villein' was attached to the glebe, as the serf now is. He was a *fixture* on the estate, and he could *not* be removed. There was no power of alienating *him* without alienating the land, his family, his neighbours, and whatever comforts he had been used to.   There was no power of separating husband and wife, and parents and children.   He was not bought and sold as an individual, and he was not regarded in the light of *property*.   He was, in some respects, recognised as a man, and even in his lowest condition had the germs of certain rights, which have grown into the condition of the now middle and respectable classes in Europe.   " The villein has become the independent farmer."   " The feudal system has in a great measure been *outgrown* in all the European states.   The third estate, formerly hardly recognised as having an existence, is become the controlling power in most of those ancient communities."*   But there is no such germ of freedom and of elevation in slavery.   There is nothing which, being cultivated and expanded, will grow into freedom.   There was nothing in slavery, as understood by the Romans, and there is nothing in it as it exists in this country, which has such a principle of liberty, advancement, and elevation, that the slave, by any natural progress, can ever emerge into liberty, or ever take such a place that there shall be recognised in him the rights of *a man ;* and though there is in the system, in many respects, a strong resemblance to the

---

* See Biblical Repertory, 1836, pp. 291, 300.

condition of a feudal 'villein,' or a Russian serf, yet these conditions are never confounded. All men know that *slavery* is a different thing. Its peculiarity is not described by a reference to the condition of society in the dark ages, or under the dominion of the Autocrat of the North.

(7.) Slavery is not the kind of property which a man has in his wife or child.[*] There may be something in common in these relations, but, except in arguments in defence of slavery, they are never confounded. In the condition of a wife and child there is indeed a want of a right of suffrage and of eligibility to office; and, in the case of the child, of a right to the avails of his labour, as in that of a slave. But (1.) the relation of parent and child is a natural relation, that of master and slave is not; (2.) the relation of husband and wife is voluntary, that of master and slave is not; (3.) in these relations wives and children are treated in all respects as human beings, slaves are not; (4.) in these relations there is no right of property in any such sense as that in which the word property is commonly used:—there is no right of sale; there is no right to sunder the relation for the mere sake of gain. It is true that some of these things have occurred in certain times and places, and that the power of purchase or sale has been understood to be connected with the relation of husband and wife, and that even parents have claimed this power over their children. But this has always been understood as an *abuse* of power, and as not fairly implied in the relation. The common sense of mankind has revolted at it; and whatever usurped power there may have been at any time, the instinctive feeling of mankind is that the 'property' which a man has in his wife or child is essentially different from that which the master has in his slave.

If none of these things constitute slavery, the question

---

* Comp. Bib. Repertory, 1836, p. 293.

then arises, what is it? What is the essential element
of the system? What distinguishes this from all other
relations? These questions can now be answered by the
single reply, that it is PROPERTY IN A HUMAN BEING. The
master *owns* the slave. He has *bought* him, and he has
a right to *use* him, or to *sell* him. He can command his
services against his own will; he can avail himself of
the fruit of his toil and skill; he can sell him or otherwise alienate him as he pleases. He regards him as his
own *property* in the same sense as he regards any thing
else as his property. He is not an apprentice, a companion,
an equal, or a voluntary servant; he is a part of his
estate, and subject substantially to the same laws as those
which regulate property in any thing else. He is his
property in the sense that either by himself, or by one
from whom he has inherited him, the slave has been
taken by force and appropriated to the use of another man—
substantially in the same way in which *property* was first
acquired by cultivating a piece of land selected from the
great *common* of the world, or fruit gathered from that
which was before common; or he has become his property in the sense that an equivalent has been paid for
him, or from the fact that the children of slaves become
property in the same way as the offspring of cattle do.
He is his property in the sense that the slave himself
has no right to the employment of his time and limbs
and skill for his own advantage, and no right to the avails
of his own labour. He is his property in the sense that
the master claims the right to himself of all that the slave
can produce by his physical strength, or by any tact or
skill which he may have in any department of labour.
He is his property in the sense that he may part with
his services to any one on such terms as he, and not
the slave, shall choose; that he may sell him for any
price in money, or barter him for any commodity, to any
person that he chooses; and that he may make a testa-

mentary disposition of him as he may of his house, his
land, his books, his cane, or his horse. This was the
doctrine of the Roman law. "The master had the entire
right of property in the slave, and could do just as he
pleased with his person and life, his powers and his
earnings." Digesta I. 19, 32. Quod attinet ad jus civile,
servi pro nullis habentur; non tamen et jure naturali,
quia, quod ad jus naturale attinet, omnes homines aequales
sunt. IV. 5, 3. Quia servile caput (civil condition of a
slave) *nullum jus* habet, ideo nec minui potest.* The
same was true in Greece. "In Greece the slave was considered ἔμψυχον ὄργανον or a κτῆμα, *a mere instrument endowed with life,* a *possession.*"†

It is true that this kind of *property* differs in some
respects from other kinds—as property in a horse differs
in some respects from property in a tree or a mine.
Property is to be regarded, in some aspects, according to
the nature of the thing which is held, and will be *treated*
in some respects according to its nature. The ownership
which a man has in a marble quarry, or in a silver mine,
or in a field or forest, is different in some respects from
that which he has in a horse or a dog; that which he
has in the latter is in some respects different from that
which he can have in a man. It will secure a different
kind of treatment, and there are still common laws, though
these are held as *property,* which a man is not at liberty
to disregard. It is observed, correctly in the main, by
the author of the article in the Biblical Repertory already
referred to (p. 293), that a man "has no more right to
use a brute as a log of wood, in virtue of the right of
property, than he has to use a man as a brute. There
are general principles of rectitude obligatory on all men,
which require them to treat all the creatures of God, ac-

---

* See Prof. W. A. Becker, in Bibliotheca Sacra, ii. p. 571.
† Ibid. p. 572.

cording to the nature which he has given them. The man who should burn his horse because he was his property, would find no justification in that plea either before God or man. When therefore it is said that one man is the property of another, it can only mean that the one has the right to use the other *as a man*, but not as a brute or a thing. He has no right to treat him as he may lawfully treat his ox or a tree."—Still, the essential thing—the right of *property* is the same. It is *ownership* of the quarry, the mine, the forest, the field, the ox, the man;—and though the *treatment* must in proper respects correspond to their nature, and though the community may feel that if a man should 'burn' his horse he would violate great laws of nature, still this does not affect the question whether he *owns* the horse and has a right to regard him as *property*. The same is true of the ownership in man. There are certain things which it is admitted the owner has no right to do, which he might do to some other species of property. He may no more 'burn' his slave than he may his 'horse;' he might not treat a slave in all respects as he *might* his horse, any more than he might treat his horse as he would an inanimate object, and still the *property* claimed in the one may be as distinct and exclusive as in the other.—He may employ him as he pleases; he may make use of all that he can produce by his labour; he may sell him, or may dispose of him, as he chooses, in his will. The slave is never regarded as a human being, with the rights of a human being, but he is regarded *as property made more valuable* BECAUSE he is a human being—just as the horse is regarded as property *made* valuable *because* he is a horse. As such the slave is to be treated as a man, not with respect to any duties or relations which he owes as a citizen, a father, a son, an heir of salvation, but only with reference to the question, how he can be rendered more valuable as a slave.

His nature is consulted in his treatment, in distinction from that of the horse, only as that of the horse is consulted in distinction from the inanimate objects of property.

This claim of *property* in the slave always involves the following things :—

1. It is wholly *involuntary* on the part of the slave. He has never conceded any such right over himself to others, and no one has done it who had any authority to do it. He has not made a voluntary surrender of himself to his master to be regarded as his; to be *owned* by him, and to yield to him the avails of his labour, and be sold by him when and where he pleases. And no one has done this who had a right to do it. The power originally asserted over him or his ancestors, was a power of usurpation or robbery; was against his consent or theirs; and was successfully asserted only because he had not the means of resistance. It was that which no parent had the prerogative of yielding, and which in most instances no parent pretended to yield. The whole system is involuntary on his part, and the property which is claimed in his person, his services, his wife, his children, was never the result of compact or voluntary agreement.

2. It is property claimed in that which naturally belongs to him, but which he is not at liberty to resume to himself. He is not at liberty to claim a property in his own time, person, family, bodily vigour, talent, or skill. There may be instances—as we are often told there are in slaveholding communities, and as we have no reason to doubt there are—in which, from kind treatment or other causes, the slave would prefer to remain with his master than to take the chances of freedom. He may see great and certain evils which would result if he were thrown upon his own resources, if, in the existing state of society, he should undertake to provide for himself and his family. Or, slavery may have so effectually accomplished its work, by destroying all that is noble in his nature, that he prefers to be a slave

to being a freeman. But while this may be true, he is not at liberty to do otherwise if he should choose, without the consent of his master. He has no independent volition in the case. A horse, if he had a choice, might prefer to remain the property of his owner by whom he was well taken care of, but he would not be at liberty to do otherwise if he chose.

3. There is a right of property in all that pertains to the slave. It is a right extending, (1.) to his time. The slave can *claim* none as his own. The hours when he shall begin his work, and when he shall close it, his master claims the right of determining, and he has no choice in the case. (2.) To his service. "When this idea of property comes to be analyzed, it is found to be *nothing more* than a claim of service either for life or for a term of years. This claim is transferable, and is of the nature of property, and is consequently liable for the debts of the owner, and subject to his disposal by will or otherwise."* There *is* "something *more*" than this in the claim of property claimed in the slave, but this concession shows, what indeed no one would deny, that the master has a claim of 'service' in the slave, which is of the nature of *transferable property*. (3.) To his bodily strength and power of labour. The master asserts a claim over these, and the *price* of the slave, that is, the value of the *property* in him, is estimated in accordance with these things. Whatever the slave has of youth, physical power, vigour of constitution, capacity for enduring labour, enters into the notion of the *property* in him—just as much as the metal, speed, bottom, and pedigree of the horse does of *his* value. (4.) To his talent or skill. If he has a tact for labour; if he has skill in any of the mechanic arts; if he has genius so that he can facilitate or abridge toil by useful inventions, it is all the *property* of the master. He is the more valuable on that account, and his superior worth is often published, when he is exposed to sale, if he

---

* Bib. Repertory, pp. 293, 294.

is a skilful and accomplished house-servant, or if he is endowed with mechanical talent. He has no *right* to avail himself of any skill which he may have in making a shoe, a carriage, or a machine. He would have no right to take out a patent for the most useful invention; he would have no right to enter a copyright for a book. Such a thing is never contemplated in the laws regulating slavery, and if a slave *had* any such endowment it would be wholly at the disposal of the master.

4. The master claims this right of property in his services without equivalent or compensation. He does not pretend to have given him any valuable consideration for the surrender of his freedom, and he furnishes him no equivalent for his labour. It is in vain to say that the food, the raiment, and the cottage of the slave are any *equivalent* for his services, or that the deficiency of these is made up by the implied pledge of the master that he will furnish him with medicine when he is sick, and that he will take care of him when he is old. None of these things are such an equivalent for his services that a freeman would be willing to contract for them by selling himself into slavery; they are not what a freeman can secure by voluntary labour. Besides, slavery is *of necessity* a system of unrequited toil. The master *expects to make something* by the slave; that is, he expects to secure more from the labour of the slave than he returns to him. The whole arrangement of the system contemplates such a profit in slave labour, or such an increase of property from it over and above what the slave himself receives, as to meet the following expenses :—First, the interest on the capital paid *for* the slave—paid, not to him, but to the one from whom he is purchased. Secondly, all the diminution of the worth of the property from advancing age, from the probabilities of sickness, and the risk of death. This is no inconsiderable sum. If a man at twenty-five years of age costs five hundred dollars, his value is constantly diminishing by advancing age, and there is a constant risk of a total loss of

the property; and to make a return to the master for this diminution and the risk of the total loss, there must be in the system a calculation to receive from the labour rendered so much over and above what the slave himself receives, as to meet the chances of this loss and this regular decrease in his value. Thirdly, there must be, according to the system, enough received from the labour of slaves over and above what *they* receive, to support the master and his family, so far as any advantage is derived from slave labour, in idleness, and usually in luxury—for the system always has been, and essentially is, one of luxury. It is not designed in the system that the master shall labour. He buys his slaves *in order* that he and his family may not be under the necessity of earning any thing. The consequence is, that there is contemplated in the system the receipt from the labour of the slave, over and above what he himself receives, enough to maintain the master himself and his family in indolence. It follows from this, that the amount of the unrequited labour of the slave on the whole is that which is necessary to meet the interest on the capital invested in him; that which is necessary to meet the regular diminution of his own value from advancing age and the risk of death; and that part of his individual labour which will be necessary to support his master. Of course, the amount involved in this latter item will be regulated somewhat by the number of slaves. Each slave is to do his part. The *system* is to support all the masters and their families in indolence, or, at least so far as the system avails, it is to release him and them from the necessity of as much labour as is gained from the unrequited labour of the slave This differs wholly from a free system, where the labourer receives what to him is a full compensation for his work. His employer has invested no capital in the person of the labourer; makes no calculation about the diminution of his value or risk from sickness; and does not contemplate being supported in indolence on unrequited labour. He *gives*

what the labourer considers a full equivalent for his work;
he *receives* what is to him of equal value with the wages.

(5.) This possession of property in the slave involves the
right to *sell* him as the master pleases. It is not a right
merely to dispose of his *service* for a term of years or for
life; it is a right to sell *the slave himself*. He sets the *slave*
up at auction—not his *services;* he disposes of the *slave*, in
his will, by name—not of his unexpired term of service. He
disposes of his person, his skill, his physical strength—all
that he has that can be of value to himself or to another.
He retains nothing to himself; he reserves no rights for the
slave. This disposal of *property* is in all respects as absolute
and entire as it is where a man sells a farm, a mill, or a
horse. He may, moreover, sell or alienate him in any way
he pleases, whether by a private bargain, by auction, or by a
testamentary disposition—as is the case in any other property.
He may sell him by sundering any ties which bind him to
others; regardless of any remonstrances of father or mother;
and irrespective of any obligations which the slave may feel
himself under to a wife, a sister, or a child. "This claim,"
says the Biblical Repertory, "is transferable, and is consequently liable for the debts of the owner, and subject to his
disposal by will or otherwise." This is the common view of
slavery the world over, and on the subject of *selling* him the
master feels himself under no more restrictions than he does
in selling his dromedary or ox.

That these are correct views of the nature of slavery, will
be apparent from a brief reference to some of the existing laws
on the subject, showing in what light slaves are regarded in
the statutes of the slaveholding states in our country. Judge
Stroud, in his "Sketch of the Laws respecting Slavery,"
says, "The cardinal principle of slavery, that the slave is not
to be ranked among sentient beings, but among *things*—
obtains as undoubted law in all these [the slave] states."
The law of South Carolina says, "Slaves shall be claimed,
held, taken, reputed and adjudged in law, to be CHATTELS

PERSONAL in the hands of their owners and possessors, and their executors, administrators, and assigns, TO ALL INTENTS, CONSTRUCTIONS, AND PURPOSES WHATSOEVER."* The Louisiana code says, " A slave is one who is in the power of the master to whom he belongs ; the master may sell him, dispose of his person, his industry, and his labour ; he can do nothing, possess nothing, nor acquire any thing but what must belong to his master."† So the Hon. J. K. Paulding, in his work on slavery, says, " Being *property*, slaves may be bought and sold by persons capable of buying and selling other property. They are held to be personal estate,‡ and as such may be levied upon and sold for the debts of the owner."§

This claim of property is not only asserted in all the books that treat of slavery, and in all the laws that regulate the system, but enters into the every-day view of the subject, and the practical working of the system. As *a matter of fact* slaves are regarded and treated as property, or as "chattels." They are bought or are inherited as such. They are advertised for sale by auction, or otherwise, as such. They are disposed of by will as such ; they may be seized as such, by a sheriff, and sold for the payment of debts. And when a slave is so disposed of, it is in the same way as any other property. There are no reserved rights to him as a man. There is no specification in the advertisement or the instrument of sale, that he differs from any other property ; there is no recognition of the fact that in any respect he is a human being, or is to be treated as such. There is no condition in the sale that any of his rights *as a man*, as a father, a brother, or a citizen, shall be regarded. It is not specified or implied that he shall exercise any of the privileges of a freeman ; that he may himself ever hold property ; that he shall be taught to read ; that the cultivation

---

* Brev. Dig. 229.   † Civ. Code, art. 35.
‡ Rev. Code, vol. i, p. 431, s. 47.   § P. 141.   See also, p. 145.

of his intellect shall be regarded; that he shall have the liberty of worshipping God. None of his rights or feelings as a son, a husband, or a father are consulted in the conditions of the sale, but his new master, like his old one, may sunder any one of these relations as soon as he pleases, and for any cause that he chooses.

THE TRUE QUESTION STATED.

The true question now is, whether this is a good institution, and one which God designed to commend and perpetuate. Is it an institution for the maintenance of which He has made arrangements in his word, and which has his sanction? Is it a system in accordance with the spirit of the religion which he has revealed, and which that religion is intended to keep up in the world? Is it such an arrangement in society that the fair influence of that religion will tend to perpetuate it, as it will the relations of husband and wife, and of parent and child? Or is it an institution which God regards as undesirable and evil in its nature and tendency, and which he intends to have removed from the world? Would the fair application of the principles of his religion perpetuate it on the earth, or remove it as an evil thing? This is the fair question now before us. According to the references made to the Scriptures, by most of the writers already alluded to, they would regard the former of these opinions as the true one—that slavery has the sanction of God; that he has from the beginning fostered and patronised the institution; that he legislates for its continuance, as he does for the relation of parent and child; and that the principles of his religion do not conflict with its perpetuity on the earth. Is this the true position to be taken on the subject?

In this view of the real question, it is not necessary to agitate the inquiry whether slavery is a *malum in se.* That question is one that has usually given rise only to perplexing logomachies, and that has contributed little to determine the

true issue in the inquiry. If it shall appear, in the course of
this discussion, that slavery is an institution which God has
never originated by positive enactment; that his legislation
has tended from the beginning to mitigate its evils; that he
has by his Providential dealings frowned upon it; that he
has asserted great principles in his word, which cannot be
carried out without destroying the system; that he has
enjoined on man, in the various relations of life, certain
duties, of which slavery prevents the performance; that
slavery engenders inevitably certain bad passions, which are
wholly contrary to religion; and that *it is the tendency and
the design of the Christian religion, when fairly applied,
to abolish the system*, it will be apparent that slavery is a
moral wrong. God does not legislate against any thing that
is good. His own Providential dealings are not against that
which is desirable in society. His Gospel is not designed
to abolish any good institution; and if it shall appear tnat
Christianity has such provisions as are designed to remove
slavery, the divine view in relation to it will be clear. To
show what *is* that view, is the sole design of this discussion.

CHAPTER III.

Slavery in the time of the Patriarchs.

IN entering directly upon the question whether slavery, as before defined, is in accordance with the will of God, and is an institution which he designs should be perpetuated for the good of society, like the other relations of life contributing to the perfection of a community, it is natural to inquire whether any thing can be determined on this question from the practice of the patriarchs. The true inquiry here is, whether the patriarchs were holders of slaves in such a sense that it can be properly inferred that God regards slavery as a good and desirable institution.

The support which the advocates of slavery derive from the conduct of the patriarchs, has already been referred to. The reader will recall the quotations from the Presbyteries of Hopewell, Harmony, Charleston Union, and Tombecbee; from the Biblical Repertory, and Paulding's work on slavery. The example of the patriarchs, Abraham, Isaac, and Jacob, is adduced as decisive on the point. Thus, as an instance, the Presbytery of Tombecbee, in their correspondence with the General Conference of Maine,* say, " On the subject of slavery we are willing to be guided by the Bible, the unerring word of truth." " In the Bible the state of slavery is clearly recognised—Abraham, the friend of God, had slaves born in his house, and bought with his money. Isaac possessed slaves, as is evident from Gen. xxvi. 14. Jacob held slaves, without the least remorse of conscience." So also Dr. Fuller† appeals with the utmost confidence to the fact that God indulged Abraham in the practice of slavery, in proof that

---

* Pp. 12, 13. † Letters to Dr. Wayland, pp. 175, 176.

it is not wrong. "He was 'the friend of God,' and walked
with God in the closest and most endearing intercourse ; nor
can any thing be more exquisitely touching than those words,
'Shall I hide from Abraham that thing which I do?' It is
the language of a friend, who feels that concealment would
wrong the confidential intimacy existing. The love of this
venerable servant of God, in his promptness to immolate his
son, has been the theme of apostles and preachers for ages ;
and such was his faith, that all who believe are called 'the
children of faithful Abraham.' This Abraham, you admit,
held slaves. Who is surprised that Whitefield, with this
single fact before him, could not believe slavery to be a sin?
Yet, if your definition of slavery be correct, holy Abraham
lived all his life in the commission of one of the most aggravated crimes against God and man which can be conceived.
His life was spent in outraging the rights of hundreds of
human beings, as moral, intellectual, immortal, fallen creatures; and in violating their relations as parents and children,
and husbands and wives. And God not only connived at
this appalling iniquity, but, in the covenant of circumcision
made with Abraham, expressly mentions it, and confirms the
patriarch in it ; speaking of those 'bought with his money,'
and requiring him to circumcise them. Why, at the very
first blush, every Christian will cry out against this statement. To this, however, you must come, or yield your
position ; and this is only the first utterly incredible and
monstrous corollary involved in the assertion that slavery is
essentially and always 'a sin of appalling magnitude.' "

The question now is, whether the facts stated in the Bible,
in reference to the conduct of Abraham, Isaac, and Jacob,
furnish an evidence that God means to sanction slavery, and
regards it as an institution which he intends should be perpetuated. It is whether one who is a slaveholder in the
United States, in the manner in which slavery exists here, is
justified in it by the example of the patriarchs.

Now those who make their appeal to the patriarchs, have

not informed us in what the strength of the argument lies, and what are precisely the considerations on which they rest such an appeal. It is possible, therefore, that injustice may be done them in an attempt to state what *they* would consider the true force of the argument. So far as I can see, however, the only bearing which the example of the patriarchs can have on the question, must consist in the following considerations :

1. That, in the cases referred to, it was truly and properly *slavery* which was sanctioned by their example. Whatever is *essential* to slavery ; whatever constitutes its peculiarity, and distinguishes it from every other species of servitude, it must be assumed in the argument, existed under the patriarchs. In an attempt to prove that *slavery* is sanctioned by their example, it is indispensable to show that the slavery which existed then was essentially the same as that which it is proposed to vindicate by it. It is indispensable to make out that whatever is proposed to be vindicated by the example, should be found in the example. If, therefore, the essential thing in slavery, as has been already shown, be the right of property, and it be proposed to vindicate or justify this, it is essential to show that this idea existed in the kind of servitude recognised among the patriarchs. It would not throw any light on the question, if the condition referred to was one of voluntary servitude ; or if it were that of a serf or 'villein,' like the relation in Russia or under the feudal system ; it must involve the essential thing *in* slavery as it exists now. It is necessarily supposed, therefore, in this appeal to the patriarchs, that the idea of *property in a human being* existed in those cases, or the argument has no force or pertinency. And that this *is* supposed, is apparent from the argument relied on by the Presbytery of Tombecbee : "Abram, the friend of God, had *slaves* bought *with money.*"

2. That the patriarchs were good men, 'the friends of God,' and that we are safe and right in following the exam-

ple of such men. The example of a *patriarch*, it is implied in the argument, must be decisive. Whatever he did, cannot be regarded as morally wrong, or a *malum in se*, and cannot be improper to be imitated in any relation of society, and at any period of the world. Unless *this* is implied in the appeal to the patriarchs, the argument has no force. For if it be admitted that they did things which would not be proper now ; that they indulged in any thing which *is* to be regarded as a *malum in se*, or that they entertained views which are *not* adapted to promote the best interests of society, and which God does *not* design to have perpetuated, it is *possible* that their conduct in regard to servitude may belong to this class. The argument, therefore, supposes that what they habitually did, is not to be regarded as a *malum in se*, or should not be called in question as morally wrong.

3. The argument must involve this idea also, that as God permitted it, and as he caused their conduct to be recorded without any expression of disapprobation, it must have been therefore right. It is not pretended that he *commanded* the purchase of slaves in the time of the patriarchs, or that he *commended* them for what they did. The argument is based on his *silence* as to any expression of disapprobation, and on his causing the record to be made. The strength of *this* argument, then, must be, that whatever God permits among good men at any time, without a decided expression of disapprobation ; whatever he causes to be recorded as a matter of historical fact, must be regarded as authorizing the same thing in others, and as a proof that he considers it to be adapted to secure the best interests of society.

I can conceive of no other grounds than these on which an argument in favour of slavery can be derived from the example of the patriarchs. It is proposed now to inquire whether this argument is valid. Does it demonstrate what it is adduced to prove, that slavery is a good and desirable institution ; that it meets with the approbation of God, and is an institution which he designs should be perpetuated ; and that

men are justified in holding human beings as property now?
In reply to these questions, I shall consider what were the
facts in the case; and then what is the real value of the
argument.

(1.) The kind of servitude referred to in the cases of the
patriarchs was doubtless common at that time. We have,
indeed, no historical documents to prove this, for we have no
other records which go back to so remote ages. But there
are some circumstances, which, in the absence of historical
documents, render this probable. One is, that in the age of
Job, who probably lived in the time of the patriarchs, the
same kind of servitude is mentioned which appears to have
prevailed in the days of Abraham. Thus in chap. i. 3, it is
said of Job, that " he had a very great *household*," (עֲבֻדָּה,
ăbŭddâ,) where the very word is used which, in various forms,
is uniformly employed to denote servitude.* This does not
determine, indeed, that those referred to were *slaves;* but it
shows that the kind of servitude mentioned in the account of
the patriarchs, prevailed in the land of Uz, that is, probably,
in Arabia Deserta, and in the country adjacent to Chaldea.

(2.) A second circumstance is, that we have mention of an
historical fact pertaining to those times, which shows that the
buying and selling of men was common. Thus when it was
proposed by the brethren of Joseph to *sell* him to the travel-
ing Ishmaelites who were engaged in commerce, they made
no more scruple about *buying* him, than they would have
done any thing that had been offered for sale; and the same
thing occurred when he was exposed for sale by them in
the Egyptian market. He was readily bought by Potiphar,
Gen. xxxvii. 27, 28; xxxix. 1. This whole transaction looks
as if the buying and selling of men was then a common thing,
and was as allowable as any other species of traffic.

(3.) A third circumstance is, that servants appear to have
been in the market, or to have been held by those who dwelt

---

* Gen. xxvi. 14; xxx. 26; xii. 16; xvii. 23; xxxix. 17, *et al.*

in the vicinity of Abraham, for it is said that he had "servants *bought* with money," Gen. xvii. 12. This would seem to show that they were held for sale by others, that is, that servitude of this kind prevailed there.

(4.) The fourth circumstance is, that as far back as we can trace the history of nations, we find the existence of slavery in some form. We find it represented in the historical paintings of Egypt, where nothing is more common than drawings of slaves or captives. We find it in the earliest stages of the history of Greece and Rome. We find it in the practice of conquerors, who were accustomed to regard the captives taken in war as the property of the captors, and who were supposed to have a right to kill them, to sell them, or to retain them as slaves at their pleasure. We find it in the earliest laws, and in the claims set up under those laws to certain persons held to servitude. Those laws are but the expressions of the early opinions on the subject, and an exponent of the prevailing practice. Thus these causes are assigned by Justinian as laying a foundation for slavery, or as making the enslaving of others proper. *Servi aut fiunt, aut nascuntur: fiunt jure gentium, aut jure civili: nascuntur ex ancillis nostris.** According to this, slaves are said to become such in three ways: by birth, where the mother was a slave; by captivity in war; and by the voluntary sale of himself as a slave by a freeman of the age of twenty. Blackstone examines these causes of slavery, and shows them all to rest on uncertain foundations; and he insists that a state of slavery is repugnant to reason, and contrary to natural law.† The foundation of this claim was undoubtedly wrong; but the fact that it was made, shows the state of feeling in the earliest times, and may be regarded as proof that slavery prevailed in the remotest periods of the world. Whatever may be said, therefore, about the state of servitude in the

* Just. 1, 3, 4.
† Comm. i. 423, 424.   Comp. Kent's Commentaries on American Law, i. 427, *seq.*

time of the patriarchs, and whatever conclusions may be
drawn from the fact that they held slaves, it cannot be held
that they *originated* the system.   It was a system which
they doubtless found in existence, and they acted only in
accordance with the customs of all the surrounding nations.

In order now adequately to understand what was the real
character of the servitude which existed among the patriarchs, on which so much reliance is placed by those who
attempt to sustain the system by an appeal to the Bible, it is
of the utmost importance to understand what is the exact
sense of the word used to designate this relation in the
Scriptures.   If the word rendered *servant* in the Old Testament necessarily means *slaves* in the modern sense of the
term, it will do something to settle the question whether
slavery as it now exists is in accordance with the will of God.
It must be *assumed* by those who bring the example of the
patriarchs in support of slavery, that the word had the same
signification then which it has now ; for if the word, as used
in their times, meant an essentially different thing from what
it does now, it is obvious that its use furnishes no argument
in support of slavery.

The Greeks, accustomed to exact distinctions, and favoured
with a language so refined as to distinguish the nicest shades
of thought, discriminated accurately between various kinds
of servitude, and designated those relations in a way which
is not common in other languages.   To serve in general,
without reference to the manner in which the obligation to
service originated, whether by purchase, by contract, by being
made a captive in war, as a subject, a dependent, they expressed by the word δουλεύω—*douleuo ;* to serve as a soldier
for reward, or to serve the gods, they expressed by the word
λατρεύω—*latreuo, (Passow) ;* to serve as a domestic or household servant, under whatever manner the obligation arose, they
expressed by the word οἰκετεύω—*oiketeuo ;* to serve in the
capacity of a hired man, or for *pay* in any capacity, they ex-

pressed by the word μισθόω—*misthoō*; to serve in the capacity of an attendant or waiter, especially at a door, they expressed by the word ὑπακούω—*hypakouō*, (*Passow*). The proper word to denote a slave, with reference to the master's right of property in him, and without regard to the relations and offices in which he was employed, was *not* δοῦλος—*doulos*, but ἀνδράποδον—*andrapodon*, defined by Passow, *Sklav, Knecht, bes. der durch Kriegsgefangenschaft in Leibeigenschaft Gerathne*—'a slave, servant, especially one who as a prisoner of war is reduced to bondage.'* Hence the Greeks used the term δοῦλος—*doulos*, to express servitude *in the most general form*, whatever might be the method by which the obligation to service originated. They used the term ἀνδράποδον—*andrapodon*, to denote *a slave* regarded as property; the term δμώς—*dmōs*, also, to denote a slave as *one conquered*, or as primarily made by capture in war;† the terms οἰκεύς—*oikeus*,‡ οἰκέτης—*oiketes*, to denote a household servant; the term ὑπήκοος—*hypekoos*, to denote an attendant, a waiter; the term μίσθιος—*misthios*, to denote a hired man, or a labourer in the employ of another; and the word λάτρις —*latris*, to denote one who served for *pay*, as a soldier. That δοῦλος—*doulos* might be a slave, and that the word is most commonly applied to slaves in the classic writers, and frequently in the New Testament, no one can doubt; but its mere *use* in any case does not of necessity denote the relation sustained, or make it proper to infer that he to whom it is applied was bought with money, or held as property, or even in any way regarded as *a slave*. It might be true also that the various terms *doulos, dmōs, andrapodon, oiketes*, and possibly *hypekoos*, might all be applied to persons who had been obtained in the same way—either by purchase, or by being made prisoners in war; but these terms, except those of

* Comp. Prof. W. A. Becker, in the Bibliotheca Sacra, vol. ii. p. 569.
† Od. i. 398; Ib. xix. 9, 333, (*Crusius, Lex.*)
‡ Od. xiv. 4, iv. 245.

andrapodon and *dmōs*, would not designate the *origin* of the
relation, or the nature of the *tenure* by which the servant was
bound.   The words used in our language—*servant, slave,
waiter, hired man*, though not marking the relations with
quite as much accuracy as the Greek words, will indicate
somewhat the nature of the distinctions.   It may be proper
to add, that the word *doulos*, as remarked above, is frequently
used in the New Testament, being found one hundred and
twenty-two times;* the word οἰκέτης—*oiketes*, occurs four
times, in three places rendered *servant*—and in one *household servant*: Luke xvi. 13, "No *servant* can serve two
masters;" Acts x. 7, "He called two of his *household servants;*" Rom. xiv. 4, "That judgest another man's *servant;*"
and 1 Pet. ii. 18, "*Servants*, be subject to your masters;"
the word μίσθιος—*misthios*, occurs in Luke xv. 17, 19, in
both places rendered *hired servants*,—"How many *hired
servants* of my father's,"—"Make me as one of thy *hired
servants;*" the word ὑπήκοος—*hypekoos*, occurs in Acts vii.
39, 2 Cor. ii. 9, Phil. ii. 8, in each case rendered *obedient;*
the word λάτρις—*latris*, does not occur, though the word
λατρεία—*latreia, service*, and λατρεύω—*latreuo, to serve*, frequently occur, applied in all cases to *religious* service; and

---

* "According to Greenfield's Schmidius, the word *doulos* occurs 122
times in the New Testament. Of these, 19 are parallel; and the remain-
ing 103 may be classed as follows:

  1. Applied to servants of men;
    [1] Of Jewish masters,   47 times.
    [2] Of masters generally without distinction,   18 "
    [3] Of a Gentile master, [Mat. viii. 9,]   1 "
    [4] To Christians as servants of each other, [Mat. xx. 27,
        2 Cor. iv. 5,]   2 "
  2. To the servants of God and Christ,   28 "
  3. To Christ as the servant of God, [Phil. ii. 7,]   1 "
  4. To the servants of sin and Satan,   4 "
  5. Used indefinitely, [Rom. vi. 16,]   1 "
  6. To those 'under the elements of the world.' [Gal. iv.,] 1 "

                                          103"

the word ἀνδράποδον—*andrapodon*, which *peculiarly* denotes
slavery, does not occur at all, though the correlative word
ἀνδραποδιστής—*andrapodistes*, occurs once (1 Tim. i. 10) with
the most marked disapprobation of the thing denoted by it :—
"The law is made for murderers of fathers and murderers of
mothers, for manslayers, for whoremongers, for *men-stealers,*
for liars," &c.

The Hebrews made no such minute distinctions as the
Greeks did. Their language was less cultivated, and much
less adapted to express nice discriminations of thought. They
used but one word, עֶבֶד *ēbĕdh*, to express *all* the relations of
servitude—somewhat as the word *servant* is used in the
slaveholding states of our own country. Among the Hebrews, however, the word was used as expressing, with propriety, the relations sustained ; in a slaveholding community
it is adopted as a mild term to avoid the use of the odious
and offensive term *slave.*

The Hebrew words עֶבֶד *ēbĕdh*, עֲבוֹדָה *ăbōdhá*, and עֲבֻדָּה
ăbŭddá, rendered commonly *servant*, *service,* and *servants,*
(Job i. 3,) are derived from עָבַד *ábădh*, meaning *to labour, to
work, to do work.* It occurs in the Hebrew Scriptures some
hundreds of times in various forms of the word, and is never
rendered *slaves*, but commonly *servants*, and *serve.* Occasionally the words derived from the verb are rendered *bondman*, or *bond-servant*, Lev. xxv. 39, 42, 44 ; Josh. ix. 23 ;
1 Kings ix. 22. The verb and the nouns derived from it are
applied to any and every kind of *service* or *servitude* which
one can render to another. The ideas of working for another, ministering to another, being bound to another, being
tributary to another, offering homage to another, will all be
found embraced in this word. The essential significations
in the use of the word are (1.) to labour or work, without
respect to the question who it is for, and (2.) to render service
to another ; that is, *to be subject to him, and to act with
reference to his will.* In accordance with this, the word, in
various forms, is used to denote the following kinds of service:

(1.) To work for another, Gen. xxix. 20, xxvii. 40, xxix. 15, xxx. 26, 1 Sam. iv. 9. (2.) To serve or be servants of a king, 2 Sam. xvi. 19, Gen. xl. 20, xli. 10, 37, 38, l. 7, Ex. v. 21, vii. 10, x. 7. (3) To serve as a soldier, 2 Sam. ii. 12, 13, 15, 30, 31, iii. 22, viii. 7, *et saepe.* (4.) To serve as an ambassador, 2 Sam. x. 2—4. (5.) To serve as a people : that is, when one people were subject to another, or tributary to another, Gen. xiv. 4, xv. 14, xxv. 23, Isa. xix. 23, Gen. xv. 13, ix. 26, 27, xxvii. 37. (6.) To serve God, or idols, Ex. iii. 12, ix. 1, 13, Deut. iv. 19, viii. 19. Under this head the word is often used in the sense of 'the *servant of* JE- HOVAH,' applied (*a*) to a *worshipper* of the true God, Neh. i. 10, Ezra v. 11, Dan. vi. 21, *et saepe;* (*b*) a *minister,* or *ambassador* of God, Isa. xlix. 6, Jer. xxv. 9, xxvii. 6, xliii. 10, Deut. xxxiv. 5, Josh. i. 1, Ps. cv. 26, Isa. xx. 3. (7) The word is often employed to denote a servant, whether hired, bought, or inherited,—one who was involuntarily held to service to another. In this sense it is frequently used in the laws of Moses ; for all the kinds of *servitude* which are referred to there, are designated by this term. As already observed, the Hebrews did not make distinctions between the various kinds of service with the accuracy of the Greeks. So far as I have been able to ascertain, they made *no* distinc- tions of that kind, except that in later times they made use of one other term besides עֶבֶד *ĕbĕdh,* which was שָׂכִיר *sâkir,* *one hired; a hired labourer;* one to whom wages was paid, Ex. xii. 45, xxii. 14, Lev. xix. 13, Isa. xvi. 14, Job vii. 1. In one passage in Job (vii. 2, 3) the two words occur in the same verse, where the distinction is marked, and yet so as, by the parallelism, to show that the persons referred to were regarded as in some respects on a level.

" As a *servant—*עֶבֶד *ĕbĕdh—*earnestly desireth the shadow,
" And as an *hireling—*שָׂכִיר *sâkir—*looketh for the reward
    of his work,
" So am I made to possess vanity,
" And wearisome nights are appointed to me.'

There were, indeed, in the Hebrew language, two words which denoted exclusively *female domestics* or *servants,* which may be regarded as a refinement peculiar to them. I do not know that it occurs often in other languages. Neither of these words, however, were designed, so far as I can perceive, to denote the *kind of service* which was to be rendered, but only to mark *the distinction of sex.* The female servant thus designated might either be hired, or bought, or inherited, or be a captive taken in war. Their condition seems to have partaken of the general nature of servitude, though for what reason a distinctive name was given to them is not certainly known. One of the names used was אָמָה, *âmâ,* rendered *maid-servant,* Ex. xx. 10, xxi. 7, 32, Job xxxi. 13, Deut. xv. 17; *bond-maid,* Lev. xxv. 44; *bond-woman,* Gen. xxi. 10, 12, 13; *maid,* Gen. xxx. 3, Lev. xxv. 6, Ex. ii. 5, Job xix. 15, Nah. ii. 7; *hand-maid,* Ex. xxiii. 12, Ruth iii. 9, 1 Sam. i. 11, xxv. 24, and often ;—and the other name was שִׁפְחָה, *Shĭphhâ,* rendered *hand-maid,* Gen. xvi. 1, xxix. 24, Prov. xxx. 23, Gen. xxv. 12, xxxv. 25, 26; *bond-maid,* Lev. xix. 20; *maiden,* Ps. cxxiii. 2; *women-servants,* Gen. xxxii. 5, 6; *maid-servant,* Ex. xi. 5, 1 Sam. viii. 16, Gen. xii. 16, xxiv. 35, xxx. 43; *wench,* 2 Sam. xvii. 17; and *servant,* 1 Sam. xxv. 41. The distinction between these two words applied to female servants, it is probably impossible now to mark.

From this examination of the terms used to denote servitude among the Hebrews, it follows that nothing can be inferred from the mere use of *the word* in regard to the kind of servitude which existed in the days of the patriarchs. The conclusions which would be fair from the use of the word, would be these, (1.) That any *service,* whether hired labour, or that rendered by one who was bought; whether that of a freeman or a slave ; whether in the house or the field, would be properly expressed by the use of the Hebrew word. (2.) That at any period of their history the word denoted *servitude as it then existed,* and its meaning in any particular age is to be sought from a knowledge of the *kind* of servitude which then actually prevailed. We can ascertain the meaning of *the word* from *the facts* in the case; not the nature of *the facts* from the use of *the word*. If the kind of servitude existed which does now in England, and to which the word *servant* is applied, it wc 'ld accurately express that; if the kind which existed under the feudal system, it would express that; if the kind which exists in Russia, it would express that; and if such a kind as exists in the Southern states of this Union, it would express that. (3.) The word *might*, therefore, denote *slavery*, if slavery at any time existed. The Hebrews would not have been under a necessity of forming a new word to denote that relation, but the term in actual use would have covered the whole ground, and would easily adapt itself to the actual state of things. But (4.) it did not *necessarily* denote that, and that signification is not to be given to it in any case unless it is clear, from other sources than from the use of *the word*, that slavery was intended. It *might* mean many other things, and it is not a correct method of interpretation to infer that because this word is used, that therefore *slavery* existed.

It follows from this, that the mere use of *the word* in the time of the patriarchs, determines nothing in the issue before us. It does not *prove* either that slavery existed then, or that it is lawful. For any thing that can be learned from the mere use of *the word*, the kind of servitude then existing may have had none of the essential elements of *slavery*.

This inquiry into the meaning of *the word* will be of use through the whole discussion, for it is important to bear in remembrance that this use of the *term* nowhere in the Scriptures of necessity implies *slavery*.

(3.) Some of the servants held by the patriarchs were '*bought with money*.' Much reliance is laid on this by the advocates of slavery, in justifying the purchase, and consequently, as they seem to reason, the *sale* of slaves now; and it is, therefore, of importance to inquire how far the fact stated is a justification of slavery as it exists at present. But one instance occurs in the case of the patriarchs, where it is said that servants were 'bought with money.' This is the case of Abraham, Gen. xvii. 12, 13 : " And he that is eight days old shall be circumcised among you, every man-child in your generations ; he that is born in the house, or *bought with money of any stranger*, which is not of thy seed ; he that is born in thy house, and *he that is bought with thy money*, must needs be circumcised." Comp. vs. 23, 27. This is the only instance in which there is mention of the fact that any one of the patriarchs had persons in their employment who were bought with money. The only other case which occurs at that period of the world is that of the sale of Joseph, first to the Ishmaelites, and then to the Egyptians —a case which, it is believed, has too close a resemblance to slavery as it exists in our own country, ever to be referred to with much satisfaction by the advocates of the system. In the case, moreover, of Abraham, it should be remembered that it is the record of a mere *fact*. There is no command to buy servants or to sell them, or to hold them as property —any more than there was a command to the brethren of Joseph to enter into a negotiation for the sale of their brother. Nor is there any approbation expressed of the fact that they were bought ; unless the command given to Abraham to affix to them the seal of the covenant, and to recognise them as brethren in the faith which he held, should be construed as such evidence of approval.

The inquiry then presents itself, whether *the fact that they were bought* determines any thing with certainty in regard to the nature of the servitude, or to the propriety of slavery as practised now. The Hebrew in the passages referred to in Genesis is, 'the born in thy house, and *the purchase of silver*,' מִקְנַת־כֶּסֶף—*miknath keseph*—not incorrectly rendered, 'those bought with money.' The verb קָנָה *kânâ*, from which the noun here is derived, and which is commonly used in the Scriptures when the purchase of slaves is referred to, means *to set upright*, or *erect*, *to found* or *create*, Gen. xiv. 19, 22, Deut. xxxii. 6; *to get for oneself*, *to gain* or *acquire*, Prov. iv. 7, xv. 32; *to obtain*, Gen. iv. 1; and *to buy* or *purchase*, Gen. xxv. 10, xlvii. 22. In this latter sense it is often used, and with the same latitude of signification as the word *buy* or *purchase* is with us. It is most commonly rendered by the words *buy* and *purchase* in the Scriptures. See Gen. xxv. 10, xlvii. 22; xlix. 30, l. 13; Josh. xxiv. 32; 2 Sam. xii. 3; Ps. lxxviii. 54; Deut. xxxii. 6; Lev. xxvii. 24, and very often elsewhere. It is applied to the purchase of fields; of cattle; of men; and of every thing which was or could be regarded as property. As there is express mention of *silver* or *money* in the passage before us respecting the servants of Abraham, there is no doubt that the expression means that he paid a *price* for a part of his servants. A part of them were "born in his house;" a part had been "bought with money" from 'strangers,' or were foreigners.

But still, this use of the word in itself determines nothing in regard to the tenure by which they were held, or the nature of the servitude to which they were subjected. It does not prove that they were regarded as *property* in the sense in which the slave is now regarded as a chattel; nor does it demonstrate that the one who was bought ceased to be regarded altogether *as a man;* or that it was regarded as right to sell him again. The fact that he was to be circumcised as one of the family of Abraham, certainly does not look as if he ceased to be regarded as a *man*.

The word rendered *buy* or *purchase* in the Scriptures, is applied to so many kinds of purchases, that no safe argument can be founded on its use in regard to the kind of servitude which existed in the time of Abraham. A reference to a few cases where this word is used, will show that nothing is determined by it respecting the tenure by which the thing purchased was held. (1.) It is used in the common sense of the word *purchase* as applied to inanimate things, where the property would be absolute. Gen. xlii. 2, 7, xliii. 20, xlvii. 19, xxx. 19.   (2.) It is applied to the purchase of *cattle*, where the property may be supposed to be *as* absolute.   See Gen. xlvi. 22, 24, iv. 20; Job xxxvi. 33; Deut. iii. 19; *and often.*   (3.) God is represented as having *bought* his people; that is, as having ransomed them with a price, or purchased them to himself.   Deut. xxxii. 6, "Is not he thy Father that hath *bought* thee?" — קָנֶךָ — *kânēkhâ—thy purchaser.* Ex. xv. 16, "By the greatness of thine arm they shall be still as a stone, till thy people pass over; till the people pass over which thou hast *purchased.*"—קָנִיתָ, *kânithâ.* See Psalm lxxiv. 2.   Comp. Isa. xliii. 3, "I gave Egypt for thy ransom, Ethiopia and Seba for thee."   But though the word *purchase* is used in relation to the redemption of the people of God—the very word which is used respecting the servants of Abraham—no one will maintain that they were held as *slaves*, or regarded as *property.* Who can tell but what Abraham *purchased* his servants in some such way, by redeeming them from galling captivity? May they not have been prisoners in war, to whom he did an inestimable service in rescuing them from a condition of grievous and hopeless bondage? May they not have been *slaves* in the strict and proper sense, and may not his act of purchasing them have been, in fact, a species of emancipation in a way similar to that in which God emancipates his people from the galling servitude of sin?   The mere act of paying *a price* for them no more implies that he continued to hold them as slaves, than it does now when a man purchases his wife or child who have been held as slaves, or than the fact that God has redeemed his people by a price implies that he regards them as slaves.   (4.) Among the Hebrews a man might sell himself, and this transaction on the part of him to whom he sold himself would be represented by the word *bought.*   Thus

in Lev. xxv. 47, 48, "And if a sojourner or a stranger wax
rich by thee, and thy brother that dwelleth by him wax
poor, and *sell himself* unto the stranger or sojourner by thee,
or to the stock of the stranger's family, after that he is sold,
he may be redeemed again." This transaction is represented as a *purchase.* Ver. 50, "And he shall reckon
with him that *bought* him, (Heb. *his purchaser,* קֹנֵהוּ
konaihū,) from the year that he was sold unto the year of
jubilee," &c. This was a mere purchase of *time* or *service.*
It gave no right to sell the man again, or to retain him in
any event beyond a certain period, or to retain him *at all,*
if his friends chose to interpose and redeem him. It gave
no right of property in the *man,* any more than the purchase
of the unexpired time of an apprentice, or the 'purchase'
of the poor in the state of Connecticut does. In no proper
sense of the word could this be called *slavery.* (5.) The
word *buy* or *purchase* was sometimes applied to the
manner in which a *wife* was procured. Thus Boaz is
represented as saying that he had *bought* Ruth. "Moreover, Ruth the Moabitess, the wife of Mahlon, have I
purchased (קָנִיתִי—*kánithi*) to be my wife." Here the
word which is applied to the manner in which Abraham
became possessed of his servants, is applied to the manner
in which a wife was procured. So Hosea says, (ch. iii. 2,)
"So I *bought* her to me (another word however being used
in the Hebrew, כָּרָה *kárá*) for fifteen pieces of silver, and
for an homer of barley, and an half homer of barley." Jacob
purchased his wives, Leah and Rachel, not indeed by the
payment of money, but by labour. Gen. xxix. 15—23.
That the practice of *purchasing* a wife, or paying a 'dowry'
for her was common, is apparent from Ex. xxii. 17; 1 Sam.
xviii. 25. Comp. Judges i. 12, 13. Yet it will not be
maintained that the wife, among the Hebrews, was in any
proper sense *a slave,* or that she was regarded as subject
to the laws which regulate property, or that the husband
had a right to sell her again. In a large sense, indeed,

she was regarded, as the conductors of the Princeton Repertory (1836, p. 293) allege, as the wife is now, as the *property* of her husband; that is, she was *his* to the exclusion of the claim of any other man, but she was his *as his wife*, not *as his slave*. (6.) The word '*bought*' occurs in a transaction between Joseph and the people of Egypt in such a way as farther to explain its meaning. When, during the famine, the money of the Egyptians had failed, and Joseph had purchased all the land, the people proposed to become his servants. When the contract was closed, Joseph said to them, "Behold I have *bought* you—קָנִיתִי *kánithi*—this day, and your land for Pharaoh," Gen. xlvii. 23. The nature of this contract is immediately specified. They were to be regarded as labouring for Pharaoh. The land belonged to him, and Joseph furnished the people seed, or 'stocked the land,' and they were to cultivate it on shares for Pharaoh. The fifth part was to be his, and the other four parts were to be theirs. There was a claim on them for *labour*, but it does not appear that the claim extended farther. No farmers now who work land on shares, would be willing to have their condition described as one of *slavery*.

The conclusion which we reach from this examination of the words *buy* and *bought* as applied to the case of Abraham is, that the use of the word determines nothing in regard to the tenure by which his servants were held. They may have been purchased from those who had taken them as captives in war, and the purchase may have been regarded by themselves as a species of redemption, or a most desirable rescue from the fate which usually attends such captives—perchance from death. The property which .t was understood that he had in them may have been merely property in their *time*, and not in their persons. Or the purchase may have in fact amounted to every thing that is desirable in emancipation, and, from any thing implied in the *word*, their subsequent service in the family of Abra ham may have been entirely voluntary. It is a very material circumstance also that *there is not the slightest evidence that either Abraham, Isaac, or Jacob ever* SOLD *a slave, or offered one for sale, or regarded them as liable to be sold.* There is no evidence that their servants even descended as a part of an inheritance from father to son. So far, indeed, as the accounts in the Scriptures go, it would be impossible to *prove* that they would not have been at liberty at any time to leave their masters, if they had chosen to do so. The passage, therefore, which says that Abraham had 'servants *bought* with money,' cannot be adduced to justify slavery as it exists now—even if this were all that we know about it. But

(4.) Servitude in the days of Abraham must have existed in a very mild form, and have had features which slavery by no means has now. Almost the only transaction which is mentioned in regard to the servants of Abraham, is one which could never occur in the slaveholding parts of our country. A marauding expedition of petty kings came from the North and East, and laid waste the country around the vale of Siddim, near to which Abraham lived, and among other spoils of battle they carried away Lot and his possessions. Abraham, it is said, then 'armed his trained servants, born in his own house, three hundred and eighteen, and pursued them unto Dan,' and rescued the family of Lot and his goods. Gen. xiv. This narrative is one that must for ever show that servitude, as it existed in the family of Abraham, was a very different thing from what it is in the United States. The number was large, and it does not appear that any persons but his servants accompanied Abraham. They were all armed. They were led off on a distant expedition, where there could have been no power in Abraham to preserve his life, if they had chosen to rise up against him, and no power to recover them, if they had chosen to set themselves free. Yet he felt himself entirely safe, when accompanied with this band of armed men, and when far away from his family and his home. What must have been the nature of servitude, where the master was willing to arm such a company ; to put himself entirely at their disposal, and lead them off to a distant land ?

Compare with this the condition of things in the United States. Here, it is regarded as essential to the security of the life of the master, that slaves shall never be intrusted with arms. "A slave is not allowed to keep or carry a weapon."* "He cannot go from the tenement of his master, or other person with whom he lives, without a pass, or something to show that he is proceeding by authority from his master, employer, or overseer."† "For keeping or carrying a gun, or powder, or *shot*, or *club*, or *other weapon whatsoever*, offensive or defensive, a slave incurs, for each offence, thirty-nine lashes, by order of a justice of the peace ;"‡ and in North Carolina and Tennessee, twenty lashes, by the nearest constable, *without* a conviction by the justice.§ Here, there is every precaution from laws, and from the dread of the most fearful kind of punishment, against the escape of slaves. Here, there is a constant apprehension that they may rise against their masters, and every security is taken against their organization and combination. Here, there is probably not a single master who would, if he owned three hundred slaves, *dare* to put arms in their hands, and lead them off on an expedition against a foe. If the uniform precautions and care at the South against arming the slaves, or allowing them to become acquainted with their own strength, be any expression respecting the nature of the system, slavery in the United States is a very different thing from servitude in the time of Abraham, and it does not prove that in the species of servitude existing

---

* Rev. Code Virg. vol. i. p. 453, § 83, 84.

† Ibid. vol. i. p. 422, § 6. See Paulding on Slavery, p. 146.

‡ 2 Litt. and Swi. 1150 ; 2 Missouri Laws, 741, § 4.

§ Haywood's Manual, 521 ; Stroud on the Laws relating to Slavery, p. 102.

here it is right to refer to the case of Abraham, and to say that it is ‘ *a good patriarchal system.*’ Let the cases be made parallel before the names of the patriarchs are called in to justify the system. But

(5.) What *real* support would it furnish to the system, even if it were true that the cases were wholly parallel? How far would it go to demonstrate that *God* regards it as a good system, and one that is to be perpetuated, in order that society may reach its highest possible elevation? Who would undertake to vindicate all the conduct of the patriarchs, or to maintain that all which they practised was in accordance with the will of God? They practised concubinage and polygamy. Is it therefore certain that this was the highest and purest state of society, and that it was a state which God designed should be perpetuated? Abraham and Isaac were guilty of falsehood and deception, (Gen. xx. 2, *seq.;* xxvi. 7;) Jacob secured the birthright, by a collusive fraud between him and his mother, (Gen. xxvii,) and obtained no small part of his property by cunning, (Gen. xxx. 36–43;) and Noah was drunk with wine, (Gen. ix. 21;) and these things are recorded merely *as facts*, without any decided expression of disapprobation; but is it therefore to be inferred that they had the approbation of God, and that they are to be practised still, in order to secure the highest condition of society ?

Take the single case of polygamy. Admitting that the patriarchs held slaves, the argument in favour of polygamy, from their conduct, would be, in all its main features, the same as that which I suggested, in the commencement of this chapter, as employed in favour of slavery. The argument would be this :—that they were good men, the ‘ friends of God,’ and that what such men practised freely cannot be wrong ; that God permitted this ; that he nowhere forbade it ; that he did not record his disapprobation of the practice ; and that whatever God permitted in such circumstances, without expressing his disapprobation, must be regarded as

in itself a good thing, and as desirable to be perpetuated, in
order that society may reach the highest point of elevation.
It is perfectly clear that, so far as the conduct of the patriarchs goes, it would be just as easy to construct an argument
in favour of polygamy as in favour of slavery—even on the
supposition that slavery existed then essentially as it does
now. But it is not probable that polygamy would be defended now, as a good institution, and as one that has the approbation of God, even by those who defend the 'domestic
institutions of the South.' The truth is, that the patriarchs
were good men in their generation, and, considering their circumstances, were men eminent for piety. But they were
imperfect men ; they lived in the infancy of the world ; they
had comparatively little light on the subjects of morals and
religion; and it is a very feeble argument which maintains
that a thing is *right, because any one or all of the patriarchs practised it.*

But after all, what *real* sanction did God ever give either
to polygamy or to servitude, as it was practised in the time
of the patriarchs ? Did he command either ? Did he ever
express approbation of either ? Is there an instance in which
either is mentioned with a sentiment of approval? The
mere *record* of actual occurrences, even if there is no declared
disapprobation of them, proves nothing as to the divine estimate of what is recorded. There is *a record* of the 'sale' of
Joseph into servitude, first to the Ishmaelites, and then to
Potiphar. There is no expression of disapprobation. There
is no exclamation of surprise or astonishment, as if a deed of
enormous wickedness were done, when brothers sold their
own brother into hopeless captivity. *This* was done also by
those who were subsequently reckoned among the 'patriarchs,' and some of whom at the time were probably pious
men. Will it be inferred that God approved this transaction ; that he meant to smile on the act, when brothers sell
their own brothers into hopeless bondage? Will this record
be adduced to justify kidnapping, or the acts of parents in

barbarous lands, who, forgetful of all the laws of their nature, sell their own children? Will the record that the Ishmaelites took the youthful Joseph into a distant land, and sold him there as a slave, be referred to as furnishing evidence that God approves the conduct of those who kidnap the unoffending inhabitants of Africa, or *buy* them there, and carry them across the deep, to be sold into hopeless bondage? Why then should the fact that there is a *record* that the patriarchs held servants, or bought them, without any expressed disapprobation of the deed, be adduced as evidence that God regards slavery as a good institution, and intends that it shall be perpetuated under the influence of his religion, as conducing to the highest good of society? The truth is, that the mere record of *a fact*, even without any sentiment of approbation or disapprobation, is no evidence of the views of him who makes it. Are we to infer that Herodotus approved of all that he saw or heard of in his travels, and of which he made a record? Are we to suppose that Tacitus and Livy approved of all the deeds the memory of which they have transmitted for the instruction of future ages? Are we to maintain that Gibbon and Hume believed that all which they have recorded was adapted to promote the good of mankind? Shall the biographer of Nero, and Caligula, and Richard III., and Alexander VI., and Cæsar Borgia, be held responsible for approving of all that these men did, or of commending their example to the imitation of mankind? Sad would be the office of an historian were he to be thus judged. Why then shall we infer that *God* approved of all that the patriarchs did, even when there is no formal disapprobation expressed; or infer, because such transactions have been *recorded*, that *therefore* they are right in his sight?

CHAPTER IV.

Slavery in Egypt.

THE will of God may often be learned from the events of his providence. From his dealings with an individual, a class of men, or a nation, we may ascertain whether the course which has been pursued was agreeable to his will. It is not, indeed, always safe to argue, that because calamities come upon an individual, they are sent as a punishment on account of any peculiarly aggravated sin, or that these calamities prove that he is a greater sinner than others, (Luke xiii. 1—5,) but when a certain course of conduct *always* tends to certain results; when there are laws in operation in the moral world as fixed as in the natural world; and when there are uniformly either direct or indirect interpositions of Providence in regard to any existing institutions, it is not unsafe to infer from these what is the divine will. It is not unsafe, for illustration, to argue from the uniform effects of intemperance in regard to the will of God. Those effects occur in every age of the world, and in reference to every class of men. There are no exceptions in favour of kings or philosophers; of the inhabitants of any particular climate or region of country; of either sex, or of any age. The poverty, and babbling, and redness of eyes, and disease engendered by intemperance, may be regarded without danger of error as expressive of the will of God in reference to that habit. They show that there has been a violation of a great law of our nature ordained for our good, and that such a violation must always incur the frown of the great Governor of the world. The revelation of the mind of God in such a case is not less clear than were the enunciations of his will on Sinai.

The same is true in regard to cities and nations. We

need be in as little danger, in general, in arguing from what occurs to them, as in the case of an individual. There is now no doubt among men why the old world was destroyed by a flood; why Sodom and Gomorrah were consumed; why Tyre, Nineveh, Babylon, and Jerusalem were overthrown; and there can be as *little* doubt, since the excavations have been made at Herculaneum and Pompeii, why those cities were buried under the ashes and lava of Vesuvius. If a certain course of conduct long pursued, and in a great variety of circumstances, leads uniformly to health, happiness, and property, we are in little danger of inferring that it is in accordance with the will of God. If it lead to poverty and tears, we are in as little danger of error in inferring that it is a violation of some great law which God has ordained for the good of man. If an institution among men is always followed by certain results; if there is no modification of it by which it can be made to avoid those results; if we find them in all climes, and under all forms of government, and in every stage of society, it is not unsafe to draw an inference from these facts on the question whether God regards the institution as a good one, and one which he designs shall be perpetuated for the good of society.

It would be easy to make an application of these undeniable principles to the subject of slavery. The inquiry would be, whether in certain results always found to accompany slavery, and now developing themselves in our own country, there are no clear indications of what is the will of God. The inquiry would be pursued with reference to the bearing of the 'institution' on morals and religion; on the industry and population of a state; on agriculture, commerce, literature, and the arts.

I propose, however, only to consider the application of the principle to one important transaction in history—the rescue of an enslaved people from Egyptian bondage. The object is to inquire what light that transaction throws on the question, *Whether God regards slavery as a good institution, and one which he desires should be perpetuated.* The *principle* on which this inquiry will be conducted is, *that if we can find a case in history concerning which God has declared his sentiments, we may draw a safe conclusion in regard to the estimate which he forms of a similar institution now.*

The case referred to is that of Hebrew servitude in Egypt. The obvious inquiries are, I. Whether there was any thing in that servitude so similar to slavery now as to make it safe and proper to argue from the one to the other; and, II. Whether the act of God in delivering the Israelites from bondage makes it proper to draw any conclusion as to his general sentiments about slavery.

I. The resemblance between the servitude of the Hebrews in Egypt and slavery now; or the inquiry whether they are so similar as to make it proper to argue from the one to the other respecting the divine will.

It is not to be denied that there were some important points in which the servitude of the Hebrews in Egypt differed from slavery now, but most if not all of those points were of such a nature as not particularly to affect the inquiry before us.

(*a*) The Hebrews were not essentially distinguished from the Egyptians, as the Africans are from their masters in this land, by colour. There could be no argument drawn from the fact that they were of different complexion, or were of an inferior *caste* of men, in favour of holding them in bondage.

(*b*) They do not appear to have been claimed by individuals, or distributed on plantations or farms as the property of individuals. It was the enslaving or oppressing of them *as a people*, or *nation*, rather than subjecting them, as is done in our country, as individuals, to the service of others. They were in the service of the government, and held *by* the government, without particular reference to the will of individuals.

(*c*) On many accounts, also, the servitude in Egypt was

much more mild than it is in this country. Though characterized as '*hard*,' '*oppressive*,' '*grievous*,' and a '*furnace ;*' and though it was such as to lead to most decided and marked interpositions of God to rescue a down-trodden people from it, yet there were features in it which greatly softened it as compared with the system in our own land. This circumstance will increase, as will be seen in the sequel, the force of the argument which I deduce from the interposition of God in the case ; for if the oppression there was so grievous as to call forth the strong expressions of God in regard to it recorded in the Bible, and to lead to the heavy judgments which fell on Egypt in order to testify his disapprobation of the system, what are we to infer in reference to the divine views of the still more grievous oppressions in our own land ? In order to see this difference, and to appreciate the force of this consideration, it is of importance to have a just conception of the nature of servitude in Egypt. The following summary, made in part by another hand, ("The Bible *vs*. Slavery, pp. 55, 56, 57,") will present this with sufficient distinctness. (1.) *The Israelites "were not dispersed among the families of Egypt, but formed a separate community.* Gen. xlvi. 34 ; Ex. viii. 22, 24 ; ix. 26 ; x. 23 ; xi. 7 ; iv. 29 ; ii. 9 ; xvi. 22 ; xvii. 5 ; vi. 14. (2.) *They had the exclusive possession of the land of Goshen, the best part of the land of Egypt.* Gen. xlv. 18 ; xlvii. 6, 11, 27 ; Ex. viii. 22 ; ix. 26 ; xii. 4. Goshen must have been at a considerable distance from those parts of Egypt inhabited by the Egyptians ; so far at least as to prevent their contact with the Israelites, since the reason assigned for locating them in Goshen was, that shepherds were 'an abomination to the Egyptians ;' besides, their employments would naturally lead them out of the settled parts of Egypt to find a free range of pasturage for their immense flocks and herds. (3.) *They lived in permanent dwellings.* These were *houses*, not *tents*. In Ex. xii. 7, 22, the two side *posts*, and the upper door *posts*, and the lintel of the houses, are mentioned.   Each family seems to have occupied a house *by itself.*   Acts vii. 20.   (4.) *They owned 'flocks and herds,' and 'very much cattle.'* Ex. xii. 4, 6, 32, 37, 38.   From the fact that *'every man'* was commanded to kill either a lamb or a kid, one year old, for the passover, before the people left Egypt, we infer that even the poorest of the Israelites owned a flock either of sheep or goats.   Further, the immense multitude of their flocks and herds may be judged of from the expostulation of Moses with Jehovah. Num. xi. 21, 22.   'The people, among whom I am, are six hundred thousand footmen; and thou hast said, I will give them flesh, that they may eat a whole month; shall the flocks and the herds be slain for them, to *suffice* them?' As these six hundred thousand were only the *men* 'from twenty years old and upward, that were able to go forth to war,' Num. i. 45, 46; the whole number of the Israelites could not have been less than three millions.   Flocks and herds to 'suffice' all these for food, might surely be called 'very much cattle.' (5.) *They had their own form of government,* and preserved their tribe and family divisions, and their internal organization throughout, though still a province of Egypt and *tributary* to it. Ex. ii. 1; xii. 19, 21; vi. 14, 25; v. 19; iii. 16, 18. (6.) *They had, in a considerable measure, the disposal of their own time.*   Ex. iii. 16, 18; xii. 6; ii. 9; and iv. 27, 29—31. (7.) *They were all armed.* Ex. xxxii. 27.   (8.) *All the females seem to have known something of domestic refinements.*   They were familiar with instruments of music, and skilled in the working of fine fabrics, Ex. xv. 20; xxxv. 25, 26; and both males and female were able to read and write.   Deut. xi. 18—20; xvii. 19; xxvii. 3.   (9.) *Service seems to have been exacted from none but adult males.* Nothing is said from which the bond service of females could be inferred; the hiding of Moses three months by his mother, and the payment of wages to her by Pharaoh's daughter, go against such a supposition.   Ex. ii. 29.   (10.) *Their food was abundant and of great variety.*   So far from being fed

upon a fixed allowance of a single article, and hastily prepared, 'they sat by the flesh-pots,' and 'did eat bread to the
full.' Ex. xii. 15, 39. They ate 'the fish freely, the cu-
cumbers, and the melons, and the leeks, and the onions, and
the garlic.' Num. xi. 4, 5; xx. 5." (11.) It does not appear
that they were liable to be sold for debt, or that they could
be disposed of by testamentary disposition. And, (12.) they
were not held strictly as *chattels*. They were oppressed
men, and were regarded as such. They were *men* held to
service ; not men reduced to all the conditions of property.

But still there were so many strong points of resemblance
between the servitude of the Hebrews in Egypt and slavery
in this land, as to make it right to argue from the one to
the other. Indeed, the resemblances are so remarkable that
they cannot fail to strike every one who reads the account in
Exodus, and the references to the servitude in Egypt which
abound elsewhere in the Scriptures. (1.) They were a
foreign race, as the African race is with us. They were
not Egyptians, any more than the natives of Congo are
Americans. They were not of the children of Ham.* They

---

* It is not admitted here that if they had been of the children of Ham, it
would have been right to reduce them to servitude; for apart from any other
consideration, the Egyptians were themselves the proper descendants of
Ham. An argument is sometimes attempted in favour of African slavery
from the curse pronounced by Noah:—(Gen. ix. 25,) "Cursed be Canaan; a servant of servants shall he be unto his brethren." See the
"Brief Examination of the Scripture Testimony on the Institution of
Slavery," by Enoch Lewis. I have not thought it necessary to notice this
weak argument, for two reasons: One is, that a mere *prediction* of
what would be, is no justification of wickedness—for the prediction of the
Saviour that he would be betrayed by Judas, and even the *command* to him
to do 'what he was about to do' *quickly*, (John xiii. 27,) did not justify the
act of the traitor; the other is, that the curse was not pronounced on *Ham*,
but on *Canaan*. What have the inhabitants of Africa to do with that?
They are not descended from the one on whom the curse was pronounced,
whatever might be the argument supposed to be drawn from that curse.
The argument, however, would be good for nothing even if they were. It
is surprising that it was ever used.

were of another family; they differed from the Egyptians, by whom they were held in bondage, as certainly as the African does from the Caucasian or the Malay divisions of the great family of man. They had no share in the government; held no appointments under the crown ; were eligible to no office; had no participation in making or administering the laws. They were dissimilar in religion, in language, in customs, in employment, (Gen. xlvi. 34,) in manners. In every thing *except* complexion, they were as unlike the Egyptians as the African is to the native American, and they had as little to do with the government and institutions of Egypt as the African has with ours. They were a race introduced from abroad, and kept throughout, and on principle distinct.

(2.) There was a strong resemblance in the nature of the claim set up over them, and in the tenure by which they were held. (*a*) The first one of the race who went down to Egypt and dwelt there, was carried there as a slave, and sold as such. He had been *kidnapped* by members of his own family; sold to men who were as willing to traffic in human flesh as in aromatics; carried by them, as an article of merchandise, to Egypt, and sold as such there. Gen. xxxvii. 25—28; xxxix. 1. This is just the way in which African slaves were introduced into the United States; and the heartless cruelty with which Joseph was made a slave, and sold, has been re-enacted millions of times in Africa, in order to procure the slaves which are now in the United States. How appropriate to the method in which slaves are procured and held in this land, would be the description which is given of the manner in which Joseph was made a slave in Egypt!

> " He sent a man before them,
> " Even Joseph who was sold for a servant;
> " *Whose feet they hurt with fetters;*
> " *He was laid in iron."*   Ps. cv. 17, 18.

Many a poor African has been consigned to slavery in the same way, but with no holy bard, like David, so patheti-

cally to record his name, and to tell the wrong of his capture,
and the manner in which he was borne to the scene of his
future toil and woes. (*b*) As it is in slavery in this land, so
there was nothing *voluntary* on the part of the Hebrews. It
was throughout the work of oppression and wrong. It existed because their masters had the *power;* not because they
had the *right*. There was nothing on their part of the nature
of contract ; there was no agreement to serve the Egyptians ;
they had never been consulted in the case. They were
' *made* to serve' with hard bondage, for they had no power
of resisting. Like slavery in this country, then, the whole
thing was distinct from the acts of freemen, and the entire
arrangement was separated from that of voluntary labour.
There was not a Hebrew who had expressed his consent to
that kind of service ; there was not one who did not groan
and sigh by reason of the bondage. Ex. i. 8—11. (*c*) It had
the essential features of *slavery*, so far as those features are
specified in the Scriptures. The same word is used to describe it which is commonly employed to denote servitude in
the laws of Moses, and evidently in the same sense. Thus
in Ex. i. 14, it is said, "And they made their lives bitter with
hard bondage"—בַּעֲבֹדָה קָשָׁה—where the same word occurs
which is commonly applied to slavery in all the forms in
which it is specified in the Scriptures. The same word
occurs in Gen. xv. 13, where the servitude in Egypt is pre-
dicted. " Thy seed shall be a stranger in a land that is not
theirs, and *shall serve them*— וַעֲבָדוּם—and they shall afflict
them four hundred years." Comp. Lev. xxv. 30, 40.

(3.) It was unrequited labour. There was no pretence
even of giving them a fair compensation for their toil.
It was a system of exaction and oppression—where severe
labour was demanded; where no pay was tendered, and
where few facilities were granted for the performance of
the prescribed task. The *method* by which this was done
bore a strong resemblance also to the arrangements in the
slaveholding portions of our own country; and the account

which is given of that, would be an accurate description of the means resorted to to compel slaves to work in this land. "Therefore they did set over them *task-masters to afflict them with their burdens.*" Ex. i. 11. Servitude has always demanded the appointment of an order of men under various names of *task-masters* or *drivers.* It appoints tasks to be done, and often too where the "tale of bricks is demanded while no straw is given." Ex. v. 8, 11. There is no *voluntary* labour. There are none of the spontaneous exertions of freemen. All the language employed to describe the servitude in Egypt, is language denoting severe oppression and wrong; language such as is proper when there are severe exactions and unrequited labour; and language that, with almost *no change*, might be employed to describe slavery in this country. It represents a state of things conducted on the same principles, and with the same ends in view; and the two are so parallel in all their essential features, that if God approves the one, he must have approved the other; if he hated the one, he hates the other. The argument here is of the same kind as we apply in other cases. The strong faith which God approved in Abraham, he approves wherever it exists now; the wickedness which characterized the race before the flood, he would equally disapprove of now; and the tyranny of Ahab he equally abhorred in Nero, in Henry VIII., and would in any future sovereign. A few of the expressions, therefore, employed when the Bible speaks of the servitude in Egypt, will show its parallelism with the state of slavery in this land, and will serve to show also how God must regard both. "And they made their lives bitter, with hard bondage in mortar, and in bricks, and in all manner of service in the field: all their service wherein they made them serve was with rigour." Ex. i. 14. "And the Egyptians evil-entreated us, and afflicted us, and laid upon us hard bondage, and when we cried unto the Lord God of our fathers, the Lord heard our voice, and looked on our affliction, and our labour, and our oppression; and the Lord brought us forth out of Egypt with a mighty hand, and with an outstretched arm, and with great terribleness, and with signs, and with wonders." Deut. xxvi. 6—8. "And I have heard the groaning of the children of Israel, whom the Egyptians keep in bondage; and I have remembered my covenant." Ex. vi. 5. Comp. Ps. cii. 20, to ascertain how the Lord will *always* regard such a state of things, or will ultimately act on the same principle.

> "For he hath looked down from the height of his sanctuary;
> From heaven did the Lord behold the earth;
> To hear the groaning of the prisoner;
> To loose those that are appointed to death."

And Ps. xii. 5:

> "For the oppression of the poor,
> For the sighing of the needy,
> Now will I arise, saith the Lord;
> I will set him in safety from him that puffeth at him.

In accordance with these declarations, are the numerous passages which speak of the servitude in Egypt as hard and oppressive bondage, and the situation of the Hebrews there as a residence in a prison. "The Lord brought us out from Egypt, out of the house of bondage." Ex. viii. 14. "I am the Lord thy God which brought thee out of the land of Egypt, out of the house of bondage." Ex. xx. 2. Comp. Deut. v. 6; vii. 8; viii. 14; xiii. 5, 10; Josh. xxiv. 17; Judges vi. 8. Let any one look at the numerous references to the servitude of the Hebrews in Egypt in these and other passages, and he cannot fail to be struck with the accuracy with which the terms employed would describe slavery in this country. There are no words used to characterize that enormous wrong—for so it is always spoken of in the Scriptures—which would not with equal accuracy and emphasis characterize oppression in this land.

(4.) In the servitude in Egypt it was necessary to adopt most harsh and oppressive measures to prevent the Hebrews from becoming so numerous as to be able to overpower their masters, and to prevent their joining their enemies in case of invasion. The measures adopted in Egypt, and the reasons why they were adopted, are distinctly specified. The alarm which was excited was on account of their growing numbers. The danger apprehended was, that, becoming more numerous than their masters, they would be able to subdue them, or that they would unite themselves with an invading army, and thus secure their own freedom, and then turn their arms on their oppressors. "And the children of Israel were fruitful, and increased abundantly and multiplied, and waxed exceedingly mighty; and the land was filled with them. And he [Pharaoh] said unto his people, Behold, the people of the children of Israel are more and mightier than we: Come on, let us deal wisely with them; lest they multiply, and it come to pass, that, when there falleth out any war, they join also unto our enemies, and fight against us, and so get them up out of the land." Ex. i. 7, 9, 10. The measures adopted to prevent this, are well known. They were first, to oppress and crush them by severe exactions; to dishearten them; and to prevent their increase by measures of excessive cruelty. Ex. i. 11, 13, 14. Then, when this failed, (Ex. i. 12,) they resorted to the still more harsh and cruel measure of putting all the male children to death, that thus they might remove the danger. These measures were adopted from what was deemed a sagacious policy, that the oppressed Hebrews might not be able to assert their own freedom. Ex. i. 15, 16.

Is there nothing like this in the system of slavery, as it exists in this land? The means resorted to are not indeed precisely the same, but they have the same end in view. It is an essential part of the system here, that there *should be* measures adopted to prevent the slaves asserting their freedom, and an extended system of things having this end in view is constantly in operation—as oppressive, as cruel, and as contrary, in some respects, to the laws of Heaven, as was the unsuccessful policy of the Egyptians. Among those measures, the following are in existence in the slave states : —preventing the slaves from being taught to read and write ; prohibiting, as far as possible, all knowledge among themselves of their own numbers and strength ; forbidding all assemblages, even for worship, where there might be danger of their becoming acquainted with their own strength, and of forming plans for freedom ; enacting laws of excessive severity against those who run away from their masters ; appointing severe and disgraceful punishments, either with or without the process of law, for those who are suspected of a design to inform the slaves that they are men, and that they have the rights of human beings ; and solemnly prohibiting the use of arms among the slaves, designed to prevent their rising upon their masters, or 'joining themselves to an enemy, to fight against their masters, and so getting up out of the land.' A very large portion of the enactments in the Southern states, have the same object in view which was contemplated and avowed by the oppressive laws and measures of the Egyptians. They are felt to be essential to the system, and so long as slavery exists, it will be *necessary* to frame such laws.

There will be occasion to illustrate each of the points referred to here under another head, when we come to consider the nature of servitude under the laws of Moses. At present, it will be sufficient to refer to a very few instances of the laws in the slave states bearing on those points, or designed to *keep* the slaves in a 'state of bondage.' (1.) *They are not to be taught to read or write.* In 1740, South Carolina enacted this law : "Whereas, the having of slaves taught to write, or suffering them to be employed in writing, *may be attended with great inconveniences*, Be it enacted, that all and every person and persons whatsoever, who shall hereafter teach or cause any slave or slaves to be taught to write, or shall use or employ any slave as a scribe in any manner of writing whatsoever, every such person or persons shall, for every such offence, forfeit the sum of one hundred pounds current money."* A similar law, except the penalty, was passed in Georgia, by act of 1770.† In the revised code of Virginia of 1819, the following statute occurs : " All meetings or assemblages of slaves, or free negroes or mulattoes mixing and associating with such slaves at any meeting-house, or houses, or any other place, &c., in the night, *or at any school or schools for teaching them reading or writing either in the day or the night,* under whatsoever pretext, shall be deemed and considered *an unlawful assembly.*"‡ (2.) *They are not allowed to assemble even for worship in any such way as shall make an insurrection possible.* In a law enacted by Georgia, 1792, it is enacted that "no congregation or company of negroes shall, *under pretence of divine worship,* assemble themselves contrary to the act regulating patrols."§ Substantially the same thing exists in South Carolina,‖ and in Mississippi.¶ (3) *No meeting whatever of slaves is to be allowed of such a number as could acquaint themselves of their own strength, or make combination possible.* If a slave shall presume to come upon the plantation of any person, without leave in writing from his master, employer, &c., not being sent on lawful business, *the owner of the plantation may inflict ten lashes for every such offence.*** " It shall be lawful *for any person* who shall *see more than seven* men slaves, without some white person with them, travelling *or assembled together,* in any high road, to apprehend such slaves, and *to inflict a whipping* on such

---

* 2 Brevard's Digest, 243. † Prince's Digest, 455.
‡ 1 Rev. Code, 424, 425. § Prince's Digest, 342.
‖ 2 Brevard's Digest, 254, 255. ¶ Rev. Code, 390.
** 1 Virg. Rev. Code, 422 ; 3 Mississippi Rev. Code, 371 ; 2 Litt. & Swi. Dig. 1150 ; 2 Missouri Laws, 741, sec. 3.

of them, not exceeding twenty lashes apiece."*   (4) *The possession of all arms or weapons of defence is strictly prohibited.* " For keeping or carrying a gun, or powder, or shot, or *a club, or other weapon whatever*, offensive or defensive, a slave incurs for each offence, thirty-nine lashes, by order of a justice of the peace."†

There are *reasons* why the same measure is not adopted here which was by the Egyptians, that of putting the male children to death. It cannot be doubted or denied that increasing humanity has done much to prevent this. But even if this had had no influence, there are other causes which *would* secure this result, and prevent a measure so cruel and wrong. They are valuable in the market. They can be sold and conveyed to places where the danger of an insurrection would be less. The surplus population of Virginia, North Carolina, and Maryland can thus be removed to Georgia, Mississippi, or Texas, instead of being thrown into the Potomac, the Rappahannock, or the Roanoke. But still, there *are* laws both numerous and appropriate, all contemplating the same end, and customs that were little, if any, surpassed in cruelty by the Egyptian law which ordained that the male children should be thrown into the Nile. Is there not many a mother who would *prefer* to see her infant son " thrown into the river," (Ex. i: 22,) to having him torn from her bosom and borne away where she would see him no more ? Is there not many a father who could see his daughter floating on the smooth current of a river, a lifeless corpse, with more calmness than he could see her wrested from his arms to be doomed to unpitied infamy and degradation in the dwelling of some planter in Texas, or made to minister to corrupt passions in a palace in New Orleans? Would a

---

* 2 Brev. Dig. 243; Prince's Dig. 554.

† 2 Litt. & Swi. 1150; 1 Virg. Rev. Code, 423; 2 Missouri Laws, 741, sec. 4; Haywood's Manual, 521. See Stroud's " Sketch of the Laws relating to Slavery," pp. 88, 92, 93, 102.

father or a mother have no pleasure in looking on the green sod that should cover the grave of an infant child, compared with the thought that he might be groaning under the lash in a distant land of bondage? And can the things ordained in this Christian land professedly to keep the slaves in bondage, and to prevent a possibility of their asserting their freedom, be less offensive to God than were similar things among the heathen of Egypt?

(5.) There is a resemblance between Egyptian and American slavery, in a remarkable feature, which has always perplexed those who have written on the subject of population—the *increase* of those who are oppressed. The growth of the Hebrews in Egypt, compared with the native population, was such as to lead to the apprehension that they would ultimately have power to bring the country under their own control. Ex. i. 7, 9. It was particularly alarming that the more they were oppressed the more they increased. Ex. i. 12. It became necessary, therefore, to resort to additional measures of rigor, to prevent their becoming so numerous as to endanger the government. Ex. i. 11, 14, 16. The similarity between this increase and that of the slaves in our own country, is such that it cannot fail to have arrested the attention of all those who have ever looked at slavery. It is sufficient, on this point, merely to refer to the undisputed fact. The increase of the population in the free states, from 1830 to 1840, was at the rate of 38 per cent., while the increase of the *free* population of the slave states was only 23 per cent. A single statement will show the *progressive* advance of the slaves over the free population of some of those states.

In 1790, the whites in North Carolina were to the slaves,
2·80 to 1; now as 1·97 to 1.

South Carolina,	1·31 " 1;	" ·79 " 1.
Georgia,	1·76 " 1;	" 1·44 " 1.
Tennessee,	13·35 " 1;	" 3·49 " 1.
Kentucky,	5·16 " 1;	" 3·23 " 1.

From this it is apparent that, in spite of all the oppressions and cruelties of slavery; of all the sales that are effected; of all the removals to Liberia; and of all the removals by the escape of the slaves, there is a regular gain of the slave population over the free, in the slaveholding states. No oppression prevents it here more than it did in Egypt, and there can be no doubt whatever that unless slavery shall be arrested in some way, the increase is so certain that the period is not far distant when, in all the slave states, the free whites will be far in the minority. At the first census, taken in 1790, in every slave state there was a very large majority of whites. At the last census, in 1840, the slaves outnumbered the whites in South Carolina, Mississippi, and Louisiana. The tendency of this, from causes which it would be easy to state, can be arrested by nothing but emancipation.

(6.) There is a striking resemblance in regard to the *numbers* held in bondage in Egypt, and those now in servitude in this country. When Moses led the children of Israel forth, the number of *men*, capable of bearing arms, was six hundred thousand. Ex. xii. 37, 38. According to this enrolment, allowing the usual proportion for age, infancy, and the female sex, there were full three millions that had been held in "the iron furnace," in Egypt. Jer. xi. 4. There are in the United States now, according to the census of 1840, 2,486,465 of a foreign race held in bondage. Of these 432,727 are *men* more than twenty-four years of age, and 391,206 are males between the ages of ten and twenty-four; and probably the number of those capable of bearing arms would be found to be nearly the same as among the Hebrews whom Moses conducted out of Egypt. As in Egypt, also, there is a vast number of women and children, and of the aged and the infirm, held in a state that, in the main, without any poetic colouring, may be called a "furnace of iron."

II. The second inquiry in regard to the servitude in Egypt, is, whether the interposition of God, in that case, was such as to make it proper for us to derive any conclusions as to his will in regard to slavery. He delivered the oppressed with an "outstretched arm, and with great signs and wonders." Is it right to infer, from this remarkable interposition in the behalf of that people, any thing respecting his views in cases of similar oppression ?   Is the case sufficiently parallel to lay the foundation of an argument on the principle on which we are accustomed to appeal to the dispensations of Providence and the course of events ?   We judge of the divine will in relation to intemperance, not only from the declarations in the Bible, but from the wo and sorrow, the poverty, rags, and disease, which God in his Providence brings upon the drunkard.   Is it right, on similar principles, to judge of his sentiments on the subject of slavery, from one of the most direct and remarkable interpositions of heaven in human affairs, which has ever occurred ?   Here stands in his word the record of these great and wonderful facts in history —millions of slaves delivered by direct divine interposition ; a series of most overwhelming calamities on those who held them in bondage ; frequent allusions to the event in the sub-sequent inspired writings ; a mighty arm stretched out from heaven to conduct the oppressed and the down-trodden to a land of freedom.   What are we to infer from these things ? Did God regard that ; does he regard a similar institution now, as a good arrangement, and as one on which he is dis-posed to smile, and which he desires should be perpetuated for the good of mankind ?   Let the following facts in the case be considered :

(1.) It would have been as just for the Egyptians to retain the Hebrews in bondage, as it is for white Americans to retain the African race.   All the *right* in either case is derived from mere power.   In the case of the Egyptians, it could not be pretended that they had a right to enslave the nation because they had purchased *Joseph* some hundreds of years before; and as little can the right to enslave the posterity of the Africans be founded on the fact that *their* ancestors were purchased in Congo.   It could not be pre-tended that they had a right to enslave them because they were a foreign race, or were of different complexion; and as little can the plea be set up to vindicate the retaining of the African in bondage. If the vindication of slavery now should be set up on that ground, it would be difficult to see why it would not apply in the case of the Hebrews as well as of the African race; nay, it would be difficult to see why this might not be imbodied in a general principle—that *all* foreigners, of a different complexion from our own, may be lawfully enslaved. Further; if the right to retain the African race in bondage be based on the laws of the land, the same plea might have been urged in the case of the Hebrews. Under the authority of Pharaoh, it had become the law of the land that the Hebrews should be held to servitude. If it be further urged that it is difficult to free the slaves in this country; that emancipation might be attended with peril to the master; that to let loose two millions and a half of slaves from a state of deep degradation might be fraught with dangerous consequences, the same thing might have been urged with equal force in regard to the servitude in Egypt. The simple truth is, that the sole claim in either case is founded in *power*, and that is just the same in the one instance as the other. The Egyptians had *power* to enslave the Hebrews, and they did it; the American has *power* to hold the African in bondage, and he does it. The right is as clear in the one case as in the other; and if God approves of slavery as it exists now in this land, he must have approved the same thing in Egypt.

Will it be said that the Hebrews were his chosen people, and that he was especially displeased with the Egyptians, not because the oppression was itself wrong, but because they oppressed his friends? And are not the Africans his people, (Acts xvii. 26;) and is there any thing that more certainly excites the sympathy and compassion of God, than the fact that an individual or a community is trodden by the foot of violence to the earth?

Will it be alleged that there is a difference in the two

cases, because the slaves in Egypt were held not by individuals but by the government, and that there was no claim of property in them—that they were not bought and sold as chattels and as things? If this is alleged, the case is not affected. God may be as little displeased that the head of a nation or a government should do wrong, as an individual. Besides, if it be alleged that the cases are not parallel because the Hebrews were not held as *chattels* and as *things*, this is all the worse for the American slaveholder; for, from this very fact, slavery here must be just so much more offensive to God than it was in Egypt. In all the acts of Egyptian oppression; in the heavy tasks imposed; in the grievous burdens laid on the Hebrews; in the murder by authority of law of all their male children, the refinement of cruelty was never thought of which has become essential in American slavery— that of reducing *a man to a chattel; an immortal soul to a thing.* The Hebrews were oppressed *men,* they were not *chattels* and *things.* And if God frowned upon slavery as it was then; if he brought ten successive judgments upon a heathen nation in order to express his abhorrence of the system, and to deliver an enslaved people, is it not right to infer that he has at least as deep feelings of indignation against a system of deeper degradation and oppression in a Christian land?

(2.) The divine declarations in regard to Egyptian bondage, and all the expressions of disapprobation of what occurred in Egypt, are applicable to the system of things in this country. No one can pretend that God approved of servitude as it was in Egypt, or that the measures which were adopted to perpetuate it were pleasing in his sight. The heavy burdens; the withholding of the material for work, and yet exacting the full amount which had been before required; the murder of the male children; and the entire series of acts designed to keep them from insurrection, and to prevent their joining an enemy, are *all* recorded with expressions of decided disapprobation. And can we suppose that God will be pleased with similar acts in this Christian country; acts that have in a great measure the same ends in view—to retain nearly three millions of people in a state of degradation and bondage? A vast and complicated system of arrangements, as has already been remarked, exists in the United States, all having for their object precisely the same thing which was contemplated in Egypt—designed to perpetuate the system; to place those held in bondage in such a condition that they can neither combine to assert their own liberty, nor be in a situation to join the army of an enemy should one invade the land. Among these arrangements are all those which are made to keep the slaves in ignorance; to withhold the Bible from them; to prevent their being taught to read; to withhold arms from them; to forbid assemblages even for worship without such a *surveillance* as to prevent all danger of combinations; to prohibit their going to other plantations without a passport; to check and arrest and punish all of their own colour, or of a different colour, who would acquaint them with their numbers, their power, and their rights; to put down all effort for the recovery of their liberty, and to bring back to servitude, to lodge in prison, or to manacle, scourge, or kill those who have attempted to escape. These, and numerous similar things, all contemplate precisely the same end which was contemplated by the arrangements made at the court of Pharaoh; and can we suppose that they are more pleasing to God in the one case than in the other? Has the lapse of three thousand and five hundred years served to reconcile the divine Mind to such measures? Are they more agreeable to the Ruler of the nations because they are resorted to in a land of *liberty*, and under the light of the Christian revelation? Were they wrong under the heathen Pharaoh; are they right under Christian masters and legislators?

Let it be remembered, too, that oppressive and cruel as were the measures resorted to in Egypt to perpetuate slavery, there are wrongs existing in this country, under the sanction of law, and which are regarded as essential to the system, which were unknown there. In Egypt, there was no withholding of the Bible; there is not known to have been any prohibition to learn to read; there was no separation of husband and wife, and parent and child, to be sold into distant servitude; there was no arrangement for confining in prison those who attempted to escape; there was no shooting down the poor man who endeavoured to assert his freedom; there was no pursuit of those who fled for liberty, with bloodhounds. Can we believe that God frowned on the arrangements made in Egypt to perpetuate slavery, and that he can look with complacency on these arrangements of augmented cruelty and oppression in our own land?

(3.) The calamities brought upon the Egyptians for holding a foreign people in bondage, and for the measures to which they resorted to perpetuate that bondage, were an expression of the views which God entertained of the system. What those calamities were, it is not needful to state. They consisted, in general, of ten successive judgments, the most desolating, the most annoying, the most humbling to the pride of a haughty people, and the best adapted to spread lamentation and wo through a nation, which the human mind can conceive. The waters of the land turned into rivers, pools, and lakes of blood; offensive and loathsome reptiles creeping into the very palaces, and filling all the implements for preparing the food even of the royal household; clouds of locusts that devoured every green thing; offensive vermin swarming everywhere; storms of hail that destroyed the labours of man; disease that swept off the cattle, and the destroying angel passing in the dead of night through all the land of Egypt, cutting off everywhere the first-born, and filling every house with grief;—these were the expressions of the divine sense of the wrongs endured by the foreign race which had been reduced to servitude.

Can any thing be inferred from this in reference to the divine views regarding slavery now? We are not now, indeed, to expect miraculous interpositions of this nature. But what if it shall be found that the existence of slavery is attended with a series of inevitable calamities to a country ? What if it leads to a diminished or enfeebled population ? What if it is destructive to the interests of industry, morals, education, and religion ? What if its effects are seen in wasted fields, in a crippled commerce, in a destruction of the interests of manufacture, in ruined credit, in bankrupt individuals and states ? What if, where the course of a river winds along through lands equally favoured by nature, one bank shall be adorned with smiling villages, and colleges, and churches, and the general aspect of neatness, thrift, and order ; and the other shall wear the aspect of ignorance, irreligion, neglect, and desolation ? Are we to be forbidden to draw an inference as to the views which God entertains of the system ? Is it wrong to draw such an inference with as much certainty as we do from the divine interpositions in Egypt ? Are not desolate fields, and a crippled commerce, and the evils of bankruptcy, and blightings and mildews, as really the act of God, as were the murrain, and the hail, and the flight of locusts, and the passing of the destroying angel over Egypt ? Are they not as certain indications of the will of God, as the rags, and the poverty, and the babblings, and the bloated and haggard form of the drunkard ? If slavery brings up a brood of evils upon a land that ' out-venom all the worms of Nile ;' that are more offensive and ruinous than crawling reptiles and annoying vermin, and that cause more permanent desolation than the sweepings of a hail-storm, is it an unfair inference that it is hateful in the sight of God ?

(4.) The deliverance of the Hebrews from Egyptian bondage shows what is the divine estimate of every similar system. He brought out an oppressed people by his own hand. He did it amidst great judgments and mighty wonders. He did it in the most public manner, and so that the fact of *his* interposition could not be mistaken. He did it in such a way that the act might be known among the nations of the earth, and that a permanent record might be made of his interposition, in order that all future ages might understand what he had done. He did it by bringing heavier judgments upon those who had been the oppressors, than had before befallen any nation. By this public act, he testified to the nations of the earth how much he *hated* the system. By this act, as well as by his own solemn declarations, he showed that he valued the freedom of the oppressed more than he did the prosperity of the royal house of Pharaoh, the preservation of the harvests of Egypt, the lives of their first-born, or even the whole land of Egypt and Ethiopia.

> "I am Jehovah, thy God;
> The Holy One of Israel, thy Saviour:
> *I gave Egypt for thy ransom,*
> *Ethiopia and Seba for thee.*"—Isa. xliii. 3.

That is, Egypt was regarded as having been given up to destruction and desolation, *instead* of the Hebrews. One of them *must* perish—either the Hebrews, under the hand of the oppressor, or the Egyptians by the hand of their deliverer; and God chose that Egypt, though so much more mighty and powerful, should be reduced to desolation, rather than the enslaved nation of the Hebrews. All the wealth of Egypt, including her armies and her king, was not *worth* so much, in the divine estimate, as the liberty of the oppressed; and God chose that the one should be sacrificed in order to secure the other—just as it *may* yet appear that God values the liberty of the oppressed in our own land more than he does the beauty of smiling harvests, a prosperous commerce, and the happiness and the wealth of the planter; and may yet suffer blighting and curses to come over the fairest portions of our own country, *in order* that the oppressed may be suffered to go free. Nor did he wait for a gradual deliverance; nor did he recommend a preparation for freedom; nor did he utter any apology for the continuance of servitude, from the difficulties attending emancipation. He demanded of the

oppressors that his people should be allowed to go free at
once.   When they would not permit this, the storms of his
wrath burst upon the guilty nation, and he led out his people
triumphantly under his own hand.

The conclusions which I am authorized to draw from this
signal interposition in behalf of an oppressed people, are, that
such oppression is hateful to God ; that the acts of cruelty
and wickedness which are necessary to perpetuate such
oppression, are the objects of his abhorrence ; that wherever
the same system of things exists which did there, it must be
equally offensive to him ; that it is his will that, if a foreign
race have been held in servitude, they should be allowed to
go free ; and that if those who hold them in bondage will not
allow them to go free when he commands it, he will, by his
own providence, bring such a series of desolating judgments
on a people, that, however hardened their hearts may have
been towards the oppressed and the down-trodden, and however much they may be disposed, like Pharaoh, to say,
" Who is JEHOVAH, that we should obey his voice to let the
people go ?" (Ex. v. 2 ;) he will make them *willing* to send
them forth, even if they pursue them with their maledictions,
as Pharaoh pursued the ransomed Hebrews with his embat-
tled hosts.   If we may draw an inference, also, from this
case, in regard to the *manner* in which God would have
such a people restored to freedom, it would be in favour of
immediate emancipation.

CHAPTER V.

The Mosaic Institutions in relation to Servitude.

THE Scriptural argument on which most reliance is placed by the advocates of slavery, is, probably, that it made a part of the Mosaic institutions. We have seen (ch. 1) that those who appeal to the Bible, in defence of the institution, make the argument from the Mosaic laws prominent, and seem to consider it decisive in the case. A single reference here to the article, so often quoted, in the Princeton Biblical Repertory, will illustrate the usual mode of making this appeal, and the manner in which reliance is placed on the argument. " The fact that the Mosaic institutions recognised the lawfulness of slavery, is a point too plain to need proof, and is almost universally admitted. Our argument from this acknowledged fact is, that if God allowed slavery to exist, if he directed how slaves might be lawfully acquired, and how they were to be treated, it is in vain to contend that slavery is a sin, and yet profess reverence for the Scriptures. Every one must feel that if perjury, murder, or idolatry had been thus authorized, it would bring the Mosaic institutions into conflict with the eternal principles of morals, and that our faith in the divine origin of the one or the other must be given up."* This may be regarded as the current method of appeal by the advocates of slavery—often expressed, indeed, in stronger language, and made more directly to bear on the institutions of slavery in our country, but still constituting, in fact, the same appeal. The argument is usually alleged as if it were decisive in the case. A bare reference to the fact that slavery existed; that it was tole-

---

* Page 287.

rated by law; that it was the subject of express enactments; that the Hebrew people might own slaves; and
that it "was no sin for a *priest* to purchase a slave with his
money,"* is generally supposed to be all that the argument
requires.   There is usually little attempt to show what
slavery *was* under the Mosaic institutions; to inquire how
it was modified, checked and controlled; to ask what privileges were conceded by law to those who were held in
servitude; to compare the Mosaic system with that which
existed in surrounding nations; and still less to compare it
with that which exists in our land.   There is little care
taken to inquire into the true spirit of the Mosaic laws on the
subject, or what *would be* the effect on slavery in the United
States if the Mosaic statutes were at once substituted in the
place of those existing here.   Yet it is plain that all this is
necessary in order to see the real force of the argument, or to
do justice to Moses.   The argument is brought to defend the
institution of slavery as it exists among us.   But how can
there be any force in it, unless it be shown that Moses was
at heart the friend of slavery as a permanent institution, and
that *his* laws on the subject, if applied now, would sustain
and perpetuate the institution as it exists among us?

The propriety, therefore, of a somewhat extended examination of this point, will be at once apparent.   It is impossible
to convince the advocates of slavery that it is in any sense
a wrong, unless the argument which they derive from the
Mosaic institutions shall be met and answered.   To do this,
it will be necessary to show, 1. What the argument *is* on
which so much reliance is placed; 2. To investigate the
Mosaic institutions on the subject, that we may understand
the system as arranged by the Hebrew legislator; 3. To
compare that system with slavery as it exists in the United
States; and, 4. To inquire how far it is legitimate to argue

---

* See the Letter of the Presbytery of Tombecbee to the Conference of
Maine, p. 14.

from the one to the other, or how far the Mosaic institutions
would countenance slavery as it exists in this country.

§ 1. *What the argument which is relied on, is.*

The argument in favour of slavery, from the Mosaic institutions, is not commonly drawn out at length, but it may be supposed to be comprised in the following particulars :—

1. That slavery in fact existed under the Mosaic institutions, or entered into institutions which had their origin in a divine arrangement.

2. That it existed there unrebuked, or that there was no express condemnation of it ; that there is to be found no explicit and positive declaration that it was wrong *per se*, or that they who practised on the system were doing wrong. The argument here is, that whatever is incorporated into a divine institution, or an institution under divine arrangement, without express rebuke and condemnation, must be regarded as in itself right.

3. That there was express legislation on the subject, recognising the relation of master and slave ; giving permission to purchase slaves ; directing the method of their treatment ; arranging their duties and the duties of their masters ; prescribing their privileges and the rights of their masters ; and, in general, legislation for this relation in the same way as there was for the relation of husband and wife, and parent and child. The inference which would be derived from this by the advocate of slavery, would be, that this relation was considered to be as lawful as any other. The argument is, that whatever is made the subject of express legislation must be regarded as right and proper by the legislator, or that it cannot be inferred that *he* regarded it as wrong or as undesirable.

4. That this arrangement extended to all classes of men under the Mosaic system. Even the *priests* might become the owners of slaves, and it was not regarded as wrong in

them to 'purchase a slave with money.'* The argument here would be, that a system *could* not be regarded as wrong in itself where even the ministers of religion were allowed, in common with all others, to participate in it.   Could God allow one to purchase a slave just as he was about to approach the very altar, and yet regard the institution as evil?   *Perhaps*, also, in this case, the appeal to the permission given to the Jewish priesthood might be urged to give a sanction to the fact that a minister of the gospel may lawfully " purchase a slave with *his* money," and to show that it is not improper that he should lend the sanction of his name and example to so good an institution.   If a Jewish priest might purchase and own a slave, how can it be inferred that the same thing is wrong for a Christian minister in the United States?

5. It would be said, in addition to all this, that there is express sanction given to the institution as one that was to be permanent, or, in the language of the Presbytery of Tombecbee, " the Bible warrants the purchase of slaves as an inheritance *for children* for ever."—p. 14.   The passage on which reliance is placed in this argument, is Lev. xxv. 44, 45, 46: " Both thy bond-men and thy bond-maids, which thou shalt have, shall be of the heathen that are round about you : of them shall ye buy bond-men and bond-maids.   Moreover, of the children of the strangers that do sojourn among you, of them shall ye buy, and of their families that are with you, which they begat in your land : and they shall be your possession.   And ye shall take them as an inheritance for your children after you, to inherit them for a possession; they shall be your bond-men for ever."

This, perhaps, drawn out at greater length, would be substantially the argument in favour of slavery derived from the Mosaic institutions.   I have designed not to do injustice to it; and indeed I have made it stronger than I have found it in

---

* Letter of the Presbytery of Tombecbee, p. 14.

any of the books to which I have access. Compare, however, Paulding on Slavery, pp. 19, 20.

What now is the real force of this argument? What weight should it be allowed to have in vindicating slavery as it exists in the United States? What are we to infer from the Mosaic institutions in regard to the divine feelings towards servitude in our own land? *Was Moses* FRIENDLY *to slavery, or was he not?* Or rather, since God was the author of the Mosaic institutions, was *he* friendly to slavery, and did he regard it as a good and desirable institution to be perpetuated on earth, as contributing to the best good of society? Or *if* he was friendly to slavery as it existed under the Mosaic institutions, is it fair to infer that he is friendly to it as it exists in the United States?

Now it will be apparent that, in order to the validity of the argument in favour of slavery from the Mosaic institutions, it is essential that the following points be made clear, viz. :—

1. That it was regarded by Moses as in itself *a good thing;* a thing which it would have been proper for him to *originate* if he had not found it already in existence. For it *may* be conceived, that, for certain reasons, he might have regarded it as proper to *tolerate* that which he found in existence, and which could not be at once removed, but which he did not regard in itself as *good* or *right,* and which he would by no means have originated. The true inquiry here, therefore, should be, whether we can find in his arrangements, any evidence that he regarded it *per se* as good and desirable ; or any evidence that he would have *originated* it as conducive to the valuable ends which he had in view. Can we infer from the Mosaic arrangements that he would have the system *originated* now where it does not already exist, or *perpetuated* where it can easily be abolished?

2. It must be shown that *God* approved the system as a good and desirable one. It must be made apparent that he did not regard it as among the *evils* that were to be removed as speedily as practicable. consistently with the preservation

of great interests which he desired should be secured. There must be some declaration, or some arrangement, by which it may be fairly inferred that it is a good *per se*, and not such an institution that he would wish it to be removed. This might be inferred, if he made arrangements for its perpetuity; if he commanded a system or set of doctrines to be propagated which would lead to its perpetuity or the enlargement of its influence; if he instituted nothing to check it; if the fair operation of the institutions which he appointed should serve to perpetuate, and not to destroy it. But if none of these things occur, it is not fair to draw the conclusion that he is friendly to the institution. If, on the contrary, an entirely opposite set of arrangements shall be found all tending to destroy the system, it will not be unfair to conclude that he does *not* regard it as a good and desirable institution; or in other words, that the Mosaic arrangement is *not* to be interpreted as in favour of slavery. We infer that the church is an institution which God approves, because he has made arrangements for its perpetuity and enlargement on earth; he has appointed ordinances which suppose that it will always be in existence; he has commanded doctrines and principles to be inculcated which will always tend to its growth; and if his injunction should be *fairly* carried out, the growth of the church would never be checked, but its influence would continually expand until the earth would be covered with organizations of this kind. It will be necessary to find some such arrangement of permanency in the Mosaic laws in order to demonstrate that he regarded slavery as a good institution, and desired it to be perpetuated on the earth.

3. It is essential to this argument, in order to show that slavery is *now* right, or that the Bible sanctions it, to be able *to argue from the Hebrew institutions to those in this country*. It is necessary to show that the Mosaic arrangements in regard to the institution were such as to justify those which are found indispensable now for its perpetuity. It is

necessary to show that the laws respecting slavery under the Mosaic code and in this land are so similar that an argument which would prove that slavery was proper *as it was then*, demonstrates that it is proper *as it is now*. This is essential, because the very purpose for which an appeal is made to the Mosaic laws by the advocate of slavery is to show that it is right now, and as it exists in the United States. There must be, therefore, in order to make the argument valid, such a resemblance as to make it proper to reason from one to the other. If the Mosaic institution was a very different thing from slavery in our country; if it was organized on different principles and for different objects; if it varied essentially in its arrangements ; and if it tended to a different result, it is evidently improper to argue from one to the other. In one word, if there was an arrangement in the one which tended to its speedy *abolition*, it is not fair to infer that the arrangements in the other which contemplate its *perpetuity*, are right.

4. It is essential to this argument from the Mosaic institutions, to prove that what is tolerated at one period of the world is always right; that what was tolerated three thousand years gc under he Hebrew system of legislation is proper under the Gospel. The argument implies that what is allowed at one period of the world, is right at all times, and in all places, and under all degrees of light and knowledge.

If these points could be made out, it would be necessary to admit the conclusiveness of the argument derived from the Mosaic institutions in favour of slavery now. The inquiry before us, therefore, is, were the arrangements among the Hebrews in regard to servitude such as to make this clear? This inquiry demands that we examine with care the laws which Moses made on the subject, and then compare them with those existing in our own land.

§ 2. *The Mosaic institutions in regard to Servitude.*

Previous to our entering on the inquiry proposed in this section, it is proper to remark that Moses did not *originate* the system of servitude which is recognised in his laws, and there is no reason to think that he would have done it. Whatever may be inferred respecting his views of the system, from his enactments, yet every thing in those enactments looks *as if* he found the institution of slavery already in existence.

That slavery had an existence when Moses undertook the task of legislating for the Hebrews, there can be no doubt. We have seen* that servitude of some kind prevailed among the patriarchs; that the traffic in slaves was carried on between the Midianites and the Egyptians, Gen. xxxviii. 25—28; xxxix. 1; and that it existed among the Egyptians. It was undoubtedly practised by all the surrounding nations, for history does not point us to a time when slavery did not exist. It was one of the earliest maxims that has come down to us, that by the common laws of war, the captive was to be a slave at the disposal of the victor. Thus the common law among the Romans says, *a quo quis vincitur, ejus servus esse tenetur.* Thus Thucydides says,† " We consider it to be of divine appointment, and conformable to reason, that one who has subdued another should have dominion over him— οὗ ἂν κράτῃ, ἄρχειν. There is even evidence that slavery was practised by the Hebrews themselves when in a state of bondage, and that though they were, as a nation, " bondmen to Pharaoh," yet they had servants in their own families who had been " bought with money." This is manifest from Ex. xii. 43—45. Comp. 51. At the very time that the law was given respecting the observance of the Passover, and before the exode from Egypt, this statute appears among others: " This is the ordinance of the Passover: There shall no

---

* Ch. iii.   † Lib. 5.

stranger eat thereof: But every man's servant *that is bought for money*, when thou hast circumcised him, then shall he eat thereof. A foreigner and an hired servant shall not eat thereof." It is clear, from this, that the institution was already in existence, and that Moses did not originate it.

The truth in regard to this point is, that Moses found servitude in existence, just as he did polygamy and the custom of divorce; that it can be no more inferred that he would have originated the one than the other; and that the fact that he legislated for the one can be no more regarded as evidence that he approved it as a good and desirable system, than the fact that he legislated for the other.

The condition of Moses as a lawgiver, in this respect, was not materially unlike that of the framers of the Constitution of the United States. When the Convention sat, in 1790, to frame that instrument, slavery existed in all the Southern states, and in not a few of the Northern states also, and had existed from the first settlement of the country. It was extensively interwoven with all the colonial institutions. The people had become habituated to it, and nearly all the existing laws tolerated it. The people of the colonies had, like the Hebrews in Egypt, been under oppression, but, like those same Hebrews, they had themselves held others in bondage. In these circumstances, it became a matter of necessity to legislate on the subject, and to admit some arrangements into the Constitution in regard to it. Hence the slave-trade itself was tolerated until the year 1808. Provision was made in the Constitution for restoring those who escaped, from one state to another, to their masters.* An important concession was made to the states where slavery existed, in regard to the ratio of representation. Though the word '*slave*' was carefully avoided in the instrument, yet it was understood that the arrangements in the Constitution pertained to slavery, and in fact *did* really pertain to it. Yet it would be very unfair to suppose from this that either the majority of the framers of that instrument were in favour of slavery, or the majority of the states which adopted it. No one would feel that he was reasoning safely, to infer from that fact that Washington, and Madison, and Franklin, and Adams were the friends of slavery, or that they would have originated the system, if it had not already been in existence. In fact, were there no other evidence in the case, it would not be difficult to make out an argument, from the very Constitution which they framed, to show that they looked on the whole institution with aversion; that they were not willing to defile the immortal instrument which they were framing with even the *name* of slavery; that they would be willing that future ages should not know, if possible, that they even tolerated it; and that they *meant* that the system should cease in the land as soon as possible. Why should we, then, any more infer that Moses was friendly to the system, from the fact that he tolerated it?

If it should be said here, that Moses had it in his power wholly to prohibit slavery in his institutions, and yet chose to admit it as a part of his system, and that therefore it is to be inferred that he regarded it as a good and desirable thing, I would make the following reply: (1) It is not absolutely certain that it could have been entirely prohibited with ease, and we know that some things were *tolerated* under his system which were not *approved*. Thus we are expressly told, on the highest authority, that the practice of divorce was permitted "on account of the hardness of the hearts" of the Jewish people, (Mat. xix. 8;) but that this was not according to the original arrangement when man was created, and was not an arrangement which God desired should be perpetuated on the earth. The Christian precept utterly abolished an arrangement sanctioned by the laws of Moses, on which he had carefully legislated, and which had been acted on, perhaps without suspicion of wrong, for many hundred years. Who can *prove* that slavery may not have been a case like this? It will not do to assume that it might *not* be, for it would seem that it would be as easy to abolish the custom of divorce, and to prohibit it for ever, as to abolish slavery and to ordain a perpetual prohibition of it.   (2) There may have been reasons, perhaps a part of them unknown to us, why Moses tolerated slavery, but which would be entirely consistent with the belief that he regarded it as an evil system, and one which he wished to have abolished as speedily as possible.   In such a case, we are not to infer from the fact that he tolerated it, and legislated for it, that he regarded it as a good and a desirable institution.   It would seem that this was the case, if the following things should be found to be true in regard to his admission of slavery into his system : (*a*) if it existed all around him in harsh and oppressive forms ; (*b*) if the condition of a slave, by being purchased by a Hebrew, would be greatly meliorated ; (*c*) if the condition there was such as to make it *an object* for slaves in surrounding countries to place themselves voluntarily under Hebrew masters ; (*d*) if by such an arrangement they might in fact become incorporated into the Hebrew commonwealth, and be made partakers of the blessings of the only true religion ; (*e*) if Palestine was made an asylum for the oppressed of all lands, and it was understood that the moment a slave crossed its borders he was secure from having the chains of heathen servitude ever riveted again on him, and the whole power of the civil arm in the Hebrew commonwealth would be stretched out for his defence and protection ; and (*f*) if it should appear that an arrangement was made by which perpetual slavery would be impracticable, and the whole system ultimately abolished.   In such a case, it would not be unfair to conclude that Moses would not have originated the system ; that he did not regard it as a desirable institution, and that it is not to be inferred that it is an institution which God approves and wishes to be perpetuated, because it was tolerated under the Mosaic dispensation.

That Moses *did* admit a system of servitude into his institutions, seems to me to be undeniable. See Lev. xxv. In
regard to the *methods* by which native born Hebrews or
foreigners might become slaves under the Mosaic system, a
full account may be found in the Constitutiones Servi Hebræi,
of Joh. Cas. Miegius, sec. 11, in Ugolin's Thes. Ant. Sacra.
tom. 26, pp. 678, seq. The modes by which those who were
native born Hebrews might become servants, were the three
following: (1.) It was a settled principle that the Hebrew could
not be made a slave to his brethren by *war*. This prohibition
is not indeed expressly found in the laws of Moses, but an
occurrence which took place in the time of Ahaz, shows that it
was a well understood principle.   In a war between the
king of Israel and Ahaz, a large number of Hebrews—more
than two hundred thousand—were made captives, and taken
to Samaria, the captors purposing to retain them as 'bondmen,' and 'bond-women.' Against this the prophet Oded
remonstrated, as a violation of the settled laws of the realm.
"And now ye purpose to keep under the children of Judah
and Jerusalem for bond-men and bond-women unto you : but
are there not with you, even with you, sins against the Lord
your God?   Now hear me, therefore, and deliver the captives
again, which ye have taken captive of your brethren : for
the fierce wrath of God is upon you." 2 Chron. xxviii. 10, 11.
It was also a settled principle among the Greeks, the Romans,
the Illyrians, and still is among the Mohammedans, that their
own countrymen could not be made slaves.   (2.) A Hebrew
might become a servant to another Hebrew by selling himself
to serve the other, on account of poverty. Ex. xxi. 2; Lev.
xxv. 39. In this case, however, it was specially provided
that he should not be made to serve with rigor. He was to
be regarded in the light of an 'hired servant,' and a 'sojourner,' and not as a 'bond-servant.' Lev. xxv. 39; comp.
Deut. xv. 7—11. This was not allowed among the early
Greeks, though in the later periods of their history it was

common.* It was permitted among the Romans;† and among the Germans,‡ and was common among the Gauls.§ (3.) A Hebrew might be sold to his brethren if he had been detected in the act of theft, and had no means of making restitution according to the provisions of the law. Ex. xxii. 3. "He should make full restitution ; if he have nothing, then he shall be sold for his theft." This is in accordance with a common legal maxim—" *Luat in corpore, qui non habet in aere.*" || The same law prevailed among the Egyptians,¶ and among the Greeks also till the time of Solon. He prohibited it by the enactment "that the body should not be bound for debt." By the laws of the Twelve Tables, the same thing was enacted at Rome. (4.) A native-born Hebrew might be a servant in a single case, in virtue of his birth. If the master had given to a Hebrew, whom he had purchased, a wife, and she had borne him children, the children were to remain in servitude after the expiration of the six years during which alone he who had been bought could be held as a servant, except by his own consent. Ex. xxi. 4. The children, however, as we shall see, would all be restored to liberty on the year of jubilee. In these methods *only* could a Hebrew be reduced to servitude, and in no instance, except the last, could he be held to servitude more than six years unless he preferred it to freedom. It was a *right* which was secured by law, and which could be enforced, that he should be entitled to his freedom at the end of six years, and in no case whatever could he be held as a slave beyond the year of jubilee.

In the laws of Moses, there is but *one* way mentioned by which a *foreigner* could be made a slave—that is, *by purchase.* Lev. xxv. 44. All kidnapping was prohibited on pain of death, Ex. xxi. 16 ; and it is remarkable that the

---

* Dio Prusœensis, Orat. 15. † See Grotius, lib. 6, c. 7.

‡ Tacitus de Mor. Ger. lib. 24 § Cæsar, Com. lib. 6.

|| Comp. Jos. Ant. book iv. ch. 8, sec. 27.

¶ Diod. Siculus, Rer. Ant. lib. 2, c. 3.

Hebrews were not permitted to make slaves of the captives taken in war. This, we have seen, was regarded as *common law* among the ancient nations, but there is no concession of this right among the Hebrews. The nations of Palestine were devoted to *destruction*, not to *servitude ;* and if they had any servants from other nations they were not to be *kidnapped*, or taken in war, but were to be the result of purchase.

Such being the facts in regard to the toleration of this institution among the Hebrews, the question then arises whether this can be adduced as a proof that slavery is lawful now. To settle this, it will be necessary to examine at some length the Mosaic institutions on the subject, and then to compare them with those existing in our own land.

The arrangements of Moses in regard to slavery, found scattered through his laws, comprise the following particulars. The results of the classification of those laws which I shall now make, and of the connected view which will be taken of them, will be to show that he greatly modified all existing systems, and that while he temporarily tolerated slavery, he originated a system of enactments, the operation of which tended certainly to exclude slavery ultimately from the Hebrew commonwealth.

1. There stands in the fore-front of the whole Mosaic system a solemn prohibition, on pain of death, of that which enters into the essential nature of slavery, and on which the whole system everywhere is based : "*He that stealeth a man and selleth him, or if he be found in his hand, he shall surely be put to death.*" Ex. xxi. 16. The *place* which this solemn prohibition occupies in the Mosaic system, and the circumstances of the Hebrew people at the time, deserve to be attentively considered. It is among the first of the precepts which were uttered after the giving of the ten commandments on Mount Sinai. It was designed to stand among the precepts which were regarded as elementary. It was uttered in such circumstances that it

must have produced a deep impression on the minds of the people.

" They had just been emancipated. The tragedies of their house of bondage were the realities of yesterday, and peopled their memories with thronging horrors. They had just witnessed God's testimony against oppression in the plagues of Egypt :—the burning blains on man and beast ; the dust quickened into loathsome life, and swarming upon every living thing ; the streets, the palaces, the temples, and every house heaped up with the carcases of things abhorred ; th҉ kneading troughs and ovens, the secret chambers and the couches, reeking and dissolving with the putrid death ; the pestilence walking in darkness at noonday, the devouring locusts, and hail mingled with fire, the first-born death-struck, and the waters blood ; and last of all, that dread high hand and stretched-out arm, which overwhelmed the monarch and his hosts, and strewed their corpses on the sea. No wonder that God, in a code of laws prepared for such a people at such a time, should uprear on its foreground a blazing beacon to flash terror on slaveholders. *He that stealeth a man and selleth him, or if he be found in his hand, he shall surely be put to death.*"*

It is not necessary here to consider the particular import of the word '*stealeth*.' It is doubtless used in the sense in which that word is commonly used—to take what belongs to another, secretly, by violence, or by fraud. To 'steal *a man*' is a phrase that will properly denote *kidnapping ;* that is, 'to steal a human being, man, woman, or child ; to seize and forcibly carry away any person whatever from his own country or state to another.'† It implies the seizing of such a person by violence, or securing him by secrecy or fraud, and appropriating him to ourselves—his person, his liberty, his ability to labour, his muscles and bones. It is, in fact, the way in which the

---

* Bible against Slavery, pp. 11, 12.   † Webster.

great mass of slaves on the earth have been made, and without which the system could never be perpetuated.

The crime referred to in this law of Moses is stated in a
three-fold form—*stealing*, *selling*, and *holding* 'a man.' All
these are put on a level, and in each case the penalty was
the same—*death*. This is, of course, the highest penalty
that can be inflicted, and this shows that Moses ranked this
among the highest crimes known to his laws. If a 'man'
was *stolen*, no matter whether he was sold, or whether he
was retained as property, he who had been guilty of the
crime was to suffer death.

It is worthy of observation, also, that Moses distinguishes
this in the strongest manner from all other kinds of theft.
In no other instance in his laws is theft punishable with
death. If property was stolen, there was to be merely a restoration. If a man had stolen an ox, and killed or sold it,
he was to restore five oxen; if a sheep, four sheep. If the
theft was found in his hand alive, he was to restore double.
Ex. xxi. 1, 4. In the case of the theft of *a man*, however,
the very first act drew down the severest penalty of the law,
and as long as the man was deprived of his rights, the
offender exposed himself to that penalty. By this statute,
therefore, Moses made the broadest possible distinction between the theft of a *man* and the theft of *property*, and his
statutes frown upon every law, and every institution, and
every view, theoretical or practical, which regards man as on
a level with the brute.

What now would be the practical operation of this law in
regard to slavery? What check would it put upon it? Or
what would be the impression which it would leave in regard
to the views which the legislator entertained of the system?
The following effects, it seems to me, would be inevitable, and
were evidently designed. (1.) It would show that the legislator did not *approve* the system. As slavery in all ages has
been originated, if not exclusively, yet to a great extent, by
theft or kidnapping, the solemn prohibition of this as subject-

ing to the highest punishment known to the laws, would be a standing declaration that the system was not approved of, *per se*. (2.) This prohibition would be a material check on slavery. If all kidnapping were at once to cease, and not another man, woman, or child were ever again to be 'stolen' on the earth, it is manifest that a very essential change would take place in regard to slavery, even if there were no other regulations to check it. The perpetuity of the system would then depend wholly on the prisoners made in war—if indeed the prohibition would not also embrace *this* method of making slaves—and on the *hereditary* character of the institutions. But, (3.) This solemn prohibition against 'stealing' a man would of course operate to a great extent to prevent the purchase of those who had been stolen. It does not require a very advanced state of morals, or a very acute moral discernment in a community, to perceive that it is wrong to participate in what is regarded as crime ; that it is not right to 'receive stolen goods ;' that it is not proper to countenance a system that is forbidden by the laws. If to steal a horse be pronounced wrong by the laws, it requires no very acute discernment to perceive that it is not right to purchase a horse knowing that it has been stolen. If the sale of horses depended materially on the fact that they were all stolen, and the stealing were pronounced to be a penitentiary offence, the moral effect would soon be to break up the traffic altogether. The friends of the laws would of course soon abstain from all such commerce, and no good citizen would feel that it was right for him to own a horse at all. (4.) This prohibition would be in the end an effectual check against slavery, on the supposition that the whole institution were to be periodically abolished. If it were to be a standing statute of the nation, that at the end of every fifty years every slave was to be free, it is clear that this prohibition would soon put an end to the system altogether. How could it be renewed again, if it were once abolished ? If it were a crime punishable by death to *steal* a man, how would there be the possibility of renewing the system to any considerable extent, after the act of abolition had taken effect? If, for example, in this country, at a specified time, and then periodically ever onward, it should be the law of the land that *all* who were then in servitude should be free, and all kidnapping should be prohibited on pain of death, how would it be possible again to renew the system to any considerable extent? Where would *slaves* be obtained in sufficient numbers to cultivate the plantations of the South? Is it not clear, therefore, that if Moses ordained that *all* the slaves in the land should be emancipated on the year of jubilee, the whole system would be abolished, and that it would be impossible to renew it? And would it not be manifest that he *meant* that it never should be, to any considerable extent, renewed? Whether he *did* ordain this, will be a matter for subsequent consideration. The only object in adverting to it now is, to show what would be the operation of the arrangement if it *were* so. If this were the fact, then it is clear that, by the statute under consideration, Moses laid the foundation for the effectual abolition of the system.

(2.) Moses secured, by law, all slaves from hard and oppressive usage. He intended that the slave should be regarded as *a man;* as having certain rights; and as having redress in cases where wrong was done him. (*a*) Servants were to be treated with humanity and kindness. Ex. xxi. 20, 21: "And if a man smite his servant, or his maid with a rod, and he die under his hand, he shall be surely punished," (Heb. '*vengeance* shall be taken on him.') Compare with this just and humane precept, the laws respecting slaves in this country. "Should death ensue by *accident*, while the slave is receiving *moderate* correction, the constitution of Georgia, and the laws of North Carolina, denominate the offence *justifiable homicide*."* (*b*) If the slave was maimed by his master, he had the right of freedom. If the

---

* Stroud, Laws of Slavery, p. 127.

master should injure him in the eye or the tooth, that is, in the spirit of the law, in any member whatever, the servant, in consequence of such treatment, had a right to his liberty at once. "And if a man smite the eye of his servant, or the eye of his maid that it perish, he shall let him go free for his eye's sake. And if he smite out his man-servant's tooth, or his maid-servant's tooth, he shall let him go free for his tooth's sake." Ex. xxi. 26, 27. (c) In connection with this, should be noticed the numerous humane provisions of the Mosaic laws in reference to the *stranger*. I do not think that the word *stranger* in the Mosaic laws refers of necessity to a slave, nor that it would be commonly so understood; but the effect of such statutes on the treatment of the slave should not pass unnoticed when we are inquiring into the bearing of the Mosaic system on the subject of slavery. The slave would, as a matter of course, be more or less regarded in the light of a *stranger*. He would be usually a foreigner. It would be felt that he was away from his own home, and in a land of strangers. All the precepts, therefore, which relate to the proper treatment of a stranger and foreigner, might be supposed to have an effect on his condition, and it would be not unnatural that, under the operation of these precepts, he should be in fact secured from all the evils from which the stranger was secured by law, and that the general commands enjoining kindness to the foreigner would have a salutary influence on his condition. Among these precepts are such as the following:—"The stranger that dwelleth with you shall be unto you as one born among you, and thou shalt love him as thyself." Lev. xix. 34. "Thou shalt neither vex a stranger nor oppress him; for ye were strangers in the land of Egypt." Ex. xxii. 21. "Thou shalt not oppress a stranger, for ye know the heart of a stranger." Ex. xxiii. 9. "The Lord your God regardeth not persons. He doth execute the judgment of the fatherless and the widow, and loveth the stranger, in giving him food and raiment; love ye therefore the stranger." Deut. x. 17, 19. "Judge

righteously between every man and his brother, and the
stranger that is with him." Deut. i. 16. "Cursed be he
that perverteth the judgment of the stranger." Deut. xxvii. 19.
These humane commands contain the general injunction that
the rights of the foreigner were to be respected no less than
those of the native Israelite ; that no advantage was to be
taken of the fact that he was in a strange land and without
counsellors or patrons ; that there was no partiality to be
shown to any one in virtue of his birth or rank in his own
country ; and that all the protection of the law of the land should
be thrown around the foreigner to secure him in his rights.
All this was enforced by a reference to their own circumstances in the land of Egypt,—a reference which could not
but have a happy bearing on the slave,—for they were slaves
in that land. "Thou shalt neither vex a stranger nor oppress
him, for ye were strangers in the land of Egypt." "Thou
shalt not oppress a stranger, *for ye know the heart of a
stranger.*" Would they, when these precepts were enjoined
with so much solemnity, be likely to treat the servant with
the same oppression which they had themselves experienced
in Egypt ? Is it not clear that Moses meant to make use of
the remarkable events of their own history—events which
could never fade from the memory—to modify the condition
of slavery, and to make the yoke as light as it could be ? A
very beautiful and affecting exhibition of the prevailing sentiments on this subject, and of the conviction that the rights
of the servant ought to be strictly regarded, occurs in one of
the solemn appeals of Job respecting his own integrity and
the sincerity of his religion.

> "If I have refused justice to my man-servant or maid-servant,
>   When they had a cause with me,
>   What shall I do when God riseth up ?
>   And when he visiteth, what shall I answer him?
>   Did not he that made me in the womb, make him?
>   Did not the same God fashion us in the womb ?"
>   Ch. xxxi. 13—15.

(3.) Moses modified the system of slavery by securing to the servant, by law, an important portion of *time* for religious and moral improvement.   During these periods of time, servants were supported by their masters, and had opportunities for receiving the same kind of instruction, and enjoying the same religious privileges, as the other members of the Hebrew community.   The law secured for them the following portions of time :—

(*a*) Every seventh year.   Lev. xxv. 4—6 : "But in the seventh year shall be a sabbath of rest unto the land, a sabbath for the Lord ; thou shalt neither sow thy field, nor prune thy vineyard.   That which groweth of its own accord of thy harvest thou shalt not reap, neither gather the grapes of thy vine undressed : for it is a year of rest unto the land.   And the sabbath of the land shall be meat for you ; for thee, and *for thy servant*, and *for thy maid*, and for thy hired servant, and for thy stranger that sojourneth with thee."   Thus, on the supposition that all the slaves in the land were to be free on the year of jubilee, here was an arrangement by which during seven whole years of their servitude they were to be released from toil.   One whole seventh part of their time was, therefore, by the statute, made entirely their own.   This arrangement would, in itself, be no unimportant modification of the system of slavery as it has commonly existed in the world, and would make it a desirable thing for those who were reduced elsewhere to this condition to become servants among the Hebrews.

(*b*) Every seventh day was, of course, secured to the servant as a day of holy rest.   In the fourth commandment, (Ex. xx. 10,) the rights of the servant in this respect are expressly guarantied :   "The seventh day is the sabbath of the Lord thy God ; in it thou shalt not do any work, thou, nor thy son, nor thy daughter, nor *thy man-servant*, nor *thy maid-servant*."   This was securing for the servant another seventh part of his time, and *so* securing it that he could not be deprived of it by his master under any circumstances.   It

was not optional with the master whether his servant should
labour on that day or not; it was a matter of express and
solemn statute that *no* labour should be done by himself, and
none exacted from his servant.

(*c*) The servant had the privilege of attending on the three
great national annual festivals. Ex. xxiii. 17. "Three times
in a year *all* thy males shall appear before the Lord God."
Ex. xxxiv. 23. "Thrice in a year shall all your male-
children appear before the Lord God, the God of Israel."
These festivals were the "Passover, which commenced on
the fifteenth of the first month, and lasted seven days, Deut.
xvi. 1—8; the Pentecost, or Feast of Weeks, which began
on the sixth day of the third month, and lasted seven days,
Deut. xvi. 10, 11 ; and the Feast of Tabernacles, which commenced on the fifteenth of the seventh month, and lasted
eight days, Deut. xvi. 13, 15; Lev. xxiii. 34, 39. As all
met in one place, much time would be spent on the journey.
After their arrival, a day or two would be requisite for various
preparations before the celebration, besides some time at the
close of it, in preparations for return. If we assign three
weeks to each festival—including the time spent on the jour-
neys, and the delays before and after the celebration, together
with the *festival week*, it will be a small allowance for the
cessation of their regular labour. As there were three festivals in the year, the main body of the servants would be
absent from their stated employments at least *nine weeks annually*, which would amount in forty-two years, subtracting
the sabbaths, to six years and eighty-four days."

(*d*) The slave was to be a guest at all the family festivals.
Ex. xii. 44. From Deut. xii. 11, 12, it would seem also that
he was to be admitted to *all* the festivals that were celebrated
in the land, or that the *entire family* was to be present.
"Then there shall be a place which the Lord your God shall
choose to cause his name to dwell there; thither shall ye
bring all that I command you; and ye shall rejoice before
the Lord your God, ye, and your sons, and your daughters,

and *your men-servants*, and *your maid-servants*, and the Levite that is within your gates." If so, then the slave attended on the festival of the *new moon*, Numb. x. 10; xxviii. 11—14; compare 1 Sam. xx. 18, 19; on the *feast of trumpets*, Lev. xxiii. 24, 25; and on the *great day of atonement*, Lev. xxiii. 27.

It is not possible to ascertain, with exactness, the whole amount of *time* which the Hebrew servant would have for himself, but it has been estimated that it would amount to about twenty-three years out of fifty, or nearly one half of his time. A considerable part of this was to be employed in religious services, when the slave was in all respects on a level with his master, and when he would enjoy all the advantages which the Jewish religion furnished, to elevate the understanding and to purify the heart. The remainder, it would seem, might be employed in any way which he might choose.

It is not surprising, therefore, that we meet with intimations that the Hebrew servant might become possessed of a considerable amount of property. If he was industrious, and if he chose to avail himself of his advantages, nothing prevented his becoming easy in his circumstances, or accumulating so much that he could properly call his own, that when the period of 'release' came, he might 'go out' in such circumstances as at once to be above dependence, and to have all the respectability attached to citizenship. In Lev. xxv. 49, it is supposed that a man who had become poor, and who was under the necessity of 'selling himself,' might procure the means of redeeming himself while in a state of servitude. "Either his uncle, or his uncle's son, may redeem him, or any that is nigh of kin unto him of his family may redeem him, or, *if he be able, he may redeem himself*." As he was forced from poverty to sell himself, it is clear that it is supposed that he might acquire considerable property *after* he became a servant. In what way this was to be done, is not indeed expressly specified, but there are some intimations in the Scriptures, that even the servant that was *bought* was to have compensation for his labour, and there are some general principles laid down, which, if applied, would lead to that. Thus, Jer. xxii. 13, "Wo unto him that buildeth his house by unrighteousness, and his chambers by wrong; that uses his neighbour's service without wages, and giveth him not for his work." Comp. Col. iv. 1; James v. 4. *If* the servant received compensation for his labour, or even if he employed the time which the law allowed him, to earn money for himself, it is evident that when he emerged into freedom, he might have had no inconsiderable amount of property.

In connection with this, we may notice a most humane and just provision of the Mosaic law securing the comfort of the slave, when, by the limitation of his service, he became a freeman. It is found in Deut. xv. 12—15: "And if thy brother, an Hebrew man, or Hebrew woman, be sold unto thee, and serve thee six years, then in the seventh year thou shalt let him go free from thee. And when thou sendest him out free from thee, thou shalt not let him go away empty: Thou shalt furnish him liberally out of thy flock, and out of thy floor, and out of thy wine-press; of that wherein the Lord thy God hath blessed thee thou shalt give unto him. And thou shalt remember that thou wast a bondman in the land of Egypt, and the Lord thy God redeemed thee, therefore I command thee this thing to-day."

We may also notice in this connection, the fact that in the patriarchal age, and possibly also under the Mosaic institutions, the servant might become the *heir* to the property of his master. Thus Abraham said, that, in default of his not having a son of his own, his servant, Eliezer of Damascus, would be the heir to his property, (Gen. xv. 2,) and in the Mosaic institutions there was nothing to prevent this.

These circumstances do much to illustrate the nature of Hebrew servitude. The large amount of time which was guarantied to the servant by law for religious and other purposes ; the possibility of securing property for himself ; the humane provision that if he became free he should not be sent out poor and pennyless ; and the possibility that he might even become the heir of his master, showed that it was the design of Moses to modify the system, as it had before existed, and that the servitude which existed in Palestine was of a milder form than that which has existed probably elsewhere on the earth. We shall have occasion to compare these provisions of the Mosaic system with those which are found in our own land.

(4.) Another important arrangement of Moses on this subject related particularly to the religious privileges of slaves. Among these privileges were the following :—

(*a*) They were admitted into covenant with God, and as members of a family were recognised as in that covenant, by the customary rite indicating that relation. This was an express ordinance in the time of Abraham, and the same is found in the Mosaic institutions. To Abraham, God gave this command when the covenant was established with him : " This is my covenant, which ye shall keep between me and you, and thy seed after thee ; every man-child among you shall be circumcised. And he that is eight days old shall be circumcised among you, every man-child in your generations ; he that is born in the house, or bought with money of any stranger, which is not of thy seed, he that is born in the house, and he that is bought with money, must needs be circumcised." Gen. xvii. 10, 12, 13. So also in the solemn covenant into which God entered with the Hebrew people in the wilderness, the servants were expressly included. Deut. xxix. 10, *seq*. " Ye stand this day, all of you before the Lord your God ; your captains of your tribes, your elders, and your officers, with all the men of Israel : your little ones, your wives, and the stranger that is in thy camp, from the hewer of thy wood unto the drawer of thy water, that thou shouldst enter into covenant with the Lord thy God."

(*b*) Slaves were guests, as we have seen, at the national

and family festivals. Of course, they would derive all the advantage of instruction, and of religious impression, contemplated in the observances of the Hebrew people. In this respect, there appears to have been no distinction, as if they appertained to a distinct class or caste. There was no special service appointed for them at unusual seasons; there were no particular places or seats assigned them, to keep up the idea of their being a degraded and dependent class; there was no withholding from them the instructions which the law of God gave about the equal rights of all mankind. The whole Mosaic arrangement, in this respect, was one that would leave the impression, that, whatever differences there might be among men in other respects, in regard to their religious rights they were on a level. In the sanctuary, at the altar, and at the family festival, they were all the children of the same Father, all sinners before God, and all dependent on the merit of the great sacrifice which was shadowed forth by the blood of the lamb that was slain. One of the most *certain* ways of mitigating the evils of servitude is an arrangement which will show to master and servant, as a practical matter, that they are on an entire equality before God. If they may approach the same altar; if they may sit, without distinction, in the same sanctuary, and partake of the same ordinances of religion; if they may be made to feel that they are alike sinners; and if they can be made to realize that God looks with as much favour upon one as the other, one of the most important steps is taken effectually to abolish the institution. This arrangement existed as perfectly as possible, it is believed, in the Mosaic institutions.

(*c*) Slaves were to be statedly instructed in the duties of morality and religion. Every seventh year, called the 'year of release,' (Deut. xxxi. 10, xv. 1, *seq.*,) the whole law was to be read through in the presence of all the people. "When all Israel is come to appear before the Lord thy God, in the place which he shall choose, thou shalt read this law before all Israel in their hearing. Gather the people together, men, and women, and children, *and the stranger that is within thy gates,* that they may hear, and that they may learn, and fear the Lord your God, and observe to do all the words of this law." Deut. xxxi. 10—12. That this law included the *servants* or *slaves* in its operation, is expressly affirmed by Josephus. "When the multitude are assembled together in the holy city for sacrifice, every seventh year, at the feast of tabernacles, let the high-priest stand upon a high desk, wherein he may read, and let him read the law to all the people, and let neither the women nor the children be hindered from hearing, *no, nor the servants neither,* for it is a good thing that these laws should be engraven in their souls."* When the law was publicly read in the time of Joshua, and a solemn covenant with God was made by the Hebrews after their entrance into the land of Canaan, all the nation was present and participated in it. "And all Israel, and their elders, and officers, and judges, stood on this side the ark, and on that side, before the priests the Levites, which bare the ark of the covenant of the Lord, as well *the stranger* as he that was born among them. There was not a word of all that Moses commanded which Joshua read not before all the congregation of Israel, with the women, and the little ones, *and the strangers that were conversant among them.*" Josh. viii. 33, 35. The word '*strangers*' in these passages would include *all* those of foreign birth that were in the land, no matter what was their condition. Thus it is often used in the Scriptures, to distinguish *all* of foreign extraction from native Israelites. Comp. Ex. xii. 49; Lev. xxiv. 22; Num. ix. 14, xv. 15, 16, 29, xxiii. 34.

(*d*) The slave might become a proselyte, and thus be admitted to the full privileges of religion. Indeed, this seems not merely to have been *permitted,* but to have been *contemplated* as a part of the arrangement. Hence, as we have seen,

---

* Ant. b. iv. ch. viii. § 12.

he was circumcised; he was admitted to all the national festivals; he was carefully instructed in the law. The arrangement seems to have been such as would lead him, of course, to become a worshipper of the true God, and to feel that his interests were identified with those of the Hebrew people. That all this was contemplated, there can be no doubt. The laws requiring them to be circumcised; to keep the Sabbath, the Passover, the Pentecost, and the Feast of Tabernacles, all suppose this. But there is no intimation that this was to be done by compulsion. It is *supposed*, all along, that they would do this as a matter of course, and consequently no arrangement is made by Moses for punishing them in case of refusal. No matter what brought them to the land where the Hebrews dwelt, it was presumed that they would become worshippers of the true God, and would regard it as a privilege to avail themselves of the religious advantages furnished them there. The following declarations of Maimonides will show how this was commonly understood by the Hebrews.

"Whether a servant be born in the power of an Israelite, or whether he be purchased from the heathen, the master is to bring them both into the covenant.

"But he that is in the *house* is entered on the eighth day, and he that is bought with money, on the day on which his master receives him, unless the slave be *unwilling*. For if the master receive a grown slave, and he be *unwilling*, his master is to bear with him, to seek to win him over by instruction, and by love and kindness, for one year. After which, should he *refuse* so long, it is forbidden to keep him longer than a year. And the master must send him back to the strangers from whence he came. For the God of Jacob will not accept any other than the worship of a *willing* heart."*

If the enjoyment of these religious privileges entered into

---

* Maimon. Hilcoth Miloth, ch. i. sec. 8.

the condition of Hebrew servitude, then it is easy to suppose that Moses designed to make that condition as mild and tolerable as possible. We shall have occasion hereafter to contrast these arrangements made *by law* under the Mosaic institutions, with those made *by law* on the same subject in the United States. In view of these dissimilar arrangements, also, we shall have occasion to ask, whether the Mosaic institutes give any sanction to the system existing in our own country? At present it is sufficient to remark, that no arrangement existed which would prevent the servant from enjoying any and every privilege of religion which existed in the land; that he might make as rapid and extended advances in religious knowledge and holiness as could be secured to any one under the Mosaic system; that he had full opportunity for performing all his duties to God and to his family; that in the great and most important transactions in which he could be engaged, he had the privilege of feeling that he was on a perfect level with his master; and that he might feel that these rights were secured to him by solemn enactments—*by the unchangeable constitution of the land.*

(5.) A fifth fundamental arrangement in regard to Hebrew servitude was, that the slave *could never be sold.* A man, in certain circumstances, *might be bought* by a Hebrew; but when once bought that was an end of the matter. There is not the slightest evidence that any Hebrew ever sold a slave; and any provision contemplating that was unknown to the constitution of the commonwealth. It is said of Abraham that he had 'servants bought with money;' but there is no record of his having ever sold one, nor is there any account of its ever having been done by Isaac or Jacob. The only instance of a *sale* of this kind among the patriarchs, is that act of the brothers of Joseph which is held up to so strong reprobation, by which they sold him to the Ishmaelites. Permission is given in the law of Moses to *buy* a servant, but none is given to *sell* him again, and the fact that no such permission is given, is full proof that it was not contemplated. When he entered into that relation, it became certain that there could be no change unless it was voluntary on his part, (Comp. Ex. xxi. 5, 6,) or unless his master gave him his freedom, until the not-distant period fixed by law when he would be free. There is no arrangement in the law of Moses by which servants were to be taken in payment of their masters' debts; by which they were to be given as pledges; by which they were to be consigned to the keeping of others; or by which they were to be given away as presents. There are no instances occurring in the Jewish history in which any of these things were done. This law is positive in regard to the *Hebrew* servant, and the principle of the law would apply to all others. Lev. xxv. 42: "They shall not be sold as bondmen."* In all these respects, there was a marked difference, and there was doubtless intended to be, between the estimate affixed to servants and to property.

If it was regarded as a settled principle in Hebrew legislation that servants were not to be *sold* again, it is easy to see what would be the effect on the system. Before he came into the hand of an Israelite, the slave might have been transferred from one to another, but here he found a resting-place. Before this, the ties which bound him to his family might have been rudely torn asunder, but here he was certain that this would never occur again. If he entered into a domestic relation while the servant of a Hebrew; if he became a husband and a father, it was certain that the ties which bound him to his wife and children would never be rudely severed. Neither himself, nor his wife, nor his children could be sold. The family bond could not be sundered except by death. This circumstance would of itself do much to modify slavery as it existed elsewhere in

* See Constitutiones Servi Hebraei, by John Cas. Miegius, in Ugolin's Thes. Sac. Ant., vol. xxvi. p. 695.

that age of the world, and make it an *object* for those who had
been reduced to this condition in other lands, to become, if
practicable, the servants of a Hebrew. So humane and
careful was the Jewish law on this subject; so averse to
sundering the ties which bind husband and wife and parents
and children together, that the law expressly provided that,
where, by the limitation of the service, the husband and
father became *free*, he might, if he chose, remain with his
family, and share their lot. Ex. xxi. 2—6.

In the Hebrew commonwealth scenes could never occur
such as are constantly taking place in the United States,
where families are separated for ever by sales at public auction, or where, at the pleasure of the master, a husband and
father may be removed to a distant part of the land, to see his
wife and children no more. It is only necessary to read the
description of such scenes as frequently occur in the Southern
states of this Union, to be forcibly impressed with the humanity
of the Mosaic law, and to see the strong contrast between
servitude under that law and slavery in our own country. It is hardly necessary to remark, what a modification it
would make in slavery in this land, if it should become a
settled principle that a slave could never be SOLD; that if he
came into the hand of an American master, he was certain
that he would never be set up by the sheriff at auction; that
he would never be consigned to another for the payment of a
debt; that he would never be exhibited and examined for private sale; and that he never could be transferred to a slave-
dealer and conveyed to a distant part of the land to endure
the evils of a harder bondage. Then he might look upon
wife and children with the feeling that nothing but death
could part them. Then he would dread the approach of no
stranger, as if he had come to purchase himself, his wife, or
child, to be removed for ever. Then he might solace his sad
hours with something of the feeling that he had *a home*, and
that however hard his lot, this most bitter of all evils was never
to be experienced by him :—that neither he nor his family could

be SOLD ; that, for the sake of gain to his master he could not be torn away from an agonized wife, or his wife from him; and that a child could never be snatched from his embrace, to be manacled, and fettered, and borne to unknown woes, more dreadful to parent and child than death itself. The slave is a man, and there are few *men* who, rather than have a son or daughter subjected to the evils of slavery in Louisiana or Texas, would not prefer to see them laid in the silent abode where

> "The wicked cease from troubling,
> And where the weary be at rest;"

and where

> "*The servant is* FREE *from his master.*"*
>
> Job iii. 17, 19

---

* If such a provision existed in the laws of this land respecting slavery, a scene such as the following would never occur. The account is given by a correspondent of the "Christian Advocate and Journal" (Methodist), and is evidently drawn from life, and is such a scene as *must* often occur under the system of slavery in this land. There is no *law* to prevent its occurring as often as a master shall find it for his convenience to part with any portion of his slaves. It could never have occurred in Palestine. The occurrence took place at Wilmington, North Carolina.

"There are at Washington City, at Norfolk, at Charleston, and perhaps some other places in the old states of the South, slave markets, where slave-dealers purchase upon speculation such slaves as they can obtain, for the purpose of resale at a profit in the extreme South.

"As I went on board the steamboat I noticed eight coloured men, handcuffed and chained together in pairs, four women, and eight or ten children, of the apparent ages of from four to ten years, all standing together in the bow of the boat, in charge of a man standing near them. Of the men, one was sixty, one was fifty-two, three of them about thirty, two of them about twenty-five, and one about twenty years of age, as I subsequently learned from them. The two first had children, the next three had wives 'and children, and the other three were single, but had parents living from them. Coming near them, I perceived they were all greatly agitated; and, on inquiring, I found that they were all slaves, who had been born and raised in North Carolina, and had just been sold to a spe-

(6.) A sixth fundamental principle of servitude among the Hebrews was, that if an Israelite had become poor, and was under a necessity of selling himself to a stranger or sojourner who had become rich, he was, at all events, to be set at liberty

---

culator who was now taking them to the Charleston market. Upon the shore there was a number of coloured persons, women and children, waiting the departure of the boat; and my attention was particularly attracted by two coloured females of uncommonly respectable appearance, neatly attired, who stood together, a little distance from the crowd, and upon whose countenance was depicted the keenest sorrow. As the last bell was tolling, I saw the tears gushing from their eyes, and they raised their neat cotton aprons and wiped their faces under the cutting anguish of severed affection. They were the wives of two of the men in chains. There, too, were mothers and sisters, weeping at the departure of their sons and brothers; and there, too, were fathers, taking the last look of their wives and children. My whole attention was directed to those on the shore, as they seemed to stand in solemn, submissive silence, occasionally giving utterance to the intensity of their feelings by a sigh or a stifled groan. As the boat was loosed from her moorings, they cast a distressed, lingering look towards those on board, and turned away in silence. My eye now turned to those in the boat; and although I had tried to control my feelings amidst my sympathies for those on shore, I could conceal them no longer, and I found myself literally 'weeping with those that weep.' I stood near them, and when one of the husbands saw his wife upon the shore wave her hand for the last time, in token of her affection, his manly efforts to restrain his feelings gave way, and fixing his watery eyes upon her, he exclaimed, 'This is the most distressing thing of all! My dear wife and children, farewell!' The husband of the other wife stood weeping in silence, and with his manacled hands raised to his face, as he looked upon her for the last time. Of the poor women on board, three of them had husbands whom they left behind. One of them had three children, another had two, and the third had none. These husbands and fathers were among the throng upon the shore, witnessing the departure of their wives and children, and as they took their leave of them they were sitting together upon the floor of the boat, sobbing in silence, but giving utterance to no complaint. But the distressing scene was not yet ended. Sailing down the Cape Fear river twenty-five miles, we touched at the little village of Smithport, on the south side of the river. It was at this place that one

in the year of Jubilee, and might in the mean time be redeemed.   That he was to be free in the year of Jubilee was
a fundamental condition of the sale.   Lev. xxv. 54.   Equally
positive was the law that he might be redeemed, and this, too,

---

of these slaves lived, and here was his wife and five children; and while
at work on Monday last his purchaser took him away from his family,
carried him in chains to Wilmington, where he had since remained in jail.
As we approached the wharf, a flood of tears gushed from his eyes, and
anguish seemed to have pierced his heart.   The boat stopped but a moment, and as she left, he bid farewell to some of his acquaintance whom he
saw upon the shore, exclaiming, ‘Boys, I wish you well; tell Molly
(meaning his wife) and the children I wish them well, and hope God will
bless them.’   At that moment he espied his wife on the stoop of a house
some rods from the shore, and with one hand which was not in the hand-
cuffs, he pulled off his old hat, and waving it toward her, exclaimed,
‘Farewell!’   As he saw by the waving of her apron that she recognised
him, he leaned back upon the railing, and with a faltering voice repeated,
‘Farewell, for ever.’   After a moment's silence, conflicting passions seemed
to tear open his heart, and he exclaimed, ‘What have I done that I should
suffer this doom?   Oh, my wife and children, I want to live no longer!’
and then the big tear rolled down his cheek, which he wiped away with
the palm of his unchained hand, looked once more at the mother of his
five children, and the turning of the boat hid her face from him for ever.
As I looked around I saw that mine was not the only heart that had been
affected by the scene, but that the tears standing in the eyes of many of
my fellow-passengers bore testimony to the influence of human sympathy;
and I could, as an American citizen, standing within the limits of one of
the old thirteen states, but repeat the language of Mr. Jefferson, in relation to the general subject, ‘I tremble when I think that God is just.’
After we left Smithport, I conversed freely with all these persons; and in
intelligence and respectability of appearance, the three men who have thus
been torn from their families ·would compare favourably with the respectable portion of our coloured men at the north.   This is a specimen of
what almost daily occurs in the business of the slave-trade; and I hesitate
not to say, that there is not a Christian in the whole South who will refuse
to unite with his brethren everywhere in the condemnation of, and in the
most effective measures to extinguish the evils of this nefarious traffic.
        “Yours in the bonds of the gospel,   A. C.”

was one of the conditions of the sale.   The privilege of being redeemed was secured to him by law, and was not at the discretion of his master.   The right of doing this was conceded to so many persons, that if the condition of servitude was at all severe, it would be morally certain that it would be done. "After he is sold, he may be redeemed again ; one of his brethren may redeem him, either his uncle, or his uncle's son, may redeem him, or any that is nigh of kin unto him of his family may redeem him, or, if he be able, he may redeem himself." Lev. xxv. 48, 49.   Every thing about this was arranged on as mild and equal terms as possible.   (*a*) It was presumed that in many cases the servant himself might, by occupying the leisure time allowed him by law, procure the means of purchasing his own freedom.   (*b*) The remotest of his kindred might claim the *right* to redeem him, and the master could not prevent it.   (*c*) It was required by the law that only a fair and equitable price should be demanded for his restoration to freedom.   A just estimate of his value was to be made in proportion to the time which remained to the year of Jubilee, and the price was to be fixed accordingly. Lev. xxv. 50—52.

This provision was an important part of the Mosaic arrangements respecting servitude.   It is true that it did not extend to those who were foreign slaves, but it was of much importance that *any* who were held as servants might be redeemed.   At all events, this feature of Hebrew servitude stands in strong contrast with all the arrangements for slavery in our land.   Here, no one who becomes a slave can be redeemed except by the will of the master.   There is no common understanding that when a man becomes a slave he may ever be redeemed, either by a relative, by a friend, or by his own labour.   There is not in any of the slave states of the Union a law making it obligatory on the master, under any circumstances whatever, to liberate a slave.   If a slave is ever in circumstances to purchase his own freedom, or if a friend is willing to do it for him, it depends wholly on the will of the master whether it can be done at all; and if he is willing that it should be done, it is at such a price as he shall choose to affix to the value of the slave. If the slave himself has succeeded in any way in purchasing his own freedom, and has a wife and children in bondage, it depends wholly on the will of the master whether he may purchase *their* freedom, though he may have ample means of doing it. The master has still absolute power to hold them in bondage, and there is no authority to compel him to part with them at all; or even if he is willing to do it, to compel him to do it on reasonable terms. A *right* of redeeming himself or his family, secured by law, and with the conditions on which it might be done specified by law, would be a feature in the system in favour of the slave which would do much to mitigate its evils. It would hold out to him at least the hope that he *might* be free, and would prevent the absolute and unbroken gloom of the thought on his soul that he must be for ever held in bondage, until he is relieved by the kind hand of death.

(7.) A seventh essential and fundamental feature of Hebrew slavery was, that the runaway slave was not to be restored to his master. On this point the law was absolute. " Thou shalt not deliver unto his master the servant which is escaped from his master unto thee. He shall dwell with thee, even among you, in that place where he shall choose in one of thy gates, where it liketh him best; thou shalt not oppress him." Deut. xxiii. 15, 16. I am willing to admit that this command probably relates only to the slaves which escaped to the country of the Hebrews from surrounding nations, and that in form it did not contemplate the runaway slaves of the Hebrews in their own land. Still, it contains most important principles on the whole subject which could not but materially modify the system. This solemn and fundamental enactment would involve the following results or effects. (1.) No law could ever be enacted in the Hebrew commonwealth by which a runaway slave could be restored to his master. No revolution of the government, and no change of policy, could ever modify this principle of the constitution. (2.) No magistrate could, on any pretence, deliver up a runaway slave. From the moment when the foot of the slave crossed the boundary which divided the Hebrews from other nations, the magistrate became his protector, and it was his business to see that he should not be oppressed or restrained. He was to dwell in such part of the land as he chose, unmolested. (3.) Palestine would thus become an asylum of freedom. Encouragement was given to all who chose to seek a refuge there, and the land of Judea was thus designed to be an asylum for the oppressed of all people. The foreigner who came there voluntarily, no matter from what place, became, from the moment that he reached the confines of Judea, a freeman. 'No matter though an Indian or an African sun had burned upon him, that moment he was free.' There was no power on earth that could again lawfully oppress him; there was none that could lawfully compel him to return to servitude. The whole authority of the divine law proclaimed him to be a freeman, and, if true to their constitution, the armies of the commonwealth would all rush to his defence, and shield him from the claims of his former master. It is not difficult to imagine what must be the effect of this arrangement on the whole system of slavery, nor to understand what Moses meant should be accomplished by it. He designed that the country, under Jewish laws, should not be regarded as a land of oppression, but a land of freedom. He meant that it should have this prominence and this honourable distinction among the nations of the earth. This was itself a most bold and independent principle in legislation, and would be so understood by surrounding nations. It was, in fact, a public invitation to the oppressed of all lands to flee from oppression; an invitation to all who were held in bondage to escape from their masters; an assurance that there was one country where they would be certain that their shackles would fall, never to be riveted again. We may imagine what the effect of this would be, by supposing that Texas, on the borders of Louisiana, had remained a separate and independent nation, and had made a similar proclamation in the face of all the states of this Union, and of all the world. If she had enacted, as a fundamental principle of her constitution, that no slave was ever to be restored; if she had made this proclamation to all the world; if she had pledged all the power of her armies and her navy that no one who sought an asylum there should ever be wrested from her grasp, what would have been the effect on the system of slavery in an adjoining state? This result would be inevitable, that there could be no security for this species of 'property.' It would be an easy matter to become a freeman. Where there was no danger of being retaken and punished, the attempt would be often made, and would be successful. The only reason why the attempt is not constantly made now, and why this kind of property is not regarded as wholly insecure, is, that the slave, if he escapes, is liable to be recaptured; that there is a compact embracing in the parties to it all the free states of this Union, by which he may be restored; and that the places where he *would* be safe are so distant, and so difficult to be reached, that he has no hope of success, and yields himself to his condition in despair. (4.) The law prohibiting the restoration of the runaway slave in the Mosaic statutes, would do much to destroy the system altogether. It could not but leave the impression that, in the eye of the law, slavery was a hard and undesirable condition; a condition from which one must escape if he would find happiness. It would operate to prevent a conscientious Hebrew from subjecting his fellow-men to a condition regarded as so harsh and severe. It would be a perpetual proclamation of the value of freedom. If a man already owned slaves, it would lead him to ask whether he ought to continue a relation, to escape from which was regarded as so desirable. And (5) we may ask whether it can be believed, in view of this law, that Moses regarded slavery as a good and desirable institution? If it were, would he not have enjoined the return of the slave to his master? Can we, moreover, regard him as supposing that the master from whom the slave had escaped, had any real *right* to hold him? If he had, would he not have enjoined his restoration? Is not this law in fact a public proclamation that he regarded the slave as *entitled* to his freedom, and to all the assistance which others could render him to secure it? Assuredly, if Moses had considered this to be a good institution, if he had regarded it as desirable for the best condition of society, if he had supposed that the master had a *right* to the slave, he would never have introduced so extraordinary a provision into his code. He would never have publicly invited the slave to escape if he could. He would never have thrown around the runaway the protecting shield of his laws. He would never have proclaimed in the face of all nations, that the moment when a man, who had fled from oppression, had reached the land overshadowed by Hebrew customs and laws, that moment he was a freeman, and that all the power of the state would be exerted to secure him from being restored to his master.

(8.) The eighth fundamental principle in the Hebrew code was, that at certain periods there was to be a total emancipation of all the slaves in the land. The provisions for securing this, were two. One was, that all *Hebrew* slaves were to be released at the close of the sixth year; the other, that *all* the slaves in the land were to be set at liberty in the year of jubilee.

First, In regard to the former of these arrangements, the law was explicit, and there is no difference of opinion as to its meaning. The Hebrew servant was, in all circumstances, to be discharged at the close of the sixth year of his service, and at the jubilee, whether he had served the six years or not, unless by submitting to a degrading ceremony he showed that he preferred to remain in a state of servitude. Moses specifies two periods at which the Hebrew servant was to

regain his freedom ; the *seventh* year (Ex. xxi. and Deut.
xv.), and the *fiftieth* year, or year of jubilee. Lev. xxv.
The meaning of these laws was this : The Hebrew servant
was in no case to serve more than six years. If the year
of jubilee did not occur during the time of his servitude, he
was nevertheless in no instance to exceed six years of service. At all events, also, he was to be free at the year of
jubilee. Even if he had *not* then served six years ; if he
had served only one, he was to be restored to liberty, for it
was a great principle of the Hebrew legislation that every
fifty years all the inhabitants of the land should be free.*
The argument to prove that the Hebrew servant was manumitted (Ex. xxi. 2 ; Deut. xv. 12 ; Jer. xxxiv. 14) on the
seventh year after he became a servant, whether this were a
sabbatical year or not, may be seen pursued at length in a
tract of John Meyer, de Temporibus, et Festis Diebus He-
bræorum, cap. xvii. 22—35, found in Ugolin's Thesaur. Ant.
Sacra. tom i. p. 697. On the year of jubilee, *all* the Hebrew servants were released, whether they had served six
years or not. The testimony of Maimonides is clear on this
point. † The Mosaic provisions respecting the Hebrew servant are thus stated :—" If thou buy an Hebrew servant, six
years he shall serve : and in the seventh year he shall go
out free for nothing." Ex. xxi. 2. " And if thy brother, an
Hebrew man, or an Hebrew woman, be sold unto thee, and
serve thee six years, then in the seventh year thou shalt let
him go free from thee." Deut. xv. 12 ; comp. Lev. xxxiv. 10
—17. If, however, during the period of his servitude, the
Hebrew had married a wife who belonged to his master, and
who was held by another tenure, and he chose to remain with
her, he was not to be thrust out with violence. He was at
liberty, by submitting to what would be a perpetual mark of
his degradation, to remain. " And if the servant shall plainly

* Comp. Michaelis' Commentary on the Laws of Moses, vol. ii. pp.
176, 177.

† See Ugolin, as above, p. 700.

say, I love my mother, my wife, and my children; I will not go out free; then his master shall bring him unto the judge; he shall also bring him unto the door, or unto the door-post; and his master shall bore his ear through with an awl, and he shall serve him for ever." Ex. xxi. 5, 6. In this case his servitude became wholly voluntary, and this can furnish no authority for involuntary servitude, or for retaining a man in bondage against his will. Any man, doubtless, has a right to become the permanent servant of another, if he chooses. In this case, however, as in all instances where a *Hebrew* became a servant, there was an express provision that he should not be regarded in the light of a *slave* or *bondman*. "And if thy brother that dwelleth by thee be waxen poor, and be sold unto thee, thou shalt not compel him to serve as a bond-servant; but as an hired servant, and as a sojourner, he shall be with thee, and shall serve thee unto the year of jubilee: and then shall he depart from thee, both he and his children with him, and shall return unto his own family, and unto the possession of his fathers shall he return. For they are my servants, brought forth out of the land of Egypt: they shall not be sold as bondmen. Thou shalt not rule over him with rigour, but thou shalt fear thy God." Lev. xxv. 39—43.

Second, The law was equally explicit that in the year of jubilee, occurring once in fifty years, there was to be a universal proclamation of freedom throughout the land. This positive law occurs in Lev. xxv. 10. "And ye shall hallow the fiftieth year, *and proclaim liberty throughout all the land* UNTO ALL THE INHABITANTS THEREOF; it shall be a jubilee unto you; and ye shall return every man unto his possession, and every man unto his family." This law does not seem to have any ambiguity, or to be easily susceptible of misconstruction. The command is positive that it should be proclaimed in every part of the land that all the inhabitants were free. It seems to be a plain matter, then, that this proclamation could not be made, and yet any part of the inhabitants of the land be retained in servitude. The word rendered *liberty* here (דְּרוֹר *děrōr*) is not of frequent occurrence in the Old Testament, but there can be no doubt about its meaning. It signifies, according to Gesenius, (1.) a swift flight, a wheeling gyration; (2.) a spontaneous flow, or flowing freely and abundantly; and, (3.) *a letting go free, freedom, liberty.* It is rendered in the Septuagint ἄφεσιν, *remission.* It is a word which is commonly applied expressly to the manumission of slaves. Thus in Jer. xxxiv. 8, 9: "This is the word that came unto Jeremiah from the Lord, after that the king had made a covenant with all the people which were in Jerusalem, to proclaim liberty (דְּרוֹר *děrōr*) unto them; that every man should let his man-servant, and every man his maid-servant, being an Hebrew or Hebrewess, go free; that none should serve himself of them, to wit, of a Jew his brother." See also vs. 15, 16, of the same chapter. So also in Ezek. xlvi. 17, the same word is applied to the year in which the slave by law was restored to liberty. The meaning of the phrase 'unto all the *inhabitants* of the land,' seems also to be plain. The Hebrew expression employed, יֹשְׁבֶיהָ—*Yōshěbēhâ*, is one which would include all that *dwelt* in the land. The LXX have used a phrase that would in itself not improperly embrace all that *sojourned* in the land from any cause, πᾶσι τοῖς κατοικοῦσιν αὐτήν. To one who should read this law, if there were no other to conflict with it, or that made it necessary to seek a different interpretation, the plain meaning of the statute would appear to be, that *all* who resided in the land from whatever motive, or whatever were their relations or employments, were from that moment to be regarded as *freemen.* So it would be now understood, if a proclamation were made in these very words throughout the United States. So also if a clause had been introduced into the federal constitution, declaring, that at the termination of fifty years from that time, 'Liberty should be proclaimed throughout all the land *to all the inhabitants thereof*,' there could have been no difference of opinion in regard to its

meaning. The courts of the land would have been unani-
mous in its interpretation. After the publication of such a
law, it is clear that slavery of any kind would have been
unlawful.

The following brief summary of remarks contains the principles on which such an interpretation is given to this word
as to make it embrace all the dwellers in the land, of all
classes and conditions. (1.) The word here rendered *inhabitants* is the one which, if that idea *had been* intended to be
conveyed, would have been employed. There is no other
word of more *general* character. in the Hebrew language ;
none which would have better conveyed the idea ; none
which a Hebrew would have been so likely to employ.
(2.) It is, as remarked above, the natural, and obvious interpretation ; that which would occur to the great mass of
readers ; that about which there would be no doubt, if
no difficulty should arise *out* of the passage itself. So it
would be understood now ; so it would have been understood
in any country or age. (3.) It is an accordance with the
usage of the word elsewhere. There is almost no word of
more frequent occurrence in the Scriptures, than the Hebrew
word (יֹשֵׁב) here employed. It occurs, in various forms, more
than eleven hundred times in the Bible,* and is employed in
the most general manner conceivable. *Any* dweller, any inhabitant, any one who resides in a place, any one who so-
journs, any one who remains only for a short time, or any
one who has a permanent residence, would be embraced by
this word. It is repeatedly applied to all that came out of
Egypt ; to all that abode in the wilderness ; to all the inhabitants of Canaan, of Edom, of Moab, of Tyre, of Kedar, of
Philistia, of the world ; and there is no word which would
more naturally embrace *all* that abode in a country, from any
cause whatever. (4.) There is nothing, as we shall see on further examination, which necessarily limits its meaning here.

---

* See the Hebrew Concordance.

For such reasons as these, it seems clear to me, that the word was *intended* to embrace *all* that dwelt in the land, whatever were their relations or employments. At certain periods of the Jewish history ALL were to be free.

The correct interpretation of this passage (Lev. xxv. 10) is of so great importance in understanding the true nature of the Hebrew institutions, that it may be proper here to submit some of the views of distinguished expositors. Vatablus explains it, "And thou shalt proclaim that all the inhabitants of the land are free, who were before held as slaves." This interpretation is adopted by Rosenmüller. Rabbi Solomon says, "Thou shalt proclaim liberty to the servants, whether the ear had been perforated with an awl or not, or whether the six years had not been completed from the time when they were purchased." The general opinion of Jewish writers has been, that at the year of jubilee all Hebrew servants at least, though they had been unwilling to be released at the close of the six years' service, (Ex. xxi.,) should then be free.* "The year of jubilee made all servants free without exception." This is the opinion of the most distinguished Jewish Rabbins.† Thus Abenezra says, in explaining the law in Lev. xxv. 41, "And he shall go out from thee, that is, he who sold himself to thee of his own accord, as well as he who was convicted of theft, and who was sold to thee on account of theft." Maimonides says, that all those whose ears had been bored, (Ex. xxi.,) and who had thus become voluntary servants beyond the period of six years, were then set at liberty. "The servant who was sold, and who had served six years, and who was then unwilling to leave his master, his ear was bored, and he was to serve *until the year of jubilee.*" ‡ Servants who had been sick through their whole time of service, or who were then confined to their

---

* See Joh. Casp. Miegius, Constitutiones Servi Hebraei, § 3, lxxxvi.

† See the instances referred to in Ugolin's Thes. Ant. Sacra. tom. xxvi. p. 793.   ‡ Avod. c. iii. § 6.

couch, were also made free at the year of jubilee.* "The servant who is sick as the year of jubilee comes in, becomes free." They who had endeavoured before to escape, but who had been prevented, were set free at the year of jubilee. "When a servant who sold himself, or who was sold by the court, made an attempt to escape, he was held to make up for these years, but he was set at liberty at the year of jubilee."† The wives and children of slaves were restored to liberty on the year of jubilee.‡ Josephus expressly states, that all the Hebrew servants whose 'ears had been bored,' and who had served their masters voluntarily more than six years, were set at liberty in the year of jubilee. § It would also appear from Josephus,‖ that on the year of jubilee, *all* slaves were set at liberty. "The fiftieth year is called by the Hebrews the *jubilee*, wherein debtors are freed from their debts, *and slaves are set at liberty;*" and though in this connection he mentions only *Hebrew* slaves, yet as he elsewhere mentions no other, it would seem that he regarded the law as general, that *all* who were then slaves should be on that year restored to freedom.

The law under consideration, (Lev. xxv. 10) is so positive and explicit in its terms, that there could have been no difference of opinion in regard to it, if there were not a permission given, which *seems* to conflict with it, and which has led many respectable expositors to maintain that the law of emancipation at the jubilee related only to the *Hebrews* who were held as slaves, and that those who were foreigners were retained for life, notwithstanding this proclamation, and that in fact, therefore, slavery among the Hebrews was a perpetual institution. It is of essential importance, therefore, to inquire whether the statute referred to demands this interpretation. It is found in Lev. xxv. 44—47: "Both thy bondmen and

---

* Maimonides, Avod. c. ii. § 5; c. iii. § 15.   † Maimonides, c. iii. § 15.
‡ See the authorities for this quoted in Ugolin, as above.
§ Ant. b. iv. ch. viii. § 28.   ‖ Ant. b. ii. ch. xii. § 3.

thy bondmaids, which thou shalt have, shall be of the heathen that are round about you; of them shall ye buy bondmen and bondmaids. Moreover, of the children of the strangers that do sojourn among you, of them shall ye buy, and of their families that are with you, which they begat in your land; they shall be your possession. And ye shall take them as an inheritance for your children after you, to inherit them for a possession; they shall be your bondmen for ever: but over your brethren, the children of Israel, ye shall not rule one over another with rigour." There can be no difference of opinion on the question whether this authorized the Hebrews to *purchase* those of the surrounding nations for slaves. The only question is, whether the slavery into which they were brought by this purchase was perpetual and hereditary, or whether those who were thus bought of the heathen came under the general operation of the law that 'liberty was to be proclaimed to all the inhabitants of the land' on the year of jubilee. The objection to this interpretation is found in the expression, " *And ye shall take them as an inheritance for your children after you, to inherit them for a possession;* THEY SHALL BE YOUR BONDMEN FOR EVER." The question is, how, in connection with the proclamation of the year of jubilee, this is to be interpreted.

It is not to be denied that many respectable names may be adduced to prove that this law contemplates that slavery should be a perpetual institution among the Hebrews, and that, while all who were Hebrews by birth were to be manumitted in the year of jubilee, this arrangement did not extend to foreign slaves. This opinion is expressed decidedly by Judge Stroud,* though he endeavours to show that "the term *perpetual,* in its proper and absolute sense, was not applicable to the slavery of the Israelites, even of the *heathen* nations, and that the heathen slaves might become *proselytes,* and thus soon obtain their freedom. It is also the opinion of

---

* Laws of Slavery, p. 63.

Thomas Goodwin,* and is the opinion of Miegius,†quoted above. Probably this would be found also to be the opinion of all in our own country who endeavour to defend slavery from the Bible. Thus the conductors of the Princeton Repertory become absolutely confident on this point, and consider it as so clear that it excludes even the possibility of reasoning on the subject. They say,

"We do not know how this passage can be rendered plainer than it is, nor can we hope that any man, who is in such a state of mind as to prevent his seeing and admitting that it authorized the Hebrews to hold slaves, could be convinced even if one rose from the dead. It is here taught, 1. That if a Hebrew through poverty sold himself, he should not be reduced to the abject state of a slave. 2. That he should be treated as a hired servant. 3. And be allowed to go free at the year of jubilee. This is the precise condition which abolitionists assign to the heathen servants among the Hebrews, whereas it is here declared to be peculiar to servants who were children of Israel; who could not be sold as bondmen, *venditione mancipii*, as the elder Michaelis translates it. Of the other class it is taught, 1. That they might be bought for bondmen. 2. That they might be held as a possession or property. 3. They might be bequeathed by their masters to the children as a possession ; *hereditario jure possidebitis*, as Michaelis renders the phrase ; or as De Wette translates it to the letter : Ihr möget sie vererben auf eure Söhne nach euch als Eigenthum. *You may bequeath them to your children after you for a possession.* 4. This bondage was perpetual. They shall be your bondmen for ever. One of the points of distinction between the two classes was, that the former could not be sold in perpetuity, the latter might. As the land of a Hebrew could not be alienated, so his person could not be re-

---

* Moses and Aaron, c. x., note 3, in Ugolin's Thes. Ant. Sacrar. tom. iii. p. 296.

† See his work, in Ugolin. Thesaur. Ant. Sac. xxvi. p. 738.

duced to perpetual bondage. At the year of jubilee he was to go free, and his inheritance reverted to him. In contrast with this, Moses allows the heathen to be reduced to perpetual bondage. Hebrews shall not be sold with the sale of a slave, *venditione mancipii*, v. 42; the heathen may be thus sold, is the very point of contrast, v. 46. If the former passage forbade reducing Israelites to the condition of slaves, the latter allowed the heathen to be so reduced. Again, both the Hebrew words and the construction in v. 39, are the same as v. 46. An Israelite 'thou shalt not compel to serve as a bond-servant;' the heathen 'shall be your bondmen.' What is forbidden in the one case, was allowed in the other."

So plain is this passage in their eyes, that it is probable that a man who should even *doubt* whether all this is so would be regarded by them as of the same intellectual capacity and attainments as he, to use their own expression, who should gravely maintain that when it is said that " John the Baptist came neither eating nor drinking, it means that he drank no water, but only milk ;" or as he who should assert that all the slaves were " ten feet high." Thus they say :—

" The attempts made to evade this plain teaching of the Scriptures are precisely similar to those which are made to prove that the Bible condemns as sinful all use of wine as a beverage, and that it pronounces even defensive war to be sinful. It is impossible to answer mere assertions. And the more extravagant the assertion, the more impossible the answer. How can a man be refuted who should say, as we know an ultra advocate of temperance did say, that the passage which speaks of John the Baptist coming neither eating nor drinking, means that he drank no water, but only milk ; whereas Christ came drinking water; though he was called a gluttonous man and a wine-bibber. So when abolitionists say in reference to all the passages above referred to, that the bondmen of the Hebrews, even from among the heathen, were voluntary servants, who received themselves the purchase money paid for them, that they were in fact hired servants, receiving wages, hiring themselves for a term of years instead of for a single year, or for a day, or week, or month, who could neither be sold nor bequeathed ; we know not how they are to be answered, any more than if they were to assert, they were all ten feet high."

To the interpretation, however, which supposes that this passage means that slavery was to be perpetual, and that so far as it pertained to foreign slaves, their condition was not to be affected by the proclamation on the year of jubilee, there stand opposed the following objections—objections of so much force as to seem to make it necessary to seek some other inter- pretation.   (1.) The positive nature of the command respect- ing the year of jubilee, " And ye shall hallow the fiftieth year, and proclaim liberty throughout all the land to all the inhabitants thereof."   This law is explicit ; the terms, as we have seen, are such as refer to freedom from servitude, and the arrangement is one which accords with the general spirit of the Hebrew institutions.   (2.) The liberty of the *Hebrew* slave was secured, by other enactments, at the termination of his six years of servitude, unless he chose to remain as a servant for a longer period, and submitted to a degrading cere- mony, as a proof that he was willing to continue in that con- dition.   Ex. xxi.   The year of jubilee, therefore, could secure no real benefit to the Hebrew servants, unless it was to the comparatively small number who should have shown themselves willing to remain in this humiliating condition.   The restora- tion to freedom of that comparative small number would have been an event by no means commensurate with the import- ance attached to the year of jubilee, as a year of universal emancipation.   It was evidently the intention of this humane and remarkable law, that on the return of every fifty years things should go back where they were half a century before ; that whatever wrongs had accumulated in society during that period should be at once rectified ; that if there were any cases of oppression and cruelty which the usual operation of the law failed to reach, they should now at once be arrested

and corrected; and that if any cases of poverty had arisen
by a reverse of circumstances, instead of becoming fixed, and
leading to the permanent debasement of the family, the evil
might be checked then, and the family have an opportunity
of beginning life again.   The idea of the great Hebrew legislator seems to have been, that in order to the perfection of a
commonwealth, there should be no *permanent* causes of degradation; that no individuals or classes in society should be
placed in such circumstances of permanent disadvantage that
they could not rise; and that in order to secure the highest
state of society it was proper that all should have the opportunity periodically of starting on life again under equal advantages.   There was to be no institution, no law, no custom,
no relation, no habit among the people, that was to become
stereotyped, and that would send a malign influence onward
inevitably to coming generations.   It was felt that evils *might*
accumulate which no ordinary operation of law would reach;
that there *might* be cases of oppression and wrong which the
usual course of jurisprudence could not affect; and that instead of allowing them to *accumulate,* there should be a time
when, by a general enactment, all these evils should cease.
It was like clearing out the channel of a river which is in
danger of being obstructed with drift-wood, that it may run
clear again; or like a law respecting a "general jail delivery,"
or the action of the court of oyer and terminer, where all un-
tried cases *must* be tried—lest otherwise some who are accused
of crime should be overlooked in the ordinary process of jurisprudence, and thus permanent injustice be done, and evils
accumulate in a community.   It is essential to society that
there should be some such enactments.   We apply them to
judicial proceedings by the writ of habeas corpus, and by
other enactments.   Moses meant that by one general arrangement all these evils should be reached at once.   He knew
nothing, indeed, of the writ of habeas corpus, or of a court
of oyer and terminer, but perhaps it would be found even now
that his *one* appointment of the year of jubilee would accom-

plish as much for the good of a community as all the devices
in jurisprudence in modern times. But it is clear that this
arrangement could not be carried into effect unless there was
a provision for *universal emancipation.* If the law had not
extended to foreign slaves, there would have been a permanent evil, diametrically opposed to the whole tenor of the
Mosaic institutions, stretching on from age to age. (3.) The
language which is employed in Lev. xxv. 46, "they shall be
your bondmen for ever," does not of necessity imply that this
refers to the perpetual bondage of the *individual slave.* It
could not, at all events, be *literally true,* nor is it necessarily
meant even that the individual was to be a slave *till his death.*
The same language precisely is used of the Hebrew slave,
who chose to remain with his master rather than to be made
free at the end of six years, and who had his ear bored as a
token of his voluntary servitude. Ex. xxi. 6 : "His master
shall bore his ear through with an awl; *and he shall serve
him for ever."* Yet it is admitted, on all hands, that this
"for ever" extended, in the case of the Hebrew servant, only
to the year of jubilee. How is it then inferred that the same
phrase should mean that the foreign individual should serve
for life, or should be perpetually a slave? (4.) All that is
fairly implied in the law of Moses (Lev. xxv. 44—46), " thy
bondmen, and thy bondmaids which thou shalt have, shall be
of the heathen that are round about you, and ye shall take
them for an inheritance for your children after you, *they shall
be your bondmen for ever,"* is, that the *permanent* provision
for servants was *not* that they were to enslave or employ their
brethren, the Hebrews, but that they were to employ foreigners.
Those who were already slaves in other nations—for *all* kidnapping, or all *making* of slaves by the Hebrews themselves
was forbidden—might be introduced into the Jewish commonwealth, under the far superior advantages which they would
enjoy there, and the greatly modified conditions of servitude
there, and it would be *a permanent arrangement* that they
might be purchased and introduced among the Hebrews, where

they would enjoy the privileges of the true religion, and where they would be secure of their freedom at the return of the jubilee. The native Hebrew was never to be regarded properly as a *slave*. He was to be considered, even when sold for debt, poverty, or theft, as "an hired servant, and a sojourner," Lev. xxv. 40; he was not "to be made to serve with rigour," (Lev. xxv. 43, 46,) and he was not, it would seem, to descend "as an inheritance," but the foreigner who was purchased might be regarded as the "money" of him who had bought him, and might be inherited as other property, until he was released by the operation of the general law when all became free. The law was a humane one, for the condition of servitude among the Hebrews, according to the Mosaic statutes, was in all respects more eligible than in the surrounding nations, and for the Hebrew to purchase a slave was in fact to secure him his freedom if he survived to the year of jubilee.

If, however, it should be conceded that this passage means that the heathen might be subjected to perpetual bondage, and that the intention was not that they should be released in the year of jubilee, still it will not follow that this is a justification of perpetual slavery as it exists in the United States. For (1.) Even on that supposition the concession was one made to *them*, not to any other people. (2.) There were particular reasons operating for subjecting the nations around Palestine to servitude, which do not exist now—they were *doomed* to servitude for *sins*, not for their complexion. (3.) No one can maintain that it would be proper to transfer *all* the Hebrew institutions to our own country, and yet the fact that any institution was found in the Mosaic code, would be just as strong in that case as in this: and, (4.) Even if we admit that it was *right* then, it would not follow that it would be right now. There is more light now than there was then. There has been an advance in the knowledge of moral truths and relations, and it would not be a safe method of reasoning to infer that what was tolerated in the period of the world when Moses lived, would meet with the divine approbation now.

The importance of this part of the subject has led me to go at considerable length into the nature of Hebrew servitude. I have done this the rather because the Mosaic institutions are constantly appealed to in defence of slavery in this country, and it seems to be inferred at once that the mere fact that Moses tolerated a system of servitude, may be regarded as a full vindication of that very different system which exists in this nation. In view of the examination which we have gone over, it is natural to ask, what would be the operation of the Mosaic laws on slavery? What would be the effect of these laws in perpetuating the system in Palestine ? What would be their operation if they were applied to the system as it exists in this land ? The following would be the inevitable results of such a system, and were doubtless such as were foreseen and intended by the sagacious Hebrew statesman.

(1.) There could be no *permanent arrangements* for the system. At certain periods, not remote from each other, all the existing forms of servitude would come to an end, and the land would be a land of liberty.

(2.) The effect of such a periodical emancipation would be to introduce a considerable number of freemen to the enjoyment of all the civil and religious privileges of the Hebrew commonwealth. The number of freemen would be augmented, and the real *wealth* of the state would be increased by all the difference in value which there is between a freeman and a slave. And this was much. Long ago it was said, by Homer,

> " Jove fixed it certain that whatever day
> Makes man a slave, takes half his worth away."

A slave, or a subject of oppression of any kind, is never worth half as much as a freeman. A man under the Turkish government, or in Russia or Persia, is not worth half as much as a mere means of increasing national wealth, as in a free country. A slave has nothing like half the value of a freeman as a means of increasing the property of a nation, or considered as a part of national wealth. In our country he is 'one-third of a freeman' in representation, but not in actual worth. The way to make a man valuable is plain. It is to impress him with the conviction that he is a freeman; to allow him to feel that his limbs, his time, his ingenuity, his sinews, are his own; to permit him to pursue his own plans in his own way, subject only to those mild restraints which a regard to the welfare of others demands; to teach him that he is responsible to his Maker alone for the manner in which he spends his time and employs his talents; to assure him, by all the safeguards which the law can throw around him, that the avails of his labour shall be his own; to give him a pledge that the whole community will come forth, if necessary, to defend him if he has been injured or wronged, and that every court of justice will vindicate his rights *to a farthing*. It is to allow him to own a piece of land on which he can tread as a freeman, and say, 'It is mine. I may keep it or sell it; I may plow it and sow it as I please. I may sit down here under the vine and the fig-tree planted by my own hands. Here, if I choose, I may build me a house where to live; and here I may dig a grave for myself and my children, which no mortal can have a right to disturb; and here I may lay me down when I die, and sleep in the hope of a glorious immortality.' An arrangement, therefore, which should have the effect to elevate periodically all to the rank of freemen, who from any cause had been depressed to the condition of bondage, would be most auspicious on a commonwealth, and there can be no doubt that Moses contemplated this in his arrangements for the regulation of affairs in the Hebrew community.

(3.) The operation of these laws would soon abolish slavery altogether, or at least would so diminish the evils of the system, as to make it practically little oppressive. After the universal emancipation at the jubilee, it would not be easy to begin the system again. It is not probable that they who were released would sell themselves again into servitude; and as all who were *slaves* were to be the result of *purchase*, and not of conquest or kidnapping, it is clear that the places of those who had been emancipated could not be soon supplied. If in this country there were an article of the constitution that there should be a jubilee once in fifty years, in which *all* who were held in slavery should be restored to freedom, even *if* it were permitted to procure slaves again by purchasing them from foreigners, it is clear that slavery would soon cease. The slave would at once lose a considerable part of his value, for he and his children would soon be free. It would be impossible at once to supply the places of those who were emancipated at the jubilee, for the most active traffic, and the most numerous importations practicable, would not meet the demand. The plantations, in the mean time, must lie waste, and all the operations usually carried on by slave labour would be suspended, unless there could be found some substitute for that labour. But here would be all those who had been set at liberty, now dignified as free-men; stimulated to make an effort for themselves and their families, *because* they were free; acquainted with the busi-ness to be done on a plantation; many of them attached to their old masters, and ready to engage in their service for a reasonable compensation. The consequence would be, that in by far the greater number of instances, there would be no desire to purchase slaves again. Those who had been slaves and who were emancipated by law, would be at once engaged, not as ' bondmen,' but as ' hired labourers,' and the same work which they performed before under the lash, they would now perform, in a better manner, under the higher incentives applicable to freemen. It may be safely said that slavery, as a system, would not survive the operation of *two* such jubilees in this land ; and the conclusion is inevitable, that Moses was not a friend of the system, and did not design its perpetuity.

I have thus examined, at length, the nature and the practical operation of the Mosaic institutions in regard to servitude. But one point remains, to settle the inquiry whether we can derive an argument from the Mosaic institutions in defence of slavery as it exists in our land, or to determine whether it is proper to infer, as is often done, that because the Hebrew institutions tolerated slavery, that, *therefore*, the system is right as it exists in the United States. This will make it necessary to compare the Mosaic arrangements already described, with those existing in this country.

§ 3. *Comparison of the Mosaic institutions in relation to Slavery with those existing in the United States.*

The Mosaic institutions are, as has been before remarked, often appealed to in support of slavery as it exists at the present time. It is inferred, that because Moses permitted it, under the sanction of God, that therefore it is lawful now. This argument supposes that slavery, as Moses tolerated it, had substantially the same features which it has now, and that consequently it is right to argue from one to the other. It is important, therefore, to bring into comparison the features of slavery as it exists now, with those which were tolerated under the Mosaic laws; for nothing can be clearer than that if an argument can be constructed at all in favour of slavery from the fact that it was tolerated by Moses, that argument can be adduced only in favour of those features of servitude which he himself imbodied in his civil code.

Before proceeding, however, to notice the things in which slavery in this country differs essentially from that tolerated under the Mosaic laws, there is one remark which it is important to make, in order to obtain a clear view of the argument. It is, that it is no certain evidence that a thing is approved, or is regarded as best, because it is tolerated. The circumstances may be such that the evil could not at once be prevented without tearing up the very foundations of society, and, therefore, it may be necessary to connive at it. The ultimate good may on the whole be more promoted, if it is permitted, with arrangements to modify it, and ultimately to remove it, than it would be if there were a violent effort to remove it at once. We have certain evidence that there were some things allowed by Moses, and for which he *legislated*, which were not regarded as arrangements most conducive to the happiness of society, and which it was never intended should always exist. Among these things we may mention (*a*) *polygamy*. Nothing can be clearer from the New Testament than that polygamy was not originally designed when man was made, (Matt. xix. 4,) and that it was not regarded as the best institution for society, or to be perpetuated for the good of mankind, (1 Tim. iii. 2; 1 Cor. vii. 2;) and yet this was practised by nearly all the patriarchs, and was tolerated by the Mosaic laws. I am aware that it is denied by the advocates of slavery,* and by some most decided abolitionists †—extremes meeting here—that Moses tolerated polygamy, or that he ever legislated for it, and that even Dr. Dwight denies it. ‡ The *argument* on which Dr. Dwight rests, and the only one, is the *marginal* reading in the English version of Lev. xviii. 18, " Thou shalt not take one wife to another." The reading in the text is, " Neither shalt thou take a wife to her sister, to vex her, besides the other, in her lifetime." But, that the reading in the text is the correct one, is apparent, (1.) because the main discussion in the chapter is not about polygamy, but about marrying near relations. Having stated the general principles on that subject, nothing was more natural than for the lawgiver to add, that though, in itself, it was not unlawful to marry the sister of a wife, and he did not mean to prohibit that—a question

---

* See the Southern Literary Messenger, for September, 1845, p. 521.
† See the Letters of the Rev. A. A. Phelps, to Professor Stowe.
‡ Theology, vol. iii. pp. 419 420

which could not but occur—yet that it was not proper to do it 'in her lifetime.' There were obvious evils and impro-prieties accompanying such a step, which would render it undesirable that it should be done. (2.) This is the fair construction of the Hebrew—וְאִשָּׁה אֶל אֲחֹתָהּ—'a wife to her sister,' and it will not properly bear any other. So the Vul-gate explicitly—Sororem uxoris tuæ in pellicatum illius non accipies—adhuc illâ vivente. So the LXX, Γυναῖκα ἐπ' ἀδελφῇ αὐτῆς, κ. τ. λ. So the Targum of Onkelos, the Samaritan, the Syriac, and the Arabic. So Coverdale renders it. Indeed, there is no interpretation of a passage better settled than this. That polygamy *was* tolerated by Moses, will further appear from the following remarks:

(1.) The act of legislation in Ex. xxi. 7—10, has reference to polygamy, and authorized it. "And if a man sell his daughter to be a maid-servant, she shall not go out as the men-servants do. If she please not her master, who hath betrothed her to himself, then shall he let her be redeemed: to sell her unto a strange nation he shall have no power, seeing he hath dealt deceitfully with her. And if he have betrothed her unto his son, he shall deal with her after the manner of daughters. If he take him another wife, her food, her raiment, and her duty of marriage, shall he not diminish." The case supposed is that of an Israelite who should sell his daughter to be a 'maid-servant,' and that the daughter thus 'sold' might be 'betrothed' to him or to his son. If, after being thus betrothed to her master, she did not please him, the law was that she should be allowed to be redeemed. In no case should she be sold to a strange people. In case she was 'betrothed' to his son, and he chose to take to himself another wife, there were certain things which were not to be withheld from her. She was not to be discarded, or deprived of support, or treated in any other way than she would have been if the 'other wife' had not been taken. "Her food, her raiment, and her duty of marriage, shall he not diminish." The argument in this passage turns on the meaning of two

words; that rendered 'betrothed,' and that rendered 'duty
of marriage.' About the former, there can be little difference
of opinion. The Hebrew word יָעַד means properly, *to point
out, to appoint, to fix.* The idea of *designating, appointing,
fixing*—as of a time or place for worship, for a meeting, for
trial, &c., is the essential idea in the word. Job ii. 11, ix. 19;
Neh. vi. 2, 10; Amos iii. 3; Jer. xlix. 19, l. 44. It is rendered in this place, by Gesenius, "to fix upon as a wife or
concubine, to betroth;" and there can be no doubt that the
thing contemplated was such a designation as a wife or as a
concubine, since she had already been 'purchased' as a maid-
servant. The case seems to have been such as would not
unfrequently occur, in which after one had been procured as
a 'maid-servant' by the promise or payment of wages, or of a
'price' to her father—with the security that she could never
be 'sold'—he who had thus secured her for his employ, or
his son, might be disposed to sustain to her the nearer relation
of a husband. The law was designed to guard that point, so
that no advantage should be taken of her condition as a servant, to oppress her, or to do her wrong. If the father who
had secured her services was not pleased with her, after
having designed to enter into this new relation, he should not
take advantage of the fact that he was the *purchaser*, and sell
her, but should allow her to be honourably redeemed, or
restored again to freedom; if the son, who had *no* claim of
purchase, he should be bound to treat her as a wife, even if
he chose to marry another. The law, therefore, was every
way humane, and was designed to prevent the worst kind of
oppression—that of an unprotected female in humble life.
The other word on which the interpretation of the passage
depends, rendered 'duty of marriage,' עֹנָה, is derived from
a verb (עוּן) which means to rest, to dwell; and the noun
means *a living together, cohabitation,* says Gesenius, "in
the conjugal sense." So the Talmud understands it in this
place. The Hebrew noun occurs nowhere else except in
Hos. x. 10, where it is rendered *furrows,* though the reading

there is doubtful, and by a different pointing the word would mean, more appropriately, *sins*. In the passage before us, the versions all sustain the interpretation which supposes that the reference is to cohabitation as man and wife. Thus the Vulgate renders it, et pretium pudicitiæ non negabit. The Septuagint, τὴν ὁμιλίαν οὐκ ἀποστερήσει—' he shall not deprive her of her marriage rites.'* The Chaldee Paraphrase has the same word as the Hebrew, and the Arabic renders it, ' *her times.*' The Syraic renders it by a word still more expressive, about which there can be no doubt, meaning *accubitus;* lying with, cohabitation. There can be no well-founded doubt, therefore, about the meaning of this passage, (ver. 10,) and if the interpretation given be correct, it proves that Moses contemplated, that in the case referred to, while the son had another wife, he should in all respects, in her food, her raiment, and in respect to the marriage rights, regard and treat *her* as his wife. He was not at liberty to treat her otherwise because he had taken another. The fair meaning of the word here, it seems to me, will not bear the interpretation proposed by Mr. Phelps,† of *habitation*, meaning that he should furnish her a *residence*. If it will not, then polygamy in *one* form was tolerated by Moses, and legislated for.

(2.) The act of legislation in Deut. xxi. 15, 16, proves that polygamy was tolerated by Moses. "If a man have two wives, one beloved, and another hated, and they have born him children, both the beloved and the hated ; and if the firstborn son be her's that was hated : then it shall be, when he maketh his sons to inherit that which he hath, that he may not make the son of the beloved firstborn before the son of the hated, which is indeed the firstborn." In this case it is supposed that a man might have 'two wives,' and the design of the ordinance is to prevent a kind of injustice which would not be unlikely to occur, when a man, in disposing of his property by will, might be induced to depart from the

---

* Thompson.　　　　　　　　† Letter to Prof. Stowe.

usual custom, and from what was right towards the lawful heir, by favouritism towards one of his wives. The only question that can be raised on this point is, whether the passage means that he *had had* two wives, either one succeeding the other, and both dead, or one still living; or whether it means that in the case supposed he had two living at the time here referred to. The literal meaning of the Hebrew, כִּי תִהְיֶין is, 'when there shall be to a man two wives;' or when a man shall have two wives; most naturally and obviously meaning, at the same time. The Septuagint expresses it in the same sense, Ἐὰν δὲ γένωνται ἀνθρώπῳ δύω γυναῖκες. It may be added here, that this interpretation is so natural, and would be so likely to be put upon the passage, that if Moses had meant to prohibit polygamy, he *could* not have used this language. He would not have left it open to so obvious and so dangerous an interpretation. It was clearly supposed that this would occur, as it had done in the time of the patriarchs; and one can hardly help believing that he had an actual case in his eye like that of Jacob. Gen. xxix. 30.

(3.) It may be added in proof that Moses tolerated polygamy, that in certain circumstances, he made it a subject of express command, in a form which no one would pretend to vindicate as proper now. Deut. xxv. 5—10. This instance at least shows, that though a man had a wife of his own, there were circumstances in which it was proper for him to cohabit with one who had been the wife of another. The point of the remark made here is that this ordinance would not have existed in a community where polygamy was in no case to be tolerated. It is true that he interdicted *many wives* to the kings who might rule over the people, (Deut. xvii. 17, "Neither shall he *multiply* wives to himself," לֹא יַרְבֶּה־לּוֹ ' he shall not have a multitude of wives;') but this very prohibition supposes that polygamy, to some extent, would be practised by a king. That polygamy prevailed in the time of Moses, see Jahn's Archaeology, § 151. The arrangements of Moses have, indeed, been shown (see Jahn) to be such that a man could not well have more than four wives, but there was nothing in his statutes which prevented an Israelite having that number, and it would seem probable that he contemplated it.* The doctrine of the Talmud and the Rabbins is, that an Israelite might have not more than four wives. The reasons for supposing that the number of wives tolerated by Moses would not exceed four, may be seen in Michaelis. They are not such as can be dwelt on here. Mohammed also limited the number of wives to four, whether for the same reason is unknown. In Deut. xxi. 15—17, it is supposed that it would not be uncommon for a man to have *two* wives, and the fact that this would occur is mentioned without any disapprobation; nay, it becomes just as much the subject of legislation as slavery is in the Mosaic institutes. "If a man have two wives, one beloved and another hated," &c. It is quite clear, however, from the Mosaic statutes, that thé Hebrew legislator was no favourer of polygamy, but that he meant gradually to mitigate its evils, and to make such arrangements that it should finally cease to be practised in the Hebrew commonwealth. He allowed an institution which he found already in existence, to be continued, 'on account of the hardness of the hearts' of the people.† The same was manifestly true in regard to slavery.

(*b*) Another of the things which were tolerated by Moses, and for which arrangement was made in his laws, was arbitrary divorce. On this subject the law was positive, but we know that it was not regarded as the best arrangement for society, or one which God approved *per se;* and yet *the whole strength* of the argument from the Mosaic institutions in favour of slavery could be urged in favour of the practice of divorce now. The Mosaic arrangement tolerated divorce,

---

* See, on this subject, Michaelis' Commentaries on the Laws of Moses, art. xcviii., and Selden *de Uxore Hebraica.*

† See Michaelis' Com., art. xcv. xcvi. xcvii.

it would seem, to any extent, and made the continuance of
the marriage relation depend wholly on the pleasure of the
husband. Deut. xxiv. 1, seq. It demanded only that the
act of divorce should be deliberate, and should be accompanied with a 'bill,' or with proper testimonials given to the
wife that she was at liberty to marry another. This requisition would prevent hasty acts, and would tend much to diminish the evil. It is evident that Moses found the practice
already in existence,* and it is also quite clear that he did
not approve of it, or regard it as an institution tending to the
best interests of society. The Saviour expresses a distinct
disapprobation of the practice ; says that " it was tolerated
only ' on account of the hardness of the hearts' of the people,
but that in the beginning it was not so." Matth. xix. 8 ;
Mark x. 5. The truth was, that Moses found this in existence
as a prevailing practice ; that it had become incorporated with
the habits of the people ; that they regarded the right of
divorce as essential to the proper authority and liberty of the
husband ; and that it would have been in vain for him to have
attempted to prohibit it entirely. All that could be done,
therefore, in the case, was to determine by statute in what
circumstances, and for what causes, it might take place ; to
prevent, as far as possible, all hasty and arbitrary acts of the
husband ; to prohibit a reunion with the former husband, if the
wife should marry again, thus securing further deliberation ;
and so to arrange every thing in regard to it, that it should be
manifest that the spirit of his institutions was against it, even
while it was tolerated. But assuredly it would be an illegiti-
mate method of reasoning to conclude that *because* Moses
tolerated polygamy and divorce ; *because* he legislated for
them, and made arrangements that they might be continued,
therefore he approved of them as necessary to the best state
of society, and meant that it should be inferred that the spirit
of his institutions was favourable to them. Still less could

---

* See Michaelis' Commentaries on the Laws of Moses, art. cxix.

it be inferred that they were to be perpetuated in *all* states of society, and at all periods of the world, as desirable arrangements for the promotion of human happiness. And yet the whole of the argument in favour of slavery, from the fact that it was tolerated in the Mosaic institutions, could be applied to polygamy and divorce. Moses sanctioned the one no more than he did the other. He made no more permanent arrangements for the one than he did for the other. He expressed no more approbation of the one than he did of the other. He wove the one no more into his system than he did the other. He 'legislated' no more for the one than he did for the other. Nay, it is manifest that he looked with a less favourable eye on slavery than he did on polygamy and divorce. He made arrangements by which slavery was periodically to cease in his commonwealth, but he made no such arrangements for divorce and polygamy. Yet who now will undertake to maintain that because these were tolerated, and legislated for, in the Mosaic statutes, therefore they are right now, and should continue to prevail for the best interests of society ?

The argument on this point from the Mosaic toleration of polygamy and divorce, has been placed in so strong a light by Dr. Wayland, that I will copy it :—

"Can the proposition, 'whatever was sanctioned to the Hebrews is sanctioned to all men at all times,' be proved from revelation ? It seems to me that precisely the reverse is the fact. To arrive at the truth in this case it is only necessary to inquire whether there were any acts sanctioned to the Hebrews by Moses which are not sanctioned to all men.

" Take, for instance, the whole Mosaic code of civil law, its severe enactments, its very frequent capital punishments, its cities of refuge, its tenure of real estate. Could any legislator at the present day enact similar laws, and justly plead as a sufficient reason that God had sanctioned, nay enacted, such laws for the Jews ? Would this be a sufficient reason for abolishing the trial by jury in a case of accidental homicide, (as for instance when the head of an axe slipped from the helve and wounded a man to death,) and enacting that the next akin might slay an innocent person if he overtook him before he arrived at a city of refuge ? I think every one must immediately perceive that this law was a humane limitation to the spirit of Oriental vindictiveness, but that it would be very wrong to put it in practice at the present day.

"But we are not left to our own reasonings on this subject. We know full well that polygamy and divorce are wrong, that they violate the obligations established by God between the sexes, and are transgressions of his positive law. On this subject I presume we can have no difference of opinion. Yet these sins were not forbidden by Moses. Nay more, laws were enacted by the Hebrew legislator in respect to both of these practices. When a man was already united to one wife, and chose to take another, the manner in which the first wife was to be put away was prescribed. The right of the first-born was also in such a case defined. When, again, a Hebrew wished to divorce a wife, the manner in which this should be done was a matter of positive enactment. The discussion of our Saviour with the Jews on this subject is given us in Matt. xix. 3—9. I will quote the whole passage. 'The Pharisees also came unto him, tempting him, and saying unto him, Is it lawful for a man to put away his wife for every cause? And he answered and said unto them, Have ye not read that at the beginning, when the Creator made man, he formed a male and a female, and said, For this cause a man shall leave father and mother and adhere to his wife, and they two shall be one flesh. Wherefore they are no longer two, but one flesh. What therefore God hath conjoined, let not man separate. They replied, Why then did Moses command to give her a writing of divorcement and dismiss her? He answered, Moses indeed, because of your *untractable disposition, permitted* you to divorce your wives, but it was not so from the beginning. Therefore I say unto you, whosoever divorceth his wife except for whoredom, and marrieth another, committeth adultery,' &c. You perceive

I have used the translation of Dr. Campbell, who seems to have understood the scope of the argument better than the authors of our version.

" Now concerning this decision of our Lord, several things are to be remarked :

" 1. Our Lord authoritatively lays down the law of marriage, defining it to be an exclusive engagement between two parties for life.

" 2. He not only does this, but he declares that this doctrine was taught from the creation, quoting Genesis ii. 24, in confirmation of his assertion.

" 3. Notwithstanding this, Moses had sanctioned divorce ; tnat is, he had not forbidden it, and had enacted laws for the regulation of it.

" 4. And moreover, the reason of this is given ; it was because of the hardness of their hearts, or their untractable disposition.

" Here then is an institution sanctioned ; that is, permitted and made a subject of legislation, which is wrong in itself, and therefore forbidden by our Saviour to them and to all men. Nay, it had been thus sanctioned, although a prior revelation had discountenanced it. It is therefore clear, that a practice may have been sanctioned to the Hebrews, which is not sanctioned to all men at all times ; nay, which before and after a particular period was not sanctioned even to the Hebrews themselves. I think, therefore, that the teaching of the Scriptures is diametrically at variance with the proposition on which the whole argument from the Old Testament is founded."[*]

Keeping the Mosaic institutions on the subject of slavery in view, I shall proceed now to compare them with those existing in our own country. It will be convenient to arrange the various topics substantially in the order in which we have contemplated them ; and the object will be to show that in all

---

* Fuller and Wayland on Slavery, pp. 54—57.

essential features, the Mosaic arrangements in regard to slavery differed entirely from those existing in this land. The inference which will be derived from such a comparison will be, that the Mosaic institutions cannot be referred to, to sanction slavery as it exists at present. The points to which I refer are the following :—

(1.) The arrangements in the two systems respecting hard and oppressive usage. We have seen that under the Mosaic institutions, the rights of the slave were carefully guarded on this subject, and that if he were subjected to such usage he had a redress by claiming his freedom. We have seen that there were express statutes requiring that slaves should be treated with humanity and kindness ; that if they were maimed by their masters they had a right to liberty ; and that there were many solemn injunctions to treat the *stranger* with kindness, no matter what relation he might sustain.

The question now is, whether there are any such provisions in the laws in this land, or whether there is any security that the slave will be preserved from hard and oppressive usage ? The question is not, whether there may not be masters who treat their slaves with kindness, but whether the *laws* furnish any security for the slave on this point? It is not whether a master may not *abuse* his power, but it is whether the law does not give him such power that the slave has no redress, as he had under the Hebrew commonwealth? If it be so, certainly the Mosaic enactments cannot, so far as this point is concerned, be adduced in defence of slavery in the United States. The following laws of the slave states of this Union will show what is the spirit of servitude here, and will illustrate the striking contrast between slavery here and in the Hebrew commonwealth.*

---

* For the laws of the slave states on this subject, I am indebted mainly to "A Sketch of the Laws relating to Slavery in the several States of the United States of America. By George M. Stroud." This work was

"THE MASTER MAY, AT HIS DISCRETION, INFLICT ANY
SPECIES OF PUNISHMENT UPON THE PERSON OF HIS SLAVE."*
In particular, (a) The murder of a slave has in general subjected
the murderer to a pecuniary fine only. "There was a time
in many, if not in all the slave-holding districts of our country, when the murder of a slave was followed by a pecuniary
fine only. In one state, a change of the law in this respect
has been very recent. At the present date, the wilful, malicious, deliberate murder of a slave, by whomsoever perpetrated, is *declared* to be punishable with death in every state."†
It should be remembered, however, that there must be great
difficulty of *convicting* a white man, and especially a master,
of such an offence. No slave is allowed to give testimony
against a white man ;‡ and of course, in most cases it would
be impossible to bring a white murderer of a slave to justice.
There might be many witnesses of the deed, and yet not one
of them be allowed to testify to what he had himself seen.
It cannot be doubted that not a few slaves have been murdered
by their masters in this land. Has there ever been a conviction for such an offence?   Has a master ever been punished
capitally for such a crime?   Is he commonly punished at all?
Is it a common occurrence to convict *any* white man for a
wrong done to a slave, except so far as the slave is regarded
as the property of another man?   On the practical operation
of the law of the slave states respecting testimony, and the

---

published in Philadelphia in 1827. It is now out of print. Of the qualifications of Judge Stroud for such a work, no one can doubt; and the
accuracy of the work has never been called in question. The slave laws
since the time of the publication of that work have undergone too unimportant changes to make the quotations now irrelevant to show the
general spirit of slavery.

  * Stroud, p. 35. The capitals are his.

  † Stroud, p. 36.

  ‡ 1 Rev. C. Virg. 422; 2 Miss. Laws, 600; Mississippi Rev. Code, 372;
2 Litt. and Swi. 1150; Maryland Laws, act of 1817, and North Carolina
and Tennessee Laws, 1777.

difficulty of convicting a white man, and the fact that those laws place a slave completely at the disposal of his master, Judge Stroud well remarks, " It [the law that no slave can be a witness against a white person] places the slave, who is seldom within the view of more than one white person at a time, entirely at the mercy of this individual, without regard to his fitness for the exercise of power—whether his temper be mild and merciful, or fierce and vindictive. A white man may, if no other individual be present, torture, maim, and even murder his slave, in the midst of any number of negroes and mulattoes.   Having absolute dominion over his slave, the master, or his delegate, if disposed to commit illegal violence upon him, may easily remove him to a spot safe from the observation of a *competent* witness."—p. 66.   (*b*) The laws of some of the slave states expressly acquit the master for killing his slave, if it be done WHEN INFLICTING MODERATE CORRECTION.   The law of North Carolina, sect. 3, of the act of 1798, on this subject, is in the following words :—" Whereas by another act of Assembly, passed in the year 1774, the killing of a slave, however wanton, cool, and deliberate, is only punished in the first instance by imprisonment and paying the value thereof to the owner, which distinction of criminality between the murder of a white person and one who is equally a human creature, but merely of a different complexion, is disgraceful to humanity, and degrading in the highest degree to the laws and principles of a free, Christian, and enlightened country : Be it enacted, &c., That if any person shall hereafter be guilty of wilfully or maliciously killing a slave, such offender shall, upon the first conviction thereof, be adjudged guilty of murder, and shall suffer the same punishment as if he had killed a free man : *Provided always, this act shall not extend to the person killing a slave outlawed by virtue of any act of Assembly of this state, or to any slave in the act of resistance to his lawful owner or master,* OR TO ANY SLAVE DYING UNDER MODERATE COR-

RECTION."* The language of the constitution of Georgia is
nearly the same. "Any person who shall maliciously dis-
member or deprive a slave of life, shall suffer such punishment as would be inflicted in case the like offence had been
committed on a free white person, and on the like proof, except in case of insurrection of such slave, and unless SUCH
DEATH SHOULD HAPPEN BY ACCIDENT IN GIVING SUCH SLAVE
MODERATE CORRECTION."† (c) If the *life* of a slave is so feebly
protected by law, it is not to be supposed that he would be
defended from wrongs done in other respects against his person. Accordingly we find, that the slave is, not only necessarily, from the nature of the case, but by the laws, almost
entirely at the disposal of the master. Wrongs done by the
master to the slave are regarded as comparatively trivial
offences, and even on the supposition that he could be convicted, the punishment is trifling. The act of South Carolina
for 1740, says, " In case any person shall wilfully cut out
the tongue, put out the eye, * * * * * *, or *cruelly* scald, burn,
or deprive any slave of his limb, or member, or shall inflict
any *other cruel punishment, other than by whipping or
beating with a horsewhip or cowskin, switch or small stick,
or by putting irons on, or confining or imprisoning such
slave,* every such person shall, for every such offence, forfeit
the sum of one hundred pounds, current money."‡ Here
we may make the following obvious remarks : (1.) The strong
contrast between this and the Mosaic law : " If any man smite
the eye of his servant, or the eye of his maid, that it perish,
he shall let him go free for his eye's sake. And if he smite
out his man-servant's tooth, or his maid-servant's tooth, he
shall let him go free for his tooth's sake." (2.) The trifling
penalty which the law imposes—of " one hundred pounds"—
for wrongs which would render a human being wretched for

---

* Haywood's Manual, 530. See also the Laws of Tennessee, act of
October 23, 1799, with a like proviso.

† Prince's Digest, 559.   ‡ 2 Brevard's Digest, 241.

life.   (3.) The permission given to inflict certain classes of wrongs at the pleasure of the master.   Thus the law expressly allows the following things : (*a*) *scalding* and *burning*, provided they be not " *cruel ;*" (*b*) *whipping* or *beating with a horsewhip, cowskin, switch, or small stick;* (*c*) *putting on irons*, and (*d*) *imprisonment*, apparently at pleasure. A similar provision is found in the new Civil Code of Louisiana: " The slave is entirely subject to the will of his master, who may correct and chastise him, though not with *unusual* rigor, nor so as to maim or mutilate him, or to expose him to the danger of loss of life, or to cause his death."*   Here, then, are *two* limitations only of the power of the master over the slave. The first is, that he shall not be at liberty to cause the *death* of the slave ; and the second is, that he shall not punish him with " *unusual* rigor."   Respecting this, it would seem that the common methods of punishing slaves on neighbouring plantations were to be the standard, and that the master was to be the sole judge whether he exceeded that.   So in Mississippi, while the laws require the " owners of slaves to treat them with humanity, and to abstain from all injuries to them extending to life and limbs," they also ordain that " no cruel or unusual punishment shall be inflicted on any slave within this state.   And any master or other person, entitled to the service of any slave, who shall inflict such cruel or unusual punishment, or shall authorize or permit the same to be inflicted, shall, on conviction, be fined according to the magnitude of the offence, in any sum not exceeding five hundred dollars."†   Here we may remark (1.) that it is, from the nature of the case, exceedingly difficult to convict a master of wrong done to a slave, from the fact above referred to, that no slave can be a witness ; and (2.) that the law authorizes the infliction of any punishment provided it be not " *cruel*," or " *unusual*."   But what horrid crimes and wrongs may be done by a master before he shall reach the point in punish-

---

* Civil Code of Louisiana, art. 173.   † Rev. Code, 379.

ment that he will himself regard as "cruel," or beyond that
which is "unusual" in slaveholding communities! So in
Missouri, the law gives the master the power of confining a
slave in prison during his own pleasure, evidently for life if
he pleases, and that without judge or jury, with none of the
privileges of *habeas corpus;* with no power of escaping.
"If any slave resist his or her master, mistress, overseer, or
employer, or *refuse* to obey his or her lawful commands, it
shall be lawful for such master, &c., to commit such slave to
the common jail of the county, there to remain AT THE PLEA-
SURE of the master, &c. ; *and the sheriff shall receive such
slave,* and *keep him,* &c., *in confinement* at the expense of
the person committing him or her."* Here the *only* security
for the slave, so far as the law goes, is the *expense* which the
master must incur for his maintenance. It may be probable
that, from the fact that the master, if cruel and vindictive,
may gratify his disposition in a manner *less expensive*, this
law will not be likely to be *abused;* yet it is clear that the
slave is, in this respect, wholly at his disposal. He is to
judge when the offence demands imprisonment, and if so,
how long; and the officer of justice, appointed in a "land
of freedom" for the execution of the laws, is to receive the
slave at his hands, and be the executioner of his will, even if
the imprisonment should continue for life. On these laws
of the slave states, Judge Stroud well remarks, "Upon a fair
review, the result is found to be : That the master's power
to inflict corporeal punishment, to any extent short of life and
limb, is fully sanctioned by law, in *all* the slave-holding states;
that the master, in at least two states, is *expressly* protected in
using the *horsewhip* and *cowskin*, as instruments of *beating*
his slave ; that he may, with entire impunity, in the same
states, load his slave with irons, or subject him to perpetual
imprisonment whenever he may so choose ; that for *cruelly*
scalding, *wilfully* cutting out the tongue, putting out an eye,

---

* 1 Missouri Laws, 309.

&c., and for any other dismemberment, *if proved*, a fine of one hundred pounds currency only is incurred in South Carolina , that though in all the states the wilful, deliberate, and malicious murder of the slave is now *directed* to be punished with death, yet as in the case of a *white* offender, none except whites can give evidence, a conviction can seldom, if ever, take place."—pp. 43—44. Let these laws be compared with those of Moses already referred to in regard to the treatment of slaves, and it will not be difficult to determine whether the Hebrew institutions furnish a sanction for slavery as it exists in this land.

(2.) In illustration of the same point we may refer to the difference of the systems respecting the *time* allowed to the slave for his own use. In the examination of the Mosaic system, we found that Moses secured for the slave *by law* an important portion of his time, either for the acquisition of property, or for intellectual, moral, or religious improvement. The slave had every seventh day ; every seventh year ; the whole of the days devoted to the national festivals, and the privilege of attending on all the family festivals. According to the estimate then made, it was supposed that the Hebrew servant would have for his own purposes something like twenty-three years out of the fifty, if he served from one jubilee to another. It is scarcely necessary, however, to remark, that in our own country no such arrangements exist, and that the *laws* do not contemplate that *any* of the time of the slave shall be his own. His entire *time*, as well as his bodily vigor and skill, is the property of his master. There is none in which he may not, according to the law, be employed in the service of his master. So far as the *law* is concerned, there is no day or hour in which he may cultivate a piece of ground for himself; there is none which he might take to read—if he can read—or to pray. The master may call him from his little patch of ground, from his family, and from his " closet" at any hour to labour in his service. The Sabbath *may* be given, and I presume usually is given, to the slave ;

but it is not secured expressly for him by law, except in Louisiana and Mississippi, as it was among the Hebrews. A half day or more in the week may be given, and we know that it *is* often given, but it is not an arrangement of *law ;* it is wholly at the discretion of the master. It may be a fact also that at certain seasons of the year, and on certain plantations, the tasks may be of such a character that they can be accomplished, so that a considerable part of the day may be secured by the slave for himself, but this is not an arrangement made *by law.* It is wholly at the pleasure of the master, and it may be confidently affirmed that there are no laws in the slaveholding states of this Union, except in Louisiana and Mississippi, which secure to the slave *any* time whatever for his own service.

(3.) In like manner, and as a consequence of this, the slave is not regarded as one who can have any right to *property.** He cannot be the legal owner of a piece of land, of a house, of a horse, of a cow, or of an article of husbandry. He could not be the proprietor of a patent for a valuable invention or improvement in machinery or agriculture, though the invention were his own. He could not be the legal holder of the copyright of a book, if he could write a book. He could have no legal right of property in the most valuable mine of silver or gold that he might discover. It would all be legally the property of his master.† The Roman law said : Servile caput *nullum jus* habet, ideo nec minui potest.‡ "In Rome, indeed, the slave could, by great diligence and economy, acquire a scanty property (peculium); but, strictly considered, all this, together with the slave himself, belonged to the master, and might be retained by him at the period of manumission."§ In this country, it is a settled principle that a slave can own *no* property. In examining the Mosaic institution, we found

---

* Comp. Ch. I.

† Comp. W. A. Becker, on Roman Slavery, in the Bibliotheca Sacra, vol. ii. pp. 572, 573.

‡ Digesta, iv. 5, 3   § Becker.

that the servant *might* become possessed of a considerable amount of property which he could regard as his own. We found that it was contemplated that he might be able to purchase his own freedom by the avails of his own labour, and that if he could do this at a fair valuation, he had the right to do it. We found, also, that when he was released by the expiration of the term of service as fixed by law, provision was made that he should be made comfortable. We found, also, that he might become the *heir* to his master, and might hope to share his property if he was faithful in his service.

Far different from the Hebrew laws are the legal arrangements in the United States. Here the slave himself is regarded as property in the most absolute sense, and of course all that he can earn becomes the property of his master, as much as that earned by the horse does. It is not even conceded that the slave *may* in any circumstances ever own property. It is expressly prohibited ; and a claim of property on his part becomes a *crime*, and there are express and solemn acts of legislation to deprive him of any little articles of property which he may have acquired. The following enactments will put this beyond dispute. Thus, in South Carolina : " It shall not be lawful for any slave to buy, sell, trade, &c., for any goods, &c., without a license from the owner, &c., nor shall any slave be permitted to keep any boat, periauger, or canoe, or raise and breed for the benefit of such slave, any horses, mares, cattle, sheep, or hogs, under pain of forfeiting all the goods, &c., and all the boats, periaugers or canoes, horses, mares, cattle, sheep, or hogs. And it shall be lawful for any person whatever, to seize and take away from any such slave, all such goods, &c., boats, &c., &c., and to deliver the same into the hands of any justice of the peace, nearest to the place where the seizure shall be made, and such justice shall take the oath of the person making such seizure, concerning the manner thereof ; and if the said justice shall be satisfied that such seizure has been made according to law, he shall pronounce and declare the goods so seized to be forfeited, and order the same to be sold at public outcry, one half of the moneys arising from such sale to go to the state, and the other half to him or them that sue for the same."* The act of the legislature of Georgia is in nearly the same words.† And lest perchance the benevolence of the master should sometimes permit the slave to hire himself to another for his own benefit, Georgia has imposed a penalty of thirty dollars " for every weekly *offence* on the part of the master, unless the labour be done on his own premises."‡ So in Kentucky, with a slight modification.§ In Virginia, if the master shall permit the slave to hire himself out, it is made *lawful for any person*, and *the duty* of the sheriff, to apprehend such slave, and the master shall be fined not less than ten dollars, and not more than twenty.‖ So in Missouri.¶ In the year 1779, North Carolina enacted as follows : " All horses, cattle, hogs, or sheep, that one month after passing this act shall belong to any slave, or be of any slave's mark, in this state, shall be seized and sold by the county wardens, and by them applied, the one half to the support of the poor of the county, and the other half to the informer."** So also substantially in Maryland,†† and Mississippi.‡‡ In the Civil Code of Louisiana it is ordained, " *All that a slave possesses belongs to his master ;* he possesses nothing of his own, except his peculium, that is to say, the sum of money or movable estate *which his master chooses he should possess.*"§§ So slaves are declared uniformly incapable of inheriting property. Thus in Louisiana, " Slaves are incapable of inheriting or transmitting property."‖‖ Slaves cannot dispose of or receive by donation inter vivos or mortis causa, unless they have been previously

---

* James' Digest, 385 b; Act of 1740.   † Prince's Digest, 453.
‡ Prince's Digest, 457.
§ 2 Litt. and Swi. Digest, 1159, 1160. See Mississippi Rev. Code, 375;
Laws of Tennessee, Oct. 23, 1813, ch. 135; Stroud's Slave Laws, p. 47.
‖ 1 Rev. Code, 374, 375.   ¶ 3 Missouri Laws, 743.
** Haywood's Manual, 526.   †† April Sessions, 1787, ch. 33.
‡‡ Rev. Code, 374.   §§ Art. 175.   ‖‖ Civil Code, art. 945.

and expressly enfranchised conformably to law, or unless they are expressly enfranchised by the act by which the donation is made to them.* " The earnings of slaves, and the price of their service, belong to their owners, who have their action to recover the amount from those who have employed them."† So in the decisions of the court of South Carolina, " Slaves cannot take property by descent or purchase ;"‡ and in North Carolina, " Slaves cannot take by sale, or devise, or descent."§

These statutes and judicial decisions settle the question in regard to the legal right of the slave to hold *any* property whatever. All belongs to his master. If he earns any thing, it belongs to the master. If he is ever hired out, the wages belong to his master. If he should make a valuable improvement in the arts, the avails of it would be his master's. If he should write a book, the copyright would be his master's. If he should find a mine of gold, or a purse, or if property should be given to him, it belongs to his master. Of course, the question about purchasing his own freedom is in every respect at the disposal of his master. He never could, *in any way*, by gift or earning, become the owner of so much property as to be able to purchase his freedom without his consent, and if he could, the question whether he could obtain it is still lodged solely with his master. As *a matter of fact*, the slave has not the means of purchasing his freedom. If he has a little piece of ground for his own cultivation, and if he is allowed to till it at night or on the Sabbath ; or if, as may be sometimes the case, the master may allow him half a day in the week to till it for himself, the utmost that he can usually earn is from twelve to twenty dollars a year ! and what hope has a man of being able to purchase his freedom by so small gains as these ? The sum of the matter is this :

---

* Art. 1462.   † Louisiana Code of Practice, art. 103.
‡ 4 Dessaussure's Chancery Reports, 266.
§ 1 Cameron and Norwood's Reports, 353.

the slave himself is held as the property of his master, as much as his horse is, and to all that he earns his master has a legal title, as much as he has to the earnings of his horse. How different this from the mild Mosaic statutes ! *Can* it be believed that God ever meant to sanction this enormous system of wrong ?

(4.) There is a very material contrast between the Mosaic institutions and those in our country in regard to the religious privileges allowed by law to slaves. In examining the Mosaic institutions in regard to servants, we found (*a*) that they were received into covenant with God, and as members of the family were recognised as in that covenant by the customary rites of religion. (*b*) They were guests at the national and family festivals. (*c*) They were statedly instructed in the duties of morality and religion. (*d*) They might become proselytes and be admitted to the full privileges of religion. (*e*) In securing to them the Sabbath, and the Sabbatical year, and the time for attending on the great festivals, there was ample *time* secured to them *by law* for the performance of all their religious duties. Between these arrangements and those existing in our own country, we shall now see there is the strongest possible contrast. In illustration of this we may remark, (1.) that the benefits of education are withheld from the slave. This is so well known that it is scarcely necessary to prove the existence of *the fact*. It is proper, however, to show that it is not the result of custom, or neglect on the part of the master, but that it is an essential part of the system, and is ordained by law. This is shown in a law of South Carolina, passed in the year **1740,** and before quoted, (pp. **92, 93,**) and in the law of Georgia, there referred to. In Virginia it is ordained, "That all meetings or assemblages of slaves, or free negroes or mulattoes mixing or associating with such slaves at any meeting-house, or any other place, &c., in the night, *or at any school or schools for teaching them reading or writing, either in the day or night,* under whatever pretext, shall be deemed and considered *an unlawful assembly*."* So in South Carolina, in addition to the law of **1740**, and in order to make the prohibition more effectual, the law was re-enacted in **1800**, with power given to any officer, at pleasure, to disperse any such assemblage. The magistrates are "required" to enter into such places where any "slaves, *free negroes*, mulattoes, and mestizoes are met together for the purpose of *mental instruction*," and to "break the doors if resisted, and to disperse such slaves," &c.; and "the officers dispersing such unlawful assemblage *may inflict such corporeal punishment, not exceeding twenty lashes, on such slaves, free negroes, &c.*, AS THEY MAY JUDGE NECESSARY FOR DETERRING FROM THE LIKE UNLAWFUL ASSEMBLAGE IN FUTURE."† Besides these enactments of law, it should also be said, that the condition of the slave is such that he could find little or no time to learn to read and write, even if the prohibition were not positive. He is doomed to toil. "Hard-worked and scantily fed, his bodily energies are exhausted; without an instructor and without books, he must of necessity remain for ever ignorant of the benefits of an education."‡ (2.) The means for moral and religious instruction are not granted to the slave, but, on the contrary, the efforts of the charitable and humane to supply these wants are discountenanced by law. There is no arrangement made by law by which the slave shall be admitted to the privileges of public worship, though in some of the states it is enacted that he may receive and profess the Christian religion, and may be baptized, and the whole matter of public worship is left at the discretion of the master. The slave has no *means* of erecting a place of worship, nor *could* he be the owner of the house erected, or of the land on which it stood, or even of the most simple communion-service, or of the Bible or hymn-book which might be used. He has no means of supporting the gospel; he has no Bible from which to give

---

* 1 Rev. Code, 424, 425.   † 2 Brevard's Digest, 254, 255.

‡ Stroud, p. 90.

instruction to his children, if he had the ability. Nay, it is well known that within a few years there have been positive prohibitions in many of the slave states against teaching the slave to read the Bible at all, and that this has been made a penal offence. If slaves have *any* religious privileges, they are not, in most of the states, secured by law, but are at the discretion of their masters, and in many of the states the dearest and most valuable of all the rights and privileges connected with religion are expressly prohibited to them. A reference to a very few of the enactments of the slave states on the subject, will show the condition of the servant in the United States, in regard to the most valuable privilege of man —that of the free worship of God. The laws of Mississippi indeed ordain, that "the master or overseer *may*, in writing, grant the slave permission to attend a place of religious worship at which the minister may be white and regularly ordained or licensed, or at least two discreet and respectable white persons, appointed by some regular church or society, shall attend."* In Maryland, permission is given by law that the slave may be baptized, with this proviso, that such permission shall not be so construed that the slave, in virtue of his baptism, should be regarded as free. "No negro or negroes, by receiving the holy sacrament of baptism, is thereby manumitted or set free, nor hath any right or title to freedom or manumission, more than he or they had before, any law, usage, or custom to the contrary notwithstanding."† In North Carolina, also, it is expressly enacted that a slave *may* be baptized. "Be it enacted, that it shall be, and it is hereby declared lawful, for any negro, or Indian slave, or any other slave or slaves whatever, to *receive* and *profess* the Christian religion, and be thereunto baptized." The same proviso is added here as in Maryland, that this shall not be construed as implying that the slave is thereby free.‡ In

---

* Rev. Code, 390.   † Act of 1715, ch. 44, § 23.
‡ 2 Brevard's Digest, 229.

Louisiana, the law enacts that, "It shall be the duty of every owner to procure for his *sick* slaves all kinds of temporal and *spiritual* assistance, which their situation may require."* In Louisiana and Mississippi, the law makes provision that the slave shall not be required to labour on Sunday. The law in Louisiana is, "If any person shall, on the Lord's day, commonly called Sunday, employ any slave in any work or labour, (work of absolute necessity, and the ordinary occasions of the family excepted,) every person so offending shall forfeit and pay the sum of ten shillings for every slave he, she, or they shall so cause to work or labour."† So in Mississippi, under a penalty of two dollars.‡ These are *all* the arrangements, it is believed, in the slave states, for the religious instruction and privileges of the slaves, made by law. That in many, or most of the states, the slaves are permitted to attend on public worship, occasionally at least, there can be no doubt; and that not a few among them become Christians, it would be as improper to doubt. Nor can it be denied that there are not a few kind and pious masters, who sincerely desire the salvation of their slaves, and who are willing to grant to them all the facilities which the circumstances of the case may permit, to secure their salvation. But I speak of the enactments of the laws; of the arrangements made by statute, and of the fair operation of the laws if they were executed according to the spirit of the enactments. In considering those laws, and in estimating the actual privileges of slaves in regard to religion, we are to bear in remembrance the following things: (1.) That in case the provisions of the few laws in favour of the slave are not complied with, the slave has almost *no* means of redress; he can never prosecute a white man, or even bear witness against him. (2.) That power is given to magistrates and others to break in upon suspicious assemblages of coloured persons, and in such a way that the slave

---

* 1 Martin's Digest, 610.   † Prince's Digest, 455.

‡ Rev. Code, 317.

would have no power of redress if wrong were done to him.
(3.) That all night-meetings are prohibited. (4.) That the law
ordains that the slave shall not be taught to read, and of course
the oral instruction which he can receive will be of comparatively little benefit to him. (5.) That slaves can never have a
church of their own, or a pastor of their own, and can never
feel that they are in any way a free congregation. (6.) That
they are a mere appendage, in most circumstances, to a
white congregation, with less advantageous seats and privileges. (7.) That in most states it is made a penal offence to
teach them to read the Bible ; and (8.) that in regard to a
preacher, they are altogether dependent on the will of their
masters, who have the power of *presentation,* and 'the
right of *patronage*,' in the most absolute and odious form in
which it has ever existed on earth. Let all these things be
contrasted with the mild and equal laws of Moses in regard
to the religious privileges of servants, and it is not difficult to
answer the question whether his institutions can be appealed
to in support of slavery in the United States.

(5.) Under the Mosaic statutes we found that there was no
provision by which a slave could be *sold,* or transferred from
one master to another. The effect of this, in modifying the
system of slavery, was also fully considered. It is hardly
necessary to attempt to *prove* that in this country directly the
reverse is true. The slave is regarded as property, so far as
the right of *selling* him is concerned, in the same sense that
a horse or a mule is property. He may be sold, transmitted
by will, or alienated in any way. He may be sold by private
bargain, or at " public outcry ;" by auction at the pleasure of
the master, or by the sheriff when seized for debt in connection with horses, sheep, or oxen. He may be sold irrespective
of the question to what place he is to be driven, or what kind
of labour he is to be employed in, or what may be the character of his new master. He may be sold irrespective of
any question whether he is a husband, or father, or brother ;
or any wishes which he may have to remain with those who

are dear to his heart. He may be sold regardless of his tears and sobs, as he is about to be separated from his wife and children for ever. Indeed, in some of the slave states, no small part of the anticipated profits of the system result from the fact that the slave *may be sold*. The only restrictions made by law on the fact that slaves may be sold at pleasure, are, (1.) the ordinances of certain states, as Delaware, Maryland, North and South Carolina, Tennessee, Kentucky, Georgia, and Louisiana, (and now of Mississippi,) prohibiting, in a great degree, the farther *introduction* of slaves;* and a law in Louisiana, by which slaves are declared to be *real* estate there, and therefore ranked among *immovable* property. It is also ordained in Louisiana, that "If at a public sale of slaves, there happen to be some who are disabled through old age or otherwise, and who have children, such slaves shall not be sold but with his or her children whom he or she may think proper to go with;" and also, "Every person is expressly prohibited from selling separately from their mothers, children who shall not have attained the full age of ten years." Of course, it follows from this, that when children *have* attained the age of ten years they may be separated from their mothers at the pleasure of their masters. With these exceptions, which do not materially affect the system of slavery, slaves may be sold like any other property.   In fact, it is well known that nothing is more common, and that the buying and selling of slaves constitutes a regular species of merchandise at the South as much as the buying and selling of woollens, cottons, and silks; of horses, sheep, and mules, in any part of the North.   One can scarcely take up a paper printed even at the seat of the federal government, without finding numerous advertisements for the purchase of slaves; and Washington and Alexandria have long been known to be places where this inhuman traffic is carried on in as regular *a business manner* as any mercantile transaction is conducted in any

---

* Stroud, p. 54.

part of the land.   Such a traffic could never have existed in the Hebrew commonwealth.   The whole spirit of its laws and institutions would have revolted at it, and a mart for the purchase and sale of slaves could not have been tolerated in any part of Palestine for a single hour.

(6.) Under the Mosaic institutions we found an important arrangement for the redemption of the servant, if he or his friends had the means of doing it, which the master was not at liberty to refuse.   The *law* provided a way by which it could be done.   If the servant could himself earn enough to pay for his freedom, or if certain of his friends chose to interpose and purchase his liberty, the law made it obligatory on his master to release him.   Lest, also, this provision should be rendered a nullity by an exorbitant price fixed by the master, the law made an express arrangement that the price should be equitable.   A just valuation was to be made of the servant in proportion to the proximity of the year of jubilee, and the master was bound to accept that as the price of his release.

Nothing like this, however, enters into American laws respecting slavery.   There is no law compelling or requiring a master to sell a slave to himself or to a friend, any more than there is requiring him to sell his horse, his ox, or his hound. When a husband and father is from any cause made free, there is no law by which he can compel his former master to release his own wife and children at *any* price, or for any consideration whatever.   If he proposes to buy them, and the master is disposed to sell them to their own husband and father, the price is entirely at the discretion of the master. No matter, also, how cruel may be the treatment of the slave, and however much he may desire a different place of residence, he has no power to obtain a change of masters.   In Egypt and Arabia, if a slave is maltreated, he may appeal to the magistrate, and *compel* his master to sell him.*   But

---

* Burckhardt's Travels in Nubia, pp. 306, 307.

nothing of this nature exists in the United States. In Judea, under the Mosaic laws, as we have seen, if a master in any way mutilated a slave; if he merely deprived him of one of his teeth, he had a right to liberty. In this country, however, neither by wrongs done to him or his family, nor by purchase by himself or his friends, can the slave claim his freedom. There exists no provision by which, under any circumstances, he can claim it as a right guarantied by law that his master shall set him up to be sold at 'public outcry,' or in any other way. Should he find a man who would be willing to purchase him at *any* price, however exorbitant, there would be no power to compel his master to dispose of him. In all the slaveholding states, it is believed, there is but a single law in which it is ever made obligatory on a master to part with his slave, and that law is of such a nature as to be practically void. It is found in the new Civil Code of the state of Louisiana. The law is in these words: "No master shall be compelled to sell his slave, but in one of two cases, to wit: first, where, being only co-proprietor of the slave, his co-proprietor demands the sale, in order to make partition of the property; second, *where the master shall be* CONVICTED *of cruel treatment of the slave,* AND THE JUDGE SHALL DEEM IT PROPER *to pronounce, besides the penalty established for such cases, that the slave shall be sold at public auction, in order to place him out of the reach of the power which the master has abused.*"—Art. 192. This law, however, must be in almost all cases a practical nullity, for (1.) it is to be remembered that by a fundamental law of slavery, no slave or coloured free person can bear witness against a white man; (2.) it is necessary that the master be 'convicted' of cruelty—a thing so difficult "that it can hardly be ranked among possibilities;" (3.) it is, after all, *optional* with the judge whether he shall or shall not make the decree in favour of the slave. But if in any cases it should be carried into effect, it furnishes no relief to the system of oppression, for (1.) the slave is not to be made *free* as the servant under the

Jewish system was, when oppressed ; (2.) there is in this case
the same view of degradation and debasement which prevails
everywhere in the notion of slavery—that the slave may be
sold—sold " at auction"—sold as property—sold as cattle are ;
and (3.) there is a possibility at least that the condition of
the slave would be in nowise benefited by such a sale.   He
would have no security whatever that he might not pass into
the hands of a master quite as cruel as his former owner was.

(7.) Slaves in the United States are to be restored to their
masters, if they endeavour to escape.   We found, among the
fundamental principles of the Mosaic law, a provision that the
slave was *never* to be restored if he attempted to do this.   He
was to find in the land of Judea an asylum.   The whole
power and authority of the commonwealth were pledged for
his protection.   It would never be lawful, even by treaty, to
make an arrangement by which he could be restored.   No
judge had the right to return him, and if an attempt was
made by his former master to rescue him, it was contemplated
that the whole power of the Hebrew magistracy would be
asserted to secure his freedom.   A practical invitation, therefore, was given to the oppressed of all lands, to seek the
enjoyment of freedom within the limits of the Hebrew commonwealth.   In examining the Mosaic institutions, I showed
what must have been. the practical bearing of this fundamental law in regard to slavery there, and what would be its
practical operation in our own land.

The law in our country on this subject is positive, and is
one of the very few provisions for the perpetuity of slavery
which it was thought important to incorporate into the Constitution of the United States.   It is probably the only thing
in the federal Constitution which comes in direct and open
conflict with any law of the Bible, or where a conscientious
man holding office would have any doubt about his duty in
obeying the Constitution of his country.   Here, however, the
provision is directly at variance with the law of God, and is
designed to prevent the very thing which was sought as a

good by the Mosaic legislation—to furnish an inducement to the oppressed to secure their freedom.   The provision of the Constitution of the United States on this subject is in the following words : " No person held to service or labour in one state, under the laws thereof, *escaping* into another, shall, in consequence of any law or regulation therein, be discharged from such service or labour, but shall be delivered up on claim of the party to whom such service or labour may be due."—Art. iv. sect. ii. 3.   That slaves are here included, there can be no reasonable doubt, and so the article has always been understood ; but two things are quite remarkable on the face of the article.   One is, that the framers of the Constitution carefully, here as elsewhere, avoided the use of the word *slave;* and the other is, that they as carefully avoided the recognition of property *in* the slave.   They speak of the individual referred to as a ' person,' not as being a *chattel* or *thing;* ' held to service or labour,' not *as property*.   And they say that the ' person' so held ' shall be delivered up on claim of the party to whom such service or labour may be due,' not that the person so held shall be delivered up to him who ' *owns*' him, or who claims him as '*property*.'

Upon the authority, however, of this provision of the Constitution, an act of Congress has been passed, dated February 12, 1793, which is the source of bitter anguish to its victims, and which, in all its details, is directly in conflict with the divine law.   The law is in these words : " When a person held to labour in any of the United States, or in either of the territories on the north-west or the south of the river Ohio, under the laws thereof, shall *escape* into any other of the said states or territories, the person to whom such labour or service may be due, his agent or attorney, is hereby empowered to seize or arrest such fugitive from labour, and to take him or her before any judge of the circuit or district courts of the United States, residing or being within the state, or before any magistrate of a county, city, or town corporate, wherein such seizure or arrest shall be made ; and upon proof to the satisfaction of such judge or magistrate, either by oral testimony or affidavit taken before and certified by a magistrate of any such state or territory, that the person so seized or arrested doth, under the laws of the state or territory from which he or she fled, owe service or labour to the person claiming him or her, it shall be the duty of such judge or magistrate to give a certificate thereof to such claimant, his agent or attorney, which shall be sufficient warrant for removing the said fugitive from labour to the state or territory from which he or she fled."* Under this provision of the Constitution, and this law of Congress, *escape* from slavery within the limits of the United States, or any of the territories of the United States, is hopeless. The arrangement is designed to secure this species of 'property,' and to render freedom for the slave impossible. It is contemplated that every magistrate in the land shall be ready to lend his support to the institution; shall be an ally of the slaveholder of the South in perpetuating the system, and shall give the sanction of his name and authority to the enforcement of a law which is directly at variance with the law of God. The law of God ordains that every man who can secure his freedom by escape from bondage, has a right to it, and should be protected in that right; the Constitution and laws of the United States suppose that he has *no* such right, and that all the authority of the civil arm is to be employed in rivetting upon him again the fetters of bondage. It would be impossible to conceive of laws more directly repugnant to each other, than, in this case, are the law of God and the law of this Christian land.

(8.) There is no provision made in this land for general emancipation. We found, in the examination of the Jewish law, that it was a fundamental provision there that every Hebrew servant was to be set at liberty at the close of the sixth year, and that there was to be a general proclama-

---

* Ingersoll's Abridgment, 310.

tion of freedom throughout the land in the year of jubilee. The practical operation of this, it was shown, would be to abolish slavery altogether, for it was seen that the system could not be perpetuated under such an arrangement.

It is not necessary to attempt to show that there is no such general arrangement in this country for freedom. It has never been contemplated, for it must be seen at once that it would be the destruction of the system. Let the Mosaic laws be applied to slavery in this land, just as they are found in the Pentateuch, and in half a century slavery in the United States would be at an end. In order, however, to see more clearly that the Mosaic statutes cannot be adduced in support of slavery in the United States, it may not be improper to refer to a few of the laws directly opposed to those sta-tutes, or which are designed to perpetuate slavery, and to prevent the possibility of emancipation. In Georgia, the *attempt* to free a slave, by any other mode than by an applica-tion to the legislature, is visited with severe penalties, as will appear by the following act : " If any person or persons shall, after the passing of this act, (1801,) set free any slave or slaves, in any other manner and form than the one prescribed herein," (i. e. by special legislative act,) " he shall forfeit for every such offence two hundred dollars, to be recovered by action of debt or *indictment*, the one half to be applied to the use of the county in which the *offence* may have been com-mitted, the other half to the use of the informer, and the said slave or slaves so manumitted and set free, *shall be still to all intents and purposes as much in a state of slavery as before they were manumitted and set free by the party or parties so offending*."* Yet, as if this enactment were not sufficiently strong to perpetuate slavery, and to prevent the *possibility* of freedom to the slave, Georgia, by an act of the year 1818, added the following statute to her code : " All and every will and testament, deed, whether by way of trust or otherwise,

---

* Prince's Digest, 457.

contract, or agreement, or stipulation, or other instrument in writing or by parol, made and executed for the purpose of effecting, or endeavouring to effect, the manumission of any slave or slaves, either directly, by conferring or attempting to confer freedom on such slave or slaves, or indirectly or virtually, by allowing and securing, or attempting to allow and secure to such slave or slaves the right or privilege of working for his, her, or themselves, free from the control of the master or owner of such slave or slaves, or of enjoying the profits of his, her, or their labour and skill, shall be, *and the same are hereby declared utterly null and void,* and the person or persons so making, &c., any such deed, &c., and all and every person or persons concerned in giving or attempting to give effect thereto, whether by accepting the trust thereby created, or attempted to be created, or in any other way or manner whatsoever, shall be severally liable to a penalty, not exceeding one thousand dollars, to be recovered, &c., *and each and every slave or slaves in whose behalf such will or testament, &c., shall have been made, shall be liable to be arrested by warrant under the hand and seal of any magistrate of this state, and being thereof convicted, shall be liable to be sold as a slave or slaves by public outcry.*"* A similar law exists in North Carolina. By an act of the General Assembly of that state, passed in 1777, it is ordained, " That no negro or mulatto slave shall hereafter be set free except for meritorious services, to be adjudged of and allowed by the county court, and license first had and obtained thereupon ; and when any slave is or shall be set free by his or her master or owner otherwise than is herein directed, it shall and may be lawful for any freeholder in this state to apprehend and take up such slave, and deliver him or her to the sheriff of the county, who, upon receiving such slave, shall give such freeholder a receipt for the same, and the sheriff shall commit all such slaves to the jail of the county, there to

---

* Prince's Digest, 466.

remain until the next court to be held for that county, and the court of the county shall order such confined slaves to be sold, during the term, to the highest bidder."* In Mississippi, it is enacted that the emancipation of a slave must be by an instrument of writing, a last will or deed, under a seal attested by at least two credible witnesses, or acknowledged in the court of the county or corporation where the emancipator resides; proof satisfactory to the General Assembly must be adduced that the slave has done some meritorious act for the benefit of his master, or rendered some distinguished service to the state, all which circumstances are but prerequisites, and are of no efficacy until a special act of the Assembly sanctions the emancipation.†

It cannot be denied that there are greater facilities for emancipation in Kentucky, Missouri, Maryland, Virginia, and Delaware, and perhaps in some of the other slaveholding states, but it is not necessary to specify the provisions particularly. In Kentucky, it may be done by a proper record in the county court of the will of the master or owner to emancipate his slaves, " *saving, however, the rights of creditors.*"‡

In reference, however, to the subject of emancipation in the United States, as contrasted with the Mosaic provisions, it may be remarked in general, (1.) That there is no provision or law for a general emancipation of all slaves as there was among the Hebrews. (2.) That in some of the states it is entirely prohibited to the owner to emancipate his own slaves, and it can take place only by a special act of the legislature. (3.) That in some of the states it can never occur unless the emancipated slave shall be removed from the limits of the state. (4.) That in all cases where it may be done, it depends on the will of the master, and there is no provision of law to compel him to do it; and (5.) That all the considerations of interest, and custom, and law, and all the circumstantial pro-

---

* Haywood's Manual, 525.   † Mississippi Rev. Code, 385, 386.
‡ 2 Litt. & Swi. 1155.

cesses of law in order to secure emancipation in any case—
the necessity of witnesses, and in many cases of legislative
enactments—go to prevent emancipation at all.   To this may
be added all the severe enactments in the slave states against
foreign interference to persuade the masters to emancipate
their slaves; all the obstructions thrown in the way of making
an appeal to the masters through the mails; all the excite-
ments against those who are suspected of being abolitionists;
all the operations of *Lynch law;* all the public denunciations
against foreign interference in the case; all the appointments
of committees of vigilance, and all the precautions against the
possible escape of those held as slaves.   *All* the arrangements
of law which are made in the slave states, are designed to perpetuate slavery, not to bring it to an end; all those in the
Mosaic statutes were intended to modify the system, and ultimately to abolish it.   Under the Mosaic system, slavery
could be, and *would be,* by the regular operation of the
laws, abolished.   Here, there is no tendency in the laws to
its abolition, but under any existing or prospective arrangement, it would continue for ever.

I have thus gone over, at considerable length, the laws of
Moses in regard to servitude, and have placed those laws in
contrast with those which exist in our own land. On this part of
my subject, therefore, it only remains to ask, what sanction the
Mosaic laws give to servitude as it exists in the United States?
Scarcely any two systems could possibly be more directly in
contrast, and how can it then be inferred that the Mosaic enactments are either proofs that Moses regarded slavery as
desirable in order to promote the best interests of society, or
that his institutions give a sanction to it as it exists in the
United States? The sanction of Moses could be adduced
only in favour of the system which *he* established, and not in
favour of one which has scarcely a feature in common with
his.   The operation of *his* laws was to modify a system which
he found in existence, and which could not at once be extir-
pated; to soften all its hard features; to bring it as far as

possible into conformity with the privileges of freedom, and as soon as practicable to abolish it altogether. The operation of the system here is to rivet the fetters of the slave; to deny to him all the privileges and rights of an intellectual and a moral being, and to perpetuate the system for ever. The application of the laws of Moses to this country would make servitude at once a mild and gentle institution, and would abolish it wholly in half a century; the regular operation of the laws now existing here would perpetuate it for ever. Here are no laws *designed* to modify and meliorate the system; there are none which contemplate emancipation. Of all the abuses ever applied to the Scriptures, the most intolerable and monstrous are those which pervert them to the support of American slavery. Sad is it, that the mild and benignant enactments of the Hebrew legislator should ever be appealed to, to sanction the wrongs and outrages of the poor African in "this land of freedom;" sad, that the ministers of religion should ever prostitute their high office to give countenance to such a system, by maintaining *or even conceding for a moment* that the Mosaic laws sanction the oppressions and wrongs existing in the United States. "*I tremble,*" said Jefferson, "*when I remember that God is just,* for God has no attributes which can take part with us in relation to this matter."

In regard to the laws existing in the United States respecting slavery, as contrasted with those of the Mosaic institutions, there are a few additional remarks which it seems proper to make in this place.

(1.) I have not copied them with any intention of exciting odium against slaveholders, or of holding the framers of those laws up to reproach. It would have been desirable to have avoided all reference to them if possible, and to have suffered them to remain scattered as they are through the law books of many states, and intermingled with other laws, so that they should not be presented under the disadvantage of being placed side by side. But it seemed indispensable that in

comparing the system of servitude under the Mosaic institutions with that in the United States, with reference to the
question whether the one sanctions the other, to compare the
laws in the two institutions.   I have endeavoured to do justice
to the Mosaic institutions in this respect by bringing together
all the laws which he enacted, and, though I have not copied
all the laws of the slaveholding states on the subject, yet it
seemed to be but a mere act of justice that the principal
enactments should be referred to.

(2.) It may be admitted that these laws in the Southern
states are not always enforced, and that in some respects
many of them become in fact a dead letter.   I am happy in
the belief that it is so ; and I admit that it is not a fair way
of judging of the system to suppose that these laws are
always rigidly enforced.   There is no doubt that in many
places almost none of them are.*   Uniform testimony goes to
show that in not a few places slaves appear to be contented,
cheerful, and happy ; that many masters are kind and truly
pious ; that on many plantations great pains are taken to teach
the slave to read the Bible, and to instruct him in the principles of religion ; that not a few slaves give evidence that they
are true Christians ; and that multitudes of them, in such
circumstances, may pass their whole lives and never feel the
weight of the terrific enactments which hang over them, or
even know of their actual existence.   It is not always fair,
I admit, to judge of the actual condition of a people by what
we find in a statute book.   Laws become obsolete.   Customs
and habits change.   The severe enactment dies away without
a formal repeal.   There is no necessity, under the advancing
state of society, to put it in execution, and it is forgotten.   There
can be no doubt that it would be possible to make quite a formi-
dable representation of the state of things in England by merely
copying the unrepealed laws in the statute book, and that by

---

* Compare on this point Dr. Fuller on Slavery, Letters to Dr. Wayland,
pp. 159, 160.

such a process an idea might be conveyed of the state of society there to which there is nothing corresponding in fact. The laws have become obsolete, though they are not repealed ; and a true judgment of the state of society there is to be formed, not by an abstract study of the law books in a distant land, but by a close observation of the actual workings of society. I have no doubt that injustice is often done to the southern states of this Union by just this process—as beyond all question injustice is done by collecting all the advertise-ments of runaway slaves ; and all the notices of their marks and brands; and all the accounts of isolated acts of cruelty and severity ; and all the instances of the whipping, the imprison-ment, and the shooting down of slaves, and by publishing them *as if* that were a fair representation of the ordinary operations of "slavery as it is." Every one of those indivi-dual instances may have occurred—perhaps hundreds of miles apart—but to collect them in a volume does no more justice to society there than would be done by collecting all the cases of rape, and riot, and burglary, and murder, and arson from the records of the courts at the North, and publishing them in a volume in order to give to a stranger a just representation of society here. I should be sorry, therefore, if by copying the laws of the Southern states as contrasted with those of Moses, I should do any thing to extend or perpetuate this injustice, or lead any to suppose that these laws are always executed, or that the state of society is to be inferred from the supposition that they are always executed, and that there is in fact *nothing* at the South of which these laws may not be regarded as the fair exponent.

(3.) It should be said, however, that while those laws exist unrepealed, they *may* be put into execution, and that the slave under them is liable to suffer all the oppression and wrong which they appear to justify. It is no uncommon thing for a man to be made to suffer under the operation of an obsolete statute of which he had no knowledge, and the remembrance of which is revived for the very purpose of doing him in justice. Whether these laws at the South shall or shall not be executed in their severity, depends on the state of the public mind, on the passions that may prevail in any community, and on the will and caprice of particular masters. This is a point over which the *slave* has no control, and in which the benevolent who might wish a better state of things, and might shudder at the wrong done, have no power. Any or all of these grievous wrongs *may* be perpetrated by a cruel master, and he will be sustained by the sanction of the laws ; and in order to a fair judgment respecting a community, we are to take into the account not only what *is* done, but what *may be* done under the sanction of law.

(4.) These laws are a fair expression of the nature of the system of slavery in its essential character. They are what the system has *produced*. They have grown out of it, as being supposed to be necessary to the best working of the system, and to its perpetuity. They are the result of long and careful legislation, in a country that boasts of being the most enlightened in the world. They are in most instances the result of experience, and are what has been found by experience to be necessary to the perfection of the system. They are what the lawgivers at the South have supposed to be requisite in order that the institution may be perpetuated in this country, and are an exponent of what the master deems to be necessary in order that his right to this species of ' property' may be best secured. For illustration, it would be fair to refer to the laws of Pennsylvania respecting the right of the owners of various kinds of property, and the ways by which they may secure themselves from wrong, as a proof of what has been found necessary in that commonwealth to promote in the best manner the security of society. Those laws are the results of long experience in the case, just as the laws of the South are the results of long experience of the best methods of perpetuating slavery. They may be referred to, therefore, as the fair *exponent* of the nature of the system.

(5.) Those laws ARE NECESSARY to the system. They are

the shield which protects it. They could not be repealed with safety. The *system* of slave laws as such could not be safely modified. The repeal of *any* of those enactments, harsh and severe as they seem to be, would be doing so much to endanger the system. To abolish them, and to introduce the great features of the Mosaic code, would be to peril the system at once. No essential modification of those laws for the better has been made in all the legislation on the subject, and the question is never agitated at the South whether the "negro code" could be meliorated consistently with the perpetuity of slavery. No proposition could be entertained suggesting that the laws should be so modified that the slave should be taught to read; that he should be allowed entire freedom to worship God; that he should be permitted to testify against a white man; that he should be considered as the owner of property; that the marriage contract should be inviolate; that he should be allowed to control his children, or that, if he escaped, he should not be returned by force to his master. Any relaxation of the system at all, bordering on such modifications, would be repelled as tending to abolition, and the nearer such modifications should come to the Mosaic statutes, the more would that danger be felt. It is not unfair, therefore, to refer to these laws as illustrating the working of the system of American slavery, or as showing WHAT IT IS.

(6.) If the system of slavery, as it exists in this country, is right, or if slavery itself is right in any proper sense of the term, then these laws growing out of the system, and necessary to its continuance, are also right. If the master possess the right which is claimed over a slave—a right to oblige him to labour for his benefit without his consent; a right to his time and to the avails of his labour and skill; a right to dispose of that time and skill, and to sell the slave himself, then he "enjoys also a right to use all the means necessary both to enforce it and to render it permanent. He has a right to protect himself against every thing that would interfere with the

exercise of this right.   If the intellectual and moral cultivation of the slave would interfere with the master's power to
enforce this right, he has the right to arrest this cultivation at
any point he chooses, or to abolish it altogether.   If the right
exist, therefore, no exception can be taken to the sternest
laws which have ever been enacted in any of the Southern
states, even though they prohibit, under the severest penalties, the education of negroes, and forbid them to assemble for
the worship of God, except under the strictest surveillance."*
To these views of Dr. Wayland, no exception, it seems to me,
can be taken, and if they are correct, then it is clear that it is
proper to place the existing laws in the slave states in contrast
with those of Moses, as illustrating the question whether
American slavery has the sanction of the Bible.

---

* Dr. Wayland's Letters to Dr. Fuller, p. 23.

CHAPTER VI.

Hebrew Servitude in the time of the Prophets.

In the previous chapters, I have gone into an extended examination of the subject of slavery or servitude as it existed among the Hebrew patriarchs, and under the Mosaic arrangements. The general conclusion which has been reached in this investigation is, that while slavery existed in the patriarchal times, and while the laws of Moses contemplated the possibility of its existence, just as they did of polygamy and divorce, yet that, so far as the Mosaic code tolerated it, it was comparatively a mild system, and one which it was the tendency of his institutions ultimately to abolish. He found it in existence, and could abolish it only by mild, but determined legislation. He made servitude under his code a different thing from what it was in surrounding nations. He made it a desirable thing for a slave elsewhere to place himself under his laws. He protected him there, and made it certain that, when once under the jurisdiction of his laws, he could never be returned again to his former master. He elevated the slave to many of the rights of a man ; regarded him *as* a man, a moral agent, a religious being ; gave him an opportunity of acquiring the knowledge of the true religion ; allowed him time for the improvement of his mind, and for the acquisition of property ; fitted him to be a freeman, and made arrangements which were incorporated in the very constitution of the commonwealth, that at certain periods, not far distant from each other, the whole land should be free from every vestige of slavery. The Mosaic institutions were thus evidently opposed to the system, and contemplated its ultimate entire abolition, in strong contrast, as we have seen, with the institutions of our own country, which contemplate its un- mitigated perpetuity.

A very important question presents itself in regard to the *working* of the Mosaic system, and on this inquiry I now enter. The inquiry extends from the period of the close of the Mosaic code, or the death of Moses, to the winding up of the Hebrew institutions—the coming of the Messiah. So far as this subject is concerned, this may be regarded as one period—whether under the judges or the kings; whether the nation was itself free, or whether it was in bondage. The inquiry is, what was the operation of the Mosaic laws respect- ing servitude? Was it regarded as consistent with the spirit of those laws? Was the Hebrew nation a nation of slaveholders? If slavery existed at any time, what was its character? Did the prophets approve and commend it? And was it a fact that under the operation of that system, the Saviour found slavery prevalent at the time of his ap- pearing?

There is some difficulty in arriving at exact views on this point, arising from the indefinite meaning of the word *servant*, and the words relating to *servitude*, in the Scriptures. That there were *servants* in the times of the prophets, and through the entire period now under consideration, no one can doubt. Any one by opening a Hebrew, a Greek, or an English Con- cordance, will find that the words עֶבֶד *ĕbĕdh*—δοῦλος *doulos*— and *servant*, occur almost numberless times, though they are used in a great variety of senses. It is necessary, there- fore, to bear in mind that the use of these words does not demonstrate that slavery existed in any proper form. The inquiry is not into the use of the *word*, but into the *thing*, and in order to this it is necessary to keep in constant re- membrance what slavery *is*. The meaning of the word ren- dered *servant* in the Old Testament has been the subject of previous examination, (Chapter III.) and the results of this examination should be borne in mind in the inquiry on which we now enter.   The result of the examination, in substance, was, that the words used to denote servitude in the Scriptures, do not necessarily denote *slavery* in the proper sense of the term, or in the sense now under inquiry, and that the mere use of those *terms* determines nothing in the issue before us. It neither proves that slavery existed then, nor that it is lawful, any more than the word *servant* in England, or in the states north of Mason's and Dixon's line, proves that slavery exists there, or is regarded as right.   We are to remember what constitutes *the thing*, (See Chap. II.) and to inquire whether there is evidence that that existed, and how it was regarded in the period under consideration.

If the view which has been taken of the Mosaic law be correct, we shall expect to find in the Hebrew commonwealth, that, if slavery existed at all, it was in a mild form.   We shall expect to find that the Hebrews did not engage in the slave-trade or traffic.   We shall expect to find that all cruelty was rebuked, and that the slave gradually rose in the public estimation, and was elevated nearer to the condition of a free-man.   We shall expect to find that the institution gradually disappeared ; that it was regarded as so contrary to the whole spirit of the Mosaic laws, that it finally ceased to be known in the nation.   These are the fair and reasonable expectations which we should form from the examination of the subject which we have gone over ; and if this should be found *not* to be the result, it would do much to make us doubt the cor- rectness of the conclusions to which we have come respecting the nature of the Mosaic arrangements.   The inquiry now is, what were the facts in the case as developed in their history? This inquiry will embrace the following points :—The treat- ment of the native inhabitants of the land of Canaan ; the foreign traffic of the nation, and the question whether dealing in slaves constituted a part of that traffic ; how it was re- garded and treated by the prophets ; and whether slavery continued to exist among the Hebrew people, or was finally abolished.

I. The inquiry in regard to the condition of the native inhabitants of the land of Palestine. I begin with this, because there is allusion to them in the sacred writings in such a way as to illustrate this subject; and because, if the Mosaic institutions had contemplated slavery as a desirable thing, and as a permanent arrangement, nothing would have been more natural than that whole people should have been reduced to permanent servitude.

To such a course there were strong inducements. They might be regarded as captives taken in war, and it was the ancient law that such captives were regarded as slaves. They were an abandoned race—a race devoted to destruction. None of them were regarded as the proper objects of mercy; none were to be considered as entitled to any privileges of citizenship, nor were they to become citizens of the Hebrew republic. Ex. xxxiv. 11—13; Numb. xxxiii. 51—56; Deut. vii. 1—5. Yet, if their institutions contemplated slavery, and it was designed that slavery should enter into the permanent arrangements of the commonwealth, what would have been more natural than to have doomed that race to servitude? Where could any class of men have been found more fitted for it, or against whose subjugation to hopeless bondage fewer objections could have been raised? In the view of the law of God, as promulgated by Moses, they had forfeited all claim to life or mercy. They might justly be driven from their land, or devoted to destruction. Yet it would seem to be a milder and more compassionate treatment to make them slaves; to permit them to live, and to give them the opportunity of becoming ultimately incorporated among the Hebrew people. This thought would certainly occur to the Hebrews themselves, if they had supposed that slavery was to be a part of their political arrangements; and if God had designed that it should enter into that system permanently, it is inconceivable why he did not at once point them to *that* people as a race that would supply them with all the slaves that they needed.

Nothing, moreover, would have been more natural than this course, if they had recalled one of the ancient predictions respecting a portion of this people—the malediction of Noah. Gen. ix. 25. "Cursed be Canaan; *a servant of servants shall he be unto his brethren.*" This passage, by a singular perverseness of interpretation, and a singular perseverance in that perverseness notwithstanding the plainest rules of exegesis, is often employed to justify the reduction of the *African* to slavery, because Ham, the *father* of Canaan, peopled Africa. Nothing can be clearer, however, than that if a Hebrew had ever thought of employing this passage to justify slavery, it would not have been applied by him to *the African*, but to *the Canaanite.* It was Canaan and not Ham that was specified; and whatever there was *in* the passage, whether of prophecy or malediction, that could be interpreted in favour of the right of subjecting any one to servitude, a Hebrew would have applied it only to the Canaanite. The plea would have been plausible, that by an ancient prediction it was foretold that the Canaanite should be a slave; that the curse of the patriarch Noah, specifying Canaan by name, would make such subjection proper; and that it was in accordance with this ancient prediction that arrangements were now made by which he should be reduced to bondage. A far more plausible argument could have been derived from *this* application of the passage in favour of fastening the chains of servitude on the Canaanite, than has ever been urged in modern times from it in favour of the subjection of the African to bondage.

Yet this application of the prophecy, so far as we know, was never made, nor did these plausible considerations in favour of subjecting the inhabitants of Palestine to slavery, ever occur to the mind of the Hebrew conquerors. No arrangements were made to kidnap them; no permission was given by Moses or Joshua to the victors to hold those taken in arms as slaves; nor was a slave-mart opened in which the captives were exposed to sale. There is not the slightest evidence that one of them was held as a slave, or was ever sold or offered for sale as a slave. They were not even attached as *serfs* or *villeins* to the soil, nor were they exported to be sold in a foreign market.

There are two occurrences referred to in their history which are decisive on this point, and which prove that not even the survivors of those tribes were regarded as slaves. The first is, the fact that a few of the inhabitants of Canaan, from the fear of death, became, by art and duplicity, *voluntary* servants to the Hebrews. I refer to the case of the Gibeonites. Josh. ix. They came to Joshua with the representation that they had travelled a great distance, and in such raiment as to *appear* as if they had come from afar. They stated to him and the elders, that they had heard of all that had been done by the Hebrews in their conquests, and they came to enter into a league of peace. The artifice succeeded, and the request was granted, and a solemn compact was entered into between them and the leaders of the Jewish host. Soon the deception was found out, (ver. 16,) and it became a serious question what course was to be pursued in regard to them. The command to destroy all the inhabitants of the land was positive; the fact of fraud in this case was undoubted; and yet a solemn league had been made with them, and the faith of the nation pledged that they should be spared. The matter was compromised, and the honour of the nation secured; since by the compact they were regarded as 'bondmen;' (literally *servitude* עֶבֶד shall not be cut off from you;' see the margin;) and they were made "hewers of wood and drawers of water" 'for the house of God.' They were employed in the service of the "congregation and of the altar," (ver. 27,) and were continued in this menial occupation. Yet there is no evidence that they were reduced to *slavery*, properly so called. They were not held as property. They were not bought and sold, nor does it appear that the obligation to servitude descended to their children. They were held in subjection, and were employed to perform the more laborious duties connected with the public services of the sanctuary. Undoubtedly they were regarded as menials, and were probably subjected to much indignity and contempt, but the essential features of *slavery* were wanting in their case. They had *voluntarily* put themselves in this position. They obtained what they asked, and though it was a laborious and debased condition, yet they preferred it to death. No argument can be derived from this in favour of the supposition that the Hebrews designed to perpetuate the institution of Slavery.

The other occurrence referred to in their history, which may illustrate the subject, is one that took place in the time of Solomon. Upon the remnant of that people in the land, who it would seem up to this time had been free, Solomon is said to have 'levied a tribute of bond-service' in building the temple. "And all the people that were left of the Amorites, Hittites, Perizzites, Hivites, and Jebusites, which were not of the children of Israel, their children that were left after them in the land, whom the children of Israel also were not able utterly to destroy, upon these did Solomon levy a tribute of bond-service (מַס־עֹבֵד) unto this day." 1 Kings ix. 20, 21. An express distinction was made between them and the children of Israel. "But of the children of Israel did Solomon make no bondmen, (עֶבֶד,) but they were men of war, and his servants," (that is, in a higher sense than the others,) "and his princes, and his captains, and rulers of his chariots, and his horsemen."—Ver. 22. Yet there is no evidence that the descendants of the Amorites, &c., were regarded as *slaves*. They were pressed into a temporary service for the purpose of procuring the materials of building the temple, and were doubtless dismissed as soon as the temple was completed. There is no evidence that they were held as property, or that they were in any case sold, or that they were held in perpetual servitude of any kind. The phrase " unto this day," ver 21, proves only that they were held until that part of the book of Kings was composed.

Two remarks, however, may be made in view of this transaction. First, that until this time they were not regarded
as slaves, or as servants of any kind. The 'bond-service' was
then laid upon them. They were before freemen, and were
now pressed into the service for a temporary purpose.
Second, slavery was not common at that time, or at least
Solomon had not slaves of his own. If that had been the
case, we should have heard something of it on an occasion
like this, and his slaves would have been required to perform
this laborious service. The fact that Solomon was obliged to
lay this burden on a people heretofore free, demonstrates that
there was no large body of slaves under his control, to whom
the work could be intrusted.

II. There was no foreign traffic in slaves. The proof of
this is as complete as it can be where there is no express declaration, and the fact is of great importance, for if there were
provisions made for the periodical emancipation of all who
were held in servitude, then it is clear that the system could
be perpetuated only by an active foreign traffic. It is needless
to say that, though chiefly an agricultural people,* the
Hebrews, especially in the time of Solomon, had considerable
foreign trade. Palestine was favourably situated for commerce,
and particularly for a commerce in slaves. It was adjacent
to the Mediterranean, and the rich productions of India, in all
ages the most desirable objects of commerce, almost of necessity passed through some part of it. It was undoubtedly to
facilitate or secure this trade, that Solomon built Tadmor or
Palmyra, and it was this which, in subsequent times, made
Tyre, and Petra, and Alexandria, and Venice what they were.
Solomon also had the advantage of a port at Ezion-Geber, on
the Red Sea, and secured also from that direction the rich
productions of India and Africa. The vicinity of Egypt to
Palestine, and the intercourse which Solomon had with that

---

* See Michaelis' Com. on the Laws of Moses, art. xxxix.

country, made it easy, if he had chosen to do it, to import
slaves from northern Africa.   An active commerce in slaves
has, in nearly all ages, been carried on through Egypt ; and
the different parts of Turkey, at the present day, are supplied
with those which are procured in the interior of Africa, and
conveyed through Nubia and Egypt.   An extensive slave-
mart is established at Shendy, in Nubia, and the slave traffic
is among the most profitable that now passes through Egypt.
The number of slaves sold annually in the slave market at
Shendy is about five thousand, a large part of whom go to
Egypt, and thence to various parts of Turkey.*   It may be
added here, that slavery has always prevailed in Egypt, and
in the adjacent countries.   " According to the most moderate
calculation," says Burckhardt, " the number of slaves actually
in Egypt is forty thousand.   There is hardly a village in
which several of them are not found, and every person of property keeps at least one.   All the Bedouin tribes also, who
surround these countries, are well stocked with slaves."—
p. 307.   It would not be possible to refer to a period in the
history of Egypt in which slavery did not exist, and in which
the traffic in slaves did not constitute an important part of the
commerce with other countries.   There was every temptation,
therefore, if the Hebrews engaged in commerce at all, to make
this a part of the traffic, and there is a moral certainty, if
slavery was regarded as in accordance with the spirit of the
Mosaic institutions, that this species of trade would have extensively prevailed.

Yet, in every allusion to the commerce which was carried
on with other nations, there is not a single instance where the
traffic in slaves is mentioned.   There happens to be quite an
extended specification of the articles of trade—a specification
which would be sufficient for a custom-house officer in ascertaining the amount and value of imports—and yet there is no
case in which a slave constituted an item in the imports.

* See this traffic fully described in Burckhardt's Travels in Nubia,
pp. 290—308.

Thus we have an enumeration in 1 Kings x. 22, of the articles which were imported in the "navy of Tharshish." "For the king had at sea a navy of Tharshish with the navy of Hiram; once in three years came the navy of Tharshish, bringing gold and silver, ivory, and apes, and peacocks." Comp. 2 Chron. ix. 21. So also Solomon had a seaport at Ezion-Geber, "on the shore of the Red Sea, in the land of Edom," (1 Kings ix. 26,) from whence the traffic with Ophir was carried on, but there is no intimation that any of those vessels were employed in the slave trade. If the traffic in slaves constituted any part of this commerce, it is incredible that "apes and peacocks" should have been specified, and no allusion to what must have been a much more important branch of commerce.

The considerations here suggested receive confirmation, if we advert to two circumstances mentioned in regard to the commerce of Tyre. The one is, that a part of the commercial operations of the Tyrians consisted in slaves. Thus it is said, (Ezek. xxvii. 13,) "Javan, Tubal, and Mesech, they were thy merchants; they traded *the persons of men* and vessels of brass in thy market." Comp. Rev. xviii. 13. The other circumstance is, that in the mention of the trade which the Hebrews carried on with Tyre, there is no allusion to any such traffic, and the enumeration of other things as the articles in which they traded, precludes the supposition that they dealt in either the purchase or sale of slaves. "Judah, and the land of Israel, they were thy merchants: they traded in thy market wheat of Minnith, and Pannag, and honey, and oil, and balm."—ver. 17. These circumstances make it morally certain that in the transactions with Tyre, and in the foreign commerce carried on from Ezion-Geber, no part of the merchandise consisted of slaves. I do not find in the whole history of the Hebrew people under the Mosaic institutions, a hint that they were ever engaged in this species of commerce. There is no enumeration of slaves among the articles of importation; there is no allusion to them in the account of the arrival of caravans or of foreigners who came to Palestine; there is no recorded instance of any public sale of slaves; there was no public mart where they were sold; there are no merchants mentioned who devoted their lives tc the business.

Now *if* slavery existed in Palestine to any considerable degree, it must have been kept up by the foreign traffic, and *if* that had existed, it is incredible that in the long time in which they existed as a separate people, no allusion is ever made to it. It would be impossible to give a correct history of the United States, without some allusion to the slave trade; and the records in regard to the importation of slaves are so deeply engraven in all our annals, that no lapse of time can ever obliterate them. If the traffic existed in Palestine in any manner at all corresponding to what exists in our own country, how can it be accounted for that in all their history there was not the slightest allusion to it?

III. The prophets felt themselves at liberty to animadvert upon the injustice of slavery, and to denounce it as entirely inconsistent with the Mosaic institutions. If this was the case, it will follow that, though slavery may have prevailed to some extent, yet it was understood that the spirit of the Mosaic institutions was opposed to it, and that they were intended to abolish it. For the prophets surely would not have denounced, as wrong, a system which the constitution of their own country was designed to perpetuate, and which the law of their God intended to sanction.

In regard to the *fact* that the prophets felt at liberty to denounce all slavery as wholly inconsistent with the Mosaic institutions, I will refer to two classes of passages of Scripture, which will make the matter entirely clear. Before I do this, it may be observed, however, that the allusions in the writings of the prophets are so infrequent as to lead us to suppose that slavery in Palestine did not extensively prevail; but that when they *do* allude to it, it is in such a way as to leave no doubt as to the views which they entertained on the subject.

(A) The first class of passages of Scripture relates to the views which were entertained about the propriety of subjecting their own countrymen to slavery ; or the question whether it was proper for the Hebrews to make slaves of their brethren. Two events which happened in their history gave occasion to the prophets to express their views on this point, and they did not hesitate to avail themselves of the opportunity. The first occurred during the reign of Ahaz, and is so important on the point that I will copy the account at length. 2 Chron. xxviii. 8—15 : "And the children of Israel carried away captive of their brethren two hundred thousand, women, sons, and daughters, and took also away much spoil from them, and brought the spoil to Samaria. But a prophet of the Lord was there, whose name was Oded ; and he went out before the host that came to Samaria, and said unto them, Behold, because the Lord God of your fathers was wroth with Judah, he hath delivered them into your hand, and ye have slain them in a rage that reacheth up unto heaven. And now ye purpose to keep under the children of Judah and Jerusalem for bondmen and bondwomen unto you ; but are there not with you, even with you, sins against the Lord your God? Now hear me, therefore, and deliver the captives again, which ye have taken captive of your brethren ; for the fierce wrath of God is upon you. Then certain of the heads of the children of Ephraim, Azariah the son of Johanan, Berechiah the son of Meshillemoth, and Jehizkiah the son of Shallum, and Amasa the son of Hadlai, stood up against them that came from the war, and said unto them, ye shall not bring in the captives hither ; for whereas we have offended against the Lord already, ye intend to add more to our sins, and to our trespass ; for our trespass is great, and there is fierce wrath against Israel. So the armed men left the captives and the spoil before the princes and all the congregation. And the men which were expressed by name rose up, and took the captives, and with

the spoil clothed all that were naked among them, and arrayed them, and shod them, and gave them to eat and to drink,
and anointed them, and carried all the feeble of them upon
asses, and brought them to Jericho, the city of palm trees, to
their brethren: then they returned to Samaria." This was
a case which settled one important question in regard to servitude. It was, that it was not in accordance with the spirit
of the Mosaic institutions, that any portion of the Hebrew
people should make slaves of their brethren who might be
taken in war. The general law in ancient times was, that
captives taken in war were the *slaves* of the victor, and
might be disposed of in any way to their advantage. This
principle prevailed all over the heathen world, and was regarded as an indisputable maxim.* Nothing was more natural than that it should be applied among the Hebrews, when
they were separated into different kingdoms, and made war
on each other; and, in the instance before us, the attempt was
made to carry out the principle in regard to their captive
brethren. The decisive rebuke of a prophet; the ready
acquiescence of the leaders in his views, and their care in
restoring the captives, all show how obviously this was a
violation of the spirit of the Mosaic institutions, and have settled
what was the spirit of those institutions, against slavery.
One such instance would for ever determine the question
whether it was proper to enslave their brethren who were
taken captive in war, and we do not hear that the attempt was
ever repeated.

A case of a similar kind, so far as the servitude of Hebrews
to other Hebrews was concerned, though not similar as to the
question whether it could be done by reducing captives taken
in war to slavery—*that* question being regarded as settled—
but which equally went to establish the point that it was
regarded as inconsistent with the spirit of the Mosaic institutions for the Hebrews to subject their brethren to servitude,

---

* See Grotius de Jure Belli ac Pacis, lib. iii. cap. vii.

occurred in the time of Jeremiah. This remarkable transaction is recorded in Jer. xxxiv. 8—20. Its importance in reference to the point before us, will make it proper to dwell upon it.

" This is the word that came unto Jeremiah from the Lord, after that the king Zedekiah had made a covenant with all the people which were at Jerusalem, to proclaim liberty unto them ; that every man should let his man-servant, and every man his maid-servant, being an Hebrew or an Hebrewess, go free ; that none should serve himself of them, to wit, of a Jew his brother. Now when all the princes, and all the people, which had entered into the covenant, heard that every one should let his man-servant, and every one his maid-servant, go free, that none should serve themselves of them any more, then they obeyed, and let them go. But afterward they turned, and caused the servants and the handmaids, whom they had let go free, to return, and brought them into subjection for servants and for handmaids.

" Therefore the word of the Lord came to Jeremiah from the Lord, saying, Thus saith the Lord, the God of Israel ; I made a covenant with your fathers in the day that I brought them forth out of the land of Egypt, out of the house of bondmen, saying, At the end of seven years let ye go every man his brother an Hebrew, which hath been sold unto thee ; and when he hath served thee six years, thou shalt let him go free from thee : but your fathers hearkened not unto me, neither inclined their ear. And ye were now turned, and had done right in my sight, in proclaiming liberty every man to his neighbour ; and ye had made a covenant before me in the house which is called by my name : but ye turned and polluted my name, and caused every man his servant, and every man his handmaid, whom he had set at liberty at their pleasure, to return, and brought them into subjection, to be unto you for servants and for handmaids.   Therefore thus saith the Lord : Ye have not hearkened unto me, in proclaiming liberty, every one to his brother, and every man to his neighbour : behold, I proclaim a liberty for you, saith the

Lord, to the sword, to the pestilence, and to the famine; and I will make you to be removed into all the kingdoms of the earth. And I will give the men that have transgressed my covenant, which have not performed the words of the covenant which they had made before me, when they cut the calf in twain, and passed between the parts thereof, the princes of Judah, and the princes of Jerusalem, the eunuchs, and the priests, and all the people of the land, which passed between the parts of the calf; I will even give them into the hand of of their enemies, and into the hand of them that seek their life; and their dead bodies shall be for meat unto the fowls of the heaven, and to the beasts of the earth."

In regard to this transaction, the following points are clear from the narrative. (1.) That at that time there were many of the Hebrews who had, for some cause, been reduced to servitude by their brethren. The reasons why this had been done are unknown, but it is probable that it had been in the manner contemplated in the laws of Moses when literally understood. It may be presumed that *poverty* was the principal cause, and in the transaction there is no intimation that it had occurred from any other. It may have been possible that there was then an unusual degree of oppression of this kind, but it does not appear that it was for any causes different from those which the literal interpretation of the Mosaic laws seemed to contemplate. The *number* of those who were thus subjected to servitude is not mentioned, but it would seem that it was so great as to demand the interposition of the prophet. (2.) A reformation from this evil was, from some cause now unknown, effected. Whether it was originated by the reigning king Zedekiah, as a civil arrangement, or by the influence of Jeremiah, as a religious movement, it is impossible to determine; but it is certain that a universal emancipation of all the Hebrews who were held in servitude was agreed upon, and was actually carried into effect. It was evidently under the patronage of the king, and he gave his sanction to it

though it may have had its origin among the religious
part of the nation, or have been urged by the prophets.
" This is the word that came unto Jeremiah from the Lord,
after that the king Zedekiah had made a covenant with all
the people which were at Jerusalem, to proclaim liberty unto
them : that every man should let his man-servant, and every
man his maid-servant, being an Hebrew or an Hebrewess, go
free ; that none should serve himself of them, to wit, of a
Jew his brother.   Now when all the princes, and all the
people which had entered into the covenant, heard that
every one should let his man-servant, and every one his
maid-servant go free, that none should serve themselves of
them any more, then they obeyed, and let them go."—ver.
8—10. It may be presumed that such an emancipation was
not effected without difficulty, and without reluctance on the
part of those who claimed their brethren as bound to servitude. We know that men are not usually disposed to emancipate those who are held in bondage, and the subsequent
transactions in regard to those here referred to, show that
they had not been restored to freedom without an effort.
Still, it was remarkable, as an instance of *voluntary* emancipation—for it was not the result of an absolute command on
the part of the sovereign, but of a covenant or compact—
" Zedekiah *made a covenant* with all the people."   It is one
of the earliest instances on record of the voluntary emancipation of large numbers held in bondage, and shows that it
may be *possible* to induce a people to act from such a sense
of justice as to release those whom they hold as slaves.   For
any thing that appears, it would have been as difficult to
bring about such an emancipation among the Hebrews by
their own consent, as it would now be in Maryland or Virginia.   (3.) After they had been emancipated, an attempt was
made to reduce them again to bondage, in spite of the solemn
covenant by which they had been set at liberty.   " But afterwards they turned, and caused the servants and the hand-
maidens whom they had let go free, to return, and brought

them into subjection for servants and for handmaids."
—ver. 11. This is a manifestation of the genuine spirit of
slavery, and shows how strong is the tendency in human
nature to relapse into it again, even when convinced that it is
wrong. So powerful is the spirit of avarice in men; so common the indisposition to labour; so constantly operating the
desire to live by the avails of the labour of others; and so
much of ease, and comfort, and luxury, is supposed to be connected with slavery, that there is scarcely any form of wrong
which men are more reluctant to relinquish, or to which they
more readily return. (4.) In this state of things, the prophet
in a most severe manner rebuked those who attempted to
subject their brethren again to servitude, and denounced on
them the severest judgments of heaven. He reminded them
of the solemn covenant into which God entered with their
fathers, when he released them from Egyptian bondage; of
the absolute command that no Hebrew should on any consideration be made to serve more than six years; and says that
for the crime of subjecting their brethren again to servitude
after they had been released from bondage, God would subject them "to the sword, to the pestilence, and to the famine,"
and would cause them to be removed "into all the kingdoms
of the earth."—ver. 17. Nothing could have shown more
decidedly the abhorrence with which the whole transaction
was viewed, or the fact that subjecting their brethren to servitude was entirely incompatible with the whole spirit of the
Hebrew institutions. If the permanent existence of slavery
had been contemplated as in accordance with the spirit of the
Mosaic institutions, no effort would have been made to secure
their release, nor would the conduct of those who endeavoured to fasten the bonds on their brethren after they had
been once broken off, have been met with so fearful a
rebuke.

The two cases now referred to, show, that though according to the exact letter of the Mosaic statutes it was lawful, in
certain cases, to hold their brethren in servitude, yet that it

was contrary to the spirit of those institutions that it should
be perpetuated; that their brethren were *not* to be made
slaves in the way which was then invariably regarded as
proper; and that any attempt to forge the chains of slavery
on them permanently must meet with the decided rebuke of
Heaven. They show that the entire subject was observed
with an eye of vigilance by the prophets whom God raised
up, and that the whole spirit of the Mosaic institutions tended
to introduce a period when no Hebrew should be the servant
of his brother.

(B) A second class of texts of Scripture will show us that
the prophets felt themselves at liberty to utter the language
of rebuke so decisively on the whole subject of slavery, as to
prove that in any and every form it was contrary to the spirit
of the Mosaic laws, and was never designed to be a permanent institution. If we find a prophet of God, in a single
instance, condemning the existence of slavery; demanding that
those held in bondage should be emancipated as an acceptable
service to God; and denouncing the whole system as oppressive, we may make use of this fact to prove that the Mosaic
laws were not favourable to it, and never intended that it
should be permanent. We find, in fact, just such an instance in the book of Isaiah, ch. lviii. 6: "Is not this the
fast that I have chosen? to loose the bands of wickedness, to
undo the heavy burdens, to let the oppressed go free, and that
ye break every yoke?" The question now is, to whom would
this be understood as referring? Who would come under
the description of the *oppressed?* Who would have obtained
release by 'breaking every yoke?' Would a compliance
with the demand of the prophet have been consistent with
the continuance of slavery? If the command of the prophet
had been obeyed in its true spirit, would there still have
remained large bodies of men in the land held as property,
and subjected to the evils of servitude? Those who suppose
that slavery was contemplated by Moses as a permanent
institution, and that it was regarded by the prophets as an

institution with which they were not to intermeddle because it was established by law, must necessarily believe that all that the prophet contemplated here could have been complied with, even if the Hebrews should have continued to be owners of slaves to any extent. It becomes important, then, to ascertain the real idea which was in the mind of the prophet.

(1.) It is clear that the evil which he desired should be removed, he considered to be a moral evil, or sin. The appropriate fast was to "loose the bands *of wickedness;*" to cease to do wrong. The eye was fixed on some prevailing form of iniquity which made it proper that there should be *fasting* on account of it, and which should be removed in order that the act of fasting might be acceptable to God.

(2.) The things which they were *to do* in relation to the various forms of evil, in order that their fasting might be acceptable, are distinctly specified, and are such as to lead to the belief that slavery was referred to, and such that *it would be understood that the prophet meant that it should at once cease.* That the expressions used by the prophet would include slavery, if it existed then, will be apparent by a brief examination of the language employed by him.

(*a*) The first thing specified is, that they should "loose the bands of wickedness." The idea clearly is, that they were to dissolve every tie which unjustly bound their fellow-men. If they were exercising any cruel authority over others; if they had bound them in any way to any service or obligation contrary to the law of God, and the demands of justice, they were to release them. This *might* refer to their holding others to contracts fraudulently made; or to their holding others to strict payment who were unable to meet their obligations; or to their subjecting others to more rigid servitude than was allowed by the laws of Moses; but it would not require a very ardent imagination for any one to see that if he held others as slaves *at all*, this came fairly under the description of the prophet. A man with a tender conscience, who held slaves, would at least have suspected that this part of the description might have been intended to include himself.

(*b*) The second thing specified is, that they should " undo the heavy burdens"—literally, ' to shake off the bands of the yoke ;' that is, the yoke of captives, of the oppressed, &c. The same word is used to denote *burden* (מוֹטָה) which in the subsequent member is rendered *yoke ;* and the verb which is rendered " undo" הַתֵּר, from נתר, is elsewhere employed to denote emancipation from servitude. See Psalm cv. 20. The idea here is, that the yoke was attached to the necks of animals by cords or bands,* and that those cords or bands were to be so loosened that the one which bore the yoke should be free. The yoke in the Scriptures is commonly employed as the emblem of oppression, or of compulsory toil or servitude, and is undoubtedly so used here. The whole phrase here used denotes the release of captives or slaves, and would, to one accustomed to Scripture language, be so understood here. Thus in Psalm cv. 17—20 :

> He sent a man before them even Joseph,
> Who was sold for a servant;
> Whose feet they hurt with fetters:
> He was laid in iron ;
> Until the time that his word came,
> The word of the Lord tried him.
> The king sent and loosed him—וַיַּתִּירֵהוּ,
> Even the ruler of the people, and let him go free.

So in Psalm cxlvi. 7 : " The Lord *looseth* the prisoners," where the same Hebrew word occurs.

(*c*) The third thing specified is, that they were to " let the oppressed go free." This language is still more emphatic and unambiguous than that before employed. The word rendered " oppressed" (marg. *broken*), is from רָצַץ *râtzătz* to break, to

---

* See Fragments to Taylor's Calmet, No. xxviii.

break down; to treat with violence, to oppress. It may apply to those who are treated with violence in any way, or who are broken down with hard usage. It may refer, therefore, to slaves, who are crushed with bondage or toil; to inferiors, who are crushed by the exactions of those above them; or to the subjects of a tyrant, groaning under his yoke. If slavery existed at the time when this word was used in the form in which it is usually found, it would be understood as including that; at least it would be so understood by the slaves themselves; for if any system properly deserves to be called *oppression*, it is slavery. This interpretation is confirmed by the use of the word rendered *free*. This word חָפְשִׁי *hhŏphshi*, evidently refers to the act of freeing a slave. The person who had been once a slave, and who had obtained his freedom, was denominated חָפְשִׁי *hhŏphshi.** The word occurs, and is so used, in the following places: Ex. xxi. 2, "And the seventh [year] he shall go out *free;*" ver. 5, "I will not go out *free;*" xxvi. 27, "He shall let him go *free;*" Deut. xv. 12, "Thou shalt let him go *free;*" ver. 13, "When thou sendest him out *free;*" ver. 18, "When thou sendest him away *free;*" Job iii. 19, "The servant is *free* from his master;" that is, in the grave, where there is universal emancipation. So in the places above referred to, respecting the freedom of the Hebrews who had been held as slaves, (Jer. xxxiv. 9, 10, 11, 14, 16,) the same Hebrew word is used. It occurs in no other places except the following: 1 Sam. xvii. 25, "And make his father's house *free* in Israel," referring to the favour that was promised to one that should slay Goliath of Gath. Job xxxix. 5, "Who hath sent out the wild ass *free?*" Ps. lxxxviii. 5. (6.) "*Free* among the dead." The word is one that would be naturally understood by a Hebrew as referring to freedom from servitude, and unless there was something in the connection that made it necessary to adopt a different signification, it would be so regarded of course. In the case before us,

* See Jahn's Archæology, § 171.

such an interpretation would be obvious, and *if* slavery at that time existed in Palestine, a Jew would understand the prophet as saying that the slave was to be released in order that an "acceptable fast" might be observed.

(*d*) The fourth thing specified is, that they were "to break every yoke." This also would be naturally understood of slavery, if it existed at that time. A 'yoke,' in the Scriptures, is a symbol of servitude or of oppression, and the prophet demanded, in order that an acceptable fast should be observed, that *every thing* which could be properly regarded as *a yoke* should be broken. This requisition, if complied with, would restore all to their equal rights.

If now this proclamation were made in the United States, and were fairly complied with, no one can doubt that it would lead to the emancipation of the slave. The language is such that it cannot well be misunderstood. The prophet demands a cessation of that which would include slavery, and specifies, in order to an acceptable fast, that that should be abandoned which has always entered into it.

These are all the cases which I have been able to find in which the prophets allude to the subject of slavery. They are not numerous, and the fact that they are *no more* numerous suggests the conclusion unavoidably that slavery was not a common thing in Palestine, or that if it prevailed it was a very mild system. But from the references which we have found to it, and the manner in which it is noticed by the prophets, we are led to the following conclusions :—

(1.) That the prophets felt themselves at entire liberty to animadvert upon it, and to state their views clearly in regard to it. They did not consider themselves restrained from doing it by the fact that it was sustained by law ; or by the plea that it was a civil institution, or that the ministers of religion had nothing to do with it. The men who were sent from God as his ambassadors to the people, did not suppose that, in lifting up their voice in opposition to it, they were doing any thing contrary to what fairly came within their notice as religious teachers, nor did they regard it as a political institution in such a sense that they were not to advert to it.

It is often said in our country that slavery is a civil institution; that it pertains solely to the states where it exists; that it is sustained and sanctioned by law; that the Constitution of the Union makes provision for its perpetuity, and that it is not appropriate for the ministers of religion, and for ecclesiastical bodies, to intermeddle with it. This plea, however, might have been used with much more propriety among the Hebrews. *Their* Constitution was, what ours is not, of divine origin, and it would have been easy for a friend of slavery to have said to the prophets that the institution was sanctioned by the laws which all acknowledged to be of divine appointment, and that arrangements were made for its perpetuity in the constitution of the commonwealth. Why would not such an argument have as much weight then as it should be allowed to have now? Yet

(2.) The prophets felt themselves at entire liberty to exhort the people to restore their slaves to freedom. They considered that slavery was as proper a subject for them to discuss as any other. They treated it as if it were entirely within their province, and never appear to have hesitated about expressing their views of it.

(3.) They never speak of it as an institution which it was desirable to perpetuate, as contributing to the welfare of the community. In the few notices which we have of it, there is a uniform representation of its nature. It is, in their view, a hard and oppressive system; a system which should be abandoned if there were acceptable service rendered to God. There is no apology made for it; no pleading for it as a desirable system, and no attempt to show that it was in accordance with the laws of the land. In their writings there is no such effort to defend it or apologize for it, as, I am grieved to say, may often be found in the preaching and the writings of ministers of the gospel in the United States. It would not be difficult to imagine what would have been the emotions of Isaiah, after he had written the fifty-eighth chapter of his prophecies, were he to read some of the apologies for slavery issued by ministers of the gospel, and by professors in theological seminaries at the present day; or should he hear the sentiments uttered in debate in ecclesiastical synods, assemblies, conferences and conventions.

(4.) From the whole view, also, it may be inferred that the prophets did not suppose that the institution of slavery was in accordance with the spirit of the Mosaic institutions, or was designed to be perpetuated. Their treatment of it is just such as would be natural on the supposition that they considered those institutions to have been so arranged that, while it was for a while *tolerated*, the tendency and design was ultimately to remove the evil entirely, and to make the Hebrews throughout a free people.

As one of the results of this inquiry, it is apparent that the Hebrews were not a nation of slaveholders. There is no evidence that they engaged in the foreign slave-trade; there is none that the domestic slave-trade prevailed; there is none that there were any marts for the purchase or sale of slaves; there is none that they purchased or sold slaves at all. There is no evidence that they even purchased of others the captives made in war; and there is none that, as was usual among other people, a Hebrew ever *sold* a captive made in war to a Hebrew brother or to a stranger. The fair inference from all this is, that the Mosaic institutions were not fitted to foster the spirit of slavery, and that while it prevailed among other people, there was some process going on in Judea adapted to separate its inhabitants from all connection with the system.

As another result of this inquiry, it may be inferred that slavery altogether ceased in the land of Palestine. On what evidence would a man rely to prove that slavery existed at all in that land in the time of the later prophets, of the Maccabees, or when the Saviour appeared? There are abundant proofs, as we shall see, that it existed in Greece and Rome; but what is the evidence that it existed in Judea?

So far as I have been able to ascertain, there are no declarations that it did, to be found in the canonical books of the Old
Testament, or in Josephus. There are no allusions to laws
and customs which imply that it was prevalent. There are
no coins or medals which suppose it. There are no facts
which do not admit of an easy explanation on the supposition
that slavery had ceased, and that the Hebrew people, though
themselves often sold into captivity as slaves, had long since
ceased all connection with it themselves. The only intimations of the existence of servitude at all between the time of the
closing of the canon of the Old Testament and the advent of
the Saviour, consist of a very few notices in the books of the
Apocrypha. Thus in the book of Judith, ch. xiv. 13, it is
said, " So they came to Holofernes' tent, and said to him that
had charge of all his things, Waken now our lord ; for *the
slaves,*" or servants, (οἱ δοῦλοι,) "have been bold to come
down against us to battle." This proves that the Hebrews
were regarded as servants to the Assyrians, for in fact
many of them, under Holofernes, had been reduced to bondage. So in 1 Macc. iii. 41 : "And the merchants of the
country, hearing of the fame of them, took gold and silver
very much, with servants, and came into the camp *to buy the
children of Israel for slaves.*" This proves that it was not
uncommon for surrounding nations to purchase slaves, about
which, indeed, there can be no dispute ; but it does not demonstrate that this was practised in Judea, or by the Jews themselves. The following passages also in the Apocrypha show
that there was servitude existing of *some* kind among the
Hebrews, but do not, unless in a single instance, determine
its nature. Wisdom, xviii. 11 ; Ecclesias. iv. 30, vi. 11, vii.
20, 21, xix. 21, xxiii. 10, xxxiii. 24, 25, 26, 30, 31, xxxvii.
11, xlii. 5 ; 2 Macc. viii. 35 ; Tobit x. 10 ; Judith, x. 23 ;
Esth. xv. 16 ; Susan. 27 ; 1 Macc. i. 6, 8 ; 2 Macc. vii. 6.
33. One of these passages only alludes to the fact that servants were bought with money. Ecclesias. xxxiii. 30 : " If
thou have a servant, let him be unto thee as thyself, because

thou hast bought him with a price." Marg. as in Gr. *in blood*, (ἐν αἵματι.) The meaning probably is, that he was a captive taken in war. In what way the others who are mentioned were obtained, or what was the nature of their servitude, is in no case stated. It is only intimated that they would escape if they could. Ecclesias. xxxiii. 25, 31. Comp. 2 Macc. viii. 35.

If, therefore, it be true that slavery did not prevail in Judea; that there is no evidence that the Hebrews engaged in the traffic, and that the prophets felt themselves at liberty to denounce the system as contrary to the spirit of the Mosaic institutions, these facts will furnish an important explanation of some things in regard to the subject in the New Testament, and will prepare us to enter on the inquiry how it was regarded by the Saviour. For if slavery did not exist in Palestine in his time; if he never came in contact with it, it will not be fair to infer that he was not opposed to it, because he did not often refer to it, and expressly denounce it. He was not accustomed to go out of his way to denounce sins with which he did not come in contact. The inquiry whether there *were* slaves in Judea in his time, will be appropriately considered in the next chapter.

CHAPTER VII.

The relation of Christianity to Slavery.

In the previous chapters, I have examined at length all that seems to refer to the subject of slavery in the Old Testament. If the train of reasoning which has been pursued is correct, we have reached the conclusion that, so far from its being true that the Mosaic system was designed to uphold and perpetuate the institution, the fact was, that under the *fair operation* of that system, slavery would at no distant period come entirely to an end. The fair and honest application of the Mosaic laws to slavery in the United States would speedily remove the evil from our country.

In approaching the New Testament with reference to this subject, the true points of inquiry may be stated in few words:—Did Christ and his apostles look benignly on the institution? Did they regard it as a good institution, or as one adapted to promote permanent good? Did they consider it to be desirable for the highest comfort of social life? Did they consider that they who *held* slaves could illustrate the power and excellence of the Christian religion in the best manner, while continuing in that relation? Did they suppose that they who *were held* in slavery were occupying the most desirable condition in life, and that they should consider that the Christian religion contemplated the continuance of that relation? Was it the design of the Saviour, that the fair application of the gospel to this system should perpetuate it in his church?

The affirmative of these questions it is necessary for the advocates of slavery to make out, in order to show that the

New Testament sustains the system. If the affirmative can be made out, and if it can be shown that slavery has flourished, and must continue to flourish, under the *fair* application of the principles which Christ and his apostles laid down, it may be inferred that Christianity is favourable to the institution; if otherwise, not.

The points which the advocates of slavery refer to as showing that Christianity is not unfavourable to the system, or that the system is not contrary to the New Testament, are the following :—

(1.) That slavery existed in the time of Christ, and that though he must often have come in contact with it, he did not condemn or denounce it. Thus it is said by the Presbytery of Tombecbee, pp. 15, 16,

" That slavery is not a moral evil, is evident from the fact, that it is nowhere condemned by the Redeemer, or his apostles in the New Testament. All principles, and all practices, which would exclude from the favour of God, and the kingdom of heaven, are recorded with great plainness without respect of persons. Witness the manner in which the scribes and Pharisees were addressed : 'For I say unto you, That except your righteousness shall exceed the righteousness of the Scribes and Pharisees, ye shall in no wise enter into the kingdom of heaven.' Matt. v. 20. In a long catalogue of denunciations against various sins by the Redeemer himself, contained in the 23d chapter of Matthew, and from the 13th to the 33d verses inclusive, not a word is said against the sin of slavery.

" How does all this come to pass, if it be so 'great an evil' as our brethren seem to think ? In the sermon on the Mount not a word is uttered against the sin of slavery. A centurion came to Jesus in Capernaum, beseeching him, and saying, Lord, my servant lieth at home sick of the palsy, grievously tormented. Jesus saith unto him, I will come and heal him. The centurion answered and said, Lord, I am not worthy that thou shouldest come under my roof; but speak the word

only, and my servant shall be healed.   For I am a man under authority, having soldiers under me, and I say unto this
man, go, and he goeth ; and to another, come, and he cometh ;
and to my servant, do this, and he doeth it.   The Lord said,
' I have not found so great faith, no not in Israel.'   Matt. viii.
5—10.   The centurion was a slaveholder, and instead of
being reproved by the Saviour, he received the highest com-
mendation."

So also the Princeton Repertory, (April 1836, p. 275,) "It
is on all hands acknowledged that, at the time of the advent
of Jesus Christ, slavery in its worst forms prevailed over the
whole world.   *The Saviour found it around him in Judea,*
&c.   *The subject is hardly alluded to by Christ in any of
his personal instructions.*"   So in the Princeton Repertory
for October, 1844, it is said, " Neither Christ nor his apostles
ever denounced slaveholding as a crime."

(2.) That slavery existed throughout the Roman world,
wherever the apostles went, and yet that they did not denounce
it as an evil, or proclaim the necessity of immediate emancipation.   So the Princeton Repertory for 1836, p. 275, " The
apostles met with it in Asia, Greece, Italy.   How did they
treat it ?   Not by the denunciation of slavery as necessarily
and universally sinful.   The apostles refer to it, not to pronounce upon it AS A QUESTION OF MORALS, *but to prescribe the
relative duties of masters and slaves.*"   So in the number
for October, 1844, it is said by the Princeton Reviewer, " At
the time of the introduction of Christianity, slavery in its worst
form prevailed extensively over the world.   The slaves are
estimated as amounting to one half or two-thirds of the population of the Roman empire ; and the severity with which
they were treated was extreme."   But "*neither Christ nor
his apostles ever denounced slaveholding as a crime.*"

So the Presbytery of Tombecbee : " In the whole catalogue of
prohibitions which disqualify for the kingdom of heaven, slavery is not once named.   Did the apostles say any thing on the
subject that justifies its existence among a Christian people ?

This Presbytery believes they did. Let every man abide
in the same calling in which he was called. Art thou called
being a servant ? Care not for it; but if thou mayest be made
free, use it rather. For he that is called in the Lord, being a
servant, is the Lord's freeman. Likewise also, he that is called,
being free, is Christ's servant. Ye are bought with a price ;
be not ye the servants of men. Brethren, let every man,
wherein he is called, therein abide with God. 1 Cor. vii. 20
—24. The Bible makes slavery a part of the domestic circle;
it is associated with husband and wife, parents and children.

" Slaves are directed in what manner they are to demean
themselves as members of the civil and social compact. Servants, be obedient to them that are your masters according to
the flesh, with fear and trembling, in singleness of your heart,
as unto Christ; not with eye service, as men pleasers, but as
the servants of Christ, doing the will of God from the heart ;
with good will doing service, as to the Lord, and not to men,
knowing that whatsoever good thing any man doeth, the same
shall he receive of the Lord, whether bond or free. And, ye
masters, do the same things unto them, forbearing threatening,
knowing that your master also is in heaven ; neither is there
respect of persons with him. Eph. vi. 5—9. Society is a
whole, formed by infinite wisdom, with all its functions and
functionaries. No honest calling is degraded, or degrading.
Each member of the social compact is to be honoured and
esteemed, while he continues to move cheerfully and usefully
in his proper sphere." And so the advocates of slavery
passim.

(3.) That the inspired teachers of the Christian religion
admitted slaveholders into the Christian church, in the same
manner as others, and regarded them, while holding slaves,
as in every respect in good standing.* This is insisted on
everywhere by the advocates of slavery, as showing that the
apostles did not regard slaveholding as a sin, or as in any way

---

* See the Princeton Repertory, 1836, p. 277.

inconsistent with the existence of true piety, and with possessing all the proper qualifications of church membership.
Thus the Princeton Reviewer says, " Did they [Christ and the
apostles] shut their eyes to the enormity of a great offence
between God and man ?   Did they temporize with a heinous
evil, because it was common and popular? *Did they admit
the perpetrators of the greatest crimes to the Christian communion?* Who will undertake to charge the blessed Redeemer and his inspired followers with such connivance at sin,
and such fellowship with iniquity ?"   This argument is stated
with much force by Dr. Fuller:—

" The demonstration furnished on this question, I need only
mention ; it is the baptism by the apostles of slaveholders,
and the admission of them into the churches.   Before baptism
they required men to repent, that is, to abandon all their sins;
yet they baptized masters holding slaves.   They fenced the
Lord's table with the most solemn warnings that men should
examine themselves, and that to eat and drink unworthily was
to eat and drink condemnation ; yet they admitted to the sup-
per masters holding slaves.   They declared that ' without
holiness no man could see the Lord,' and at once condemned
all the darling sins of the day.   Idolatry was interwoven with
the very elements of society, yet they spared it not, but at
the sight of 'a city given to idolatry' their 'spirits were
stirred,' and they told the people plainly that they worshipped
devils.   They abhorred the thought that ' the temple of God
could have any agreement with idols ;' and stigmatized idolatry as one of the 'works of the flesh,' 'as to which,' said
they, ' we tell you before, as we have told you in times past,
that they which do such things shall not inherit the kingdom
of God.'   Voluptuousness reigned in city and country, and
even philosophers considered it innocent ; but the heralds of
Christ assailed it everywhere.   In a word, going in the
strength of the Lord God, they, with lion-hearted dauntless-
ness, struck at and warred with the superstitions of the Gentiles and the prejudices of the Jews.   They attacked the

passions of the vulgar and the pride of the noble. They defied the priests, and confronted the Sanhedrim, and thundered before unjust and licentious princes, ' of righteousness, and temperance, and judgment to come.' Yet as to slavery, they not only never forbade it, but received believing masters into the churches, and declared them ' faithful and beloved,' brethren in Christ Jesus."*

(4.) It is said by those who maintain that slavery is not inconsistent with the spirit of the New Testament, that the apostles " legislated" for it in the same way as they did for the other allowed relations of life. They recognised the relation of master and slave in the same manner as they did that of husband and wife, and parent and child, and monarch and subject, and in language that implied no more disapprobation in the one case than in the other. They prescribed the duties of both, *as if* the relation was not improper. It is argued further, that they never " legislated" for a *sinful* relation ; that they never made similar laws in reference to polygamy or concubinage ; and that the fact that they thus made laws contemplating this relation, showed that they could not have designed to express disapprobation of the system. This argument is much urged by the advocates of the system, and is deemed by them conclusive on the point. In support of it, they refer to such passages of the New Testament as Eph. v. 22, 33 ; vi. 1—9 ; Col. iii. 18—25 ; iv. 1 ; 1 Tim. vi. 1—5.

(5.) It is urged that to suppose slavery to be a sin, and yet to suppose that Christ and the apostles failed to denounce it as such, is a gross reflection on their character, and entirely inconsistent with their moral honesty. This argument is urged with great zeal by the Princeton Reviewer, as being decisive in the case. Thus the author of the article in the Repertory for 1836 says on this point : " It requires no argument to show that sin ought to be at once abandoned. Every thing, therefore, is conceded which the abolitionists

* Dr. Fuller's Letters to Dr. Wayland, pp. 196, 197.

need require, when it is granted that slaveholding is in itself a crime. But how can this assumption be reconciled
with the conduct of Christ and the apostles? Did they shut
their eyes to the enormities of a great offence against God
and man? Did they temporize with a heinous evil, because
it was common and popular? Did they abstain from even
exhorting masters to emancipate their slaves, though an imperative duty, from fear of consequences? Did they admit
the perpetrators of the greatest crimes to the Christian communion? Who will undertake to charge the blessed Redeemer and his inspired followers with such connivance at
sin, and such fellowship with iniquity? Were drunkards,
murderers, liars, and adulterers thus treated? Were they
passed over without even an exhortation to forsake their sins?
Were they recognised as Christians? It cannot be that
slaveholding belongs to the same category with these crimes;
and to assert the contrary, is to assert that Christ is the minister of sin." And again, on pages 283, 284, he urges the
argument with renewed energy: "Let us, however, consider
the force of the argument as stated above. It amounts to this.
Christ and his apostles thought slaveholding a great crime,
but they abstained from saying so for fear of the consequences. The very statement of the argument, in its naked
form, is its refutation. These holy men did not refrain from
condemning sin from a regard to consequences. They did
not hesitate to array against the religion which they taught,
the strongest passions of men. Nor did they content themselves with denouncing the general principles of evil; they
condemned its special manifestations. They did not simply
forbid intemperate sensual indulgence, and leave it to their
hearers to decide what did or what did not come under that
name. They declared that no fornicator, no adulterer, no
drunkard could be admitted into the kingdom of heaven.
They did not hesitate, even when a little band, a hundred
and twenty souls, to place themselves in direct and irreconcilable opposition to the whole polity, civil and religious, of

the Jewish state. It will hardly be maintained that slavery was, at that time, more intimately interwoven with the institutions of society than idolatry was. It entered into the arrangements of every family; of every city and province, and of the whole Roman empire. The emperor was the Pontifex Maximus; every department of the state, civil and military, was pervaded by it. It was so united with the fabric of the government that it could not be removed without effecting a revolution in all its parts. The apostles knew this. They knew that to denounce polytheism was to array against them the whole power of the state. Their divine Master had distinctly apprised them of the result. He told them that it would set the father against the son, and the son against the father; the mother against the daughter, and the daughter against the mother; and that a man's enemies should be those of his own household. He said that he came not to bring peace, but a sword, and that such would be the opposition to his followers, that whosoever killed them, would think he did God service. Yet in view of these certain consequences the apostles did denounce idolatry, not merely in principle, but by name. The result was precisely what Christ had foretold. The Romans, tolerant of every other religion, bent the whole force of their wisdom and arms to extirpate Christianity. The scenes of bloodshed which, century after century, followed the introduction of the gospel, did not induce the followers of Christ to keep back or modify the truth. They adhered to their declaration that idolatry was a heinous crime. And they were right. We expect similar conduct of our missionaries. We do not expect them to refrain from denouncing the institutions of the heathen, as sinful, because they are popular, or intimately interwoven with society. The Jesuits, who adopted this plan, forfeited the confidence of Christendom, without making converts of the heathen. It is, therefore, perfectly evident that the authors of our religion were not withheld, by these considerations, from declaring slavery to be unlawful. If they did

abstain from this declaration, as is admitted, it must have
been because they did not consider it as in itself a crime.
No other solution of their conduct is consistent with their
truth or fidelity."

This argument seems to have had a peculiar value in the
eyes of the conductors of that periodical.   After having slum-
bered unnoticed and unappreciated for some eight years on
its pages, it was deemed important that so valuable a specimen of reasoning should not be lost to the generation that
was about to come on the stage, and that the world should at
least be reminded that there *was* such a cogent argument
which might be urged in favour of the system ; and accordingly it is reproduced, somewhat enlarged, though with no
additional strength, in the same work for October, 1844.*   In
that article the reviewer urges the point before us with augmented zeal.   He says, " They [that is the abolitionists]
say, in substance, that the apostles concealed the truth, that
they were afraid of consequences, that they acted from policy,
or motives of expediency.   Our answer to this is, 1. That
such conduct would be immoral.   For men professing to be
inspired teachers of truth and duty, to appear among men
living in the daily commission of 'a heinous crime in the

---

* Why, after the lapse of so many years, it was deemed necessary to
republish it substantially in the same periodical, is not stated.   The character of the article, being the undisguised production of a northern man,
was such as not soon to be forgotten at the North ; and having been re-
published in a pamphlet form at Pittsburgh by southern gentlemen, it
seemed scarcely necessary to refresh the memory of those who reside at
the South with the fact of its existence.   It is one of the characteristics
of the *theology* at Princeton, that it never changes ; and perhaps the object of the republication was to certify to the world that its views of slavery
are as changeless as its divinity.   Whatever may have been the motive,
however, its republication without material change, and with no additional
strength, may be regarded as *a sign* that in the apprehension of the conductors of the Princeton Repertory, the argument which palliates slavery
is exhausted.

sight of God,' and never once tell them it was a crime ; to allow
them to go on in this course of iniquity, to the ruin of their
souls, is a supposition which shocks the moral sense. Nothing but the explicit declaration that slaveholding was a
crime, and immediate emancipation a duty, could satisfy the
demands of conscience, in such a case.   Men were constantly
coming to the apostle to ask, what they must do to be saved,
what God would have them to do; and if they did not answer
those questions openly and honestly, according to their real
convictions, they were bad men.   Such conduct in any other
case would by all men be pronounced immoral.   Suppose
our missionaries among the heathen, in teaching the gospel,
should, from motives of policy, abstain from telling them the
truth, should fail intentionally to inform them that idolatry,
adultery, child-murder, or any like crime, was a grievous sin
in the sight of God, would not all the world pronounce them
unfaithful ?   Do not abolitionists condemn southern ministers
for not explicitly stating that slaveholding is a crime, and immediate emancipation a duty ?   Would they not view with
abhorrence the minister who really coincided with them in
his views, and yet through fear of consequences, held his
peace, and allow his hearers to sin on in security ?   Would
not, on the contrary, the world ring with their shouts in
praise of the man who, in fidelity to God, and in love to man,
should openly preach the truth on these points to a congregation of slaveholders, even though it brought sudden destruction on his own head ?   We fear, however, we are only
obscuring the clearness of a self-evident truth, by multiplying
illustrations.   The conduct of the apostles is absolutely irreconcilable with moral honesty, if they believed slaveholding
to be a heinous crime in the sight of God.   They were either
bad men, or they were not abolitionists, in the American
sense of that word.   2. But again, the course ascribed to the
apostles in reference to slavery, is not only base in itself,
but it is contrary to their conduct in all analogous cases.
Slaveholding is the only sin familiar to those to whom they

preached, and about which they wrote, that they failed to denounce. Idolatry was a crime which was more prevalent than slaveholding; more implicated in all the institutions of life, in support of which stronger passions were engaged, and in attacking which they could not look for the support of one-half or two-thirds of the community. Yet idolatry they everywhere proclaimed to be a crime, inconsistent with Christianity and a bar to salvation. The consequence was, the apostles were persecuted even to death. It is not true that they kept back the truth for fear of suffering. They called God to witness that they declared the whole counsel of God, and were clear of every man's blood. It is said that the cases of idolatry and slavery are not parallel, because it was more dangerous to denounce the latter than the former. Admitting the fact, is the degree of danger attending the discharge of a duty the measure of its obligation? Must a religious teacher, in explaining the way of salvation, keep back the truth—one of the most effectual methods of teaching falsehood—because he may incur danger by inculcating it? We do not, however, believe the fact. We believe that the apostles might have taught that slaveholding is a sin, with far less danger than that which they incurred by teaching that what the heathen sacrificed they sacrificed to devils. We need not conceive of their adopting the system of agitation, and the whole 'moral machinery' of modern times. They adopted no such course with regard to idolatry. But they might doubtless, with comparative safety, have told slaveholders that it was their duty to emancipate their slaves. They could as well have enjoined them to set their servants free, as to command them to render to them what is just and equal. Many men, without any great exhibition of courage, have taught and do still teach the moral evil of slaveholding in the midst of slaveholders. And even now, any man who, in a meek, sincere, and benevolent spirit, should say to southern planters, that the relation they sustain to their slaves is contrary to the will of God, and incompatible with their own salvation, would meet with no greater disturbance than the Quakers have experienced in making their annual testimony against slavery.

"The course ascribed to the apostles is not only inconsistent with fidelity, and contrary to their uniform practice, but it is moreover opposed to the conduct of the messengers of God in all ages. The ancient prophets never failed to reprove the people for their sins, and to exhort them to repentance, no matter how strong the attachment of their hearers to their iniquity, or how powerful the interests leagued in its support. Elijah did not fail to denounce the worship of Baal, though Ahab and Jezebel were determined to kill the prophets of God; nor did John the Baptist fail to tell Herod that it was not lawful for him to have his brother's wife."

(5.) Another consideration relied on is, that the apostles nowhere exhort masters to liberate their slaves; they speak of the relation as one of comparatively little account, and as one attended with few disadvantages. Thus the Princeton Reviewer says,

"The subject is hardly alluded to by Christ in any of his personal instructions. The apostles refer to it, not to pronounce upon it as a question of morals, but to prescribe the relative duties of masters and slaves. They caution those slaves who have believing or Christian masters, not to despise them because they were on a perfect religious equality with them, but to consider the fact that their masters were their brethren, as an additional reason for obedience. It is remarkable that there is not even an exhortation to masters to liberate their slaves, much less is it urged as an imperative and immediate duty. They are commanded to be kind, merciful, and just; and to remember that they have a Master in heaven. *Paul represents this relation as of comparatively little account.* 'Let every man abide in the same calling wherein he was called. Art thou called being a servant, (or slave,) care not for it; though, should the opportunity of freedom be presented, embrace it. These external relations, however, *are of little importance,* for every Christian is a freeman in the highest and best sense of the word, and at the same time is under the strongest bonds to Christ.' 1 Cor. vii. 20—22."

If the relation is a mild one, and on the whole not very undesirable, and if masters are never exhorted to disturb it by any act of voluntary emancipation, it seems to be inferred that the New Testament is not inimical to it, and that it is an institution which it is desirable to perpetuate for the best interests of society.

(6.) As a final argument to show that the apostles were not hostile to slavery, and that the institution is not opposed by Christianity, an appeal is made to the case of Onesimus, referred to in the epistle to Philemon. The argument relied on is, that Onesimus was a slave; that he had escaped from his master, and was a *runaway;* that he was converted under Paul; that he sent him back without any wish or concurrence on the part of Onesimus, and with a view that he might remain as a slave with Philemon. It is *inferred* from these supposed facts, (1.) That Paul regarded the relation as proper and desirable. (2.) That it is wrong for a slave to leave his master without his consent. (3.) That the effect of conversion should be to make a runaway slave willing to return to a state of bondage. (4.) That it is a duty to send back a runaway slave to his master; and, (5.) That the act of Paul in restoring Onesimus to his master, fairly proves that he supposed the relation was to be perpetual.*

It is on such arguments as these that those who maintain that slavery is not inconsistent with Christianity, rely. It is of importance, therefore, to examine the force of this reasoning, and to inquire whether the Saviour and his apostles meant to represent slavery as a desirable system for the best interests of society; as a system which is congenial with the gospel which they sought to propagate; as one which the gospel would serve to extend, and as so destitute

---

* Compare Dr. Fuller's Letters to Dr. Wayland, p. 195.

of the elements of evil, that they would desire to see it perpetuated in connection with the Christian religion. I shall,
therefore, examine these points at some length, with a view
to ascertain the exact relation of Christianity to slavery, and
particularly to the system as it exists in our own country. If
Christianity would sustain and perpetuate that system, it may
be assumed that the institution is not evil; if it would not, it
is not a very forced conclusion that it is to be regarded as sinful and wrong.

I. THERE IS NO EVIDENCE THAT CHRIST HIMSELF EVER CAME IN CONTACT WITH SLAVERY.

The first inquiry which meets us here is, whether there is
evidence that Christ himself ever came in contact with slavery.
If he did, and regarded it as wrong, in the same sense as hy-
pocrisy and sensuality are wrong, it is to be presumed that he
would have denounced it in the same way as he did those
things; and if he did *not* express his disapprobation of it, it
seems to be a fair inference that he did not regard it as wrong.
If, however, he never came in contact with it, nothing can be
safely argued in favour of it from his silence, any more than
it can be inferred that he was favourable to the sports of the
amphitheatre at Rome, or to the orgies which were celebrated
in honour of Bacchus, or to the claims to inspiration of the
oracles of Dodona or Delphi. We can only argue in respect
to his sentiments on such points, from the *principles* which he
laid down of a general character, or from the incidental
remarks which he made when discoursing on other topics.

In endeavouring, then, to ascertain the views of the Saviour
on this subject, I would make the following remarks :—

(1.) There is no conclusive evidence that he ever came in
contact with slavery at all. If the train of argument which
has been pursued in regard to the tendency of the Mosaic institutions is well-founded, there is every probability that
slavery had ceased in the Hebrew commonwealth long before
the advent of the Saviour. There is no proof which I have

seen referred to from any contemporary writer, that it existed
in Judea in his time at all; and there is no evidence from the
New Testament that he ever came in contact with it. The
only instance that is ever referred to of the kind, and the only
one that can be, is the case of the Roman centurion who had
a servant sick at Capernaum. Matt. viii. 5, seq. But this
case does not prove the point for which it is adduced; for (*a*)
the *terms* which are used as descriptive of the case, do not
prove it. The centurion himself applies to the sick servant
at home the term ὁ παις—*pais*, (Matt. viii. 5,) which is a word
much too general to demonstrate that he was a slave. It was
rarely applied to a slave at all, and when it was, it was only as
the term *boy* now is in the slaveholding states of this Union.
The term which the centurion uses in ver. 9, implying
that he had *servants* under him, also, does not demonstrate
that they were slaves: "And I say to my servant—τῷ δούλῳ
—do this, and he doeth it." This word, as has been shown,
(Ch. III.) is also too general to make it certain that he refers to
slaves. If it should be said that it is *probable* that this sick
man was a slave, still it is obvious to reply, that what is necessary to the argument derived from the fact that the Saviour
did not express disapprobation of the system, is, *that he
actually came in contact with a case,* and did not condemn it.
Even then it might be questioned whether his not expressing
a sentence of condemnation on the system could be construed
as an argument that he did not disapprove of it; but in order
that the argument should have any force, it is necessary to
know that he actually encountered slavery. (*b*) It may be
urged further, that it is by no means certain that a Roman
officer, such as the centurion was, would have a *slave* to accompany him. That he would have a servant of some kind
is not improbable, for it is still common in the East for officers
in an army, and even for the ordinary cavalry, to have servants to attend them, to wait upon them, and to take care of
their horses. But these are not commonly *slaves*. They are
persons in the employ of the government, assigning such

persons to the use of the army, to be paid by the government.
(*c*) Considering the facilities for escaping in passing through
foreign countries on a march, it is hardly probable that the
attendants on Roman officers would be slaves. At all events,
there is not the slightest *proof* that this man was a slave, and
if not, then there is not the slightest *proof* that the Saviour
ever came in contact with slavery at all, either in public or
in private life. The only evidence which I have seen that
there were any slaves in Palestine about the time of the
Saviour, is the statement of Josephus, (Hist. 19,) that "King
Agrippa exhibited at one time in Judea seven hundred pair of
gladiators." But (1.) There is no evidence that the Saviour
ever witnessed any such scene, nor is it probable that he did.
(2.) If his silence in such a case may be construed as a proof
that he did not disapprove of slavery, it may for the same
reason be construed as a proof that he did not disapprove of
gladiatorial exhibitions.

(2.) Nothing then can be inferred from the silence of the
Saviour on this subject. It was by no means his method to
go out of his way to denounce sins which prevailed in other
parts of the earth, however great they might be, or however
much it may be inferred that he disapproved of them. He condemned the sins of his own age and country as he encountered
them, and laid down great principles of truth which would
be of easy application to all others as his gospel should spread.
But to infer that he approved of every thing on which he
maintained silence, or which he did not expressly condemn,
would be a violation of all the principles by which we judge
of a religious teacher or philosopher, and would be doing
him manifest injustice. Are we to infer that he approved of
the sports in the amphitheatre at Rome ; of the conflicts of
gladiators, and the bloody struggles between captives in war
and wild beasts ? Are we to infer that he approved of the
scenes of the Roman Saturnalia, or the modes of worship on
the Acropolis at Corinth, because he was silent in regard to
them ? To hold him to this, would be a violation of every

rule of right; yet they in fact do no less, who infer that, because he did not denounce slavery, *therefore* he was not unfavourable to the system.

(3.) He never uttered a word which can be construed *in favour* of slavery. It is remarkable that the advocates of the system never appeal to any thing that fell from his lips in his instructions; to any principle or doctrine that he laid down in his religion, in defence of the institution. If there were nothing else in the world than the discourses of Jesus Christ to form the opinions and direct the conduct of men, no one would ever dream that such a system was desirable or proper. In his discourses, there is not a sentiment which can be tortured by any ingenuity of exegesis into an approval of the system. No one, under the fair influence of the doctrines which he laid down, ever yet made a man a slave; no one ever supposed that he could justify such an act by any thing that the Saviour ever did or taught. Not even a *hint* can be found in all that he said, on which a man who was about to embark in the slave trade, or who designed to raise slaves for sale, or who meant to purchase a slave, or who meant to keep one already in his possession, could rely to sanction his course. Never were any discourses or writings in the world more entirely free from any thing which would lend such a sanction, than the recorded discourses of the Redeemer.

(4.) While this was true—true that he in no way intermeddled with the system any more than he did with the regulations of the Roman Coliseum, or the laws respecting the harem in a Persian court, it is also true that he laid down principles which are entirely inconsistent with slavery, and which would tend to its rapid abolition. In another part of this argument from the New Testament, I shall have occasion to inquire into the effect of Christianity on the abolition of slavery. At present, all that it is necessary to observe is, that there are fundamental principles laid down by the Saviour which are opposed to the whole system of slavery, and which it is necessary constantly to violate in order to its perpetuity. Among those principles are the following :—

(*a*) The doctrine that all the race are on a level before God ; that all are redeemed by the same blood ; that all are equally the heirs of life ; that all are moral and responsible beings ; that all are descended from the same parent. The instructions of the Saviour do not go against all distinctions in life. They recognise the relations of father and son ; of ruler and subject ; of the rich and poor, as those which are not inconsistent with his grand fundamental position—that in the matter of redemption all men are on a level. In these relations all are to be recognised as men : as capable of redemption ; as free moral agents ; and no one by nature is supposed to have any priority or superiority over the other. But slavery *always* supposes that there is a distinction among men in these respects—a distinction *different* from that which arises from regarding them as sustaining the relation of parent and child ; as qualified to govern or not, and as fitted for different occupations of life where all may be free. It is supposed to be such a distinction in nature as to make it proper that one should be a master and the other a slave ; that one should be regarded as a freeman, and the other ' a chattel and a thing ;' that one should have a right to buy and sell, and that the other should be bought and sold. It is impossible, in the nature of things, that the advocate of slavery should regard *all* men as, in every respect, on a level in regard to redemption. There is inevitably, in his apprehension, some reason, in the nature of the case, just in proportion as there is any reason for the existence of slavery *at all*—*why the present master* SHOULD BE *the master, and the present slave* SHOULD BE *the slave ;*—why the *white man* should be the master, and why the *man of colour* should be the slave. Yet it is clear that this view of the matter is entirely at variance with the fundamental doctrine in the plan of redemption.

(*b*) Under the gospel, and in accordance with its principles, no relation was to exist, which would be inconsistent with the honest recognition of all who bore the Christian name and image as *brethren*. They were to be regarded as Christian brethren in all respects, and there was to be nothing in their condition which would make the application of the term to any and to all improper. Matth. xxiii. 8. "One is your master—καθηγητής: *and all ye are brethren—*πάντες δὲ ὑμεῖς ἀδελφοί ἐστε.* 'Ye *all:'*—that is, 'all who profess to be my followers—all who compose the true church, no matter what their rank, colour, condition, age. There is to be nothing in your condition or relations which shall be inconsistent with the fair and honest application of the word *brethren—*ἀδελφοί. Any thing which would *not* allow that, would be a violation of the principles of my religion.' This is the uniform language of the New Testament. Now, the employment of this term is entirely appropriate in *all* those relations where freedom is enjoyed. There is nothing to hinder its *fair* use when the rich address the poor, or princes their subjects, or preachers their people, or men of years and experience those who are just entering on life. But there *is* much to prevent its fair use when applied by masters to their slaves, *or still more by slaves to their masters*. It *cannot* be used except it be constructively and metaphorically, by those who regard their slaves as chattels and as property, and who have the constant feeling that they are at liberty to sell them at any moment, as they do their cattle. To apply the term *brethren* to those who are *slaves*, is a departure from all just use of language, and is a mockery of the feelings which it is condescendingly designed to soothe. Does it *ever* occur that slaves address their masters in this manner; and would they be allowed to do so?

---

* It is remarkable that even here the Saviour is careful not to employ a term which would even *suggest* the relation of *master and slave*. He uses the term καθηγητής—*a leader, conductor* (Anführer, Anleiter, *Passow:*) a leader, guide, teacher, master, (*Robinson, Lex.*), and not the term expressive of the relation of *master*, in contradistinction from a servant or slave—δεσπότης.—1 Tim. vi. 1, 2; Titus ii. 9; 1 Pet. ii. 18.

(c) One of the great and leading principles of the religion of the Saviour is expressed in the golden rule: "Whatsoever ye would that men should do to you, do ye even so to them; for this is the law and the prophets." Matt. vii. **12.** This rule he evidently designed should be incorporated into his religion as essential to the system, and it is manifest that nothing inconsistent with the fair application of it can be in accordance with the spirit of Christianity. Yet its bearing on slavery is obvious. Its influence in securing the emancipation of all those now held in bondage, if fairly applied, would be certain and inevitable. (1) No one, under the influence of this rule, ever made a man a slave. No one ever felt that in tearing him away from his home, in separating him from country and friends, in exposing him to sale, and in dooming him to perpetual bondage for no other crime than that of being

"Guilty of a skin not coloured like his own,"

he was doing that which he would wish another man to do to him. (2.) No one in exacting from another unrequited toil, or feeding him on coarse fare, or clothing him with coarse raiment, far inferior to what he himself possesses, or in depriving him of the privileges of reading the Bible, or of rising in political life, or of being eligible to office, ever did that which he would wish others to do to him. (3.) No one ever subjected a fellow-being to the operation of the laws of servitude, as they exist in this country, by the fair operation of this rule. He would not wish any one to subject him or his children to the operation of these laws. (4.) It may be added, that few or none, under the fair operation of this rule, would ever continue to hold another in slavery. Those cases must be exceedingly rare on the earth, where a man would desire that he himself should be in the condition of his slave, or that, *if* he were already a slave, the bonds of servitude should be riveted perpetually on him. Freedom is sweet to man; and it cannot be doubted that if a man were in all circumstances to act towards those under him, as *he* would desire to be treated if in their places, the bonds of servitude would soon be loosed.

If these principles are correct, then it is clear that neither the example nor the silence of the Saviour can never be referred to as sanctioning slavery.   It is one of the plainest of all propositions, that if we had had *only* his instructions and his example to guide us in this matter, slavery would never have been originated ; and that where it *had* before existed, it would soon cease.   The application of these principles to the system in this country, as we shall see in another part of the argument, would inevitably abolish the system.

II. The manner in which the Apostles treated the subject of Slavery.

§ 1. *They found it in existence when they organized churches out of the limits of Judea.*

We have seen above, that there is no evidence that when the Saviour appeared, slavery in any form existed in Judea, and consequently there is no proof that he ever encountered it. We have also seen that his silence on the subject cannot be construed as any evidence that he did not disapprove of the system, and did not design that the principles of his religion should abolish it, wherever it might be found.   It is of great importance, therefore, to inquire how his apostles treated the system when they encountered it, and whether the manner in which they met it can be construed as an evidence that *they* regarded it as a good institution, and as one which it was desirable to perpetuate in the world.

There can be no doubt that slavery existed in the countries to which they went to preach the gospel, and that they often encountered it, and were called to act in view of it in organizing churches.   There are evidences of this, as we shall see, in their epistles ; and from what is known of the condition of the Roman empire at that period, it cannot be doubted 'hat

they came in contact with it, and that in preaching the gospel
they would be called to address those who sustained the relation of master and slave.

It is unnecessary to enter into a proof that slavery abounded
in the Roman empire, or that the conditions of servitude were
very severe and oppressive.   This is conceded on all hands.
If any one desires to see it *demonstrated* beyond the possibility of a doubt, he may consult an article by Professor B. B.
Edwards, in the American Biblical Repository for October,
1835, pp. 411—436.   The purpose of my argument does not
require me to go into an examination of this point, in detail.
All that the argument does require, whatever conclusion we
may reach as to the manner in which the apostles treated the
subject, is, the admission of the fact that slavery everywhere abounded ; that it existed in forms of great severity
and cruelty ; that it involved all the essential claims which are
now made by masters to the services or persons of slaves ;
that it was protected by civil laws ; that the master had the
right of transferring his slaves by sale, donation, or testament ; that in general he had every right which was supposed
to be necessary to perpetuate the system ; and that it was
impossible that the early preachers of Christianity should not
encounter this system, and be constrained to adopt some principles in regard to the proper treatment of it.

In order to allow to those who suppose that slavery is sanctioned by the New Testament, and that the conduct of the
apostles may be appealed to in justification of the system as
it exists in this country, all the advantage in the argument
which can be derived from the actual state of slavery as they
found it, it seems necessary, however, to advert to the *form*
in which slavery was found when they preached the gospel.
It is proper to concede that the state of things was such that
they *must* have encountered it, and that it then had all the
features of cruelty, oppression, and wrong which can ever
exist to make it repellant to any of the feelings of humanity,
or revolting to the principles of a Christian.   It is fair that

the advocate of the system should have all the advantage which can be derived from the fact that the apostles found it in its most odious forms, and in such circumstances as to make it proper that they should regard and treat it as an evil, if Christianity regards it as such at all. It is proper that it should be seen that their method of treating it was not prompted by the fact that it was of so mild a type as to be scarcely worthy of their attention. It is to be admitted that if there can be wrongs in slavery anywhere which should rouse the spirit of a Christian man, they existed to as great an extent in the countries where the apostles propagated the gospel; that if the system as it exists in our own land is contrary to the spirit of Christianity, the system as they found it was no less contrary to it; that if now, in any of its forms and influences, and in any of the means adopted to perpetuate it, it is opposed to the gospel, it was no less so then; that if it can be regarded now as desirable that the system should come to an end, it was no less desirable then; and that if Christians now should labour to bring it to a termination, it was no less desirable and proper that they should do it then. This, it seems to me, is all that the advocate of slavery can ask to have conceded on this point.

The features of slavery in the Roman empire, so far as it is necessary to refer to them to illustrate this point, were summarily these :—

1. Slavery existed generally throughout the Roman empire, and the number of slaves was very great. "Some rich individuals possessed ten thousand, and some as many as twenty thousand of their fellow-creatures," who were held as slaves.* In Italy, it was computed that there were three slaves to one freeman, and that in this part of the empire alone their number amounted to more than twenty millions. The number, therefore, throughout the Roman empire must have been immensely great; and if so, it is impossible that the apostles

---

* Professor B. B. Edwards.

should not have encountered it. Gibbon* says "that the slaves were at least equal in number to the free inhabitants of the Roman world. The total amount of this imperfect calculation [of the inhabitants of the Roman empire] would rise to about one hundred and twenty millions." Of course, according to this, the number of slaves could not have been less than sixty millions in the Roman empire, at about the time when the apostles went forth to preach the gospel. Respecting the number held by individuals, Gibbon remarks, (p. 26,) that "it was discovered on a very melancholy occasion, that four hundred slaves were maintained in a single palace of Rome. The same number of four hundred belonged to an estate, which an African widow, of very private condition, resigned to her son, while she reserved to herself a much larger share of her property. A freedman, under the reign of Augustus, though his fortune had suffered great losses in the civil wars, left behind him three thousand six hundred yoke of oxen, two hundred and fifty thousand head of smaller cattle, and, what was almost included in the description of cattle, four thousand one hundred and sixteen slaves." "Scaurus possessed above four thousand domestic, and as many rural slaves. In the reign of Augustus, a freedman, who had sustained great losses during the civil wars, left four thousand one hundred and sixteen slaves, besides other property." "Slaves always composed a great part of the movable property of individuals, and formed a chief article of ladies' dowries." "It was fashionable to go abroad attended by a large number of slaves. Horace† says, "habebat sæpe ducentos, sæpe decem servos." Besides the domestic and agricultural slaves, there were the gladiators, who were chiefly slaves, and who were extremely numerous at different periods. Julius Cæsar exhibited at one time three hundred and twenty pairs. Trajan exhibited them for one hundred and twenty-three days, in the course

---

* Dec. and Fall, vol. i. p. 27, ed. New York, 1829.
† Lib. 1, Sat. iii. v. 11.

of which ten thousand gladiators fought. Chrysostom says, that under Theodosius the Great, and Arcadius, some persons had two or three thousand slaves. From the time of Augustus, we may allow three slaves to one freeman; we shall thus have a free population in Italy of 6,944,000, and of slaves 20,832,000; total, 27,776,000.*

(2.) The methods in which men became slaves, in the Roman empire, were the following:—

(*a*) By war. This was almost a universal custom. In general, prisoners of war were sold as soon as possible after their captivity. " On the descent of the Romans upon Africa in the first Punic war, twenty thousand prisoners were taken. On the great victory of Marius and Catullus over the Cimbri, sixty thousand were captured. When Pindenissas was taken by Cicero, the inhabitants were sold for more than £100,000. Augustus, having overcome the Salassi, sold as slaves thirty-four thousand, of whom eight thousand were capable of bearing arms. Cæsar, in his Gallic wars, according to the moderate estimate of Velleius Paterculus, took more than four hundred thousand prisoners."

(*b*) Slaves were acquired by commerce. " The slave-trade in Africa is as old as history reaches back. Among the ruling nations of the North coast,—the Egyptians, Cyrenians, and Carthagenians,—slavery was not only established, but they imported whole armies of slaves, partly for home use, and partly, at least by the Carthagenians, to be shipped for foreign markets. They were chiefly drawn from the interior, where kidnapping was just as much carried on then as now. Black male and female slaves were even an article of luxury, not only among the above-named nations, but in Greece and Italy. For the building of the public works at Rome, vast numbers of slaves were procured. In raising such a structure as the Mausoleum of Adrian, thousands of wretched men, torn from their own firesides, were toiled unto death. For a long period,

---

* Bibl. Repos. as above, pp. 413, 414.

great numbers of slaves were drawn from Asia Minor, particularly from Phrygia and Cappadocia.   *Slave* and *Phrygian*
became almost convertible terms.   So great a multitude were
carried into slavery, that but few towns were planted; the
country was rather a pasturage for flocks.   In most countries
it was common for parents to sell their children into slavery.
Man-stealing was, at all times, a very common crime among
the ancients."   The following places are mentioned either as
emporia for slaves, or countries from which they were procured:—Delos, Phrygia, and Cappadocia; Panticapaeum,
Dioscurias, and Phanagoria on the Euxine or Black Sea;
Alexandria and Cadiz; Corsica, Sardinia, and Britain; Africa
and Thrace; and, indeed, almost every part of the world furnished slaves for the Roman people.*

(*c*) Freeborn Romans might be reduced to slavery by law.
Criminals doomed to certain ignominious punishments, were,
by the effect of their sentence, deprived of citizenship, and
reduced to servitude. Those who did not give in their names
for enrolment in the militia, were beaten, and sold into slavery
beyond the Tiber. Those who did not make proper returns
to the Censor, were liable to be visited with the same punishment. An indigent thief was adjudged as a slave to the injured
party. Children that were exposed by their parents, and left
to perish, became, by law, the slaves of any person who chose
to take them up and support them. Freedmen, if guilty of
ingratitude towards their former masters, might be again reduced to slavery.

(*d*) Persons became slaves by birth. The Roman law on
this subject was, that the condition of the child depended on
that of the mother alone—*partus sequitur ventrem.* "The
father of a natural child, by his bond-woman, was the master
of his offspring, as much as any other of his slaves."

(3.) In regard to the *condition* of slaves under the Roman

---

* Comp. Bib. Repos. as above, pp. 416, 417.

laws as they existed in the time of the propagation of Christianity, it may be remarked,

(a) That the master had the power of life and death over the slave. Thus the Codex Justinian says, "All slaves are in the power of their masters, which power is derived from the law of nations; for it is equally observable among all nations, that masters have had the power of life and death over their slaves."

Prof. W. A. Becker, of Leipsic, in an article translated for the Bibliotheca Sacra, (vol. ii. p. 571,) says, "With the Romans, a slave passed indeed for a human being, but one without any personal rights; in the legal sense he had no *caput*, no legal rights, no legal capacity. The master had the entire right of property in the slave, and could do just as he pleased with his person and life, his powers and his earnings.

"In regard to the power of life and death, it was unlimited. The master could use the slave for any purpose that suited his own pleasure. He could punish him, put him to pain and torture, and, free from all obligation to give account of his actions, could put him to death in any way that pleased him. This right of unlimited dominion continued down to a late time, and certainly through the whole period of the republic, and it can be safely assumed that it was in less actual exercise in the earlier than in the later periods of Roman history. The arbitrary exercise of this power, which had been previously subject only to censorial animadversion, was gradually limited, at first by the operation of the Lex Petronia, which forbade that any one should give up his slave arbitrarily, (*sine judice,*) to fight with wild beasts, (*ad bestias depugnandas ;*) perhaps even in the time of Augustus, though the story of the cruelty of Vedius Pollio* seems to prove, that up to that time there was no legal restriction on the right of the master." The whole article of Prof. Becker may be consulted with advantage.

---

* Dio Cas. liv. Seneca de Irâ, iii. 40.

(*b*) They were permitted to hold no property as their own, whatever they acquired being regarded as the property of their masters. Thus the Codex Just. says, "Whatever is acquired by the slave, is acquired for the master." "Whatever our slaves have at any time acquired, whether by delivery, stipulation, donation, bequest, or any other means, the same is reputed to be acquired by ourselves, for he who is a slave can have no property. And if a slave is instituted an heir, he cannot otherwise take upon himself the inheritance, than at the command of the master."

(*c*) Slaves were not permitted to marry. "Servile relations are an impediment to matrimony." The only sexual connection was a *contubernium*, a mere living together, without any of the legitimate rights of marriage.*

(*d*) They were not allowed to give testimony. "Those persons are allowed to be good witnesses, who are themselves legally capable of taking by testament; but yet no woman, *slave*, interdicted prodigal, no person under puberty, &c., can be admitted a witness to a testament."

(*e*) They were exposed to the most unrelenting barbarity, being wholly unprotected by law, and left entirely in the power of their owners. They were liable to every kind of torture; and cruel masters sometimes kept on their estates tormentors by profession, for the purpose of punishing their slaves. Burning alive was sometimes resorted to, and crucifixion was frequently made the fate of a slave for trifling misconduct, or from mere caprice. The truth was, that slaves were considered in no other light than as representatives of so much value, and were in all cases liable to be disposed of as any other property was, with no respect whatever to their being moral and intellectual beings. Hence, it is not wonderful that they should have been slain as food for fishes, or that the question should have arisen whether, in a storm, a man should sacrifice a horse, or a less valuable slave.†

---

* See Bibliotheca Sacra, vol. ii. p. 572.

† Comp. Wayland's Letters on Slavery, pp. 86, 87.

Among the modes of punishment enumerated by Professor Edwards as practised on slaves, were the following :—" The lash and rod were in frequent use.   If a slave spoke or coughed at a forbidden time, he was flogged by a very severe master. The toilet of a lady of fashion was a terrible ordeal for a slave. A stray curl was an inexorable offence, and the slave's back was punished for the faults of the mirror.   Burning alive is mentioned as a punishment in the Pandects and elsewhere. Tertullian says it was first used for slaves alone.   Vine saplings, as instruments of punishment, were the least dishonourable ; next to them rods—*fustes* or *virgæ*, scourges—*flagella* or *flagra*, sometimes loaded with lead—*plumbata*.   Chain scourges were used, with weights at the end, all of bronze or tin.   The *equuleus* was a terrible instrument of torture.   Dislocation was one of its effects.   There were also the *fidiculæ*— lyre strings, the *ungula* and *forceps*, &c.   A slave taken among soldiers was cast from the Capitoline rock, having been first manumitted that he might be worthy of that punishment. Cruel masters sometimes hired torturers by profession, or had such in their establishments, to assist them in punishing their slaves, or in extorting confessions from them.   The noses, ears, teeth, or even eyes were in great danger from an enraged master.   Crucifixion was frequently made the fate of a wretched slave, for trifling conduct, or for mere caprice."   " Hortensius cared less for the health of his slaves, than for that of his fish. It was a question put for ingenious disputation, whether, in order to lighten a vessel in a storm, one should sacrifice a valuable horse, or a worthless slave."

It is to be conceded, therefore, that slavery existed in its most revolting forms in the time of the apostles, and that they often came in contact with it, in preaching the gospel, and in organizing churches.   It is to be admitted that it existed under laws as severe and arbitrary ; laws which gave to the master as absolute power over the slave, and which subjected him to as great oppression and wrong, as the laws in the slave states of this Union.   Whatever may follow from this, either for or against slavery as it now exists, the fact cannot be denied, and that fact is not to be called in question in our reasonings on the subject.

It has recently been made a question whether slavery existed in those parts of the Roman empire where the apostles founded churches, and consequently whether they ever in fact came in contact with it. Indeed, it has been maintained by some of the friends of the anti-slavery cause, that there is no reason to think that it existed in Asia Minor in the time of the apostles, and that, consequently, when, in addressing 'masters and servants' in the Epistles to the Ephesians, to the Colossians, and in the first Epistle of Peter, there is no evidence that *slaves* were intended, but that the reference is to a condition of voluntary service. If this could be made out; if it could be demonstrated that there was no slavery in those places to which those epistles were addressed, it would be indeed fair to suppose that the terms used by the apostles did not relate to slavery, and that it could not be proved from those epistles that the apostles ever admitted the masters of slaves to the communion of the church. But even then the whole difficulty would not be met, for in the epistles to Timothy, (1 Epis. vi. 1—3,) and to Titus, (ii. 9, 10,) there is a reference to the same relation, and those epistles have no special reference to Asia Minor, but contain general directions to those who were ministers of the gospel in the church at large.

But, it seems to me, that it is wholly improbable that there were no slaves in Asia Minor, and, at all events, it cannot be demonstrated that there were none ; and if this is so, then it is to be admitted that the passages in those epistles refer to those who sustained the relation of master and slave—and that whatever advantage can be derived from that fact, if any, by the advocates of slavery, the *fact* is to be conceded. The reasons for this are briefly these : (1.) It is highly improbable that when slavery prevailed so extensively throughout the Roman empire, it should not have existed in Asia Minor. There were no influences at work there, as in Palestine ; no institutions of religion ; no principles of liberty to prevent it. (2.) We have seen above that large numbers of Phrygians and Cappadocians were taken as slaves to Rome, and it is a rare thing, perhaps a thing that never has occurred, that slavery did not prevail in a country which furnished slaves for another country. The very fact that Phrygia and Cappadocia were understood to be places from which slaves could be obtained for the capital, would make it necessary to keep them for the market. (3.) There is direct evidence which makes it more than probable that slavery had an existence in the provinces of Asia Minor. It undoubtedly existed all around it, and in such a way that it would naturally exist there also. Thus Timæus asserts that, in early times, before Athens had obtained possession of the commerce of the seas, Corinth had four hundred and sixty thousand slaves. In Sparta, slaves abounded, and the name *Helot* was synonymous with that of *slave*. In Attica there were about eighty thousand citizens, and four hundred thousand slaves. After the fall of Corinth, the island of Delos rose into importance as a commercial place, and especially as a mart for slaves. The slave-trade there was so brisk that the port became proverbial for the traffic, and was capable, says Strabo, of importing and re-exporting ten thousand slaves in a single day.* As a matter of fact it is asserted that " there were six thousand slaves which belonged to the temple of a goddess in Cappadocia." Hence the words of Horace, " Mancipiis locuples, eget æris Cappadocum rex."† These facts make it morally certain that slavery must have existed in Asia Minor, and that it undoubtedly existed at Ephesus and Colosse. It should be added, (4.) That the most natural and obvious interpretations of the passages in those epistles, is to refer them to the relation of master and slave. This will be shown in the sequel. I am persuaded that no-

---

* See an article in the Biblical Repository on " Slavery in Ancient Greece," by Professor B. B. Edwards, vol. v. pp. 138, seq.

† See Biblical Repository, vol. v. p. 416.

thing can be gained to the cause of anti-slavery by attempting to deny that the apostles found slavery in existence in the regions where they founded churches, and that those sustaining the relation of master and slave were admitted to the churches if they gave real evidence of regeneration, and were regarded by the apostles as entitled to the common participation of the privileges of Christianity. If the argument from the Scriptures against slavery cannot be sustained without admitting that, I do not see that it can be sustained at all.

§ 2. *The Apostles did not openly denounce Slavery as an evil, or require that those who were held in bondage should be at once emancipated.*

In inquiring into the manner in which the apostles treated the subject of slavery, it is clear that they did not openly and everywhere denounce it as an evil; that they did not make immediate and direct war upon it; that they did not declare that a slaveholder could in no possible circumstances be a Christian; that they did not demand the emancipation of slaves as an indispensable condition of admission to the church; that they did not forbid all fellowship with those who held slaves, or require others wholly to separate from them; and that they did not encourage efforts to promote insurrection among the slaves themselves. These things seem to me to lie on the face of the New Testament, and whatever argument they may furnish to the advocates of slavery, or whatever difficulty they may present to the enemies of slavery in disposing of these facts, it seems plain that the facts themselves cannot be denied.

More particularly, in reference to this point, the following things must be regarded as indisputable :—

1. That slaveholders were admitted by the apostles to the Christian church, and were not subjected to immediate discipline for holding slaves; in other words, that where those were converted who held slaves, as probably many were, it

was not required of them in all cases to emancipate their slaves in order that they should become members of the church. This is clear, because (*a*) it is undeniable that they preached to many who were slaveholders; (*b*) there is no direct evidence that they required them to emancipate their slaves in order to their being admitted to the church; (*c*) they addressed those to whom their epistles were directed as in fact still sustaining this relation, though they were members of the church. Eph. vi. 9; Col. iv. 1; 1 Tim. vi. 2, and Titus ii. 9, 10. The passage in 1 Tim. vi. 2, makes this so clear, it seems to me, that it cannot be denied by any one who will candidly and carefully examine the direction of the apostle: "And they that have *believing masters*, let them not despise them, because they are brethren; but rather do them service, because they are *faithful and beloved.*" The same thing is taught with equal clearness in 1 Cor. xii. 13: "For by one spirit are we all baptized into one body, whether we be Jews or Gentiles; whether we be *bond or free.*" Here, it is evident, that as there were in the church those who had been Jews, and those who were of Gentile origin, so there were those who were properly described by the word 'bond'—δοῦλοι—and those who were described by the word 'free'—ἐλεύθεροι. It is true, that the latter term does not necessarily prove that they were *masters* or *owners* of slaves, still the use of the term 'bond and free' in the same connection would most naturally suggest that. I do not think that an argument could be based on the mere *words* used here, to prove that they were slaveholders; but in a community where slavery abounded—for example, like that in South Carolina or Georgia, the phrase, 'the bond and the free,' used in any connection, would most naturally be understood as referring to masters and slaves. The only question which can be raised on this point is, whether the term used in the passages just referred to, οἱ κύριοι, and the corresponding term used in 1 Pet. ii. 18, δεσπότης—and rendered in every instance *masters*, refers to *masters* in the sense of

proprietors of *slaves,* or masters in the sense of having those
in their employ who were voluntary or hired servants.   I
admit that so far as the *words* themselves are concerned, they
do not necessarily imply that those to whom they are applied
were masters in the former sense, for they would be used,
and were often used, to denote those who had those under
them who were voluntary servants, and would be the terms
which would be naturally employed to denote *such* a relation.
But there are three circumstances which seem to make it
clear that the words are used here as denoting those who
were the owners of slaves.   1. One is, that the condition
of those towards whom they are represented as sustaining
the relation of *masters,* was evidently that of *slavery.*   No
one, it seems to me, can doubt that they were slaves.
Their condition is not described as one of voluntary service, but as a much harder service—in which they were
‘ under the yoke ;’ in which they were subjected to great
hardships ; and from which it is said that it would be desirable to be delivered if possible.   The evidence of this will
appear in another part of the argument.   But if this be so,
then it will follow that the terms used in addressing *masters*
were such as denote the owners of slaves.   2. A second
thing is, that considering the universal prevalence of slavery
where the gospel was preached, it is not probable that any
very considerable number would be found who were masters
and servants in the sense of a *voluntary* servitude on the
part of the latter.   The great mass of those who sustained
the relation of master and servant, were those among whom
the terms would denote *slavery,* and it is morally certain that
many of them would be brought under the power of the gospel.   In other words, it is absurd to suppose that the gospel
would be preached in so discriminating a manner that only
those would be converted who stood entirely aloof from slavery
—both as masters and servants.   But unless these terms are used
in that sense, there is no reference to the relation in the New
Testament, and nothing can be inferred about the views of

the apostles in the case, one way or the other. **3.** A third circumstance is, that this is the interpretation which would be put, and *is* put, on these expressions by the great mass of the readers of the New Testament—by plain Christians in all lands and times who have no theory to support :—one of the best of all evidences that the interpretation is correct.

Whether this fact would make it proper to treat slavery in the same manner now, is indeed quite another question, and one which it is not necessary to argue here. There are many things to be considered in reference to that before it would be legitimate to draw the conclusion, that *because* the apostles admitted slaveholders to the church in the state of things which existed in the world in their time, *therefore* it would be proper to do it in all circumstances, and at all periods of the world, and in all countries. It is quite conceivable at least that circumstances may so change, that what would be wise and expedient at one time would be in the highest degree unwise and inexpedient at another; and it is casting no imputation on the moral integrity of an apostle to suppose that, under the laws of the Roman empire, amidst institutions which had been sanctioned for ages, and in a state of things where they had no agency in making the laws, some things might have been tolerated which they would not have deemed it best to tolerate in a community like that existing now in the United States. Nay, it is conceivable that going as they did as missionaries among the heathen—poor, friendless, unknown, with no powerful protectors, there might have been arrangements admitted into the church which they would not have judged to be the best possible for all circumstances, or which they would regard as on the whole the most desirable. This certainly occurred in regard to some things ; it *may be* that it was so in regard to slavery. It might be, therefore, an unfair inference to conclude, that *because* the apostles admitted slaveholders to the communion, *therefore this should be contemplated as a permanent arrangement* in a well-organized Christian community, or that a Missionary Board

in this age should contemplate this in their missions among the
heathen.   The only *fair* inference from their conduct is, that
slavery, in all conceivable circumstances, is not to be regarded
as *a sin*.   Whether in any circumstances, however, it is, or
is not, is a legitimate subject of inquiry.   Whether this conduct on the part of the apostles was consistent with moral
honesty, and with a real hatred of slavery, will be the subject of subsequent consideration.

2. In like manner, the apostles did not deny that those who
were the holders of slaves might be true Christians.   This is
implied, indeed, in the fact that they were admitted into the
church, but there is more direct and independent proof of it.
Thus, in 1 Tim. vi. 2, they are addressed as such : "And
they [that is those servants who are under the yoke] that
have *believing masters*, let them not despise them, because
they are brethren."   Here, there are three terms employed
which imply that, though sustaining this relation, they were
regarded as real Christians.   The first is found in the phrase
'*believing masters*'—πιστοὺς δεσπότας—a phrase which would
be properly applied only to those who were true Christians.
Comp. Luke xix. 17 ; John xx. 27 ; Acts x. 45 ; xvi. 1, 15 ;
2 Cor. vi. 15 ; Gal. iii. 9 ; Eph. i. 1, *et al.*   The second
term is *brethren*—' let them not despise them because they
are *brethren*,'—a term also which denotes that they were regarded as fellow-Christians, or were to be regarded by the
'servants under the yoke' as *their* brethren.   The third term
or phrase is, '*faithful and beloved*,'—showing that they had,
and that they deserved, the confidence of those who were
Christians.   No one can doubt that there are many such
masters of slaves in our own country, who on account of their
Christian virtues are, and deserve to be, *greatly beloved*.
The exhortation to the servants that they should not despise
them because they were brethren, is based on the fact that there
might possibly spring up in their minds, unless they were
properly instructed, a want of respect for their masters if they
were regarded as ' brethren ;' or from the fact that the master

and the servant had embraced the same religion, and were to be regarded as in the most important respects on an equality. It would not be wholly unnatural that this truth should be so perverted by ill-designing persons as to make servants insubordinate and disrespectful; and it would be easy for such persons to allege, that as they were equal before God, the master had no right to control the servant, and the servant was under no obligation to obedience. While, therefore, the apostle admitted in the fullest sense that, *as* Christians, they were equal, and were to regard each other as brethren, he designed to guard the servant from the inference which some might derive from this fact, that *all* distinctions were at once to be broken down between them. This passage then proves that those who had owned slaves in accordance with the prevailing laws of the Roman empire, might be converted to the Christian faith, be admitted to the church, and be addressed as Christian brethren. It does not prove, however, that they might buy and sell slaves *after* they were converted; nor does it state how long they might *continue* to hold slaves and yet be regarded as true Christians; nor does it of necessity imply that they might contemplate this as a permanent arrangement, and contentedly hold their fellow-men in bondage with no purpose to restore them to freedom. Though they were regarded as truly converted, and though they are addressed as ' brethren,' yet nothing in this passage forbids the supposition that it might be a duty for them to cause this relation to cease as soon as it could be done. Whether that was so, must be determined by an independent inquiry.

3. In like manner, it is to be conceded that the apostles did not openly and publicly proclaim that slavery was an evil : that the Roman laws on this subject were wrong; that the whole institution was contrary to the gospel; that the system was replete with every form of monstrous error; and that it was the duty of every man who owned slaves at once to set them at liberty. They never used harsh and severe language

in regard to it ; never denounced civil government as wholly evil, because it upheld the institution ; never spoke of those who held slaves as thieves, or murderers, or infidels, or adulterers, or open abettors of vice and immorality.   The simple proof of this is to be found in an appeal to the New Testament.   Such violent denunciations and such severities of language are not to be found there ; and as it is to be presumed that in the Acts of the Apostles we have a *fair* representation of their usual manner of preaching, and a statement of the topics which they insisted on in their public discourses ; and as in their epistles we have a fair illustration, undoubtedly, of the usual method in which they addressed the churches, the inference is clear that such violent denunciations formed no part of *their* preaching.   It cannot fail, I think, to strike every one, that there is a most marked difference between the manner of the apostles in this respect, and the style of address of many who are the advocates of emancipation at the present day.   There is a severity of language which finds no countenance in the New Testament.   There are severe reproaches cast on the owners of slaves, which find no parallel in the Acts of the Apostles and in the Epistles.   There is a style of denouncing civil government, and ecclesiastical bodies, and churches, and ministers of the gospel, and private Christians, which is utterly foreign to the methods of discussing these questions employed by the apostles.   No calm and dispassionate inquirer, it seems to me, can doubt that in their methods of discussing this subject, many who are called ' abolitionists' have departed far from the example of the apostles ; and, indeed, I apprehend, not a few of them would openly avow it.   But it is *as* clear that their course has been wrong in itself, and has been adapted to defeat the very end in view.   Indeed, it would seem that if Satan had resolved to employ his highest ability in forming a scheme by which the fetters of the slave should be riveted for ever on the unhappy children of Africa in this land, he could not have devised a more effectual way than by producing just the mode of treating it which prevails at the South and the North. Never, it seems to me, has a good cause been more wretchedly managed in the main than the cause of anti-slavery in the United States. Any man will do a good service to his generation who can contribute to bring his fellow-citizens, by exhortation or example, to a more calm and kind way of meeting this great evil. The following remarks of the late Dr. Channing, in his work on Slavery, should command the assent of all thinking men.

" The abolitionists have done wrong, I believe ; nor is their wrong to be winked at, because done fanatically, or with good intentions ; for how much mischief may be wrought with good designs ! They have fallen into the common error of enthusiasts, that of exaggerating their object, of feeling as if no evil existed but that which they opposed, and as if no guilt could be compared with that of countenancing and upholding it. The tone of their newspapers, as far as I have seen them, has often been fierce, bitter, and abusive."—p. 133. " The abolitionists might have formed an association ; but it should have been an elective one. Men of strong principles, judiciousness, sobriety, should have been carefully sought as members. Much good might have been accomplished by the co-operation of such philanthropists. Instead of this, the abolitionists sent forth their orators, some of them transported with fiery zeal, to sound the alarm against slavery through the land, to gather together young and old, pupils from schools, females hardly arrived at years of discretion, the ignorant, the excitable, the impetuous, and to organize these into associations for the battle against oppression. Very unhappily, they preached their doctrine to the coloured people, and collected them into societies. To this mixed and excitable multitude, minute, heart-rending descriptions of slavery were given in the piercing tones of passion ; and slaveholders were held up as monsters of cruelty and crime."—p. 136. One great principle which we should lay down as immovably true, is, that if a good work cannot be carried on by the calm, self-controlled, benevolent spirit of Christianity, then the time for doing it has not come. God asks not the aid of our vices. He can over-rule them for good, but they are not the chosen instruments of human happiness."—p. 138.

4. It is to be admitted, that, in meeting this subject, the apostles gave instructions to those who sustained the relation of master and slave, respecting their duties while *in* that relation. The passages already referred to contemplate the performance of certain duties *in* that relation, or while that relation continued. Thus, in regard to the duty of *masters*, they are enjoined (Eph. vi. 9) to do "the same things" towards their servants which had been enjoined on them; to wit, to exhibit the same kindness, fidelity, and respect for the will of God. They were to "forbear threatening;" that is, they were to avoid a fretful and dissatisfied temper—a disposition to govern by terror rather than by love. They were (Col. iv. 1) to "give unto their servants that which is just and equal, remembering that they had also a master in heaven." These, I believe, are all the direct commands which are addressed to masters in the New Testament, but they imply that the relation did exist, and that there were important duties to be performed *in* that relation. There are undoubtedly many *general* precepts addressed to Christians, as such, which masters would be expected to apply to themselves to regulate their conduct in their treatment of their slaves, but these are all that directly bear on the subject, unless the case of Philemon, which will be examined at length in the sequel, be one. It is indeed quite remarkable, that, considering the fact that there were so many slaves in the countries where the gospel was preached, and the probability that not a few masters would be converted to the Christian religion, *so little* is addressed to them in the epistles, and that *so little* is said implying that the relation existed at all. Still, these passages *do* seem to make it certain that the relation existed among *some* who were members of the church, and

that the master owed important duties to his servant while sustaining that relation.

There are, however, more passages which refer to the duty of slaves, and which seem to imply that, as might be supposed, more slaves than masters were converted. Thus in Eph. vi. 5—8, they are instructed to be " obedient to their masters according to the flesh, with fear and trembling, in singleness of heart, as unto Christ, not with eye-service, as men-pleasers, but as the servants of Christ, doing the will of God from the heart; with good-will doing service, as to the Lord, and not to men." In Col. iii. 22—25, also, a direction very similar to this occurs. In 1 Tim. vi. 1, 2, it is said, "Let as many servants as are under the yoke count their own masters worthy of all honour, that the name of God and his doctrine be not blasphemed. And they that have believing masters, let them not despise them, because they are bre-thren; but rather do them service, because they are faithful and beloved, partakers of the benefit." In 1 Pet. ii. 18, it is said, " Servants, be subject to your masters with all fear; not only to the good and gentle, but also to the froward." It should be said respecting this passage, however, that it is less clear that it refers to slavery than the others which have been adduced. The Greek word is not that which is com-monly used, δοῦλοι, but οἰκέται, a term which means merely *do nestics*, *house-companions*, or *household servants*—from οἶκος, *nouse*. (See Ch. III.) They might have *become* such domestics, either by purchase or by voluntary agreement. The word would properly apply to *any* persons who were employed about a house as domestics, in whatever way they entered into that relation. It may be admitted as probable ' that most of those who were thus engaged were slaves, and that such are referred to here by the apostle. But that fact is not conveyed by the *word* which is used.

Whatever consequences may follow from these passages; whatever argument may be fairly deduced from them by the advocates of slavery, it cannot, it seems to me, be denied that the apostles addressed those to whom they sent their epistles, as sustaining the relation of master and slave, and gave to each instructions in regard to their duty *in* that relation. They doubtless meant to be understood as teaching that *in* that relation they owed important duties to each other. It is also to be admitted, that in giving these directions, they did not encourage among the slaves insurrection against their masters, or insubordination, or an attempt to escape by ' running away ;' and, in like manner, it is to be admitted, in whatever way it may be explained, that they did *not* enjoin on the masters the duty of emancipating their slaves immediately in all possible circumstances. This is to be admitted, because no instructions of that kind can be found in their writings, and it is not to be presumed that they gave one species of instruction to them in oral intercourse, and another in their letters.

The question now is, whether, these things being so, the conduct of the apostles shows that they regarded the system as consistent with the best good of society, and as one to be tolerated and perpetuated in the church; or, is their treatment of this matter consistent with the fact that they regarded the whole system as evil, and that they sincerely desired its extinction ? If they *did* so regard it; if it is indeed sinful and evil, can their conduct be vindicated as honest men ? If they regarded it as wrong, if they desired its extinction, if they meant that their labours as Christian men should abolish it, can their conduct in the points now referred to be shown to be consistent with common honesty, and with that openness and boldness in exposing sin which their character as apostles demanded ?

These are certainly very important questions, and on all sides they should be met with candour and fairness. They constitute the very gist of the whole inquiry respecting slavery, so far as the New Testament is concerned. The advocates and apologists for slavery, as a scriptural institution, would probably be willing to leave the argument here, as decisive in the case.   The argument on which they rely rests essentially on two grounds :—

I. That the apostles ' legislated for slavery,' as they did for the relations of husband and wife, and parents and children ; and,

II. That if they were in fact opposed to slavery, and regarded it as a moral evil, and yet pursued this course, it was not consistent with moral honesty, and involved one of the worst forms of what is now known as Jesuitism.   It is the duty of those who entertain the views which I am advocating, to meet these arguments.   They cannot be evaded without being fatal to the cause.   Let us then inquire whether these things are so.

I. The first argument from these admitted facts is, that the apostles *legislated* for slavery as they did for the relations of husbands and wives, and parents and chi'dren.   By this it is meant, that they made laws for those who sustained that relation in such a way that they must have intended that the relation should be permanent in the church ; and that they could not have done this if they had regarded the institution as sinful, and had not intended to lend their sanction to it.   It is said in support of this argument, that though polygamy prevailed, yet that they never legislated for that relation— that they never prescribed the duties of husbands in such a sense that it was supposed a man would have two wives— and that they never prescribed the duties of the wives of one man to each other, or the duties of a plurality of wives to the same husband.   It would be said further, perhaps, that they never prescribed the duties of pirates, and robbers, and thieves in the business to which they had devoted themselves, nor the duties of idolaters to their idols or their priests, nor the duty of men in any other sinful relation.   When John, as recorded in Luke iii. 12, seq., prescribed the duties of ' publicans' *in* the employment in which they were engaged, it is said, that it is

fair to suppose that he did not regard that employment as
necessarily sinful; when he prescribed the duties of soldiers,
it is implied that he did not regard the occupation of a soldier
as necessarily wrong.   If he had so regarded these employments, instead of prescribing the duties of these persons *in*
them, he would have directed them at once to leave them, and
to seek some honest and honourable occupation.   The argument is, that a relation in life with respect to which the Bible
has 'legislated,' and in reference to which it has prescribed
duties *in* that relation, may be permanently continued, consistently with the best interests of society and the world.

I need not say that this argument is greatly relied on by the
advocates for slavery and the apologists for it, and that it is
usually considered to be enough merely to *refer* to it, without
drawing it out to even the length in which I have stated it.
I have not intended to do injustice to it; and I have not, in fact,
found it so strongly expressed as is done in the language
which I have now used.

In reply to this argument, I would make the following remarks :—

(1.) It is not true that the apostles '*legislated*' for slavery,
or for its existence, in any proper signification of the word
legislate.   The word *legislate* means "to make or enact a
law or laws."*   Now, in what sense is it true that the apostles *made* or *enacted laws* respecting slavery?   Did they ever
take up the subject as a new thing; as a matter about which
arrangements were to be made; as an institution concerning
which they were to make laws to be of permanent observance
in the church?   Assuredly, they did none of these things.
They did not prescribe it as one of the regulations of the
church; they did not even utter sentiments formally permit-
ting it in the church; they did not attempt to make laws
respecting it at all.   It may be said that Moses legislated for
it; and that the Roman senate legislated for it; but there is

* Webster.

no intelligible sense in which it can be said that the apostles legislated for it. They prescribed the duties of the *master* in a relation already existing—but that was not legislating for *slavery;* they prescribed the duties of *slaves*, in a relation which the gospel did not originate, but in which it found them—but that was not laying down laws for the permanent continuance of the institution. The permanency of the institution can derive no support from what they said on the subject, and in no manner depends on it. The permanency of the relations of husband and wife, and of parents and children, does not depend on the fact that the apostles *legislated* for those relations, or on the fact that they prescribed the duties of those who sustained these relations. The question whether it was contemplated that those relations should be permanent in the earth, lies back of the fact that the apostles prescribed the duties of parents and children. They made laws for the master—as responsible to God—not for slavery: for the slave—as a redeemed man and a sufferer—not for the perpetuity of the system which oppressed him.

(2.) It is not fair to infer from the manner in which they prescribed the duties of masters and slaves *in* that relation, that they approved the system, and that they desired its perpetuity. To prescribe the duties of certain persons while sustaining a certain relation to each other, cannot be construed as an approbation of the relation itself. It might not be desirable for him who gave directions about the right mode of acting *in* a certain relation, to attempt to disturb it at that time, or it might be impossible at once to remove certain evils connected with it, and yet there might be important duties which religion would enjoin while that relation continued. Thus, to direct masters to render to their servants that which is just and equal; to forbear threatening, knowing that they had a master in heaven; to be kind, equal, and just in their dealings with their servants—which is the extent of the 'legislation' of the apostles in respect to them—cannot with any justice be construed into an approval of the system: for as long as that relation continued, whatever might be their duty about *dissolving* it, there were certain duties which they owed to those under them, and which the Christian religion made it imperative on them to perform.   And in like manner, to direct servants to be obedient to their masters according to the flesh ; to obey in all things their masters according to the flesh ; to count their masters worthy of all honour ; to direct them to please their masters well in all things, not answering again, not purloining, but to show all good fidelity ; and to be subject to them with all fear, not only to the good and gentle, but also to the froward—which is the extent of their ' legislating' for slaves—cannot be construed as an approbation of the system, or as expressing the opinion that it would be desirable that this relation should always continue.   While it continued, there were certain duties which religion required of them, whether it were to be dissolved or not; for it was in an eminent manner desirable that they should show the fair influence of religion on the heart.   Even on the supposition that the apostles regarded the system as a great evil, and desired the immediate abolition of slavery, *as long as* the relation continued, they would have required that this spirit should be manifested.   It is the same spirit, certainly, which the great body of the most decided abolitionists in this country would desire that those who are held in slavery should evince, though this fact cannot be construed into an argument that they approve of slavery.

That this is a just view, will appear from two considerations.   (*a*) The apostles ' legislated' in a manner quite as decisive respecting the relation between Nero and his subjects, (Rom. xiii. 1—7 ; 1 Pet. ii. 13—17,) and yet it would be doing them great injustice to infer that they approved of his government, or desired that it should be perpetuated on the earth. It would be very unfair to conclude from the views which they expressed, that such a despotism would be the best kind of government for the United States, or that it would be desirable that it should be established everywhere, or that it was such as God approved, or even that in any sense it was right. And yet, whatever obligations Christians might be under to modify that government if they had any power to do so, while the relation which they sustained to it continued, there were important duties which they owed to the government under which they were, *as such;* for even under the hardships of such a government, they were under obligation to evince such a spirit as would do honour to the gospel. And even if the apostles had given just the instructions to Nero which they did to Christian masters, it would not have proved that they regarded his administration as a good one, or that God desired that *such* a government should be perpetuated. If they had directed him, as they did Christian masters, to ' render to his subjects that which was just and equal,' and to evince kindness, and tenderness, and fidelity, ' forbearing threatening,'—' legislating' for *him* in that relation, it would by no means demonstrate that his conduct towards his subjects was such as God approved, or that there was not something essentially wrong in the kind of government which he endeavoured to maintain over the Roman people. (*b*) The same remarks are applicable also to cases of persecution. The apostles ' legislated' for those who were suffering under persecution; that is, they recognised the fact that Christians were persecuted; they made laws for those who were persecuted; they enjoined on them the performance of certain duties *in* that condition, as much as they did for those who were held as slaves. They enjoined on them the duty of showing proper respect for their superiors; a spirit of subordination and submission; patience under the reception of wrongs, just as they did on slaves in respect to the wrongs and oppressions which they received from their masters. But assuredly, it would be doing the apostles great injustice to infer that because they did this, they approved of the laws which made the persecution of the saints inevitable, or that they desired that the system under which those laws were enacted should be perpetuated. And even if the apostles had enjoined

on persecutors the same thing which they did on Christian
masters, it could not be construed as expressing an approbation of their conduct in maintaining a system which subjected
so many innocent Christians to so grievous wrongs.   *If* they
had enjoined on them the duty of being kind, and of 'forbearing threatening,' and of 'rendering to all that which is
just and equal'—'*legislating*' for them in the case, it would
be a very inconclusive method of reasoning, to infer that they
approved of the persecuting system, and wished to be understood as desiring its perpetuity.

(3.) But it is not *true* that in any sense the apostles 'legislated' for slavery as they did for the relation of husband and wife,
and parent and child.   It is not true that they ever represented
those relations as parallel, or as equally desirable and acceptable
to God.   I shall have occasion to refer to this again, but would
here notice the following things in regard to their legislating
for those who were ·in this relation—in all which their instructions differ from those respecting the relation of husband
and wife, and parent and child.   (*a*) They uniformly represent servitude as a *hard* condition, and as in itself undesirable.
1 Cor. vii. 21 ; 1 Pet. ii. 18—23.   Comp. the injunctions to
masters, Eph. vi. 9 ; Col. iv. 1.   But where do they represent
the condition of a wife or child as necessarily a *hard* and *undesirable* condition ?   (*b*) They enjoin on slaves submission
to their condition as a hard one, and one in which they were
constantly liable to suffer wrong.   1 Pet. ii. 18, 19 : "Servants, be subject to your masters with all fear ; not only to
the good and gentle, but also to the froward, *for* this is
thankworthy, if a man for conscience toward God *endure
grief* [i. e. that which is fitted to produce grief,] *suffering
wrongfully.*"   1 Cor. vii. 21 : " Art thou called being a
servant ? *Care not for it.*"   That is, 'though it is a hard
condition, yet let it not be a subject of deep anxiety
and distress ; in the humble lot in life where God has
placed you, strive to evince the Christian spirit, and show
that you are able to honour religion, rejoicing in the hope

of immortal freedom in a better world.' But where does an apostle attempt to console a wife or a child by telling them not to ' *care for it*' that they are in such a condition? How would a child interpret such a direction, that *though he* had a father over him when he became a Christian, yet that he ought not to ' care for it,' but to endeavour in that hard condition to perform his duties as well as he was able, and to console himself with the reflection that after all he was a child of God, and was in that more important sense free? (*c*) The principal virtue which the apostles enjoin on slaves to cultivate, is that of *patience under wrong*—a mild, gentle, and kind spirit, even when conscious that they were enduring wrong. See the passages already referred to. Comp. particularly 1 Pet. ii. 18—23: "This is thankworthy, if a man for conscience toward God endure grief, suffering wrongfully. For what glory is it, if, when ye be buffeted for your faults, ye shall take it patiently? But if, when ye do well, and suffer for it, ye take it patiently, this is acceptable with God. *For even hereunto were ye called.*" Ye were called by your Christian profession, and after the example of your master— the Lord Jesus—"who, when he was reviled, reviled not again; when he suffered, he threatened not; but committed himself to him who judgeth righteously," to evince a spirit of patience under wrongs, and to bear them submissively, by committing your cause unto God. But what other relation of life is there in which the leading virtue recommended to be cultivated, is *patience under the infliction of wrong?* Is that the crowning virtue recommended in the marriage relation? Is that described as the cardinal virtue of a son or daughter? (*d*) They represented it as desirable to escape from servitude if it could be done; or as more desirable to be free than to be in that condition. Thus, in 1 Cor. vii. 21, the apostle Paul says, "Art thou called being a servant? Care not for it: *but if thou mayest be made free, use it rather.*" But where is any thing like this said respecting the condition of a wife or child? Where is it implied that such a relation was so hard and oppressive that it would be desirable to escape from it if possible?

If these things are so, then it is clear that the apostles did *not* 'legislate' for slavery in any such sense as they did for the relation of husband and wife, and parent and child. They never regarded the relations as similar. Every thing that they said in the way of *legislation* is entirely consistent with the supposition that they disapproved of the system, and desired that it might cease as soon as possible.

II. The second argument relied on, from the facts respecting the manner in which the apostles treated the subject of slavery as specified above, is, that if they were opposed to slavery at heart, and regarded it as sinful, their course was inconsistent with moral honesty, and that it was in fact one of the worst forms of what is now known as Jesuitism.

This argument is greatly insisted on by all the advocates of slavery, and by all who apologize for it as a scriptural institution. It is in fact the strongest argument which has been adduced on that side of the question. It is stated in as strong a manner probably as it can be, in the Princeton Biblical Repertory, in the passages already quoted, pp. 234—240. It is also urged with great confidence by Dr. Fuller in his Letter to Dr. Wayland; and in order that the full force of the argument may be seen in the present connection, I will copy it as it is presented by this eminent Baptist divine.

" In the remark just made, I supposed, of course, that you admit some sort of slavery to have been allowed in the Old Testament, and suffered by Jesus and his apostles. A man who denies this will deny any thing, and only proves how much stronger a passion is than the clearest truth. Both Dr. Channing and Dr. Wayland, with all respectable commentators, yield this point; but if this point be yielded, how can it be maintained that slaveholding is itself a crime? No one can regard the noble president of Brown University with more esteem and affection than I do; from his arguments, however, I am constrained to dissent. His position is this :* the moral precepts of the gospel condemn slavery ; it is therefore criminal. Yet he admits that neither the Saviour nor his apostles commanded masters to emancipate their slaves; nay, they 'go further,' he adds, 'and prescribe the duties suited to both parties in their present condition ;' among which duties, be it remembered, there is not an intimation of manumission, but the whole code contemplates the continuance of the relation. Here, then, we have the Author of the gospel, and the inspired propagators of the gospel, and the Holy Spirit indicting the gospel, all conniving at a practice which was a violation of the entire moral principle of the gospel! And the reason assigned by Dr. Wayland for this abstinency by God from censuring a wide-spread infraction of his law, is really nothing more nor less than expediency— the apprehension of consequences. The Lord Jesus and the apostles teaching expediency! They who proclaimed and prosecuted a war of extermination against all the most cherished passions of this guilty earth, and attacked with dauntless intrepidity all the multiform idolatry around them— they quailed, they shrank from breathing even a whisper against slavery, through fear of consequences ! ! And, through fear of consequences, the Holy Spirit has given us a canon of Scriptures, containing minute directions as to the duties of master and slave, without a word as to emancipation!!! Suppose our missionaries should be detected thus winking at idolatry, and tampering with crime in heathen lands.

"Dr. Channing also says,—'Paul satisfied himself with disseminating principles which would slowly subvert slavery. 'Satisfied himself!' but was he so easily satisfied in reference to any act which he regarded as a dereliction from duty? Hear how he speaks: 'If any man that is called a brother be a fornicator, or covetous, or an idolater, or a railer, or a drunkard, or an extortioner, with such an one no not to eat.'

---

* I need hardly say that the argument is the same as Paley, b 3 ch. 3.

'Be not deceived ; neither fornicators, nor idolaters, nor adulterers, nor effeminate, nor abusers of themselves with mankind, nor thieves, nor covetous, nor drunkards, nor revilers,
nor extortioners, shall inherit the kingdom of God.' 'Whoremongers and adulterers God will judge.' 'In the name of
our Lord Jesus Christ, when ye are gathered together, and
my spirit, with the power of our Lord Jesus Christ, to deliver
such an one unto Satan for the destruction of the flesh, that
the spirit may be saved in the day of the Lord Jesus.'
Such was Paul's language; nothing but this unyielding, un-
compromising condemnation of every sin could content him;
yet, as to the 'unutterable abomination of slavery,' he is a
temporizing palterer! As to slavery, which 'violates every
article in the decalogue,' although the apostle saw it all
around him, and members of the church guilty of it, he
declined uttering a word—he is cowed into a time-server, a
worker by concealed and tardy indirections! He 'satisfies
himself,' while millions on all sides are sinking into hell
through this crime—he 'satisfies himself' with spreading
principles which would slowly work a cure! Craven and
faithless herald! and after this, with what face could he say,
'I have kept back nothing'—'I have not shunned to declare
the whole counsel of God?' Arguments like these refute
themselves ; they are the signal failures of minds masterful
for the truth, but impotent against it; and will convince
every sincere inquirer that to denounce slaveholding as necessarily a sin, is to deal in loose assertion, and practically to
range one's self with the infidel and scoffer.''*

These are strong positions, expressed both by Dr. Fuller
and by the author of the article in the Repertory, in vigorous
language. The argument is not capable of being urged in
any clearer manner, and if it can be shown, as thus presented,
to be unfounded, it will remain disposed of for ever. It is in
the highest degree important to reply to it, not only to vindi-

---

* See Fuller's Letters, pp. 4, 5, 6.

cate the character of the apostles, but also to ascertain the true relation of the New Testament to the subject of slavery, and also to furnish instructive lessons about the wisest course of meeting great and appalling evils in the world.

The true question is, whether, on the supposition that the apostles regarded slavery as an evil institution ; as undesirable for the good of society ; as contrary to the spirit of the religion which they preached ; as so offensive in the sight of God that he desired its removal; and as an institution which the religion which they promulgated was intended to remove from the earth, it was *morally honest* for them to pursue the course which they did—to admit slaveholders to the communion ; to baptize them ;* to speak of them as ' brethren beloved ;' and to give them counsel for their conduct *in* that relation, without apprising them that they were living in gross sin, or requiring them at once to emancipate their slaves.

This inquiry resolves itself essentially into two questions. (1.) Whether they meant to have it supposed that they approved of the system, and desired it to be perpetuated on the earth, in the same sense that they desired that the marriage institution, and the relation of parent and child should be perpetuated as desirable for the best interests of society ; and, (2.) If they did not, whether their treatment of it was originated by a false notion of expediency ; by the fear of the consequences of exposing its evil, and in fact left a false impression on those whom they addressed, in regard to it.

On the supposition, then, that they regarded the system as evil, and desired it to be abandoned, and meant that religion should undermine it and remove it from the world, what in their circumstances was the path of wisdom and of honesty ? What did Christian integrity demand of them in the accom plishment of their object ? In reply to these questions, and in order fairly to meet the argument, I would make the following remarks :—

---

* See Fuller's Letters, p. 196.

(1.) It will be admitted on all hands, that whatever were the reasons which induced them to meet slavery in the manner in which they did, it was not from any fear of the consequences of an opposite course. Their whole conduct shows, that, whatever motives may have influenced them in respect to any existing evil, it was not the dread of a loss of popularity, or of comfort, or of life. It *is* true in reference to the prevailing evils of the world, as the conductors of the Biblical Repertory say, that "they did not keep back the truth from the fear of suffering. They called God to witness that they declared the whole counsel of God, and were clear of every man's blood." It *is* true that, as Dr. Fuller says, "they proclaimed and prosecuted a war of extermination against all the most cherished passions of this guilty earth, and attacked with dauntless intrepidity all the multiform idolatry around them."   On all hands it will be agreed by those who are acquainted with the principles on which the apostles acted, that they were not restrained from denouncing what they regarded as wrong, from fear of personal consequences. If it *be* a fair inference from this, as Dr. Fuller and the conductors of the Princeton Repertory suppose, that they did *not* regard slavery as "a heinous crime in the sight of God," then the inference cannot be denied. *Whatever* conclusion follows, it is to be conceded that the method in which the apostles met it did not arise from the fact that "they quailed, or shrunk from breathing even a whisper against slavery, through fear of consequences."*

(2.) It is incumbent on those who believe that slavery is inconsistent with the spirit of Christianity, and that God regards it as an evil and undesirable thing, to show that the manner in which the apostles met it was honest; that it did not imply connivance at an acknowledged evil; that it was not a course fitted to produce deception ; and that there were reasons for meeting the subject in this manner, which did not exist in the case of idolatry and other sins.

---

* Dr. Fuller.

In illustrating this point, therefore, and in endeavouring to show that the conduct. of the apostles was consistent with the belief that slavery was an evil, and that the spirit of the religion which they propagated was opposed to it, and yet that their course was honest, I would submit the following remarks :—

(a) There were reasons for meeting this evil in this manner, which did not exist in the case of other evils. In other words, it was expedient, and yet honest, to meet it without making an open and violent assault on the institution, and without denouncing it as at all times, and in all circumstances a sin, and without denying that in *any* circumstances one who held slaves could be a good man. Or, in other words, there was a propriety in their meeting it by inculcating fundamental truths, which would gradually but certainly remove the evil, rather than by an open opposition to the laws in the case, and a denunciation of it as always sinful. The general principle is, that they adopted the best method of ultimately removing the evil under the influence of Christianity, without lending to it any such sanction as to leave the impression that they regarded it as a good and desirable institution.

There are two kinds of *expediency*, one of which is consistent with moral honesty, and the other of which is not. Expediency may be employed in a good cause and to accomplish good ends ; or it may be employed in a bad cause and to accomplish evil purposes. The word " *expedient*" means that " which tends to promote the object proposed ; fit or suitable for the purpose." An " *expedient*" is " that which serves to promote or advance ; any means to accomplish an end." " *Expediency*" is " fitness or suitableness to effect some good end, or the purpose intended ; propriety under the particular circumstances of a case."* In itself, therefore, *expediency* is not inconsistent with entire honesty, and with the most manly independence. It is, in itself, a characteristic

---

* Webster.

of wisdom, and we could hardly respect a man who did not do that which is *expedient*, in the sense of adopting means *suitable* to the end which he proposes, and *adapted* to secure that end. "A man would hardly be deemed of sound mind unless he obeyed the dictates of such an expediency. Nay, if he failed to avail himself of such means, he might be morally delinquent. For instance, if a man were charged with the accomplishment of some good design, and neglected to use the means suitable to effect it, or still more, if he used means of a directly opposite tendency, we should all declare him culpable. His conduct would show that his interest in the work was not sufficient to prompt him to the use of the proper means to insure his success."*

There may be cases, then, in which *expediency* is right and proper ; and there may be cases, also, as we all know, in which it may be "mean, contemptible, cowardly, and wicked." *When* it is wicked and mean, the evil must arise from some cause aside from the fact that the act seems to be *expedient*. It must be because there is some wrong in the object aimed at, or because there is something dishonest, cowardly, mean, or wicked in the measures adopted to secure it ; something which in that case is 'expedient,' not because it is fit and suitable to the end, but because it involves some improper conceal-ment of the truth ; some false pretence, or some dishonest trick to secure the end in view. In such a case, an act would be as wicked, as an honest and wise expediency would be virtuous.

Suppose, for instance, a man goes among the heathen to preach the gospel. If he should study the character of the people ; if he should be prudent and not needlessly rouse their prejudices ; if he should conform himself to their modes of dress and style of living ; if he should evince such an inte-rest in them as to win their confidence and affections ; and if he should present the gospel with sound sense and practical

* Dr. Wayland's Letters to Dr. Fuller, p. 64.

good judgment, he would be pursuing a wise expediency, for he would be pursuing a course that was adapted to secure the end in view, and every thing which he did would be consistent with the strictest honesty. But suppose he should rely on pious frauds, and invent false testimonies to his doctrines, and pretend to work miracles, this would be an 'expediency' that would be manifestly dishonest. And suppose even that it might be attended with some conversions, still that would not alter the case. The thing itself would be condemned by all honest men.

In like manner, suppose that in propagating the gospel, I *adopt* some of the evil customs of the heathen ; that I attempt to avail myself of their known reverence for sacred shrines, and forms, and places; of their superstitious regard for holy vestments, and for those who sustain a priestly character among them, and should attempt to transfer all this at once to Christianity to secure its success, it is equally clear that this would be a wicked expedient. It would be relying on what I knew to be false, though they did not know it, and though perhaps they might never perceive it. There is no honest mind which would not condemn it—except just so far as any of these things might be in exact conformity with the principles of the religion which I sought to propagate.

Suppose, further, that in my efforts to spread my religion, I should, for the sake of not arousing opposition or endangering my life, leave *a wholly erroneous impression* of the moral character of certain things which I found prevailing among the people—as, for instance, of the crimes of idolatry, infanticide, or intemperance. If my conduct could be *fairly* so construed as to imply approbation of these things; if I did not leave a distinct impression that I regarded them as evil; if I should connive at them with a view to extending my principles; and if I should make distinct and definite arrangements contemplating their perpetuity, and leave it to be so understood, there could be no difference of opinion in regard to my conduct. It might be *possible* that some such course would secure my personal safety, and it may even be conceived that this might do something to conciliate the favour of the heathen, and dispose them to look favourably on me and my doctrines, but no one could hesitate to say that *such* an expediency would be morally wrong.

So, if, to accomplish my ends, I should attempt to make my message acceptable, by *totally* withholding a part of the truth; or by modifying it; or by adding to it; or by adapting it to what should be demanded by popular clamour, no one could hesitate to say that I did wrong. It would be acting from expediency in such a sense that no one could approve of it.

Such and similar cases are instances in which to act from 'expediency' implies guilt. It arises from fear; it involves the suppression of truth; it leaves a false impression; and no man can look upon it but with disapprobation, and no one who acts in this way can hope to meet the approbation of God. If the apostles really believed that slaveholding was wrong, and yet concealed their opinion of it from any of these motives, or so acted in regard to it that they left the impression that it was a good and desirable institution, it would be impossible to vindicate their conduct.

But, on the other hand, there may be cases where expediency is a virtue, and where it is entirely consistent with honesty and sincerity. In such cases, there is no designed suppression of the truth; there is no bad motive; there is no withholding of offensive doctrines under the influence of fear, or from the dread of the consequences; and there is no false plea by which it is sought to advance the cause in hand. Such cases are the following :—(a) Instances in which there is conformity to some custom or habit among a people that is not sinful, with a view not to excite prejudice or needless opposition. Such was the case of Paul, who 'became all things to all men that he might by all means save some; who to the Jews became as a Jew, that he might gain the Jews; and to them that were under the law as under the law, that he might gain them that were under the law; and to them who were

without law as without law, that he might gain them that
were without law.' (1 Cor. ix. 21, 22.) Thus he perfo med
a vow at Jerusalem, (Acts xxi. 24 ;) and thus he and the other
apostles and early Christians of Hebrew origin all continued
to conform to the Jewish customs after they had ceased to be
binding, in order that they might not alarm the prejudices of
the Jews, and give rise to the charge that they were hostile to
the Mosaic institutions. Every man, who is wise, does the
same thing. He does not needlessly arouse opposition. He
does not make war on things which are indifferent. He does
not unnecessarily give occasion for charges against himself,
which would defeat the whole end which he has in view.
While he does not do that which is morally wrong, or abandon
any principle of truth, he at the same time adapts himself to
the habits of thinking, the mode of living, the manners and
customs of those whom he seeks to influence, in order that
his views may meet with no unnecessary opposition. (b) Another case of obviously justifiable expediency is that of in-
sinuating our views by parables or fables which will convey
the truth in such a way as to disarm opposition, and secure
the assent of the mind to some principle which involves all
that we wish to inculcate, before the proposition itself is openly
stated. Such was the parable with which Nathan addressed
David ; such were the parables of our Saviour ; such were
the fables of Æsop. The bare and bold statement of the truth
which it was desirable to get before the mind would have
created revulsion, and the attention is therefore arrested by an
interesting narrative, and the assent gained to some important
principle of easy application, before the particular truth is
stated which it is designed to convey to the mind. This is
allowable ' expediency ;' and this has been practised among
all people. Prejudice is disarmed, and the end is reached
without producing revulsion. (c) A similar method is that
of laying down important principles, and suffering them to
produce a certain effect which is foreseen, and which will
operate ultimately to remove an existing evil. Instead of

attacking the evil at once, when the only effect would be to defeat the end in view, it may be far better to lay down certain fundamental truths, the operation of which shall be to place the evil ultimately in a proper light, and to lead by certain consequence to its removal. It may be that the thing which we regard as wrong is not so seen by others; it may be that they have had a training which has sanctioned it in their minds; it may be that they hold principles in regard to it which, if *they* are correct, make that which we would wish to remove correct also. To secure our object, therefore, it is necessary that more correct *principles* should be held, and a patient work of moral instruction becomes absolutely necessary. The object could not be reached in any other way. The evil has been so long practised; it is so interwoven with other important interests; in the defence of it there is such a blending of truth and error, that it is necessary to disentangle the skein, and to bring out the truth by the faithful inculcation of correct principles. It is in this way that God has in fact removed most of the evils of the world by a *gradual* development of principles which strike on great wrongs existing in society, thus preparing the world for the higher developments of his will; and it is in this way that wise *men* commonly approach a deep-rooted evil. It is the *expedient* and the *wise* course. The other would be *inexpedient* and *unwise;* for it would not be that which would be necessary to moral honesty, and would defeat the end in view. These principles can be justified by the example of the Saviour. His parables, as before remarked; his treatment of the prejudices of the Jews, and his methods of meeting the blindness and errors of his own disciples, all illustrate them. Thus also he said, at the close of his ministry, respecting his mode of teaching, "I have yet many things to say unto you, *but ye cannot bear them now.*" John xvi. 12. So the apostle Paul, (1 Cor. iii. 1, 2,) says, "And I, brethren, could not speak unto you as unto spiritual, but as unto carnal, even as **unto** babes in Christ. I have fed you with *milk,* and not with *meat ;* for hitherto *ye were not able to bear it, neither yet now are ye able.*"

This principle has been so well illustrated by Dr. Wayland— to whom I am indebted for some of these thoughts—that I cannot do better than copy a few of his remarks on the subject.

" This form of expediency—the inculcating of a fundamental truth, rather than of the duty which springs immediately out of it, seems to me *innocent.* I go further : in some cases it may be really *demanded.* Thus, suppose a particular wrong to have become a social evil, to have become interwoven with the whole framework of society, and to be established by positive enactment and immemorial usage ; suppose that all departments of society have become adjusted to it, and that much instruction is necessary before any party can avail itself of the advantages of a righteous change ; suppose also the whole community to be ignorant of the moral principles by which both the wrong is condemned and the right established. In such a case, the wrong could only be abolished by changing the sentiments and enlightening the consciences of the whole community. Here it seems to me that it would be not only allowable, but a matter of imperative duty, to inculcate the principles on which the duty rested, rather than the duty itself. The one being fixed in the mind, would necessarily produce the other; and thus the end would be in the most certain manner accomplished.

" It is in this manner that the New Testament has generally dealt with the various forms of social evil. Take for instance civil government. At the time of Christ and his apostles, the only form of government known in the civilized world, was a most abominable and oppressive tyranny. Yet the New Testament utters no precepts in regard to forms of government, or the special duties of rulers. It goes further. It commands men everywhere to obey the powers that be, so far as this could be done with a good conscience towards God. But it at the same time inculcates those truths concerning the

character, rights, responsibilities, and obligations of man, which
have been ever since working out the freedom of the human
race; and which have received, as I believe, their fullest
development in the principles of the American Declaration of
Independence. Indeed, in no other manner could the New
Testament have become a system of religion for the whole
human race, adapted to meet the varying aspects of human
depravity. If it had merely taught precepts, whatever was
not forbidden must have been taken as permitted. Hence,
unchecked wickedness would soon have abounded, and the
revelation of God must have become a nullity. But by teaching principles of universal application, it is prepared to meet
every rising form of moral deviation, and its authority is now
as all-pervading as at the moment when it was first delivered.
Our Saviour, as it appears to me, carries out this principle to
the utmost, when, setting aside as it were all other precepts,
he declares that our whole duty is summed up in these two
commandments, ' Thou shalt love the Lord thy God with all
thy heart, and thy neighbour as thyself; for this is the law
and the prophets.' That is, I suppose him to mean, that
cherishing these principles in our hearts, and carrying them
out into all our actions, we shall do the whole will of God
without any other precept."*

A very material question then arises here which is vital to
the whole argument. It is this. On the supposition that the
apostles regarded slavery as contrary to the spirit and principles of the religion which they wished to propagate; as a
system which they desired to destroy, and which they believed
Christianity was intended to destroy; in other words, on the
supposition that they were enemies of slavery and wished its
abolition, what, in the circumstances in which they were
placed, was it proper for them as honest men to do? What
would be the wisest and the best course to reach the end in
view? Would the proper course be at once to attack and

---

* Letters to Dr. Fuller, pp. 73, 74, 75.

denounce it, and to declare that no slaveholder could *in any possible circumstances* enter into the kingdom of heaven? Would it be to insist that every master should emancipate all his slaves as an indispensable condition, of being admitted to the Christian church? The apostles were strangers in the lands where they published the gospel; they had no civil power; they had no agency in making the laws; they had no power to change them. Slavery had existed for ages; its propriety was not doubted; it was defended by lawgivers and moralists; it was interwoven with every custom and habit of social life; it entered into all the arrangements for agriculture, for the mechanic arts, and for war; and it was supposed to have the sanction of religion. What *would* have been the effect of denouncing it, and of proclaiming in so many words, that it 'was a heinous sin in the sight of God,' cannot be a subject of doubt. They would have been regarded as disturbers of the public peace; as travelling entirely beyond the conceded rights of religious teachers; and as intermeddlers with the laws: and they would have been banished at once from every slaveholding community—just as abolition agents are now at the South.

Would not the following principles, in conformity with the views relating to expediency above laid down, be all that could be required of the honest enemies of slavery, in their circumstances?

First, *not* to pursue such a course as would defeat the very end in view, *while it was not yet admitted that it was wrong or a moral evil* by those among whom slavery prevailed. If it *had* been conceded to be a wrong—to be sinful; if it had been or would be at once admitted, as it would be in the case of idolatry, and drunkenness, and murder, and falsehood, and incest, to be an open and flagrant violation of the laws of God, then the case would be different. Then it would be plain that it could not be tolerated for a moment; that it would be proper to meet it as an indisputable evil, and to require its immediate abolition. Thus it was with the sins just referred to. They were plain cases; things positively forbidden by the laws of Heaven; things which men would at once perceive and feel to be wrong. There was no defence which could be set up for them; there could be no difference of opinion about their impropriety.

Second, it would be obviously demanded of honest men in such circumstances *never to express any approbation of the system;* and I will add, never to do that which could be *fairly* construed, when all the circumstances were considered, as implying approbation of the system. Either of these things, even on the supposition that they should be regarded as *expedient*, would be an instance of *dishonest expediency.* On the supposition, for example, that by representing to a large slaveholder that slavery was entirely consistent with the law of God and the principles of the religion which they preached, in order that he might thus be led to look favourably on the new system of religion, and induced to embrace it, it would be such an 'expedient' that no honest man, who regarded the system as evil, could adopt. No considerations could have justified upright men in adopting any such course in reference to lying and licentiousness.

Third, it would be obviously demanded of honest men in these circumstances, that they should lay down such fundamental principles of morality as, when fairly applied, would show that the system was evil, and that the religion which they aimed to promulgate was opposed to it, and would ultimately remove it. It would be clearly improper that they should advance any principle which, if *fairly* applied, would tend to sanction or to perpetuate it. Thus, it would have been improper that they should state any principle which would, when fairly applied, tend to sustain polygamy, or idolatry, or which would *not* tend to remove them from the world.

Fourth, it would be obviously demanded that, as honest men, they should make such statements and such arrangements, as should leave the *fair* impression on the minds of those to whom they were made, that they desired that the system should cease, and that their instructions could not fairly be pleaded as sanctioning the system. This would be met by their stating such views of man and of redemption as would be inconsistent with the permanent relations of slavery ; by enjoining such duties on the masters as, if *fairly followed*, would lead them to emancipate their slaves as soon as possible ; by such statements as would preserve Christians from the purchase and sale of others ; and by showing that there were duties incumbent on all men, and which all were under obligations to God to perform, which it would be seen would be interfered with by the continuance of the system, and which in fact could *not* be performed while the relation continued.

If these things were done, would not their course be entirely *honest*, on the supposition that they were opposed to the system of slavery ? Would not this be a course which would fall in with the rules of justifiable 'expediency,' as explained above ? Would it not be in fact all that could be demanded in the case ? But one other thing could *possibly* be supposed to be required of them as honest men—to denounce it always; to exclude from the church, in all circumstances, those who were engaged in it ; to proclaim that in every instance it was wholly inconsistent with the possession of the Christian hope ; to publish that, at all hazards, it was every man's duty at once to emancipate all his slaves, and that it was the duty of every one who was a slave to rise on his master and assert his freedom. But was *that* demanded ? If so, why was it not demanded of them that they should denounce all the crimes of the Roman emperor, and proclaim the evils of such a government, and exhort the nations to free themselves from this oppressive yoke ? Why was it not demanded that they should denounce the evils of the gladiatorial shows, and the other barbarous amusements of the amphitheatre, and the thousand other evils which abounded in the Roman world ? Was any thing more required in these cases, than that, in all honesty, they should lay down principles, the fair application of which would bring these barbarous sports to an end?

It is still asked, however, why, if they regarded slavery as 'a heinous sin,' they did not treat it as they did idolatry, and murder, and theft, and licentiousness? How *could* they tolerate it any more than they could those evils? How *could* they admit a man to the church who practised the one, more than he who practised the other? Would they admit an idolater to the church? They never did. Would they receive to the communion one who made his living by piracy? They never did. Would they give directions to one who was living in the practice of adultery, or incest, how to conduct *in* that relation? They never did. Would they address such a one as 'faithful and beloved?' Assuredly not. To this I may reply: (1.) All those were acknowledged and undisputed sins. No one could set up a defence of them; no one could urge any thing in their favour, or in vindication of them. They were open and palpable violations of the law of God, and in no possible circumstances could they be right. It was not so with slavery. It would not at once be seen and admitted to be wrong. (2.) There are certain things, in accordance with this view, which are evil and wrong, but which require patient *instruction*, and much *discussion of principles* before the wrong will be perceived, and where, if denunciation be employed instead of argument, the whole object will be defeated. An instance of this sort has occurred in our own times. It is now generally admitted that the manufacture and sale of intoxicating drinks, for the purpose of being used as a beverage, is wrong; that it tends to produce evil and only evil; that it is not a kind of business which should be pursued by a Christian; and that it is the duty of a church to keep itself pure in this respect. But to reach the present views on this subject, has been the result of a long process of argumentation, and of an examination of principles, demanding the patient and profound inquiries of some of the best intellects in the world—for the whole business was regarded as honourable and lawful; it was sustained by the laws and by public sentiment, and it was patronised by numbers of the best men in the church. And yet what church is there now that would deem it best or right to go back to the views which prevailed on this subject thirty years ago? *Drunkenness,* indeed, was always condemned, alike in the New Testament and by all Christians—but how slow a process has it been to perceive the wrong of that business which *tends* to produce drunkenness, and which steadily operates to keep it up in the world. Oppression and cruelty, and the withholding of wages which are due, have in like manner always been condemned, alike in the New Testament and by all Christians; but there were reasons why there should be *as* slow a process in arriving at the conclusion that that system which *involved* oppression and cruelty and the withholding of wages, is wrong, as existed in the case of the manufacture and sale of intoxicating drinks. It may, indeed, be fairly *inferred* that the apostles would not have approved of the manufacture and sale of alcoholic liquors as a beverage, but where do they expressly condemn it? (3.) There *are* evils—great and acknowledged evils —which the apostles treated just as they did the subject of slavery, in respect to which they laid down great principles, and left them to the certain operation of time to secure the changes which they desired. Such was the case in regard to polygamy—a usage which indubitably prevailed in their time, and in the countries where they preached the gospel; and yet it would be as difficult to find a distinct declaration in the New Testament condemning it, as it would be to find one that openly condemns slavery. Such was the case also in regard to the barbarous sports of the amphitheatre—the gladiatorial shows, and the conflicts with wild beasts for the amusement of the Roman senators and matrons. Such things abounded. The apostles knew of their existence. *It came in their way to speak of them*—for Paul was once at least condemned to fight with wild beasts at Ephesus, and often had occasion to allude to the sports which prevailed in the Roman

world.   And yet it would be impossible to find in the New
Testament one single text which expressly condemns these
things, any more than one which expressly condemns slavery.
Are we, therefore, to infer that the apostles approved of these
things, or that they wished them to be perpetuated, or that
they would have deemed it right for Christians to be engaged
in them ?   Such, too, was the case in respect to civil government.   Can any one suppose that the writers of the New
Testament approved of the government of Nero ?   That they
regarded his cruelties and abominations with complacency ?
That they thought it would be desirable that such a government should be perpetuated ?   Or that there were no evils in
existing governments which they expected that time, under
the operation of the principles which they laid down, would
correct ?   And yet, where in the New Testament shall we
look for a distinct condemnation of the atrocities of Nero's
reign ?   There were many deep social evils on which Christianity made war, and which it intended to remove, and yet
the way in which it was done was by laying down principles
which would ultimately effect the change, and not by direct
and open denunciation.   (4.) The apostles as freely and
openly condemned many things *in* slavery, and indispensable to it, as they did idolatry or any thing connected with it.
They condemned the making of a slave, (1 Tim. i. 10); they
condemned all oppression, cruelty, and wrong ; they expressed
their views on these points without ambiguity or hesitancy ;
and since these *always* entered into slavery then, as they do
now, it follows that they expressed themselves in a way on
this subject which could not be misunderstood.   *How* they
did this, will be seen in a subsequent part of this argument.

The conclusion which seems to follow from these considerations, is, that there were many existing things which the
apostles regarded as wrong, and which they intended the
Christian religion should abolish, which they met, not by open
denunciation, and not by maintaining that those which practised them could in no possible circumstances be Christians,

and should in no case be admitted to the privileges of church membership, but by condemning certain things which were always connected with them, and by laying down such general principles that they could not fail in the end to secure their removal. Even some things, in respect to the morality of which there could be no difference of opinion, appear to have been left in this manner. Thus, every thing pertaining to the barbarous sports of the amphitheatre were left to the slow but certain operation of Christian principle to remove them. Many things pertaining to idolatry were left in the same manner. Whether it was right to partake of the meat that was offered in sacrifice to idols, was a question that was left to be determined by the operation of Christian principle. Evils strike their roots far into the social organization. They become sustained and sanctioned by customs, habits, and laws, and it is not possible to remove them at once without changing the whole framework of society. It is necessary to advance slowly to the work, to state the elementary principles of morals, and to trust much to the gradual but certain operation of those principles to effect in silence the work of reform.

I have thus endeavoured to show, that, on the supposition that the apostles regarded slavery as evil, and that they designed that the religion which they preached should ultimately remove it, there were reasons arising from a just 'expediency,' why they should treat it as they did; and that the method which they adopted cannot be regarded as evidence that they approved of the system, or that they desired its perpetuity.

(b) I would observe, therefore, in the next place, that this is the very course which is recommended now by many who would not wish it to be understood that they are the advocates of slavery, or that they regard it as a good institution. The course which they recommend is that of patiently inculcating principles, and instructing the master in his duty, and trusting to the silent influence of the gospel; and they wish it to be understood that they regard this as consistent with the idea

that they are opposed sincerely to slavery, and that they believe the gospel will ultimately abolish it. They would be
by no means willing that the course which they recommend
should be construed as implying that *they* are the friends of
slavery, or the apologists for it.* But if they insist that this
construction should not be put on *their* recommendations, why
should it be on the course pursued by the apostles? If in
their case this course is consistent with the belief that they
regard slavery as an evil, why should it not be in the case of
the apostles?

That this course *is* recommended by many at the present
day, it is unnecessary to prove. Equally at the South and
the North it is demanded that there shall be no rude and violent attack made on the system; that the owners of slaves
shall not be denounced as men who cannot be Christians;
that they shall not be excluded from the church because they
hold slaves, and that they shall not be held up to public
opprobrium and scorn. At the same time, it is maintained that
the silent operation of the Christian religion will gradually
remove the system, and that all that is necessary to be done
is to go on patiently inculcating the fundamental principles
of the gospel, and that in due time that gospel will remove
slavery from our country and from the world. The views of
the conductors of the Princeton Repertory, who may be
regarded as giving utterance to the sentiments which prevail

---

* Thus the conductors of the Princeton Repertory are quite indignant
at the supposition that the course which they and their friends pursue
should be construed as implying that they are in any way the advocates
of slavery. They say, (Repertory, 1844,) "The very title of the book to
which we have so often referred is 'A Review of Dr. Junkin's Synodical
Speech *in defence of American Slavery.*' Dr. Junkin's speech, however,
is simply an argument to prove that slaveholding is not a crime, and therefore that 'believing masters ought not be excommunicated from the church
of God.' This is called a defence of American slavery! i. e. of the whole
system of slave laws now in force in this country. *There is no help for
men who will act thus.*"

on this point at the South, are expressed in the most decisive language. Thus, in a passage already quoted, they say :

" It is on all hands acknowledged, that, at the time of the advent of Jesus Christ, slavery in its worst forms prevailed over the whole world. The Saviour found it around him in Judea ;* the apostles met with it in Asia, Greece, and Italy. How did they treat it ? Not by the denunciation of slave-holding as necessarily and universally sinful. Not by declaring that all slaveholders were men-stealers and robbers, and consequently to be excluded from the church and the kingdom of heaven. Not by insisting on immediate emancipation. Not by appeals to the passions of men on the evils of slavery, or by the adoption of a system of universal agitation. On the contrary, it was by teaching the true nature, dignity, equality, and destiny of men ; by inculcating the principles of justice and love ; and by leaving these principles to produce their legitimate effects in ameliorating the condition of all classes of society."

Again they say :

" We think, therefore, that the true method for Christians to treat this subject, is to follow the example of Christ and his apostles in relation both to despotism and slavery. Let them enforce as moral duties the great principles of justice and mercy, and all the specific commands and precepts of the Scriptures."

And again, in their article in 1844, they reiterate these views still more distinctly :

" It is also evident, that acting in accordance with these principles would soon improve the condition of the slaves, would make them intelligent, moral, and religious, and thus work out to the benefit of all concerned, and the removal of the institution. For slavery, like despotism, supposes the actual inferiority and consequent dependence of those held in subjection. Neither can be permanent. Both may be prolonged

* There is no evidence, however, as I have endeavoured to show, of that.

by keeping the subject class degraded, that is by committing sin on a large scale, which is only to treasure up wrath for the day of wrath. It is only the antagonist fanaticism of a fragment of the South, which maintains the doctrine that slavery is in itself a good thing, and ought to be perpetuated. It cannot by possibility be perpetuated."

But from these views, so plainly expressed, shall we infer that the conductors of the Repertory wish to be understood as the advocates of American slavery? Shall we infer that they regard it as an institution which it is desirable to perpetuate, and which the Christian religion is adapted and designed to perpetuate? However such a conclusion would *seem* to follow from some portions of their reasoning, and however certainly such an impression will go forth from *some* of their statements, adapted to soothe the consciences of slaveholders at the South, yet there are other portions of their argument with which such a conclusion would be entirely at variance; portions in which they distinctly express the opinion that the system is an evil, and that the effect of the gospel would be gradually to remove it, *because* it is so. Thus they say :—

"We have little apprehension that any one can so far mistake our object, or the purport of our remarks, as to suppose *either that we regard slavery as a desirable institution*, or that we approve of the slave laws of the Southern states. So far from this being the case, the extinction of slavery, and the amelioration of those laws, are as sincerely desired by us, as by any of the abolitionists.

"If it be asked what would be the consequence of thus acting on the principles of the gospel, of following the example and obeying the precepts of Christ? We answer, the gradual elevation of the slaves in intelligence, virtue, and wealth; the peaceable and speedy extinction of slavery; the improvement in general prosperity of all classes of society, and the consequent increase in the sum of human happiness and virtue. This has been the result of acting on these prin-

ciples in all past ages ; and just in proportion as they have
been faithfully observed.

"Besides the two methods mentioned above, in which
slavery dies a natural and easy death, there are two others
by which, as history teaches us, it may be brought to an end.
The one is by the non-slaveholders, in virtue of their authority in the state to which the slaves and their masters belonged,
passing laws for its extinction. Of this, the Northern states
and Great Britain are examples. The other is by servile
insurrections. The former of these two methods is of course
out of the question, as it regards most of the Southern states ;
for in almost all of them the slave-owners have the legislative
power in their own hands. *The South, therefore, has to
choose between emancipation by the silent and holy influence
of the gospel, securing the elevation of the slaves to the
stature and character of freemen,* or to abide the issue of a
long-continued conflict against the laws of God."

Now if it is fair to conclude that the views entertained by the
conductors of the Repertory, when they recommend the inculcation of the relative duties of the master and the slave, and
the silent influence of the gospel, are not inconsistent with the
belief that *they* do not regard "slavery as a desirable institution," and that they suppose the gospel would produce its
certain extinction, it is fair to infer the same thing of the
apostles, and to conclude that *they* did not regard it as "a desirable institution," and that they supposed they were adopting the most wise and judicious means to remove what they
considered as an evil. Moreover, if the course which is
pursued by the conductors of the Repertory be such as to
free *them* from the charge of Jesuitism and dishonest dealing,
while they are recommending a method adapted to secure the
entire removal of the system—by a quiet influence—by the
inculcation of principles—by the silent operation of the system
'producing the gradual elevation of the slaves in intelligence,
virtue, and worth, and the *peaceable and* SPEEDY *extinction of
slavery*'—why should they have inferred that the very same

course, if pursued by the apostles, would have been dishonest and Jesuitical? Why should it be charged on *them* as wrong, when the same course is recommended by those who admit that the gospel would remove it as 'an undesirable institution,' and who become indignant when it is suggested that they are the advocates of slavery or the apologists for it? Would they *not* desire that it should be understood that, while they recommend this course, they are the friends of liberty; that they prefer freedom for themselves and their children to bondage; that they suppose that the gospel will promote liberty wherever it has its fair influence in the world, and that it contains principles which are hostile to slavery? Would they wish it to be supposed that they desire that slavery should be extended and perpetuated on the earth? Assuredly not— for they express the belief that the effect of the silent influence of Christianity would be to remove it entirely from the world; that is, that it is *an evil*—for Christianity removes nothing that is good. The doctrine of the Princeton Repertory, as I understand it, is, that men are to go into those portions of our country in which slavery exists, and to inculcate the truths of the gospel; to instruct the master and the slave in their respective duties; to lay down principles which will gradually remove the evils of the system, and ultimately abolish it altogether; and to do this *with a view and intention that this shall be the result*. Is this course honest, or is it Jesuitical? If honest now, was it not in the days of the apostles? If it is consistent now with a sincere aversion to the system, and a belief that the principles of the gospel are opposed to it, was it not then? Would it be exactly right for any one, from the course which they recommend, to represent the conductors of the Repertory as the friends and advocates of slavery, and as desiring its perpetuity? If it would not, is it proper to represent the apostles, when pursuing just such measures as they recommend, as the friends of the system, or as Jesuitical in their manner of treating it? The whole matter on this point is clear. If the apostles supposed that the gospel which they preached would ultimately abolish the system, they regarded it as an evil. If they left that impression as fairly deducible from their writings, then they were honest men, and cannot be charged with duplicity.

(c) I would remark, then, that they did *not* leave a false impression on this subject. They did not leave it to be fairly deduced from their conduct or their writings that they regarded it as a good system, or as desirable to be perpetuated. This point will be more fully considered in another part of the argument. Here, it may be observed, in general, that they never enjoin it as a duty, or speak of it as proper or desirable, for Christians to hold slaves; they never express any approbation whatever of the system; they never speak of it as they do of marriage and similar institutions, as honourable; they never enjoin it on the masters to continue to hold their slaves in bondage; they never even say to a slave that it is *right* for his master to hold him in bondage, or recommend obedience or submission on that ground; they never leave the impression on his mind that liberty would not be better than servitude. They represent it as a hard system; lay down principles which would lead every Christian master, if he followed them, to emancipate his slaves as soon as possible; endeavour to comfort slaves as in a condition that was hard and undesirable; advise them to avail themselves of the opportunity of becoming free if it is in their power, (1 Cor. vii. 21, εἰ καὶ δύνασαι); and direct them, if they cannot obtain their freedom on earth, to look forward to that world where every fetter will be broken, and they will be free for ever. If it shall appear, as I trust it will, that the apostles gave *this* representation of slavery, then it is doing them great injustice to speak of them as friends of the system, or to say that their conduct was chargeable with pusillanimity or duplicity.

(d) One other remark should be made here, in inquiring whether they were honest men if they were really opposed to slavery, and how far their conduct should direct us in the treatment of this subject. It is, that they were all *foreigners* in those countries where slavery prevailed. They had no agency in making or administering the laws. We have. We make and administer the laws ourselves. The apostles could not change the state of things then existing by a vote. The American people can. They *had* no vote; they could effect changes in a community only by a slow moral influence. The people of the slaveholding states *can* produce changes on this subject at the polls; can make any changes which they please. Their responsibility, then, was of a different kind from that of the people of the slaveholding states. The only thing which they could do was to lay down principles; to mould the public mind by a moral influence; and to leave the impression of their opinions on the age in which they lived. The responsibility of the people where slavery exists in our land is of a different character altogether. The question is whether they shall sustain the system by their votes; or whether, in connection with such moral influences as may be used, they shall use the power which they have, and put an end to it: and whatever may be their duty on that point, it is clear that they cannot refer to the example of the apostles to guide them in it. They never could cast a vote that could in any way affect slavery; they could do nothing in making or administering the laws which sustained it.

§ 3. *The question whether the general conduct of the Apostles is consistent with the belief that they approved of Slavery, and desired its perpetuity.*

A very material question here presents itself, which is, whether the general conduct of the apostles, above referred to, is consistent with the supposition that they regarded slavery as a good institution, and desired that it should be perpetuated? Was it such as to make a Christian master feel that he was doing right, or acting consistently with his religion, in asserting a claim of property over those who were his fellow Christians?

In examining the method in which they treated the subject, with reference to these points, I would make the following remarks :—(1.) No argument in favour of slavery can be derived from *any express statements* in the New Testament affirming its justice or propriety. This is not pretended by any of the advocates of slavery, and obviously cannot be. There *are* no such statements of its propriety ; of the desirableness of the relation ; of the purpose of God that it should be perpetuated in the world. It is impossible for an advocate of slavery to appeal to the New Testament to sustain him in the right which he claims over a slave, in any such sense as a man can appeal to the New Testament to sanction his right to worship God ; to search the Scriptures ; to enjoy the avails of his own labour ; to form his own opinions ; to control his children, &c. And this, in the circumstances of the case, is much. At a time when slavery prevailed everywhere, it could not but have occurred to those to whom the gospel was preached, to inquire whether it was right and proper, and whether it was consistent with the Christian religion. There would be tender and troubled consciences on the subject. It was in fact a matter of discussion among the heathen themselves whether it was right, and many of their philosophers had declared themselves decidedly against it.* Thus, Alcidimas, the scholar of Gorgias of Leontium, says : "All come free from the hands of God ; nature has made no man a slave." Philemon says : "Though he is a slave, yet he has the same nature as ourselves. No one was ever born a slave, though his body may be brought by misfortune into subjection." Aristotle, indeed, vindicated slavery, on the ground of the natural superiority of one man over another. Xenophon and Socrates raised no objection against the institution of slavery. Plato, in his Republic, only desires that no Greeks may be reduced to slavery. The question, therefore, among

---

* See the article of Prof. B. B. Edwards on "Slavery in Ancient Greece," in the Biblical Repository, vol. v., pp. 155—160.

the Greeks was unsettled, and it was regarded as a debatable
matter whether slavery was right or wrong.   Many of the
philosophers had doubts of its justice and propriety, and un-
questionably many more of the common people had.   Now,
in these circumstances, it is much that there is no express
permission of it in the New Testament; that there is no unequivocal assertion in favour of the system; that there is
no unqualified declaration of an apostle that would have put
these scruples to rest.

   Equally clear is it that there is no express *permission*
given to Christians to hold slaves.   There is, in the New
Testament, no reference to the fact that it was tolerated in the
Mosaic institutions; there is no statement that it had ever
been or was right that men should be bought and sold; there
is no intimation that it was regarded as a good and desirable
institution, and that it was intended that it should be perpetuated.   If it shall appear that the apostles laid down any
principles which would *seem* to militate against the institution, and to raise any scruples in the minds of conscientious
men who held slaves, they were at no pains to explain
themselves, or to give ease to a conscience that might be
troubled, on the subject.   And if a Christian master at the
present time, either from the workings of natural humanity in
his soul, or from the influence of the principles laid down in
the New Testament, should be troubled in his conscience in
regard to his *right* to hold slaves, there is no part of the
apostolic writings to which he could turn to allay his feelings
and calm his scruples, by any thing like a distinct declaration
that slavery is *right*.   Now, in regard to *such* an institution,
so much *apparently* against human rights, and against the
principles of the New Testament, it is not too much to
demand of those who suppose that it is sanctioned by the
apostles, that they should adduce some *express statement*
to that effect, or some distinct *permission* to Christians to
hold their fellow-men in bondage.   But it is clear that if

the continuance of slavery depended on this, universal freedom would be inevitable.

(2.) No argument in favour of slavery can be derived from the precepts of the apostles to the *masters*.

I have already conceded that the apostles admitted holders of slaves to the church, on evidence that they were truly converted; and that they addressed important precepts to them *in* that relation; and that among those precepts they did not *require* them immediately to emancipate their slaves, as a condition of good standing in the church.

The question now is, whether this fact can be fairly construed as demonstrating that they regarded slavery as right, and designed that it should be perpetuated. The affirmative of this is confidently maintained by the advocates of the system. Thus Dr. Fuller* says:

"I come now to what I have announced as proof on the question before us. It is the precepts to masters. And here let it be still remembered, that the Old Testament is constantly referred to by the apostles as of divine origin, and that there slavery had, by express precept, been sanctioned ; and I put it to any one, whether the precepts to masters, enjoining of course their whole duty, and not requiring, not exhorting them to emancipate their slaves, are not conclusive proof that the apostles did not consider (and, as a New Testament precept is for all ages, that no one is now justified in denouncing) slaveholding as a sin. These precepts are so regardful of the slave that they even require the master to 'forbear threatening,' yet not an intimation as to emancipation. These precepts were to men anxious to know the whole will of God, and ready to die (as multitudes did die) rather than commit sin, and who were not prevented by law, as we are, from giving liberty to their bondmen. Yet the apostles do not even insinuate that slaveholding is a sin. The apostles solemnly took heaven to witness that they had 'kept back nothing;' and in addressing, not only the people, but the pastors, who were to

---

* Letters to Dr. Wayland, pp. 194, 195.

teach the people and bequeath their ministry to their successors, they asserted their purity from the blood of all men, because they 'had not shunned to declare the whole counsel of
God.' Yet they had shunned even to hint to masters that
they were living in a 'sin of appalling magnitude;' and had
kept back truth, which, if you are right, was of tremen-
dous importance. Lastly, a whole epistle (to which you do
not allude) was addressed to a pious master, whom Paul styles
a 'brother dearly beloved;' and its entire contents were about
his slave. This letter was written, too, when the apostle
styles himself 'Paul the aged,' sixty or seventy years after the
first promulgation of the gospel, and when surely the spirit
and principles you speak of ought to have begun to operate."

The supposed argument from the epistle to Philemon, on
which much reliance, also, is placed, will be considered in
another place. In reference to the other portions of the argument, I would make the following remarks :—The precepts
addressed to masters, as such, in the New Testament, are two,
and two only : Eph. vi. 9, "And ye, masters, do the same things
unto them, forbearing threatening, knowing that your master
also is in heaven; neither is there respect of persons with
him;" and Col. iv. 1, "Masters, render unto your servants that
which is just and equal, knowing that ye also have a master
in heaven." There are no other passages in the New Testament which can be considered as directly addressed to the
owners of slaves ; and if a slaveholder can take shelter under
any such address to himself, as sanctioning his claim, it must
be found in these two verses. Let us inquire, then, whether
an owner of slaves could find a sanction for continuing this
relation in these passages of the New Testament. To determine this, it is necessary to look at them in connection with
certain *other* declarations of the New Testament, which the
owners of slaves could not but regard as demanding their
attention.

(*a*) What do these passages really prove ? What sanction
do they give to slavery ? What right do they give to the

master to continue the relation? They simply inculcate on masters the duty of treating their slaves as they would wish to be treated, and to remember that they have a master in heaven. Do they say that the master has a right to hold them in bondage; to regard them as property; to sell them to whom he pleases; to avail himself of their unrequited labour; to make all their religious privileges and rights dependent only on his will? They say no such thing; they imply no such thing; fairly interpreted, they would go against any such claim.

And yet it is on such passages as these that the master must ground his right to continue to hold his fellow-men in bondage, if he founds that right on the precepts addressed to him in the New Testament; for there are no other. It is implied in the argument which is derived from these passages, that they sanction the whole system of domestic slavery, and grant a universal permission to establish and maintain it at all times, and in all lands, and are proof that it was the intention of the Author of the Christian religion that the system should be perpetuated. They are supposed to sanction the right of one man, who has the power, to compel a human being, a fellow-creature, a man redeemed by the blood of Christ, and an heir of salvation, to labour for him, without his own consent, and to be subject wholly to his will. They are supposed to sanction all the claim which is set up by the master over such a man—the right to withhold from him the Bible; to forbid his marrying the object of his affections; to regulate his food and clothing and mode of living; to control his children; and to give him a right, when he pleases, to sunder his connection with his wife and children for ever, and to sell him, or her, or them, to any one whom he pleases. They are supposed to sanction the right to all that such a man can earn, and all by which he can in any way contribute to the wealth, the ease, or the luxurious indulgence of the master. Every thing that enters essentially into the system of slavery, all the claims which a master asserts over his slaves; all the laws which go to uphold the system,—all these are supposed to be sanctioned by these two injunctions.

Well may we ask, in the words of Dr. Wayland, (pp. 83, 84,) whether there was " ever such a moral superstructure raised on such a foundation ? The doctrine of purgatory, from a verse of Maccabees ; the doctrine of the papacy, from the saying of Christ to Peter ; the establishment of the Inquisition, from the obligation to extend the knowledge of religious truth,—all these seem as nothing to it. If the religion of Christ allows such a license from such precepts as these, the New Testament would be the greatest curse that ever was inflicted on our race."

(*b*) But in order to see the exact bearing of these precepts, and to understand whether they could properly be regarded by a Christian master as sanctioning his claim over a human being, they should be considered in connection with other things, in which he would feel himself to be concerned, and certain representations made in the New Testament which he could not but regard as having an important bearing on him, and on the question of his duty to his slaves. The object now is to obtain a just view of the attitude in which a master would be placed, with *all* the statements of the New Testament before his mind that could be considered to relate to his duty to his slaves. What would he do, or how would he esteem this system, under the influence of *all* the doctrines and precepts laid down in the New Testament that could be regarded as applicable to him in this relation ? To see this, let the following things be borne in mind :

(1.) The right of the master to the slave, as already observed, is never once recognised, either in so many words, or in any expressions which fairly imply it. It is not found in any statement of his right in general, or in detail. It is never said that he is the lawful *owner* of the slave, or that the relation is good and desirable, or that it is contemplated by Christianity that it should be continued ; nor is it anywhere said that he has the right to avail himself of the labour of the slave, or to interfere with his relations to his wife or children, or to prescribe the time or the mode in which he shall worship God. There is not one thing which enters essentially into the nature of slavery, for which an explicit precept of the New Testament can be pleaded. It is not said that he has a right to *enforce* obedience, or even to *require* it of his slaves. It is indeed enjoined on servants that they be obedient to their masters, as it was on subjects to be obedient to the laws of Nero; but there is no authority given to masters to require or enforce such obedience, any more than there is to Nero, or any other bloody tyrant. What was the duty of the servant in the premises, and what were the obligations of the master, are different questions, and the one throws no light on the other. When a man strikes me, it is my duty to receive the blow with a proper spirit; but this furnishes no sanction for his conduct.

Now this undeniable fact, that the right of the master over the person and the services of the slave is never recognised *at all* in the New Testament, is a most important fact, and in the circumstances of the case could not but have an important bearing on the whole subject in the view of the early Christians. How could it be that he would not be led to ask the question, as already remarked, whether the apostles regarded it as right? If an owner of slaves in the United States were now to appeal to the New Testament to justify what is actually done, to what part of the New Testament would he look? Where would he find a distinct precept, giving him a right to *buy* a fellow being? Or to hold him as property? Or to sell him? Or to separate him from his wife and children? Or to withhold from him the Bible? Or to feed him on coarse fare, and to clothe him in coarse raiment, in order that he himself and his family might be supported in indolency and luxury? For not one of these things will he find a direct precept or permission in the New Testament; and yet *all* of them are things which are unlawful *without* such a precept or permission.

(2.) The New Testament lays down the doctrine, in terms so plain that a holder of slaves could not be ignorant of it, that all men are by nature equal in regard to their rights; that there is no distinction of blood, or caste, or complexion that can justify such an institution as that of slavery. It is one of the fundamental doctrines of Christianity—a doctrine on which the whole system is based, and which sends its influence into every portion of the system—that God "hath made *of one blood* all nations of men for to dwell on all the face of the earth." Acts xviii. 26. They are descended from the same earthly ancestors, and are children alike of the same heavenly Parent. Whatever distinction of complexion there may be, it is a doctrine of the Bible that all belong to one and the same great family, and that in the most important matters pertaining to their existence they are on a level. By nature, one is no more the favourite of Heaven than another; one has no rights over another. Now, this doctrine, which lies everywhere on the face of the Bible, could not but be seen by a conscientious Christian master in the times of the apostles, to strike at one of the *fundamental* conceptions on which slavery is based—the essential superiority of one class of men over another. It was on this ground professedly that Aristotle advocated slavery;* and if it were not for this conception, slavery could not long exist at all. I need not say that extensively at the South now in our own country, it is maintained that the negro belongs to a race essentially inferior to the white man, and that by his physical incapacity it may be demonstrated that he was designed by his Creator to be in a condition of servitude; nor need I say that this idea of essential inferiority contributes much, even among good men, though often unconsciously to themselves, to perpetuate the system. All over the world it would probably be found that one of the essential things on which the institution of servitude rests, is this supposition of the natural inferiority of one class to another, and

---

* See Biblical Repository, as above.

the moment when that shall be made to disappear, and the conception shall fully enter the mind, that, whatever difference of
complexion or physical characteristics of any kind there may
be, there is essential equality; that all are the children of
God alike; that the same blood flows in all human veins;
that every human being is *a brother*—that moment a death-
blow will be given to slavery, from which it will never
recover. I need not say that whatever support the system
was supposed to derive among the ancients from the inequa-
lity of men, or the inferiority of one class to another, or whatever it may be supposed to derive from the same consideration now, this receives no countenance from the New
Testament. It would be impossible for a Christian master to
derive the least sanction to his claim to the service of others,
from any intimation of the kind in that book.

(3.) The New Testament lays down the doctrine that all
are alike in a more important respect than in the equality of
natural rights, and their being of the same family. All are
redeemed by the same blood, and are heirs of the same glorious
immortality. The same great sacrifice has been made for the
slave which has been made for his master; and so far as the
purchase made by redemption affixes any stamp of value on the
human soul, it proclaims that the soul of the slave is worth as
much as that of the master. In every respect as a redeemed
sinner; as an heir of heaven; as a child of God, the slave is
on a level with his master. He has the same right to worship God; to partake of the ordinances of religion; to pray;
to read the Bible. In the highest of all senses they are
brethren—ransomed in the same way, and destined, if they
are Christians, to live in the same heaven. It is unnecessary
to attempt to prove this from the New Testament, for it lies
on the face of the volume, and no one can call it in question.

Yet it is impossible not to see what would be the bearing
of this truth on the mind of a Christian master, and on the
whole question of slavery. In spite of all reasoning to the
contrary, the feeling *must* cross the mind of such a master

that he has no right to hold *a Christian brother* in bondage ·
to regard him as property; to sell him to others; to break up
his domestic relations; to interfere with any of his rights as a
husband, a father, a son, or a Christian. The feeling will
cross the mind that, as a redeemed man, he has the same rights
as any other redeemed man; that as Christ died for him, he
is to be treated in every way as an heir of life; that as all
hope for the same heaven, no one has a right to rivet the
fetters of bondage on another. A Christian master, in order
to his having perfect peace in asserting his claims over a
redeemed man as a slave, *must* feel that there ought to be
some *explicit warrant* for this in the New Testament; and
if there is any thing for which such a plain, unequivocal
warrant should be adduced, it is for the asserted right of hold
ing a Christian brother,—a fellow-heir of life—a candidate for
heaven,—as *property;* the right to sell him or to keep him,
to alienate him by contract or by will; to appropriate all the
avails of his labour to our own use; to regulate exactly his
manner of living; to separate him from wife, and children, and
home; and to determine the times and seasons, if any, when
he may worship God. And when we ask for this explicit
warrant, this unambiguous authority in the case, we are
referred to two texts of the New Testament, enjoining on
masters 'to do the same things to them, forbearing threatening, knowing that they have a master in heaven;' and 'to
render to their servants that which is just and equal.' And
this is all. This is the whole authority which is or can be
adduced for reducing one for whom Christ died to bondage,
and holding a Christian brother in the chains of perpetual
servitude. Verily, a Christian master should be able to refer
to some more explicit authority than this.

(4.) The fair influence of the injunctions on this subject in
the New Testament, so far as a Christian master would feel
himself addressed in them, would be to induce him to emancipate his slaves. If there was no explicit authority given
to him to hold them in bondage; if they were considered to

be n all respects by nature on an equality with himself, and as having the same rights as he; if they were regarded as Christian brethren, redeemed by the same blood, and heirs of the same eternal life, the effect on the mind of a conscientious man would be inevitable. However he might have felt before he was made acquainted with the Christian system, when these great doctrines of the cross were revealed to him, and he had embraced them, he could not but have felt their silent influence on the mind, leading him to the conclusion that Christianity designed that all should be free. The influence of these doctrines may be illustrated by a supposed case. At a time when it was the law of nations that all prisoners of war should be regarded as slaves, we may conceive of a man who had early left his home and country, and gone to a distant land. While there, among the captives which might be exposed to sale, might be a bright and beautiful female child. Impressed with the common sentiments respecting the rights over the captives taken in war, he may have purchased her without scruple, when exposed to sale, as his slave. What now would be his emotions, and what his views about the propriety of retaining her in bondage, if he should learn that she was his own sister; born after he had left his home; the daughter of his own beloved mother? Would he suppose that he had a right to retain her as a slave; to hold her as property; to sell her to whom he pleased? Much like this was the effect which Christianity was fitted to produce on the feelings and views of men in regard to slavery. Up to the time when its truths were made known, the great mass of mankind had no scruples about its propriety. They regarded one portion of the race as inferior to the other, and as born to be slaves. Christianity disclosed the great truth that all were on a level; that all were equal; that all were brethren. When this truth dawned on the soul, what must have been its effect on those who held their fellow-men in bondage? That effect must have been not a little like that in the supposed case of the man who had unwittingly purchased his own sister, and now held her as a slave.

If we look more closely at the very precepts which the apostles gave to 'masters,' and on which reliance is placed to justify them in holding their fellow-men in bondage, it must be apparent that this effect would follow from those very precepts, even if there were no other on the subject in the New Testament. One of them (Eph. vi. 9) enjoins it on masters to ' do the same things unto them, forbearing threatening, knowing that they had a master in heaven, and that *there is no respect of persons with him.*' Would the effect of *this* precept be to lead him to infer that slavery was a good thing, and was to be perpetuated ? The manifest object of the apostle in this passage is, to secure for servants a proper treatment ; to require the master to evince towards them the same spirit which he had enjoined on servants ; and to teach them to remember that they had a master in heaven who would require a strict account ; for ' *there was no respect of persons with him.*' But this great and central truth of the Christian religion, that 'there is no respect of persons with God,' is one which is by no means favourable to the perpetuity of slavery. A man who should have this constantly before his mind, and allow it to have its full influence on his heart, would not be long the owner of a slave. The direct tendency of it is to show him that his slave, in the sight of God, is equal to himself, and that before his high and impartial tribunal the rights of the slave would be regarded as much as those of the master. The other passage is still more decisive : " Masters, render unto your servants *that which is just and equal;* knowing that ye also have a master in heaven." Col. iv. 1. What would be the fair effect of this on the mind of a conscientious Christian master? What *would* be ' just and equal' to a man in these circumstances ? Would it not be (*a*) to compensate him fairly for his labour ; to furnish him an adequate remuneration for what he had earned ? But this would strike a blow at the root of slavery, for one of the elementary principles of the system is, that there *must* be 'unrequited labour;' that is, *the slave must earn as much more than he receives, as will do his part in maintaining his master and his family in idleness.* If he and they were disposed to earn their own living, they would not need the labour of slaves. (*b*) If a man should in fact render to his slaves 'that which is just and equal,' would he not restore them to freedom? Would any thing short of this be *all* that is just and equal? In the case of our own sons, if they were reduced to slavery, could we feel that any thing *short* of restoration to freedom would meet the claims of justice? Have not slaves in every instance been deprived of their liberty by *injustice?* Are they not retained in their condition by a practical denial of their *equality* with other men? Is it not now both *unjust*, and a denial of their *equality* with others, to continue that relation any longer? And would not *justice* to them restore them to freedom? What has the slave done to forfeit his right to liberty? What has he or his forefathers done to make it 'just' that it should be contemplated that he and his posterity should be held in bondage *for ever?* And is he not now retained in his present condition, every day and hour, by withholding that which is 'equal?' *Has* he now 'equal' rights, and 'equal' privileges with other men? Has he not been cut off from them by *denying* him the equality to which he is entitled in the arrangements of God's government? Can he be held at all without violating all the just notions of *equality?* This passage, therefore, contains a *principle* which would 'lay the axe at the root' of slavery everywhere.

Now, suppose a man to be fairly under the influence of these undoubted principles of Christianity. Let him be imbued with the conviction that God has made of one blood all the human race; that all are by nature equal before him; that all have been redeemed by the same great sacrifice on the cross, showing no respect to colour, caste, or rank; that all true Christians are *brethren*—belonging to the same family and fellow-heirs of the grace of life ; and that it is a duty to render to all that which is just and equal ; and to these things let him add the golden rule of the Saviour, and what sanction would these two passages (Eph. vi. 9, and Col. iv. 1) really give to the system of slavery ? What would be the fair influence of all the precepts of Christianity which *the master* could regard as appropriate to him, and bearing on his duty ? Would it be—could it be, to satisfy his conscience that the apostles meant to teach that it was right for him as a Christian man to hold his brother—his fellow Christian—*as property ;* and to regard him as, in *any* sense, a 'chattel' or a 'thing ?' *Could* he feel this—when it is never *said*, and when it is never even *implied ?* No ! no man under the full and fair influence of these principles could feel thus.

The case of Onesimus, the servant of Philemon.

In pursuing the inquiry whether the precepts addressed to masters furnish a sanction for slavery, there is a propriety in examining, with a somewhat more rigid attention, the case of Onesimus, the servant of Philemon. This is especially important, from the reliance which is reposed on that case by the advocates of slavery. The epistle to Philemon is often referred to by them as full proof that the sanction of the New Testament is given to slavery ; and, indeed, it would seem to be regarded as so clear on the point, that all that is necessary is to *name* this epistle as settling the whole matter in debate. The points which it is supposed to prove are two :—*first*, that slavery is right, since it is assumed that Onesimus was a slave, and that Paul, in writing to his master Philemon, does not intimate that the relation was contrary to the spirit of Christianity ; and *second*, that it is our duty to restore a slave to his master, if he runs away—since it is assumed that Paul did this in the case of Onesimus.* This argument is con-

---

* Comp. Dr. Fuller on Slavery, in his Letters to Dr. Wayland, pp. 194, 195.

stantly referred to by the advocates of slavery at the North as well as at the South.

It cannot be denied that this view of the matter would be sustained by most of the commentaries on this epistle ; but it is time to inquire whether that exposition is the true one, and whether this epistle gives any sanction to slavery in these respects. Perhaps a not less important inquiry also would be, whether the common interpretation put on this epistle, as sustaining slavery, could be made to commend itself to the innate sense of mankind as what a revelation *would* teach ; and especially whether it could be so commended to slaves themselves as to make them feel that a book which taught the doctrine commonly supposed to be taught in it, *could* be a revelation from God.* In order to this, it is important to

---

* A very affecting illustration of the use which is often made of this epistle at the South in defence of slavery, and of the innate conviction of the slaves themselves that a revelation from God *cannot* inculcate the doctrine that is derived from it, and of the distrust and suspicion excited in the minds of slaves against the ministers of the gospel when they declare that this epistle *does* sanction slavery, is found in the Tenth Annual Report of the "Association for the Religious Instruction of the Negroes in Liberty county, Georgia." In that report, the missionary, the Rev. C. C. Jones, frankly says:—" Allow me to relate a fact which occurred in the spring of this year, illustrative of the character and knowledge of the negroes at this time. I was preaching to a large congregation on the *Epistle to Philemon;* and when I insisted upon fidelity and obedience as Christian virtues in servants, and, upon the authority of Paul, condemned the practice of *running away,* one half of my audience deliberately rose up and walked off with themselves, and those that remained looked any thing but satisfied, either with the preacher or his doctrine. After dismission, there was no small stir among them: some solemnly declared ' that there was no such epistle in the Bible ;' others, ' that it was not the gospel;' others, 'that I preached to please masters;' others, 'that they did not care if they ever heard me preach again.'"—pp. 24, 25. This is a very instructive passage on the subject of slavery. Mr. Jones has shown himself by his labours to be a sincere friend of the coloured man, and to be truly desirous of his welfare, and has been making a very interesting

know exactly what was the state of the case in relation to
these points—for in interpreting the New Testament it should
not be *assumed* that any part of it is in favour of slavery, any
more than it may be assumed in respect to polygamy, profaneness, adultery, or any other sin.   The points which it is
necessary to make out, in order to prove that the epistle of
Philemon may be urged in favour of slavery, are, that Onesimus was actually a slave ; that Paul returned him against his
will to his former master ; that he sent him back because he
supposed he had done wrong by escaping from servitude ;
that he so expressed himself in the letter to his master as to
show that he was not unfriendly to the system, or regarded it
as not inconsistent with the spirit of the Christian religion ;
and that he meant that Onesimus should continue to be held
as a slave, after his return to Philemon.   Now, in regard to
these points, I would make the following remarks :—

---

experiment—which, from the nature of the case, must ultimately be a
failure—to see whether true religion can be propagated and maintained
among a people by *mere oral* instruction, and where the slave is forbidden
by law to have free access to the oracles of God.   If Mr. Jones had been
trained under different influences, and had adopted a different method of
interpreting this epistle ; if he had been able, consistently with his views
of truth, in expounding it to his congregation of slaves, to have said that
there was no certain evidence that Onesimus was a slave at all; that when
he was away, and had been converted to Christianity, he may have felt
that he had wronged Philemon, and on many accounts wished to return
to him ; that there is no proof that Paul sent him back against his will,
or even advised him to go, but that, seeing he was desirous to return, he
gave him a kind letter to Philemon, to induce him to be willing to receive
him again ; and that, even supposing he had been a slave, Paul expressly
directed him *not* to regard and treat him any more *as* a slave, but as in all
respects a Christian brother, it cannot be doubted that his audience would
have all retained their seats.   *That* view would have accorded well enough
with their common sense, and with what they would expect to find in a
revelation from the Father of all mankind ; it is no wonder that they
could not be persuaded that the other view was any part of a revelation
from heaven.

(*a.*) There is no positive or certain evidence that Onesi-mus was a slave at all. Even if it should be admitted to be *probable* that he was, it would be necessary, in order that the epistle might be adduced in favour of slavery, that the fact should be made out without any ground of doubt, or the argument is worthless—for the only conceivable force *in* the argument is, that he was a slave. Just so far as there is any doubt about that, so far is the argument of no value. It is clear that the epistle can, under any circumstances, be adduced in favour of slavery only *so far* as it is certain that Onesimus had been a slave. But that is not certain. It cannot be made to be certain, and it should not be taken for granted. Either of the suppositions that he was bound to service till he was of age by a parent or guardian, or that he had voluntarily obligated himself to serve for wages, if true, would be fatal to the argument derived from this epistle in favour of slavery ; and in order to that argument, it must be shown by fair exegesis that *neither* of these suppositions accord with what is said of him by the apostle.

What, then, is the evidence that Onesimus was a slave? *All* the proof that there can be on that point must be derived from ver. 16, and *all* the evidence *in* that verse is in the fact that he is there called "*a servant*,"—δοῦλος. "Not now as a servant." What evidence that verse affords that, *if* he were a slave, Paul did not mean that the relation should be continued, will be considered hereafter. The question now is, whether the mere application of the term "servant" to him— δοῦλος—necessarily proves that he was a slave?

From the remarks which I have before made on the meaning of the Greek word rendered *servant*—δοῦλος—it is evident, I trust, that nothing certain can be determined, from the mere use of this word, in regard to the condition of one to whom it is applied. It is not the peculiar and distinctive word which in the Greek language denotes a *slave*—though like our word *servant*, it was often, perhaps usually applied to a slave Like that word, it is of a general character, and would be applied to *any one* who was engaged in the service of another, whether bound by a parent or guardian, or whether he engaged voluntarily to serve another, or whether he was purchased as a slave, or whether he was a *serf* attached to the soil. The word denotes *servant* of any kind, and it should never be assumed that those to whom it was applied were slaves. Unless there is some circumstance stated which will enable us to determine what *kind* of a servant any one was, it can never be ascertained by the mere use of the word. In the instance before us, there is no circumstance mentioned by which it can be determined whether Onesimus was a voluntary or involuntary servant, and no advocate of slavery has a right to assume that he was a slave. It cannot be inferred, from the fact that he had run away from his master, that he was a slave, for indented apprentices often do this; and those who have made a voluntary contract to labour for others do this, and by doing it are guilty of all the wrong here charged on Onesimus. It cannot be inferred, from the fact that Paul sent him back to his master, that he was a slave, for this might have occurred if he had been a bound servant, an apprentice, or even one who had voluntarily agreed to labour in the employment of Philemon; and, as we shall see, there is no evidence whatever that Paul compelled him to return against his will. *All* that is said of him in ver. 16 of the epistle, or in any other part of the epistle, would be met by the supposition that he was a *voluntary servant*, and that he had been in fact intrusted with important business by Philemon. No man has a right to *assume* that when the word δοῦλος—*doulos*—occurs in the New Testament, it means a *slave*, or that he to whom it was applied was a slave; (comp. Mark x. 44; Luke ii. 29, xvii. 10; Acts ii. 18, iv. 29, xvi. 17; Rom. i. 1, vi. 16; 2 Cor. iv. 5; Rev. i. 1, ii. 20, &c. &c.;) and yet, *without* such an assumption, it is impossible to prove that Onesimus sustained this relation.

(*b.*) There is not the least evidence that Paul used any force, or even persuasion, to induce Onesimus to return to

Philemon. It cannot be inferred from the epistle, that he even *advised* him to return. All that even *looks* like evidence on this point is found in ver. 12 of the epistle: "Whom *I have sent again:* thou therefore receive him, that is, mine own bowels." But all the circumstances of the case make it probable, or certainly not improbable, that this was at his own request, and there is nothing in the expression which will not be fully met by such a supposition. (1) The language does not necessarily imply that he *compelled* him to go, or even *urged* him to do it. It is just such as would have been used on the supposition, either that he *requested* him to go and convey a letter to Colosse, or that Onesimus *desired* to go, and that Paul sent him, agreeably to his request. Comp. Phil. ii. 25, "Yet I supposed it necessary *to send* to you Epaphroditus, my brother and companion in labour," &c. ; Coloss. iv. 7, "All my state shall Tychicus declare unto you, who is a beloved brother, and a faithful minister, and fellow-servant in the Lord : whom *I have sent* unto you for the same purpose, that he might know your estate," &c. But Epaphroditus and Tychicus were not sent against their will, nor is there any more reason to think that Onesimus was. Comp., for a similar use of the Greek word πέμπω, which does not differ in sense from the word here used, ἀποπέμπω, (*to send up, to send back,*) so far as the point before us is concerned, Luke vii. 6, 10, 19, xx. 13; Acts x. 5, xv. 22; 1 Cor. iv. 17; 2 Cor. ix. 3; Eph. vi. 22; Phil. ii. 19, 23, 28. The word here employed by the apostle is of such general import, that on the supposition that Onesimus had a *desire* to return, or that Paul wished him to bear a message to a friend there, or to do any other service for him, this would be the very word which would be employed. There is nothing in the statement which forbids us to suppose that Onesimus was *disposed* to return to Philemon, and that Paul sent him at his own request. (2) Paul had no *power* to send Onesimus back to his master, unless he chose to go. He had no civil authority; he had no guard to send him with; he could intrust

him to no sheriff to convey him from place to place, or to con-
fine him in jail, if he were disposed to escape; and he had
no means of controlling him, if he chose to go to any other
place than Colosse. He could, indeed, have sent him away
from himself; he could have *told* him to go to Colosse, but
there his power ended. Onesimus then could have gone
where he pleased. But there is no evidence that Paul even
told him to go to Colosse against his own inclination, or that
he would have sent him at all, if he had not requested it.
And if he had, what probability is there that he would have
been so pliant and passive as to return *to a state of slavery?*
How many runaway slaves are there now, who would return
to their masters on being merely *told* to do so? Who ever
saw one that would be willing to do it, even on the authority
of an apostle?* (3) There may have been many reasons why
Onesimus *desired* to return to Colosse, and no one can prove
that he did not express that desire to Paul, and that Paul sent
him in consequence of that request. He may have had relatives and friends there; or, being now converted, he may

---

* An instance, illustrative of this, occurred once in my own experience.
About twelve or fourteen years since, as I was entering the gate of my
church, to go into my study, early in the morning, a fine-looking coloured
man, apparently about twenty-five or thirty years of age, met me, and told
me that he was a runaway slave, from Maryland, and wished some assistance. Influenced by feelings which commonly prevailed at that time, and,
as I then thought, in accordance with the Bible, and probably having this
very case of Onesimus in my eye, I endeavoured to show him the impropriety of his leaving his master, and to convince him that he ought to
return. But I could make not the least impression on his mind, and all
my arguments had no force in his view whatever. For the error which I
committed in that case, I have for years felt regret, and have increasingly
felt that I was bound to do something to help my fellow-men everywhere
to the enjoyment of freedom, in every proper way; and from that case, I
am satisfied that it would be no easy thing to persuade a man, who had
escaped from bondage, to return to it, even on apostolic authority. What
slave has there ever been in the world, who has been induced to return by
any such reasoning?

have become sensible that he had, in some way, wronged his former master, and that he ought to return, and repair the wrong; or he may have been poor, and a stranger in Rome, and may have been greatly disappointed in what he expected to find there when he left Philemon, and may have wished to return to the comparative comforts of his former condition. It is no uncommon thing for a runaway apprentice to be disappointed in the expectations which he cherished when he left his master, and to feel that it would be better for him if he could again return to his former home and employment. It is no very uncommon thing for one who has done wrong to another, and who has fled away, if he should be converted, to desire to return and repair the wrong. And since any one of these, or of many other supposable causes, may have induced Onesimus to desire to return to his master, it should not be *assumed* that Paul sent him against his will, and thence *inferred* that he was in favour of sending back runaway slaves *against their* will. There are many points to be proved, which cannot be proved, in order to make that a legitimate conclusion. (4) It may be added, therefore, that this passage should not be referred to, to prove that we *ought* to send back runaway slaves to their former masters against their own consent ; or to vindicate the laws, which require magistrates to do it ; or to show that they who have escaped from slavery should be arrested and forcibly detained; or to *justify any sort of influence over a runaway slave, to induce him to return to his former master.* There is not the least evidence that any of these things occurred in the case before us, and if this instance is ever referred to, it should be *to justify what Paul did*—AND NOTHING ELSE. The passage shows that it is right to aid a servant of any kind to return to his master, if he desires it ; and that it is right to give him a " letter," and to plead earnestly for his favourable reception, if he has in any way wronged his master—for Paul did this. On the same principle, it would be right to give him pecuniary assistance, to enable him to return—for there *may* be cases where one who has fled from servitude would wish to return. There may be instances where one has had a kind master, with whom he would feel, that, on the whole, he could be more happy than in his present circumstances. Or there may be instances where one may have relatives that are in the neighbourhood, or in the family of his former master, and the desire to be with them may be so strong, that he would prefer to be a servant, as he was before, rather than remain as he is now. In all such cases, it is right to render aid—for the example of the apostle Paul goes to sustain this: but it goes no further. Nothing more can be *proved;* nothing more is necessary to be believed, in order to a fair interpretation of the epistle.

(*c.*) There is no evidence that Paul meant that Onesimus should return *as* a slave, or with a view to his being retained and treated *as* a slave. Even supposing he had been so formerly, there is not the slightest intimation in the epistle that when he sent him back to his master, he meant that he should throw himself into the chains of bondage again. No man can take this epistle and prove from it that Paul *would* have sent him at all, if he had supposed that the effect would be that he would be reduced to slavery again. If *such* had been his expectation, the expression of such a desire would have found a place in the epistle; at least, the epistle would not have been so framed as almost of necessity to lead to a different result.

(*d.*) There is very satisfactory evidence, besides this, that Paul did *not* mean that Onesimus should be regarded and treated as a slave. This evidence is found in ver. 16, of the epistle : " Not now as a servant, but above a servant, a brother beloved, specially to me, but how much more unto thee, both in the flesh, and in the Lord." It would be impossible for Philemon to comply with the wish expressed here, and yet retain Onesimus as a slave, and regard him as property ; as a 'chattel ;' as a ' thing.' For (1) *if* he had been formerly a slave; if this is the fair meaning of the word δοῦλος, (*doulos,*) then this is expressly declared,—" *Not now as a servant,* (οὐκέτι ὡς δοῦλον.) If he had been a slave before, he did not *wish* that he should be received as such now, or regarded as such any longer. The adverb rendered 'not now,' (οὐκέτι,) means, *no more, no farther, no longer.* It implies that in regard to the condition in which he had been before, he was not to be so any more. He was to be received and treated as sustaining another kind of relation hereafter, that of a Christian brother. Comp. Matt. xix. 6, "They are *no more* twain ;"— the same Greek word. They were once so, but they are not to be regarded as such now. Matt. xxii. 46 : "Neither durst any man from that day forth, ask him *any more* questions," (ἐπερωτῆσαι αὐτὸν οὐκέτι.) They once did it, but now they did not dare to do it. Luke xv. 19 : "Am *no more* worthy to be called thy son ;"—though I once was. John vi. 66 : "And walked *no more* with him ;"—though they once did. See also John xi. 54, xiv. 19, xvii. 11 ; Acts viii. 39 ; Gal. iv. 7 ; Eph. ii. 19. How *could* Philemon comply with this wish of the apostle, on the supposition that Onesimus had been before a slave, and yet regard him still as such ? The very attempt to do it would be directly in the face of the desire expressed by the apostle, and every moment he held him as such he would be disregarding his wishes. Suppose that Paul, after a short interval, had actually gone to the residence of Philemon, as he expected to, (ver. 22,) and had found him regarding and treating Onesimus *as a slave ;* would he have felt that he had complied with his wishes ? Did he ask this of him ? Did he *not* ask just the reverse—that he would not do it any more ? Would it not be natural for him to say that he had *not* received him as he wished him to do ? And how could Philemon have replied to this ? (2) He desired him to receive and treat him, in all respects, as a Christian brother ; as one redeemed ; as a man : "Not now as a servant, but *above* a servant, *a brother beloved ;*" that is, as a Christian brother. See 1 Tim. vi. 2, where this same phrase is applied to Christian masters, and where it is claimed justly, as has been already noticed, by the advocates of slavery, that it proves that those to whom it was applied were real Christians : " Let them not despise them, because they are *brethren ;* but rather do them service, because *they are faithful and beloved*." The phrase implies that he was a Christian, and was entitled to be treated, in all respects, as a Christian brother, and in no respect as a servant. But how could he do this, and yet regard and treat him as a slave ? *Is* it treating one in all respects as a Christian brother, to deprive him of freedom ; to consider him as an article of merchandise ; to exact his labour without compensation ? Would the man himself who makes another a slave, suppose that *he* was treated as a Christian brother, if *he* were reduced to that condition ? Would he feel that his son was so regarded, if *he* was made a slave ? There are no ways of reconciling these things. It is *impossible* for a man to regard his slave as, in the full and proper sense of the phrase, ' *a Christian brother*.' He may, indeed, esteem him highly as a Christian ; he may treat him with kindness ; he may show him many favours ; but— *he regards him also* AS HIS SLAVE ; and this makes a difference wide as " from the centre thrice to the utmost pole" in his feelings towards him and other Christians. He is *not* on a level with himself *as* a Christian. He has not the same rights in his own family, and in regard to his time, and to the avails of his labour, and to the privilege of reading the Bible, which the master supposes the Christian religion to guarantee to himself : and in relation to these things he could not but feel that he was deprived of the rights which religion confers, if *he* were placed in the same condition in which his slave is. The idea of his being *his slave* mingles with all the feelings of the master towards him, and gives a colouring to all his views of him. He cannot but feel, if he is under the influence of religion, that that slave, if he were treated in *all* respects as a Christian, would be as free as himself ; would have the same right to his time, and skill, and liberty ; would be permitted to form his own plans, and to enjoy the avails of his

own labour ; and would be as secure from the possibility of
being *sold*.

If it should be objected here, that when the apostle (ver. 16)
requests Philemon to receive Onesimus " not as a servant, but
above a servant, a brother beloved," he adds " specially to me,
but how much more unto thee, *both in the flesh*, and in the
Lord," and that this phrase ' *in the flesh*' proves that he had
been a slave, and that he meant that he should still be so considered, though at the same time he was to be regarded as a
Christian brother ; I would reply, that the phrase ' in the
flesh' may be properly used in reference to *any* relation which
may exist pertaining to this present world, as contradistin-
guished from that which is formed primarily by religion, and
which would be expressed by the phrase ' in the Lord.' This
latter phrase denotes relations formed by religion, or in which
religion lies at the basis. (Comp. 1 Cor. vii. 39, ix. 1 ; Rom.
xvi. 2, 22 ; Eph. vi. 21 ; Phil. i. 14 ; 1 Thess. v. 12, *et al*.)
The other expression, ' in the flesh,' denotes any relation pertaining to the present life, or founded on any thing else but
religion. See 1 Cor. vii. 28, x. 18 ; Rom. ix. 3, xi. 14 ;
Gal. iv. 23. It might, in itself, refer to any natural relation
of blood, or to any formed in business, or constituted by mere
friendship, or by family alliance, or to any relation having its
origin either in voluntary or involuntary servitude. It will
not do to *assume* that it refers to any one of these, without
more evidence than is conveyed in the mere expression ; and
from the mere use of the phrase, it will not do to infer that he
to whom it is applied was a slave. It is not necessary to suppose, in order to meet the full force of the expression, either
that Onesimus had been a slave, or that he would be continued
to be regarded as such. Any relation of the kind referred to
above which may have existed before between him and Philemon, or which might be afterwards formed, would be appropriately denoted by this phrase. The new and more interesting relation, which they were now to sustain to each other,
which was formed by religion, is expressed by the phrase

'in the Lord.' In *both* these, Paul hoped that Onesimus would manifest the appropriate spirit of a Christian, and be worthy of his entire confidence. It may be added also, that there are many relations of a voluntary kind subsisting between one man and another, involving the obligation even to render service, which are entirely consistent with the feeling that he who renders it is in all respects a Christian brother; but none, except the natural relations of kindred, of an involuntary kind. A labourer on a farm; a journeyman mechanic; a scrivener employed to do a piece of writing; a book-keeper or a salesman in a store; a lawyer 'retained' to manage a cause; a minister of the gospel employed as a pastor—engaged all of them in a voluntary service; and a son from his natural relations bound to labour for his father to a certain period of life—each of these may be regarded in all respects as a Christian brother;—a slave never.

(*e.*) The principles laid down in this epistle to Philemon, therefore, would lead to the universal abolition of slavery. If all those who are now slaves were to become Christians, and their masters were to treat them ' not as slaves, but as brethren beloved,' the period would not be far distant when slavery would cease. This would probably be admitted by all. But if this is conceded, then all is conceded that my argument requires. It would follow from that, that slavery is *not* a thing which it is desirable to perpetuate—is *not* a thing which Christianity tends to perpetuate—and is therefore evil and sinful. For, a state of things which would be destroyed by Christianity is not right at any time. Christianity, even in its highest influences, interferes with nothing that is good, and would annihilate nothing which is not wrong. That which is true, pure, and just, and which is best for the welfare of man, will survive in all the relations of life, when Christianity spreads all over the world; and to say that Christianity, when fairly applied in an individual case, as that of Philemon, would destroy the system of slavery, is to say that Christianity would everywhere destroy it, and that it i always wrong—for what would have existed in that one family, in reference to this relation, under the fair influence of the gospel, would exist in every family on the face of the earth.

3. No argument in favour of slavery can be derived from the injunctions addressed by the apostles to slaves themselves.

The argument on this point in favour of slavery is often referred to, and is relied on, among others, as conclusive, in proof that slavery is not to be regarded as sinful. Thus it is adduced by Dr. Fuller :—

"The New Testament is not silent as to slavery; it recognises the relation, and commands slaves to obey their masters; and what I now affirm is this, that, when we consider the previous permission by the Old Testament, such commands to slaves are not only a *suppressio veri*, but a *suggestio falsi* —not only a suppression of the truth, but a suggestion of what is false—if slavery be a sin of appalling magnitude. Let it be borne in mind that the previous sanction had been both by God's conduct and express precept, and demanded, therefore, a countervailing revelation of no equivocal sort. Yet, not only is no condemnation uttered, but slaves are addressed as such, and required to obey.

"'Is any man called,' says the apostle, 'being circumcised? let him not become uncircumcised. Is he called in uncircumcision, let him not be circumcised. Circumcision is nothing, and uncircumcision is nothing, but the keeping of the commandments of God. Let every man abide in the same calling wherein he was called. *Art thou called being a servant? care not for it;* but if thou mayest be made free, use it rather. For he that is called in the Lord, being a servant, is the Lord's freeman : likewise, also, he that is called, being free, is Christ's servant.' 1 Cor. vii. 18—22. His ardent soul on fire with the great salvation, and the anticipations of the glory to be revealed, Paul declares that the true spirit of the gospel, instead of interfering with social relations, should cause the believer to soar above them; and that the

advantages and disadvantages of all earthly conditions ought
to be forgotten and swallowed up in the thought of those
transports and raptures to which he is hastening.   In the
verse just copied, while he says liberty is to be preferred to
slavery, yet he adds that, in the light of faith, the soul alone
has true value, and even the hardest bondage is nothing at all,
the most cruel treatment nothing at all, not worth a thought,
if the slave has been called to the glorious liberty of the
gospel.   And he classes the distinction between master and
servant in the same list with circumcision and uncircumcision, which made no sort of difference."*

The passages relied on in this argument are these, and
these only :—

1 Cor. vii. 20—24: "Let every man abide in the same
calling wherein he was called.   Art thou called being a servant ? care not for it : but if thou mayest be made free, use
it rather.   For he that is called in the Lord, being a servant,
is the Lord's freeman : likewise also he that is called, being
free, is Christ's servant.   Ye are bought with a price ; be not
ye the servants of men.   Brethren, let every man, wherein he
is called, therein abide with God."

Eph. vi. 5—8: "Servants, be obedient to them that are
your masters according to the flesh, with fear and trembling,
in singleness of your heart, as unto Christ; not with eye-service, as men-pleasers ; but as the servants of Christ, doing
the will of God from the heart ; with good will doing service,
as to the Lord, and not to men : knowing that whatsoever
good thing any man doeth, the same shall he receive of the
Lord, whether he be bond or free."

Col. iii. 22—25 : "Servants, obey in all things your masters according to the flesh ; not with eye-service, as men-
pleasers ; but in singleness of heart, fearing God : and whatsoever ye do, do it heartily, as to the Lord, and not unto men ;
knowing that of the Lord ye shall receive the reward of the

---

* Dr. Fuller's Letters to Dr. Wayland, pp. 188, 189, 190.

inheritance : for ye serve the Lord Christ.   But he that doeth wrong shall receive for the wrong which he hath done : and there is no respect of persons."

1 Tim. vi. 1—5 : " Let as many servants as are under the yoke count their own masters worthy of all honour, that the name of God and his doctrine be not blasphemed.   And they that have believing masters, let them not despise them, because they are brethren ; but rather do them service, because they are faithful and beloved, partakers of the benefit.   These things teach and exhort.   If any man teach otherwise, and consent not to wholesome words, even the words of our Lord Jesus Christ, and to the doctrine which is according to godliness, he is proud, knowing nothing, but doting about questions and strifes of words, whereof cometh envy, strife, railings, evil surmisings, perverse disputings of men of corrupt minds, and destitute of the truth, supposing that gain is godliness : from such withdraw thyself."

Titus ii. 9, 10 : " Exhort servants to be obedient unto their own masters, and to please them well in all things ; not answering again ; not purloining, but showing all good fidelity ; that they may adorn the doctrine of God our Saviour in all things."

1 Peter ii. 18—20 : " Servants, be subject to your masters with all fear ; not only to the good and gentle, but also to the froward.   For this is thank-worthy, if a man for conscience toward God endure grief, suffering wrongfully.   For what glory is it, if, when ye be buffeted for your faults, ye shall take it patiently ? but if, when ye do well, and suffer for it, ye take it patiently, this is acceptable with God."

The question now is, whether these passages are to be regarded as evidence that the apostles approved of slavery, and desired that it should be perpetuated ?   Whether the design of these passages was to induce the slaves themselves to believe that their condition was a desirable one ; that all that Christianity could do for them was to meliorate their circumstances *in* that relation ; and that it was contemplated by it, that one portion of the members of the church should always be held in bondage to another portion ?

If the passages quoted can be regarded as proof on this point, the proof must either lie in the fact that they enjoin submission to their masters ; or that they do not enjoin it on slaves, as a duty, to assert their freedom ; or that they do not even declare that the slave had a right to freedom.   In reference to this argument, I would make the following remarks :

(*a*) The main duty which they enjoin on the slaves is that of patience, meekness, fidelity, kindness, truth, and honesty— duties which are. obligatory on Christians towards all men, whatever may be their relations, and of course towards masters.   There were certain vices to which servants were particularly exposed—as pilfering, lying, purloining, eye-service ; and the apostles enjoin on them, as Christians, to avoid those vices.   So they enjoin a patient and kind spirit towards their masters ; but this does not prove that their masters were right in doing that which made the virtues of patience and meekness necessary.   When the Saviour enjoins on me to turn my cheek to him that smote me, it does not prove that he was right who smote me ; when he commands me to give my coat to him who had taken away my cloak, it does not prove that he had a right to either of them.   There is a Christian duty which *I* am to perform in the circumstances in which I am placed, whatever may be the conduct of others ; but that fact does not prove that others are right in what they do to me. The injunctions of the apostles addressed to slaves do no more to sanction the evils of slavery, than the directions addressed to those who are persecuted sanction the conduct of Nero and Mary.   The fact that religion requires martyrs to be unresisting, and to allow themselves to be led to the stake, does not demonstrate that they are right who lead them to the stake ; and yet the argument in that case would just as much prove that the conduct of the persecutor is in accordance with the spirit of Christianity, as in the other, that slavery is.

(*b*) If these passages, enjoining obedience and patience on the part of slaves, prove that slavery is right, and will go to justify it, they prove that it was right as it then existed—for the apostles do not discourse about any *abstract* duty of obedience, but of obedience in the circumstances in which they then were placed. These injunctions, then, go to justify the whole system of Roman servitude, and to show that the apostles meant to lend their sanction to all the abominations that were practised in connection with Roman slavery. But it is presumed that there are no men now, who will pretend that that system was in accordance with the spirit of the gospel. Yet that is the *only* system in reference to which the apostles inculcate obedience.

(*c*) If these injunctions, to be obedient, honest, and patient, prove that slavery is consistent with the gospel, the similar injunctions addressed to Christians to be submissive to civil rulers will prove that all the abominations of the government of Nero were right, and that Christians were to submit to them *as being right*. The commands to obedience, patience, and fidelity, addressed to Christians under the administration of that monster of iniquity, are as positive and explicit as any addressed to slaves to be submissive to their masters. Thus the apostle Paul says, (Rom. xiii. 1—6,) "Let every soul be subject unto the higher powers. For there is no power but of God: the powers that be are ordained of God. Whosoever therefore resisteth the power, resisteth the ordinance of God: and they that resist shall receive to themselves damnation. For rulers are not a terror to good works, but to the evil. Wilt thou then not be afraid of the power? do that which is good, and thou shalt have praise of the same: for he is the minister of God to thee for good. But if thou do that which is evil, be afraid; for he beareth not the sword in vain: for he is the minister of God, a revenger to execute wrath upon him that doeth evil. Wherefore ye must needs be subject, not only for wrath, but also for conscience' sake. For, for this cause pay ye tribute also: for they are God's ministers, attending continually upon this very thing." It would be as proper to adduce this passage, to prove that the tyranny of Nero was a good and desirable government; that it was the design of Christianity to perpetuate such a government; that it would be wrong to attempt to throw it off and establish civil liberty, as to adduce the injunctions addressed to slaves to prove that slavery is a good institution. The injunctions in the one case are as positive as in the other.

(*d*) In these injunctions addressed to slaves, it is worthy of special observation, that *the right of the master is never conceded, or even referred to.* The obligation to obedience and fidelity is never put on the ground that slavery is right; that it is a good institution; that there is a natural inferiority of one to another, or that the master has in any way a claim to the service of his slave. The ground on which obedience and fidelity are enjoined is altogether different. It is, that, whatever treatment we may receive from others, *we* are to manifest a spirit of submission and meekness; we are to do our duty to our God, as Christians, in *any* circumstances in which we may be placed in life. In this case, if the apostles *did* believe that slavery is right, and in conformity with the spirit of Christianity, it is unaccountable that they did not put the obligation to obedience on that ground. That would at once have repressed any insubordination among the Christian slaves, and would have prevented any bad effect on their minds from certain doctrines, which they did lay down, which *seemed* to be adverse to slavery, and which a slave would be *likely* to construe as favourable to his natural equality with his master, and to his right to freedom. If the apostles believed that slavery is right, and meant to be understood as teaching that it is to be perpetuated, they have been guilty of a most unaccountable concealment in holding back this fact from the slaves themselves, and in never alluding to it, even in the remotest degree.

(*e*) The apostles, so far from intimating to slaves that they regarded the system as a good one, constantly represent it as a hard and undesirable condition, and exhort them to conduct themselves in this relation as under the infliction of a wrong. They exhort them to the exercise of just such virtues as they are bound to manifest who are constantly enduring wrong— the virtues of patience and meekness, and the manifestation of a spirit not disposed to take revenge. Thus Peter says, "Servants, be subject to your masters with all fear; not only to the good and gentle, but also to the froward. For this is thank-worthy, if a man for conscience toward God endure grief, suffering wrongfully. For what glory is it, if, when ye be buffeted for your faults, ye shall take it patiently? but if, when ye do well, and suffer for it, ye take it patiently, this is acceptable with God." So Paul represents it as a hard and undesirable condition, though he exhorts servants not to be anxious about it, but to remember that they will soon be delivered from it in heaven. 1 Cor. vii. 21: "Art thou called being a servant? care not for it; but if thou mayest be made free, use it rather. For he that is called in the Lord, being a servant, is the Lord's freeman." That is, 'Let him not be concerned about the hardships of his present condition, but let him patiently submit to them. He is already free in a higher and more important sense than it would be to be emancipated from temporal bondage, and let him, in the possession of that more valuable liberty, patiently bear the evils connected with his humble and trying situation in life, rejoicing that he is endowed with higher freedom—freedom from the degrading servitude of sin and Satan.' Now, what *other* relation of life is there which is described in this manner? What other is there, in which the principal virtues recommended are those which grow out of the patient endurance of wrongs? What other is there, in which the apostles exhort those who are in that relation 'not to care for it,' but to rejoice rather that they are free, in a higher and more important sense? What would have been thought if the same kind of exhortation had been addressed to wives, or to children, and it had been represented that the principal virtue to be exhibited by a wife or child was patient endurance of wrong? What would be inferred about the apostolic view of those relations, if the apostles had said to wives and children that they were not to 'care' anxiously on account of their condition, but that they were to rejoice in the feeling that they were 'free' in a higher sense, and that the ills of the condition of a wife or child, therefore, should be patiently borne? And what would be inferred, if he had told them that if they might be 'free' from a husband or father 'to use it rather?' But no such exhortations as these are found in the New Testament, and the relation of master and slave, therefore, is *not* like other relations.

(*f*) Slaves were directed, if possible, to obtain a release from their hard condition. They were taught to prefer freedom, and to obtain it, if they could consistently with the manifestation of the spirit of the gospel. Thus the apostle Paul expressly says, (1 Cor. vii. 21,) " Art thou called being a servant? care not for it: but if thou mayest be free, use it rather." Here there is a distinct assertion that freedom is preferable to slavery, and that the slave should not regard his condition as the best and most desirable, though, in comparison with the higher freedom which the gospel imparts in delivering the soul from sin, he was to regard his servitude as *comparatively* unimportant. This *might* be, and yet it might be true that slavery was a *great* evil. Yet the command is clear, that if it was in the *power* of the slave to become free, (εἰ καὶ δύνασαι ἐλεύθερος γενέσθαι,) he was to avail himself of the privilege. If either the laws or his master set him free; if he could purchase his liberty; if a friend would purchase it for him; if in *any* way that was not *sinful* he could obtain his freedom, he was to embrace the opportunity. But where is there any representation like this in regard to a wife or child? What should we think of the condition of a wife or child if there *had* been such a representation? But there is none. It is never said or implied that their condition, as such, is a hard or undesirable one, and that they should, if possible, escape from it.

(*g*) To all this is added, in regard to the slave, that, if he could *not* be free, he was to comfort himself with the reflection that he had been emancipated from the greater evil—*sin*, and therefore was to bear with patience the lesser temporary evil—*servitude;* that *in* his condition it was possible for him to serve Christ acceptably ; that the evils of his hard lot did not prevent his becoming a true Christian, and cherishing the hope of eternal life ; and that he should patiently bear those evils, submitting to the arrangements respecting them over which he had no control, as to any other wrong. 1 Cor. vii. 22 : " For he that is called in the Lord, being a servant, *is the Lord's freeman.*" ' He is manumitted, made free, endowed with liberty by the Lord.' The meaning is, ' You are blessed with freedom from the bondage of sin by the Lord. *That* servitude was far more grievous, and far more to be lamented, than the bondage of the body. You are now a true freeman, the freeman of the Lord. Your spirit is free ; while those who are not slaves, and perhaps your own masters, are even now under a more severe bondage than yours. You should rejoice, therefore, in deliverance from the greater evil, and be glad that in the eyes of the Lord you are regarded as *his* freeman, and are endowed by him with more valuable liberty than it would be to be delivered from the servitude under which you are now placed. You will soon be admitted to the eternal liberty of the saints in glory, and will forget all your toils, and privations, and wrongs, here below.' But, where, I may repeat, is there any such representation made to a wife, or a child, or even to the subject of a civil government ? Where are they told to console themselves in their hard condition with the reflection that they, by deliverance from sin, have been released from *a far greater evil* than the condition of a wife or child, and that, therefore, they should not regard the evils of their condition with solicitude ? Where are they told that though under the law of a husband, a parent, or a civil ruler, they were ' the Lord's freemen,' and should now bear patiently the lesser evils of their bondage in these relations, exulting in their higher liberty as the freemen of the Lord? There *are* no such exhortations in the New Testament, and the apostles never designed to represent the relations of husband and wife, and parent and child, and master and slave, as similar, or to leave the impression that the one was as proper and as desirable for the good of a community as the other.

From the arguments thus far presented in regard to the relation of Christianity to slavery, it seems fair to draw the conclusion that the Christian religion lends no *sanction* to slavery; that it is not adverted to in the New Testament either as a good and desirable relation, or as one that religion would have originated for the good of society, or as one which it is desirable to perpetuate in order that society may reach the highest point in its progress which it can reach. It would be clearly impossible to find a *hint* that would be the slightest basis of an argument to prove from the New Testament that either Christ or his apostles would have *originated* slavery, or that they regarded it as a good and desirable institution. There is but one point, then, necessary to complete the argument, which is to inquire whether they expressed any views, or laid down any principles, which, if fairly acted on, would tend to its abolition.

§ 4. *The principles laid down by the Saviour and his Apostles are such as are opposed to Slavery, and if carried out would secure its universal abolition.*

In addition to what has already been said, which might be appropriately introduced under this head, I would make some additional remarks. The inquiry is, what was the *intention* of the Saviour in regard to this institution? What would be the result of a fair application of the principles of his religion in regard to it? Did he design that it should be understood to be a good system, and one which his religion was intended to sanction and perpetuate?

To show that the institution of slavery is contrary to the Christian religion, and inconsistent with its spirit ; that it is regarded as an evil which religion was designed to remove from the world ; and that it cannot be perpetuated consistently with the fair influence of the gospel, I would now submit the following considerations :—

(1.) The Saviour and his apostles inculcated such views of man as *amount* to a prohibition of slavery, or as if acted on would abolish it. In other words, they gave such views of man, that, under their influence, no one would make or retain a slave. This argument I cannot express in a better manner than is done by Dr. Wayland :—

" In what manner, then, did the Saviour and his apostles deal with this universal sin ? I answer, by promulgating such truths concerning the nature and destiny of man, his relations and obligations both to man and to his Maker, as should render the slavery of a human being a manifest moral absurdity ; that is, a notion diametrically opposed to our elementary moral suggestions. Let us observe how strangely they are in contrast with all that was then known of the *character* and *value* of a man.

" To men who had scarcely an idea of the character, or even the existence, of a Supreme Intelligence, and whose objects of adoration were images of ' gold and silver and stone, graven with art and man's device,' and whose worship consisted in the orgies of Venus and Bacchus, the gospel revealed the existence of one only living and true Jehovah, all-wise, all-just, all-holy, everywhere present beholding the evil and the good, knowing the thoughts and intents of the heart, who will bring every secret thing into judgment, whether it be good or whether it be evil, and who has placed us all under one and the same law, that law which declares, ' Thou shalt love the Lord thy God with all thy heart, and thy neighbour as thyself.'

" To men who had scarcely an idea of existence after death, whose notions of futurity were the fables of Charon's boat, the Styx, and Tartarus—fables which were already held up as objects of inextinguishable laughter—the gospel revealed the doctrine of man's immortality; it taught that every human being was a never-dying soul; that the world to come was a state either of endless and inconceivable happiness or of wo; that for this infinitely important state, the present brief existence was the probation and the only probation that God had allotted to us; and that, during this probation, every one of our race must by his own moral character determine his destiny for himself.

"To men who had scarcely formed an idea of their moral relations, the gospel revealed the fact that our race were universally sinners, and were, without exception, under the condemnation of that law which denounces eternal death as the desert of every transgression; that God placed such an estimate upon a human soul, nay, that he so loved the world that he gave his only-begotten Son, that whosoever believeth on him should not perish, but have everlasting life; and that, in consequence of this atonement, eternal salvation is freely offered to every human being, who, repenting of his rebellion, will return to the love and service of God.

"To men steeped in the most debasing and universal sensuality, whose motto was, 'Let us eat and drink, for to-morrow we die,' the gospel revealed the truth, that while this salvation was thus freely offered to all, yet still every individual of our race was placed on earth to work out his salvation with fear and trembling; that he was still, in the strictest possible sense, in a state of probation; and that in a world lying in wickedness, surrounded by every temptation to sin, exposed to all the allurements of vice, and assailed by all the arts of the adversary of souls, he must come off conqueror over every moral enemy, or else he will after all perish under a most aggravated condemnation.

"And lastly, to men who esteemed the people of another nation as by nature foes whom they had a right to subdue, murder, or enslave, whenever and in what manner soever they

were able, the gospel revealed the fact that all men are, by the
act of their creation, *brethren ;* that all are equally beloved
by the same Father of all ; that Christ died equally for all ;
that all are equally exposed to the same perdition ; that to all
is equally offered a mansion in the same Father's house, and
that the title to that inheritance, the same to all, can be secured
in no other way than by obedience to the universal law of
love, a law enforced by the solemn sanction, ' Inasmuch as ye
did it not *to one of the least of these,* ye did it not *unto me.'*

"Such, then, were some of the effulgent truths which the
gospel poured upon the moral darkness of the heathen world.
Such was the entire revolution (the word, you perceive, is
feebleness itself when applied to such a case) which the gospel effected in all the notions which were then entertained
respecting the character, the destiny, the responsibilities, and
the *inestimable value* of a man. We feel at once that the
highest seraph around the throne would not dare to violate
the meanest right of the meanest creature who stood in such
a relation to God ; infinitely less would he dare, for the sake
of his own temporary convenience, to interfere with any of the
means to which such a creature was entitled, for ascertaining
and doing the will of God, and thus escaping eternal death,
and laying hold on everlasting life. ' Are *they* not all ministering spirits, sent forth to minister to those that are heirs of
salvation ?' What shall we say, then, if a creature of yesterday, himself subject to the same law, exposed to the same
condemnation, and going to the same judgment-seat, abolishes,
at his own pleasure, and on the authority of physical force,
the social, intellectual, and moral rights of his brother ; and
for the sake of pecuniary gain interferes with the most solemn
relations which can exist between the God and Father of us
all, and his child here on earth—a child redeemed with the
precious blood of his only-begotten Son.

"It is obvious that such principles as these, instilled into
the public mind, must of necessity abolish slavery, and every
other form of wrong. Just in so far as slavery is, either in

its principles or its practice, at variance with these elementary truths of revealed religion, it is forbidden. Whether it be thus at variance, let every man judge."*

To these remarks I would add, that the Christian religion teaches that "God hath made of one blood all the nations of men for to dwell on all the face of the earth," (Acts xvii. 26,) and that as the children of the common Father they are regarded as equal. All the right which one human being has ever been supposed to have over another, in virtue of any superiority in rank, complexion, or blood, is evidently contrary to this doctrine of the Bible in regard to the origin and equality of the human race. The *common nature* which man has, is not affected, in any respect, by the colour of his hair or his skin, by the difference of his stature, by national physiognomy, or by any ethnographical distinctions in the form of the skull. This common nature, as distinct from the brute creation, remains the same under every external appearance, and every form of intellectual and moral development. A man may be wiser or less wise than I am ; he may have more or less property ; he may have a more richly endowed, or an inferior mental capacity, but this does not affect our common nature. He is in every respect, notwithstanding our difference in these things, as completely a human being as myself ; and he stands in precisely the same relations towards the Creator and Father of all. He, like myself, has an immortal soul, and is placed in a state of probation, as a candidate for everlasting happiness or everlasting wo. He has an intellect capable of an endless progression in knowledge ; and God has given him the right to improve it to the utmost. He is endowed with a conscience, which, like his immortal intellect, for ever constitutes an impassable line between him and the inferior races of the animal creation. In virtue of this endowment, it is his right and privilege to seek to know the will of God, and to act always with reference to the future

---

* Fuller and Wayland on Slavery, pp. 90, 91, 92, 93.

state on which he is soon to enter. He is a sinner, and, as such, is placed in substantially the same circumstances with all others before God, in reference to the rewards of heaven or the pains of hell. It was with reference to this *common nature* that redemption was provided. It was our common nature which the Son of God assumed when he became incarnate, and, *in* that assumption, and in all his sufferings for man, he regarded the race as having such a common nature. He was not a *Jew*, except by the accident of his birth ; but he was a *man*, and in his human frame there was as distinct a relation to the African and the Malay, as there was to the Caucasian. The blood that flowed in his veins, and that was shed on the cross for human redemption, was the blood of a human being—a descendant of Adam—and had as much reference, when it warmed his heart with benevolence, and when it was shed on the cross, to a descendant of Ham as to the posterity of Japheth or Shem. Every human being has a right to feel that when the Son of God became incarnate he took *his* nature upon him, and to regard him as the representative of that common humanity. It is on the basis of that common nature that the gospel is commanded to be preached to 'every creature,' and any one human being has a right to consider that gospel as addressed to him with as specific an intention as to any other human being whatever. It is on the basis of that common nature also that the Holy Spirit is sent down from heaven to awaken, convict, and convert the soul ; and any human being, no matter what his complexion, may regard the promise of the Holy Spirit to be as much addressed to him as to any other one—though that other one may have a more comely form or complexion; may be clothed in the imperial purple, or may wear a coronet, or a crown. In *all respects* pertaining to our common origin; to our nature as distinct from the brute creation ; to the fall and to redemption; to the rights of conscience and to the hopes of glory, the human race is regarded in the Bible as on a level. There is an entire system of things which contemplates *man as such* as

distinguished from the inferior creation; not one of which
pertains to a brute, however near the brute may seem to ap-
proximate a human being, and each one of which is as applicable to one human being as to another.

If these views are correct, then all the reliance which the
system of slavery has ever been thought to derive from the
supposed fact that one class of human beings is essentially
inferior to another, is a false reliance. At all events, such
views will find no support in the Bible, and they must be left
to be maintained by those who recognise the Christian Scriptures as of no authority. A man acting on the views laid
down in the Bible on this subject, would never *make* a slave;
a man acting on these views would not long *retain* a slave:
and Christianity, by laying down this doctrine of the essential
equality of the race, has stated a doctrine which *must* sooner
or later emancipate every human being from bondage.

(2.) The gospel regards every human being as invested
with such rights as are inconsistent with his being held as a
slave; that is, these rights, as recognised in the New Testament, always have been violated where slavery exists; are
liable to be violated at any time; and there is no way of effectually guarding against such violation, for the power to violate
them enters into every proper conception of slavery. In other
words, it is involved in the notion of the system that the slaveholder has power to violate what are undoubted laws of God,
and to interfere with and annul the arrangements which he
has instituted for the good of man. If this be so, it will be
conceded that the New Testament does not contemplate
slavery as right, or as an institution to be perpetuated for the
good of society.

Among those rights which are liable to be violated at the
pleasure of the slaveholder, and against the violation of which,
from the very nature of slavery, it is impossible to guard, are
the following :—

(a) The rights involved in the marriage relation. The
master necessarily holds the power of preventing its being

formed, or of annulling it at his pleasure. This results from
the very nature of slavery, and never has been forbidden, and
never can be, while slavery retains its essential features. It
results from the right of *property ;* for the right to buy a thing
implies a right to sell it again ; and as a man in purchasing
one slave is under no obligation to purchase another, though
it be the wife or child of the former, so it is in regard to the
sale. As in procuring slaves originally, whether by the conquests of war, by kidnapping, or by purchase, no respect was
had to the relations which they might sustain to their families,
or any duties which might grow out of such relations, so there
is no reference to any such duties or relations in the tenure
by which they are held. On this very obvious principle all
the laws pertaining to slavery in this land are founded. The
right to separate husband and wife, parent and child, and
brother and sister, is nowhere forbidden, and this power is
constantly acted on. It is not known that an *attempt* has
ever been made to regulate this by law, and the only influence
by which it is sought to control it is by an appeal to the humanity of masters. There are doubtless thousands of cases
where the master *would not* separate a husband from his wife
by selling one without the other, but this does not prove that
the law does not regard them as having the power, and is not
to be taken into the account in estimating the character of the
system.

Even supposing, moreover, that the husband and wife are
not actually separated from each other, and the marriage bond
wholly disregarded, still there are duties enjoined in reference
to this relation in the New Testament which the recognised
power of the master wholly sets aside. In the New Testament, the husband is declared to be the " head of the wife, as
Christ is the head of the church," (Eph. v. 23, 1 Cor. xi. 3,)
and as such has a right to rule in his family. The wife, *as
such,* is commanded to be subject to her husband ; to recognise
his authority ; to obey him ; to love him ; to submit to him
in all things. " As the church is subject to Christ, so let the

wives be to their own husbands in every thing." Eph. v. 24. Comp. Eph. v. 33; Titus ii. 4, 5; 1 Pet. iii. 1. Now this command is practically nullified in every case where slavery exists. The *master*, not the *husband*, possesses supreme authority in relation to every slave, male or female, and *his* will is to be obeyed, and *not* that of the husband, if they ever come in conflict. The master, too, by the laws of *all* slaveholding communities, has the power of *enforcing* obedience by punishment, even when it is against every wish and will of the husband. This power extends to her manner of employing her time; to her whole domestic arrangements; to her hours of labour and of rest; to her food and raiment; to her habitation, and to every comfort. Even when the husband is *sick*, there is no power of enforcing any right which the wife has by the laws of marriage in the Bible, to attend on him, and soothe his sorrows; and though it may be that the duties which a wife owes to her husband in such cases may not often be prevented by an absolute interference on the part of the master, yet the fact that it is not, is not to be traced to any mercy in the institution of slavery, or the laws, but to the mercy of our common humanity. Nothing *prevents* the master from setting at naught the whole law of God on the subject.

(*b*) Slavery interferes with the natural right which a father has over his children. This results, too, from the nature of *property* implied in the relation. The primary and the controlling notion is, that the child is *owned* by the master, not that he is placed under the control and authority of his father. The master, not the father, is supreme. The Bible recognises certain duties as growing out of the relation of a father and child, which are never acknowledged in the code of slavery; and enjoins certain duties which the father can never perform, except at the pleasure of the master. The father is displaced from the position where God has assigned him, and the master is substituted in his place. The Bible has laid down certain duties as binding on the parent, as such, and which properly grow out of the relation of parent and child. The parent is to "command his children and his household after him," (Gen. xviii. 19;) he is to "bring them up in the nurture and admonition of the Lord," (Eph. vi. 4;) he is to "provide for his own, and specially for those of his own house," (1 Tim. v. 5;) he is to instruct them in the ways and duties of religion, to lead their devotions, to seek to prepare them for heaven, to be their counsellor and adviser in regard to the perplexities and duties of life. Children, on the other hand, *all* children, are to 'honour their father and mother, that their days may be long in the land,' (Ex. xx. 12;) they are to 'obey their parents *in all things*,' (Col. iii. 20;) they are to 'obey their parents in the Lord,' (Eph. vi. 1.) Now, it is impossible to secure the discharge of these duties under the system of slavery. The whole question whether a father *may* perform these duties at all, rests with the master. The father's own time is not at his disposal; he is at liberty to select and appoint no hours when he will instruct his children ; he has no right to designate any time when he will even *pray* with his family; and the whole business of 'providing for his own' is entirely taken out of his hands. The master provides, and is the agent appointed by the laws to do it. The father is under no obligation by the laws even to *attempt* it. It is not presumed that he *can* do it. It is not understood that he ever *will* do it. He violates none of the obligations contemplated by slavery, if he makes *no provision whatever* for his children while he himself shall live, or after he is dead; if he leaves them to suffer without one sympathizing look or word; if he provides no physician for them in sickness, or even if he does not see them decently buried when they are dead. Food and raiment; medicine and physicians; shrouds, coffins, and graves are to be provided by the master. It is not contemplated by the law that the slave can ever be the owner of *property* enough to furnish his child a coffin or a grave. So also in the whole duty of training the child for heaven. If time is to be taken for that, it is to be at the pleasure of the master; if a religious teacher is to be employed, it is only at his pleasure, and under his direction.

The law of God is perhaps still more entirely nullified, in regard to the duty which the child owes to its parent. Here it is impossible for him to obey the command of God requiring subjection to his parent, if the will of the master comes in conflict with his. It is not designed that *the parent* shall be obeyed. The master has the absolute authority, and has the right to counteract any of the requirements of the father. The master, not the parent, directs in regard to the employment of the time, and appoints every task that is to be performed. The master has authority in the whole matter of discipline, and punishment is administered, not because the laws of a father have been disregarded, but because the will of the master has been disobeyed. The spirit of the whole institution is, not that the *father* is to be obeyed, but the *master;* and if the father is *not* obeyed, the law lends no help to secure the respect and obedience of the child. The law has displaced the father from the position which *God* gave him, and has substituted the authority of another.

(c) Slavery interferes with the natural right which every human being has, to worship God according to his own views of what is true. That this right is recognised in the Bible, it would be needless to attempt to prove. See Acts iv. 18—20, v. 29; John v. 39; 1 Cor. x. 29; 1 Thess. v. 21; 1 John iv. 1; Prov. iv. 13; Luke xi. 52; Deut. x. 12, xiii. 4. The right to do this is everywhere now conceded, and is regarded as one of the great and inalienable principles of Protestantism and of liberty. It is the most important position which society has taken in its progress toward that state of perfectness which it is destined to attain; the last point which society is to reach in this direction—the *ultima Thule* of human hopes and prospects on this point. To establish this principle has cost more than any other which enters into just notions of liberty—for it is the result of discussions and inquiries pursued for ages; of all the persecutions and martyrdoms that have been endured; of all the self-denials and sacrifices in the cause of freedom. To maintain and enjoy the right of the undisturbed privileges of religion; the right to worship God unmolested; the right to hold what opinions they pleased; to worship God where, and when, and however they pleased; our fathers came to this western land, and endured all the sacrifices incident to the perilous voyage across the deep, and the peopling of what was then a vast and inhospitable wilderness. There is no other right for which an American citizen, at the North or the South, would more cheerfully lay down his life; none from which he would not sooner part.

And yet this right, so invaluable, is practically denied to the slave wherever the institution exists. The abundant quotations which I have made, in the former part of this work, from the laws of the Southern states, show, that, whatever kindness there may be on the part of many masters, this great right, so far as the slave is concerned, is denied him. Every thing pertaining to the worship of God—the time, the place, the manner—is entirely in the hands of the master; and there is not a company of slaves in the land that, according to the laws, can act *freely* in the worship of their Maker. The condition in which the early Puritans were placed in England, in the times of Elizabeth, James, and Charles I.; the condition in which the Nonconformists and Quakers were, in the time of Charles II.; the condition in which the Pilgrim Fathers were, in England and Holland—a condition so severe, that they sought the inhospitable shores of New England, in the dead of winter, rather than endure it—all these are nothing, when compared with the absolute right which the master has over his slaves in the Southern states. The world, even in the worst times of civil oppression, has never seen any thing worse than this; any thing which more entirely interferes with every sacred right of conscience.

And can any man believe, that it was the design of God to sanction such a system, or that it is in accordance with the principles of the New Testament, and is to be perpetuated for the good of society? Can it be believed, that God meant to put the authority to regulate entirely the manner in which he should be worshipped, into the hands of any man? The whole chivalry of the South would be in arms, if an attempt were made, from any quarter, to impose on them the same restrictions in regard to the worship of God which the laws make necessary respecting the slaves; and there is not on earth a class of men that would be more ready to shed their last drop of blood in opposition to such an attempt, and in defence of the very principles which are set at naught by their own laws respecting three millions of human beings—as free, by nature, to worship God in the manner which they prefer, as themselves.

(*d*) Slavery interferes with the rights of *property*. If any principle is clear, not only from reason, but from the Bible, it is, that a man has a right to the avails of his own labour. This is founded on the right which he has to *himself*, and of course to all that he himself can honestly earn. If any portion of this is taken away by taxes for the support of government, it is not on the principle that another *man*, though at the head of the government and ruling over him, has any right to it, but it is, that he himself is *represented* in that government; and that it is, to all practical purposes, an appropriation by himself, of his own property, to make himself, his family, and the remainder of his property more secure. It is not taken *from* him; it is committed *by* him to others, to be employed in his own service, and in the protection which he receives there is a full equivalent for all that is rendered to the government. He is still regarded as the lawful owner, and as having a right to all the avails of his own industry, until it is thus surrendered to other hands.

This right, while it enters into all our notions of liberty, and while the denial of it led to all the sacrifices which secured American Independence, is abundantly recognised in the Bible. An attempt to prove it is scarcely necessary;

but the following passages show what are the current statements of the Scriptures on the subject : "Wherefore I perceive that there is nothing better than that a man should rejoice in his own works ; for that is his portion : for who shall bring him to see what shall be after him." Eccl. iii. 22. "Behold that which I have seen : it is good and comely for one to eat and to drink, and to enjoy the good of all his labour that he taketh under the sun all the days of his life, which God giveth him : for that is his portion." Eccl. v. 18. "Behold the hire of the labourers who have reaped down your fields, which is of you kept back by fraud, crieth ; and the cries of them which have reaped are entered into the ears of the Lord of Sabaoth." James v. 4. "Thou shalt not defraud thy neighbour, neither rob him ; the wages of him that is hired shall not abide with thee all night until the morning." Lev. xix. 13. "Rob not the poor because he is poor ; neither oppress the afflicted in the gate : for the Lord will plead their cause, and spoil the soul of those that spoiled them." Prov. xxii. 22, 23. "For I the Lord love judgment, I hate robbery for burnt-offering." Isa. lxi. 8. "The people of the land have used oppression, and exercised robbery, and have vexed the poor and needy ; yea they have oppressed the stranger wrongfully. And I sought for a man among them that should make up the hedge, and stand in the gap before me in the land, that I should not destroy it : but I found none. Therefore have I poured out mine indignation upon them ; I have consumed them with the fire of my wrath ; their own way have I recompensed upon their heads, saith the Lord God." Ezek. xxii. 29—31. "Wo unto him that buildeth his house by unrighteousness, and his chambers by wrong ; *that useth his neighbour's service without wages, and giveth him not for his work.*" Jer. xxii. 13.

Now it is unnecessary to attempt to prove, that this essential principle of the right of property is wholly at variance with slavery as it exists in this land, and indeed with all proper notions of its nature, wherever it exists. It is a fundamental doctrine in the idea of slavery, that the slave can be the legal owner of no property; can have no right to the avails of his own labour. This has been abundantly demonstrated in the quotations which have been made from the laws of the slaveholding states. The slave can own neither farm, nor house, nor ox, nor ass, nor any thing which his hands can earn. He can own no copyright of a book, and claim none of the avails of a book. He can buy nothing, and can sell nothing. He can contract no debt that could be collected of him; he can collect no wages from another for services rendered; he can make no will that the law would recognise as valid. There is even no little memento of kindness, which he may have received from his master or from others, which he can claim as his own; there is no such token, which the master might not legally appropriate to himself. The slave has no right to any portion of the corn or the cotton which his own hands have raised; nor can he ever look on a tree, a rose-bush, or a flower, and say, legally, that it is his own.

Now, if the principles of the Bible on the subject of property are permanent principles, it is clear that the system of slavery is not in accordance with the word of God, and that it is not the intention of Christianity to perpetuate the system in the world. The fair application of these principles would soon bring the system to an end. Can it be believed that the New Testament sanctions the power of making void the marriage relation; of abrogating the authority of parents; of nullifying the command which requires children to obey their parents; of interfering with the right which every man has to worship God according to his own views of duty and truth; and of appropriating to ourselves entirely the avails of the labour of another man? Whatever may be the abstract views which any man may defend on the subject of human rights, yet no one can seriously maintain—I know not that any one has ever attempted to maintain—that these things are sanctioned by the New Testament. And yet, they are *essential* to the system. Slavery, in the proper sense of the term, never has existed without some or all of these things; it never can.

(3.) The gospel, and the Bible generally, prohibits, in the most positive manner, many things which are always found in slavery, and which are inseparable from it.

Among these things are the following:—

(a) *Stealing a man is forbidden; and the precepts of the Bible on that subject are necessarily violated by slavery.* This, as we have seen, was prohibited, in the most solemn manner, in the Old Testament: "And he that stealeth a man, and selleth him, or if he be found in his hand, he shall surely be put to death." Ex. xxi. 16. It is forbidden, in an equally positive manner, in the New Testament: "The law is made for *menstealers*"—ἀνδραποδισταῖς. 1 Tim. i. 9, 10. The meaning of this word has been before considered. It needs only to be remarked here, that the *essential* idea of the term is, *that of converting a freeman into a slave.* Thus Passow defines the word ἀνδραποδισμός—*andrapodismos*—Verwandlung eines freyen Mannes in einen Sklaven, besonders durch Verkauf, Unterjochung, u. s. w.:—*a changing of a freeman into a slave, especially by traffic, subjection, &c.* Now, *somehow* this 'conversion of a freeman into a slave'—the sin forbidden in the passage before us—occurs essentially in the case of every one who ever becomes a slave; for it is a truth no less in accordance with the Bible, and with all the principles of natural religion, than with the declaration of American Independence, "that all men are *created* equal; that they are endowed by their Creator with certain inalienable rights; that among these are life, *liberty*, and the pursuit of happiness." This was also the doctrine of the Roman civil law: Quod ad jus naturale attinet, *omnes homines æquales sunt.* Digesta, i. 19, 32.

If this right is ever disturbed, so as to deprive a human being of the liberty with which he was created, it must be by some power coming in between his creation, contemplated as the work of God, and his future condition in fact; practically and really 'converting the freeman to a slave,' and constituting the very offence forbidden in the passage before us. He was made a freeman; he is held a slave. The one is the act of God; the other is the act of man. Now this process of converting a freeman to a slave may be either by the conquests of war, or by kidnapping, or by the laws of a land. It may be either the act of *an individual* or of *a community ;* an act of direct and immediate wrong by an individual, or an effect of the legalized workings of a system.

It is clear, however, that neither one method nor the other can make it right, or reconcile it with the statement of Paul in 1 Tim. i. 9, 10. The mere act of a legislature in *legalizing* the conversion, or sanctioning the original robbery, does not make the prohibitions here inapplicable to it, or make it *cease* to be a violation of the law of God; nor is the case changed by the fact that the original perpetrator of the wrong is dead, and that it is now a part of an organized system. *Somewhere,* the wrong is done to the man whom *God* made free; to each individual who is made a slave : and in every instance, either some individual, or the society which sanctions and legalizes the wrong, is responsible. If the inhabitants of Georgia, living on the borders of the Cherokee country, had been long in the habit of committing depredations on the farms of the Cherokees, and carrying off their horses, it is clear that there would be a wrong done in the case of every horse that was stolen. The wrong would not be removed, if the legislature of Georgia at the time had authorized the outrage, or should legalize it afterward; nor would any lapse of time, or any number of legal enactments, make the act of depredation right. *Somewhere,* either in the individual or in the society, the guilt of the wrong would remain, nor could it ever be removed by any legal enactments. The case might be made still stronger, though on the same principle, by a reference to property of a different kind. When Napoleon invaded Italy, a large portion of the celebrated paintings and statues of that land were plundered and removed to Paris. On the supposition that the invader had no right himself to rob churches and palaces ; that he violated every principle of common justice, and every sentiment of what the Earl of Chatham calls ' honourable war,' it is clear that no lapse of time, no amount of legal enactments, and no number of transfers of the property by sale or by bequest, could ever convey a moral right to those works of art. The claim of one robber might be legally good against another, or the claim of one French proprietor might be legally good against another inhabitant of France, or an inhabitant of Russia or England, but it could never be morally good against the Italian church or convent that had been plundered. *Somewhere*, in spite of all the forms of law, the *wrong* is perpetuated and extended, nor can it ever be obliterated but by a restoration. It may be that one who inherited one of these paintings may have been guilty of no wrong in *becoming* the recognised legal owner—for he had no agency in it ; it may be that he could hold it against another claimant—a pretended heir at law of the estate ; it may be that a restoration to the original owner might be for a time impracticable ; but none of these things sanction the original wrong, or abolish the moral claim of the original owner.

These principles are still more clear, in the case of stealing a man—a human being—a fellow-traveller to eternity. The injury is greater to him, and to every one descended from him, who, in virtue of an unhappy connection with him, shall be involved in the wrong, than can possibly be in the case of a horse or a work of art. The guilt of *converting the freeman to a slave* exists somewhere ; and if in any case it does not rest on the individual who becomes an involuntary inheritor of the wrong, it rests on the community which provides for this by its laws. The *thing* is forbidden. It is contrary to the whole spirit of the New Testament.

(*b*) *Oppression is forbidden ; and just the kind of oppression which always enters into the idea of slavery.* " For the oppression of the poor, for the sighing of the needy, now will I arise, saith the Lord ; I will set him in safety from him

that puffeth at him." Ps. xii. 5. "He shall judge the poor
of the people, he shall save the children of the needy, and
shall break in pieces the oppressor. For he shall deliver the
needy when he crieth ; the poor also, and him that hath no
helper." Ps. lxxii. 4, 12. "I know that the Lord will maintain the cause of the afflicted, and the right of the poor." Ps.
cxl. 12. "What mean ye that ye beat my people to pieces,
and grind the faces of the poor ? saith the Lord of hosts." Isa.
iii. 15. "Wo unto them that decree unrighteous decrees, and
that write grievousness which they have prescribed ; to turn
aside the needy from judgment, and to take away the right
from the poor of my people, that widows may be their prey,
and that they may rob the fatherless. And what will ye do
in the day of visitation, and in the desolation which shall come
from far ? To whom will ye flee for help ? And where will
ye leave your glory ?" Isa. x. 1—3. Comp. also Amos viii.
4—7 ; Ex. iii. 7—9 ; Eccl. v. 8 ; Isa. lxi. 8 ; Jer. v. 26 ;
Ezek. xxii. 12 ; James ii. 13, v. 4 ; Job xxvii. 13 ; Jer. xxii.
13, xxxiv. 17.

There is almost nothing which is more frequently adverted
to in the Bible, than *oppression*. And yet, the idea of *oppression* enters into the very conception of slavery, and is imbodied in all the laws that pertain to it. Indeed, if it were
the design to originate a system of laws for *the very purpose*
of oppression ; if a legislature should wish to frame a series of
enactments which should accomplish that in the most effectual
manner, the slave laws of this country would be the very ones
which would be needed for such a purpose. Scarcely any
modification would be necessary to accomplish such an end ;
scarcely a new element of cruelty and wrong could be introduced into these laws. Let any one read over the laws of the
slave states as I have quoted them in a former part of this
volume, and this will be apparent at a glance.

It is clear, also, that if all that properly comes under the
name of *oppression* were removed from those laws, slavery,
as a system, would soon come to an end. There might, in-

deed, be found a few now held as slaves who are in such circumstances that they do not regard their condition as oppressive, and who would prefer to remain with their masters rather than at once to be set at liberty. But their condition would not invalidate the truth of the general remark. Slavery, as a system, could not live a day, if there were not in it the elementary idea of oppression; and if so, it is clear, that a fair application of the principles of the Bible would soon bring it to an end; that is, that it is contrary to the principles of the Bible, and therefore wrong.

(c) *Depriving one of his lawful wages, is forbidden in the New Testament.*—Such a withholding of the proper wages due to the labourer is involved in the very idea of slavery, and in order to show that the Christian system is opposed to it, and would abolish it, it is necessary to show that the application of the principles laid down on that subject in the New Testament would bring the system to an end.

This point has already been partially illustrated under a previous specification, in showing that the system of slavery interferes with the essential rights of property. It is proper, however, to add a few words in regard to this specific form of the evil, in order to show, not only that it violates the essential rights of the labourer, by denying that the slave can be the *owner* of any property whatever, but that it furnishes no such *compensation* for labour as the principles of the New Testament give a man a right to receive.

The principles of the Bible on the subject are stated in the following language: " Behold the hire of the labourers who have reaped down your fields, which is of you kept back by fraud, crieth; and the cries of them which have reaped are entered into the ears of the Lord of Sabaoth." James v. 4. " And I will come near you to judgment; and I will be a swift witness against the sorcerers, and against the adulterers and against false swearers, and against those that oppress the hireling in his wages, the widow, and the fatherless, and that turn aside the stranger from the right, and fear not me, saith the Lord of hosts." Mat. iii. 5. "Wo unto him tha. buildeth his house by unrighteousness, and his chambers by wrong; that useth his neighbour's service without wages, and giveth him not for his work." Jer. xxii. 13. "The labourer is worthy of his reward." 1 Tim. v. 18. "The labourer is worthy of his hire." Luke x. 7.

In all these passages the same principles essentially are laid down. They are these: (*a*) that where labour is performed, or service rendered, a fair equivalent is due to the labourer; (*b*) that he to whom the service is rendered is not to withhold that fair equivalent; (*c*) that we are not to avail ourselves of the forced or unrequited labour of others. He who renders the service is to receive a *fair* equivalent; that is, he is to receive what is worth as much to him as the labour is; and he in whose behalf the service is rendered is to bestow on the labourer as much as the service rendered is worth to him.

Now, it is not true, in the system of slavery anywhere, that it is contemplated that a fair equivalent shall be rendered to the slave for the service which he performs. It is presumed, in the very nature of the system, that the master shall receive from the toil of the individual slave, or from his slaves collectively, so much *more* than he gives to them for their work, as to be sufficient to free him from the necessity of toil, and to enable him, so far as that is concerned, to live in indolence. It is not true that an equivalent is paid to the slave. What he receives is *not* what he would be willing to contract to do the work for. It is not what freemen receive for the same amount of work. No one can pretend that the coarse raiment, and the hard fare, and the rude cottages, and the scanty furniture, and the implied pledge of medical attendance in sickness, and of support in old age, can be any proper *equivalent* for the service which a slave renders. It is not what *any* freeman would contract to do the work for. If it *were* an equivalent, the whole system would be unprofitable, and must soon come to an end.

As long, therefore, as slavery exists in any community, it

is a standing violation of these precepts of the New Testament, and an honest application of these precepts would at once bring the system to an end. Let all slaveholders adopt the principle which prevails where there is free labour, of giving to those employed a *fair* compensation for their toil; an honest equivalent for their work, and the system must at once cease. It follows, therefore, if these principles are correct, that all that is received by the master *above* such an equivalent, is to be set down to the fact that the master has *power*, and 'can enforce the wrong;' and is as *unjustly* appropriated to himself as if it were taken by robbery in any other form, from the earnings of another. Why is it more justifiable than any other mode of availing ourselves of the labour of others without their consent, and without rendering to them a fair equivalent? There is not on earth any other condition of things to which the passage in James v. 4 is so applicable as that of slavery; and if the rebuke *in this one passage of the word of God* were regarded, slavery would at once come to an end. Let it be imagined to be addressed to slaveholders, and how distinctly does it seem to refer to every feature of injustice and wrong in the system. " *The hire of the labourers which have reaped down your fields, which is of you kept back by fraud, crieth ; and the cries of them which have reaped, are entered into the ears of the Lord of Sabaoth.*"

(d) *The withholding of instruction is forbidden in the New Testament.* Nothing is more definite in the Bible, or more in accordance with all our views of what is proper and right, than the declarations that all men have a clear right to know the truth ; to receive instruction, to have free access to the oracles of God. Luke xi. 52: " Wo unto you, lawyers ! for ye have taken away the key of knowledge: ye entered not in yourselves, and them that were entering in, ye hindered." John v. 39: "Search the Scriptures ; for in them ye think ye have eternal life, and they are they which testify of me." Prov. xix. 2: " That the soul be without knowledge, it is not good."

The precepts in the Bible which speak of the value of knowledge, and of the obligation to search for the truth, apply to all men. It is everywhere supposed that all have a right to the privilege of obtaining the knowledge of God; and, in the laws of the Mosaic economy, we have seen the solicitude which was manifested that all persons in the Hebrew commonwealth should have the benefits of religious instruction.

Yet the laws of the slave states in this Union are a direct violation of all these precepts, so far as slaves are concerned. It is not contemplated that they shall have sufficient knowledge even to read the Bible. There are numerous laws which are enacted with the express design that they shall not have that knowledge. Those laws have been enacted on the principle that they are *necessary* to perpetuate the system; that there is no other way of preserving the slaves in subordination; that were they to allow them to be acquainted with the Bible, it would make them restless and dissatisfied, and would tend to the ultimate subversion of the whole system. It is understood everywhere in the slaveholding states that nothing would be more fatal to the existence of slavery there, than to establish a system of common-school instruction; and that the whole institution would be perilled if all the slaves were taught to read the Bible. It would be impossible to press through a single legislature of the slaveholding states an act *authorizing* the free instruction of all the slaves to such an extent that they might be able to read the word of God; much less to institute a system of common-school instruction that should embrace all the slaves. Even the efforts which are made by not a few worthy philanthropists, of a recent date, in the South, to benefit the slaves by giving them instruction, contemplate only *oral* instruction;* and the experiment has been undertaken—an experiment which cannot but be destined to certain failure in the end, benevolent and well-meant though it be—to see whether this mode of instruction can be made to answer

---

* See the Reports of the Rev. Mr. Jones.

the purpose of the plan which God has adopted, and which he has revealed as the right of every human being, in the sense that no one can deprive him of it, and as the only thing adapted to meet the wants of the human soul—the ability to *read* the Bible, and the unrestricted *right* to do it.

The laws prohibiting the instruction of the slaves are essential to slavery. Slaveholding legislators believe, that if those laws should be repealed, the system could not be perpetuated. In this opinion every intelligent person must unite with them. Nothing can be clearer than this ; there is no point on which less doubt can be entertained.

But if this be so, then two things follow also, with entire clearness. (*a*.) One is, that the essential laws in the slave-states are opposed to the Bible on this point ; or in other words, the Bible is essentially opposed to slavery. That is, laws are *necessary* to support the system, which are a direct violation of the principles of the word of God.

(*b*.) The second thing is, that the framers of those laws, and the advocates of slavery, have no real belief that the system of slavery is sanctioned by the word of God. If they had, the very best thing which they could do, would be forthwith to teach all their slaves to read the Bible. If this system is in accordance with the Scriptures ; if it is clear that it is meant that it shall be perpetuated ; if the relation of master and slave is one that is recognised as a desirable one, and one that is to be continued, then the Bible is *the very book* to put into the hands of the slaves, and then the master is doing both himself and the slave a great wrong that he does not do it. For the slave often feels that his condition is a hard one. He often feels that, being a human being, he has a right to freedom. He is chafed, and discontented, and dissatisfied with his condition. He often feels—he cannot help it, with the measure of light which he has—that God made him for higher ends ; for the privileges and immunities of freedom. His spirit is restless and disturbed, and he is in constant danger of being tempted to take measures to burst his chains, and to enjoy the

sweets of liberty. Now, if the Bible is friendly to slavery;
if it is wholly opposed to all efforts to produce universal
emancipation; if it never speaks of slavery as *sinful*, then
the best thing that can be done to calm down the restless
feelings of the slave, is, to put this book into his hands, and
let him see what is *the will of God* in the case; to bring the
sanctions of *religion* on the side of the master, and to let the
slave see that he is only obeying the injunctions of his Maker.
One of the best methods of calming down the rebellious feelings
of those who are afflicted by the loss of health, property, or
friends, is to put the Bible in their hands, and let them see
that it is the will of God that his people should be tried.
Nothing does so much to still the murmurs of a troubled soul,
and to produce peace, as to know that God has appointed
these trials, and that in obedience to his will they should be
patiently borne. So, if slavery be countenanced in the Bible,
and it is there regarded as an institution having the divine
approbation, nothing would do so much to soothe every murmuring feeling; to produce universal contentment; to silence
every complaint against the master, and to make the slave
happy, as to instruct him so that he could read the Bible, and
see all this with his own eyes. Masters of slaves are doing
themselves great wrong, by leaving the *suspicion* on their
minds, that something would be found in the Bible which
would lead them to doubt whether God designed that they
should be held in that condition. The 'schoolmaster' would
thus do a good service if he were 'abroad' all over the South.
The Bible Society should be heartily countenanced by the
masters and legislators there, and would deserve their warmest
thanks if it should follow in the steps of the schoolmaster, and
put a Bible into the hands of every murmuring and dissatisfied
slave, and into the hands of all the children there born to be
slaves. Nothing could do so much to prevent trouble—and
especially to prevent the propensity now so prevalent with
them to escape to the North.   .

(4.) It is conceded that the gospel, if fairly applied, would remove slavery from the world : it is therefore wrong. This is admitted in the Princeton Biblical Repertory.

" It is also evident, that acting in accordance with these principles would so soon improve the condition of the slaves, would make them intelligent, moral, and religious, and thus work out to the benefit of all concerned, and the removal of the institution. For slavery, like despotism, supposes the actual inferiority and consequent dependence of those held in subjection. Neither can be permanent. Both may be prolonged by keeping the subject class degraded, that is, by committing sin on a large scale, which is only to treasure up wrath for the day of wrath. It is only the antagonist fanaticism of a fragment of the South, which maintains the doctrine that slavery is in itself a good thing, and ought to be perpetuated. It cannot by possibility be perpetuated."

The same sentiments are expressed in the Princeton Repertory for 1836, pp. 302, 304. This same concession would be made by most of those who suppose that slavery was tolerated in the church by the apostles, and who are most offended at its ever being denominated a sin. Even Dr. Fuller, the ablest defender of the institution of slavery of modern times, candidly makes the following concession : " If you had asserted," says he, addressing Dr. Wayland, "the great danger of confiding such irresponsible power in the hands of *any man*, I should at once have assented. There is quite enough abuse of this authority to make me regret its *general existence.*" Again he says, " You must already have perceived, that, speaking abstractly of slavery, I do not consider its perpetuation *proper, even if it were possible.* Nor let any one ask, why not perpetuate it if it be not a sin ? *The Bible informs us what man is, and, among such beings, irresponsible power is a trust too easily and too frequently abused.*"* It is evident from these passages, that even this distinguished defender of slavery, as a scriptural institution, would not regard it as de-

---

* Fuller and Wayland on Slavery, p. 157.

sirable or 'proper' that it should be perpetuated; that he 'regrets' the general existence of the institution; and that he regards its perpetuation as 'impossible.' Even Dr. Fuller, therefore, must suppose, that a fair application of the principles of the Bible would remove the system ultimately from the world, since he would rely on nothing to correct what is evil in man, or permanently to modify society, but the influence of religion.

I have myself repeatedly conversed with intelligent gentlemen of the slaveholding states on the subject, and I have never seen one who did not admit that the gospel would ultimately remove slavery entirely. They have, indeed, been opposed to violent measures—to denunciation, to harsh words, to a disorganizing spirit, and to making the mere fact of sustaining the relation of a master a test of admission to the church or a ground of excommunication from it—as in fact most of the opponents of slavery at the North are; they have in general maintained that the North had no right to intermeddle with it, and that it pertained wholly to the states where the institution exists; they have insisted that it is not proper for ecclesiastical bodies to interfere with the subject, even by bearing testimony against it; but they have conceded that the gospel, by its mild and gentle influence, would ultimately abolish the system. It may be set down as the undoubted belief of the great mass of private Christians, and Christian ministers at the South, that the *fair* effect of the gospel, if applied in a proper manner, would be first to meliorate the condition of the slave, and ultimately to effect his entire emancipation. The concession would be made, in accordance with the views in the Princeton Repertory, that "the consequence of acting on the principles of the gospel, of following the example and obeying the precepts of Christ, would be the gradual elevation of the slaves in intelligence, virtue, and wealth; *the peaceable and* SPEEDY *extinction of slavery;* the improvement in general prosperity of all classes of society, and the consequent increase in the sum of human happiness and virtue."* Most persons also would accord with the opinion so emphatically expressed in the same work, that, "The South has to choose between emancipation *by the silent and holy influence of the gospel*, securing the elevation of the slaves to the stature and character of freemen, or *to abide the issue of a long continued conflict with the laws of God*."—p. 304.

These views, of what the tendency of the gospel would do if fairly applied, though they seem to be entirely contradictory to the opinion, so commonly defended at the South, that it is an institution sanctioned by the Bible, would be strengthened by a reference to the effect which the gospel, when first promulgated, had on the system of Roman slavery. It has been commonly admitted, even by the advocates of the opinion that slave-holding is not necessarily sinful, that the effect of Christianity was to abolish slavery throughout the Roman empire, and the manner in which the apostles treated it has been supposed to have contributed essentially to this result.

This opinion, so greatly conceded to be true, has, however, been recently called in question, by Dr. Fuller. The *bearing* of the concession that the gospel ever *did* abolish slavery, could not but be seen by a mind as clear as his. He therefore expresses himself in the following decisive language :

"'Slavery was at last abolished throughout the whole Roman empire ; and, by the admission of all, this was purely the result of the gospel.' *Answer*. Even if this statement were correct, it would not affect our discussion. But I submit to you that it is inaccurate. At first, myriads of slaves were procured by war ; and then the law of self-preservation occasioned the greatest severities. When all nations had become consolidated into one empire, this source of supply almost ceased, and, masters depending on the natural increase, slaves became more valuable, and their treatment more kind. Through this cause the laws were mitigated, and, in the reign of the Antonines, edicts were published protecting slaves.

---

* Vol. viii. pp. 303, 304.

This was in the second century, nor can this change be at all ascribed to the gospel. In process of time Christianity seconded the humane working of this system, and infused its mild and benevolent spirit into the institution, making it quite a different thing. But slavery never was abolished throughout the Roman empire. In its latest days there were millions of slaves in the empire, and a living writer thinks, that their number was one of the causes which conspired in producing that most astonishing catastrophe, the subjugation of Rome by the Northern barbarians."*

It becomes, then, an important inquiry just here, what *was* the effect of the Christian religion on the system of slavery as it existed in the Roman empire? Did it in any way modify it, or tend to remove it? Was it understood to lend its sanction to it, so that it was regarded as a good and desirable institution? Was it understood that it was improper for Christian ministers to preach on the subject, or synods and councils to bear their testimony against it? Are there any facts to show that its tendency was to promote universal emancipation, or was it a common belief in the Christian church, that it was to be perpetual? If all Christian ministers and churches should act now on what was understood by the early Christians to be the proper way to act, would the system be vindicated and perpetuated?

In reply to these questions, I would observe that the *facts* in the case, so far as I have had the means of ascertaining them, were these:

(*a*) The attention of Christians was early turned to the subject of slavery, and to the evils of the system. In the second epistle of Ignatius of Antioch to Polycarp of Smyrna, are the following words: "Overlook not the men and maidservants; neither let them be puffed up; but rather let them be the more subject to the glory of God, that they may obtain from him a better liberty. Let them not desire to be set

free at public cost, that they be not slaves to their own lusts."
In the general epistle of Barnabas, ch. 14, v. 15, he says,
" Thou shalt not be bitter in thy commands towards any of
thy servants that trust in God ; lest thou chance not to fear
him who is over both ; because he came not to call any with
respect of persons, but whomsoever the spirit prepared."*

(b) Freedom, under the influence of Christianity, was regarded as a great blessing, and the desire to promote it led to
great sacrifices on the part of the early Christians.   The
prevailing views of the early Christians may be regarded
as expressed in the following passage of Clemens, in his
epistle to the Corinthians : " We have known many among
ourselves, who have delivered themselves into bonds and
slavery, *that they might restore others to their liberty ;* many
who have hired out themselves servants unto others, that by their
wages they might feed and sustain them that wanted."   The
following facts also will show with what feelings the early
Christians regarded slavery.   " Paulinus, bishop of Nola, ex-
pended his whole estate, and then sold himself, in order to
accomplish the same object.   Serapion sold himself to a stage-
player, and was the means of converting him and his family.
Cyprian sent to the bishop of Numidia, in order to redeem
some captives, 2500 crowns.   Socrates, the historian, says,
that after the Romans had taken 7000 Persian captives, Aca-
cius, bishop of Amida, melted the gold and silver plate of his
church, with which he redeemed the captives.   Ambrose of
Milan did the same in respect to the furniture of his church.
It was the only case in which the imperial constitutions allowed
plate to be sold."†

(c) Emancipation became a very common thing in the early
Christian church, and was attended with such ceremonies as
to show that it was regarded as a matter of great importance,
and that an invaluable privilege was thus conferred on the slave.

---

* Bib. Repos. for 1835, pp. 432, 433.
† Bib. Repos. Oct. 1835, p. 433.

Thus, when a slave became, with the consent of his master, a minister of the gospel, he was, by the very act, regarded as emancipated.* Emancipation came to be performed in the church, attend d with the impressive rites of religion,† and every thing relating to it was such as to make a deep impression of the desirableness of restoration to freedom.

(d) Under the influence of Christianity, the laws were greatly modified, and many of the former oppressive and harsh treatments came to an end. " After the establishment of Christianity, under Constantine, slaves partook of all the ordinances of religion, and their birth was no impediment to their rising to the highest distinctions of the priesthood. At first, indeed, it was required that a slave should be enfranchised before ordination ; but Justinian declared the simple consent of the master to be sufficient. Slaves were fully protected in the exercise of worship, and to a certain extent in the observance of religious festivals. If a Christian slave fell into the hands of a heathen master, the latter was prohibited from interfering with his spiritual concerns."‡

(e) It is admitted that the tendency of things under the Roman empire, in the early ages of Christianity, was to bring slavery to an end ; and that, in fact, it brought it almost to a termination. Indeed, such were the facilities for manumission in the Roman state, and such numbers were actually emancipated *before* Christianity exerted any influence, that it came to be necessary, as it was supposed, to restrict the right of emancipation, in order to limit the dangerous number of freedmen. Cicero induces us to believe, that good slaves usually attained their liberty after six years' service.§ It was usual for a wealthy master to give freedom to a number of slaves upon joyful occasions.‖ The posthumous vanity of masters was

---

* Blair's Slavery amongst the Romans, p. 168.

† Pliny vii. epist. 16.

‡ Bib. Repos. ut supra, p. 434.   § Philip. viii. 11.

‖ Ammi. Marcell. xxii.; Libianus Paneg. Jul. i. 21; Cassiod. Varior. vi. ep. 1.

gratified in their funeral procession being swelled by a crowd of slaves, to whom they left their freedom by testament, and hundreds were sometimes thus emancipated at once.* The number of freedmen found in Rome, at the close of the civil wars, was so large that Augustus, desirous to re-establish the relative importance of the pure civic classes, imposed various restrictions on their manumission, and several of his successors acted on similar views. The Fusian law, passed probably under Augustus, limited the proportion of slaves that a proprietor might emancipate by will, and fixed one hundred as the *maximum*, not to be exceeded by any single owner.† The exact provision of this law was, that for one or two slaves, there was no limitation; but between the numbers three and ten, one half could be emancipated; of any number under thirty, a third; under a hundred, a quarter; under five hundred, a fifth part, and in no case whatever more than a hundred.‡

This tendency to emancipation was much increased by the influence of Christianity. The feelings of the early Christians, as we have seen, prompted them to it; and the obstacles to emancipation were finally removed, to a great degree, by Justinian.§ So strong was the tendency to emancipation, so decisive was the influence of Christianity, that, if slavery was never entirely brought to an end in the Roman empire, it was nearly so; and if the progress of things had not been interrupted by the invasion of the Northern hordes, there is every reason to think that it would have wholly ceased within the limits of the Roman power. Thus, Gibbon expressly says, that it "had *almost ceased* under the peaceful reign of the Roman emperors." (See Fuller on Slavery, p. 221.) Thus Dr. Fuller himself says: "In process of time Christianity seconded the humane working of this system, and infused its mild and benevolent spirit into the institution, making it

---

* Blair, ut supra, p. 173.   † Ibid. p. 174.
‡ Becker on Roman Slavery, in the Bibliotheca Sacra, Aug. 1845, p. 579.   § Blair, ut. sup. p. 174.

quite a different thing."—p. 220. Thus also, Prof. B. B. Edwards[*] says: "The spirit of the Christian religion effected a glorious triumph in almost every part of the imperial dominions. There was no instantaneous abandonment of the system of servitude. But its contrariety to the precepts of the New Testament was gradually seen. Clergymen vindicated the rights of the oppressed. The codes of slave-law were gradually ameliorated, till finally the rescripts of Justinian nearly accomplished the salutary reform." On the influence of the invasions of the Goths and Vandals in checking the progress of emancipation, and perpetuating slavery, the whole of the article just referred to may be consulted with great advantage. It is evident, that whatever influence those invasions had in perpetuating slavery should be regarded as counteracting the tendency of the Christian religion.

From the above statements in regard to slavery in the Roman empire after the gospel was preached, it is manifest that slavery was considered to be adverse to the spirit of the gospel; that the early Christians were willing to make great sacrifices to impart freedom to those who were enslaved; that emancipation was regarded as a most important and desirable thing; that the tendency of Christianity was to meliorate the laws pertaining to slavery, and to 'make it quite a different thing;' that under the influence of Christianity slavery ' had almost ceased' in the Roman empire; and that there is every reason to suppose that it would have ceased entirely, if the progress of things so auspiciously commenced had not been arrested by the incursions of the Northern barbarians.

The result of this investigation in regard to Roman slavery is, therefore, in entire accordance with the statement in the Princeton Repertory, *that the fair application of the Christian religion would ultimately bring the institution to an end.*

But, if this be so, it is a legitimate conclusion that slavery is sinful, and that the gospel does not contemplate that it shall

---

[*] Bibl. Repos. Jan. 1836, p. 441.

be perpetuated for the best interests of society. It is clear, that the most rigid application of the principles of the gospel will destroy nothing that is good, and that it will interfere with no desirable relation in society. It makes war only on evil; its tendency is to remove only that which is sinful. Regarding the gospel as a system of truth revealed from heaven, all that is necessary to prove that any thing is wrong, is to show that the fair application of the gospel would abolish it. It makes no difference as to this point, whether it be by a gradual process, or whether it would do it immediately; whether it would be by effecting a change in the laws, or by acting directly on the individual consciences of those who are guilty of the wrong; the fact that the gospel would abolish its existence, proves that it is wrong. The Christian religion disturbs nothing that is good ; it destroys no relation which it is desirable should be perpetuated for the best interests of man. All the arguments, therefore, in the Princeton Repertory, and elsewhere, in favour of slavery, when the admission is made that the gospel would abolish it, are grossly inconsistent. At one moment it is maintained that it is not condemned in the Bible ; that slavery has been countenanced in all ages ; that it is not to be regarded as *per se* an evil ; that it is wrong for ecclesiastical bodies to legislate on it ; that slaves may be held with propriety by Christian ministers and by other Christians ; that the war which Christianity makes on it is not on the system, but the ' *abuses* of the system'—the unjust and oppressive laws on the subject ;* and at another, it is admitted, in the clearest manner, that the fair application of the Christian religion would bring the system ' SPEEDILY' to an end,—as if the gospel would abolish any thing that is good and right. If Christianity would bring it to an end, there must be some *reason* why it would ; and the only reason that can be assigned as drawn from the nature of Christianity is, that

* Princeton Repertory, April, 1836, pp. 302, 303.

it is contrary to the will of God, and a thing that is morally wrong.

It is a fair conclusion, therefore, that if Christianity would abolish it, slavery is sinful. It demonstrates the point before us, that it is contrary to the Bible, and cannot be defended from the word of God. To show that it is *not* contrary to the Bible, it should be maintained that, under the fair operation of Christianity, the system would be extended and perpetuated ; and that the best way to keep it up on the earth would be to promulgate the principles of the Christian religion as plainly and as extensively as possible. There are few men, it is to be presumed, who would be disposed to take that ground.

The force of the argument here referred to may be seen by applying it to two classes of objects.

(*a*) There *are* things, indubitably, which the application of Christianity would bring to an end, and which, wherever it has prevailed, have been abolished. Such, for example, are polygamy, gladiatorial shows, intemperance, concubinage, profaneness, piracy, highway robbery, duelling, fraud, licentiousness of manners. Christianity will bring them to an end, because they are wrong; and the fact that it will do so, *proves* that they are wrong. If it would also abolish slavery, would it not prove that it is to be classed with the same evils as those just referred to ? Is it the tendency of the system to abolish alike the evil and the good ? Is it 'a fountain which at the same place sends forth sweet water and bitter ?'— James iii. 11.

(*b*) There *are* things which it would not abolish ; which it has no tendency to abolish, but which it only confirms in their influence. Such are the relations of the marriage covenant ; of parent and child ; of brothers and sisters ; of neighbours and friends. The most rigid application of the principles of Christianity would do nothing to abolish the relations of husband and wife in a community, or those of parent and child. The Christian system would only perpetuate and do honour to those relations ; nor is it possible to conceive that the time will ever come, under the application of Christianity, when they will cease in the world. Does not this prove that they have the sanction of God, and are designed to be perpetuated for the good of man? And if the relation of master and slave had equally the sanction of God, would not the fair application of Christianity be to extend and perpetuate it also? Why should it perpetuate the one and abolish the other?

These considerations seem to me to be conclusive proof that Christianity was *not* designed to extend and perpetuate slavery, but that the spirit of the Christian religion is against it; and that the fair application of the Christian religion would remove it from the world, BECAUSE *it is an evil, and is displeasing to God.*

CONCLUSION.

I HAVE thus gone through with the subject which I proposed to examine—the scriptural argument on the subject of slavery. There is another line of argument on the subject which might be pursued, in order to confirm the views which have been taken, derived from the *working* of the system. This would consist of an examination of the bearing of the system on the various questions pertaining to agriculture, commerce, arts, manufactures, education, morals, and political prosperity. It would be easy, on these points, to show that there is not a valuable interest of society which does not suffer from the influence of slavery, and that our own country, in the comparative increase and prosperity of the free and slave states, furnishes abundant illustration of this truth. This course of argument would be proper, in accordance with the object which I proposed, only as it would be a *confirmation* of the views taken in interpreting the Bible. If the teachings of the Bible are against the system; if in the word of God it is *not* regarded as a good and desirable institution; if it appears from the Scriptures that it was not his intention that it should be perpetuated ; and if the fair application of the Christian principles would be to abolish it, it may be presumed that these views would find confirmation in the events of his Providence ; and that in respect to those things on which the best interests of society depend, and which will enter into its highest condition, those portions of the world where slavery prevails will be found to be falling behind those which are free from it. This argument might be pursued at length, and with the clearest demonstration. With certain classes of minds it would have more force than any thing which I have advanced. But it does not fall directly within my design in ascertaining the true sense of the Bible on the subject.

I have not thought it necessary for me, in this argument, to go into any examination of the question in what way our country can be delivered from this great evil, or what is the duty of those who now hold slaves who would be desirous of dissolving all connection with the system, or what is their duty in seeking the modification of the laws on the subject. There is one great preliminary matter first to be settled, and that is, to secure the conviction everywhere, in the church and out of it, that slavery is evil, and only evil; that it is contrary to the spirit of the Bible; that the fair influence of the Christian religion would be to bring it to an end; and that it is a system which cannot be defended by any fair and honest interpretation of the word of God. The examination which I have pursued has conducted us, if I mistake not, to the conclusion that slavery cannot rest for its support on the teachings of the Bible. The fair influence of the Bible; the application of the principles of the Christian religion, would bring the system to a 'speedy' end. This is felt everywhere at the North; and is probably felt in the consciences of the great majority of persons at the South. Few men, even there, would have the boldness to undertake to maintain that the Bible sanctions *the system of American slavery, as it is.* The great mass of the friends of religion there would admit that the mild and gentle influence of Christianity would bring it to an end. Thousands of Christians there, I doubt not, are looking forward to the time when this shall be accomplished, and are praying most sincerely that the gospel *may be* so applied to all classes there—to the master and the servant; to the legislators and the people; to the churches and the community at large—that the evils of this system may be ultimately

banished, and that all the South may be truly a land of freedom. They sigh over wrongs and woes which they yet see
no method of removing.

That the South, moreover, is sensible that the fair influence
of the Bible is against the system, and would bring it to an
end, is manifest from all the laws which exist there to prevent
the truths of the Bible from coming in contact with the minds
of the slaves themselves. If the Bible is favourable to the
system, and would sustain it, the most obvious course to continue it, as has been before observed, would be to cause every
slave to be taught to read, and to place the Bible in every
negro cottage in the plantations of the South. But this cannot be done. The laws are against it; the public sentiment
is against it, and against it only because it is known that the
slave, if allowed to be his own interpreter of the word of God,
would *not* draw the conclusion that the master often does,
that the Bible is in favour of slavery. Well is it known that
the Bible would teach him that he is a man; that he is a
redeemed heir of life; that he was born as free as others;
that he has a right to his own time, and to the fruits of his
own toil; and that if he had all the rights which he ought to
have, he would be as free as his master. Well is it known
that the influence of the Bible, while it would make him
patient under his trials and wrongs, would awaken in his
bosom an inextinguishable love of liberty. It would be impossible to repress in the soul the aspirings after freedom; and
with the Bible everywhere in his hands, it would be impossible to keep down the feeling that the master was guilty of
oppression and wrong.

Now this conviction that slavery is contrary to the spirit
of the Christian religion, and that that religion will ultimately
bring it to an end, is destined most certainly to increase and
prevail. Nothing is more sure than that, on this subject, the
human mind will become strengthened in this conviction
until it becomes universal. There is but one result every-

where to be anticipated in the progress of knowledge, and in the careful investigations of the Scriptures on this subject, and that is the result which was reached by the minds of Penn, and the younger Edwards, and by Wilberforce and Clarkson, that the system of slavery is contrary to the spirit of the Bible. The progress towards this result may be temporarily checked. Many minds may for a while hesitate; many, swayed by interest, may doubt it; but the world will come to it, and will yet admit that the system which proclaims that man may be held as a chattel, cannot be sustained by the word of God. With reference to so certain a result, we may apply to this anticipated triumph of truth, the eloquent language with which Dr. Fuller closes his letters to Dr. Wayland, on slavery.

" The knowledge of God and our Saviour Jesus Christ, we are assured, shall fill this guilty and polluted earth, as the waters cover the face of the deep. And it is with that knowledge, too, as with those waters, when the sea is rolling in. Wave after wave breaks, and is driven back; but the ocean is advancing; and before its majesty and strength, impotent must every barrier prove;—vainly shall nations rage, and rulers take counsel together, and all the kings of the earth set themselves, saying, Hitherto shalt thou come, but no further, and here shall thy proud billows be stayed."

It is deeply affecting to see such a mind as that of Dr. Fuller—large, generous, highly cultivated, and well-disciplined—labouring to defend the system of slavery, yet deeply impressed with its undeniable evils; with the fact that the current of public feeling is setting against it; and that he can find little sympathy in the spirit of the age while maintaining such an argument, pouring itself forth in the following pensive and disconsolate words :—

" I have done ; and mine has been an irksome and cheerless task. You have had the popular side of the question, and the Reflector has accompanied your letters with accounts of the enthusiasm produced by them at the North. May you ever be animated in your pious labours by multitudes who love and admire you,—among whom I shall always be found, when conscience permits it. For me, I have long been schooled to say, ' *My soul, wait thou only upon God; for my expectation is from Him.*' I expect no enthusiasm from the North, and little even from the South. I ask only the calm and honest reflection of wise and good men for truth, which may not be welcome, but is truth for all that. Easily could I have composed papers which would have been copied and applauded here, but truth forbade it. Nor can I approve of the fanaticism of the South, any more than that of the North, on the subject which has been before us. I only wish, in fact, that, instead of employing my humble efforts in refuting an untenable, and mischievous, and monstrous dogma, I had been occupied in the more congenial work of attempting to excite masters to a sense of their fearful responsibility, and to the discharge of their solemn duties."

How much more in accordance with such a mind would it be, to engage in showing how the system debases all that is noble in man, and how contrary it is to the spirit of the Lord Jesus, and to all the principles of that religion which he came to establish in the world. For such a mind *must* perceive that there is a current setting against slavery, which nothing can resist. There are great and well-established principles in society, which are constantly pressing harder and harder on the system. The progress towards universal freedom is onward. The spirit of the age; the settled principles of liberty; the advances in intelligence and in benevolent feeling, all are against the system, and it cannot survive the shock when all these are fully arrayed against it.

The defence of slavery from the Bible is to be, and will soon be abandoned, and men will wonder that any defence of such a system could have been attempted from the word of God. If the authors of these defences could live a little longer than the ordinary term of years allotted to man, they would themselves wonder that they could ever have set up such a defence. Future generations will look upon the defences of slavery drawn from the Bible, as among the most remarkable instances of mistaken interpretation and unfounded reasoning furnished by the perversities of the human mind.

One thing further is settled. If the Bible could be shown to defend and countenance slavery as a good institution, it would make thousands of infidels—for there are multitudes of minds that will see more clearly that slavery is against all the laws which God has written on the human soul, than they would see that a book sanctioning such a system had evidence of divine origin. If slavery is to be defended, it is not to be by arguments drawn from the Bible, but by arguments drawn from its happy influences on agriculture, commerce, and the arts; on the increase of population and national prosperity; on morals and social intercourse; on the military strength which it gives a people; on the smiling villages, the neat dwellings, the school-houses and churches, which it rears and adorns; on its influence in promoting chastity and purity of life; on its elevating the black man, and making him more intelligent and happy than he would be in his own land; on its whole benevolent bearing on the welfare of the slave, in this world and the world to come. Whether these considerations in its favour are sufficient to defend the institution, may be safely left to the results of an examination by those who are disposed to engage in it.

From the whole train of reasoning which I have pursued, I trust it will not be considered as improper to regard it as a position clearly demonstrated, that the fair influence of the Christian religion would everywhere abolish slavery. Let its principles be acted out; let its maxims prevail and rule in the hearts of all men, and the system, in the language of tne Princeton Repertory, 'would SPEEDILY come to an end.' In what way this is to be brought about, and in what manner the influence of the church may be made to bear upon it, are points on which there may be differences of opinion. But there is one method which is obvious, and which, if everywhere practised, would certainly lead to this result. It is, *for the Christian church to cease all connection with slavery.* Happily we have, on this subject, one most beautiful and instructive example of what might be done by all Christian churches—the example of the Society of Friends. Humbly commending that example to the churches of the Lord Jesus Christ in this land, as one eminently prudent, Christian, and wise, I would submit this whole argument to the candid judgment of the Christian public, to all who love liberty and value the rights of man.

The history of emancipation among the Quakers is an exceedingly interesting and instructive portion of the history of our country; and in the calm, and prudent, and persevering measures which they have adopted, is probably to be found the true way in which our country can be, and is to be, freed from this great evil. They have aimed at two things—and two only—both of them legitimate, both of them prudent and wise :—*first* to remove slavery from their own body; and *then* to bear their solemn testimony, in regard to the evil, to the world. The first object was pursued year after year by patient and manly discussion, and by faithful and affectionate dealing with their brethren;—and the period at last arrived—a most triumphant period in the history of their body—when they could announce to the world that the evil of slavery was not attached to any portion of their denomination; when there was not a "Friend" who claimed a right of property in his fellow-man. The other object they have as steadily pursued. They have borne, without ambiguity, and without hesitancy, and with nothing of a spirit of denunciation, their 'testimony' in regard to the evil of the system before the world. They offer no forced interference. They use no harsh words. They impugn no man's motives. They interfere with no rights protected by law. But they are a plain-spoken people. They use intelligent language. They do not attempt to blink the subject, or to cover up the evil. They make no apology for slavery; they never speak of it as right; they never speak of it as sanctioned by the Bible; they never even speak of the difficulty of emancipation; they use no metaphysical distinctions on the question whether it is a moral, or a political, or a social wrong, or on the question whether it is in all cases a sin. They leave the impression that *they* regard it as a wrong in every sense of the word, and that they themselves deemed it *so great* a wrong that they were willing to make great sacrifices, that their own denomination might be freed from it totally and for ever; and they leave this solemn testimony to go forth to the world for what it is worth.

Now here, I am persuaded, is a wise model for all other denominations of Christian men, and the true idea of all successful efforts for the removal of this great evil from the land. Let all the evangelical denominations but follow the simple example of the Quakers in this country, and slavery would soon come to an end. There is not vital energy enough; there is not power of numbers and influence enough out of the church, to sustain it. Let every religious denomination in the land *detach itself* from all connection with slavery, without saying a word against others; let the time come when, in all the mighty denominations of Christians, it can be announced that the evil has ceased *with them* FOR EVER; and let the voice from each denomination be lifted up in kind, but firm and solemn testimony against the system—with no 'mealy' words; with no attempt at apology; with no wish to blink it; with no effort to throw the sacred shield of religion over so great an evil—and the work is done. There is no public sentiment in this land—there could be none created, that would resist the power of such testimony. There is no power *out* of the church that could sustain slavery an hour if it were not sustained *in* it. Not a blow need be struck. Not an unkind word need be uttered. No man's motive need be impugned; no man's proper rights invaded. All that is needful is, for each Christian man, and for every Christian church, to stand up in the sacred majesty of such a solemn testimony; to free themselves from all connection with the evil, and utter a calm and deliberate voice to the world, AND THE WORK WILL BE DONE.

THE END.